TURNER

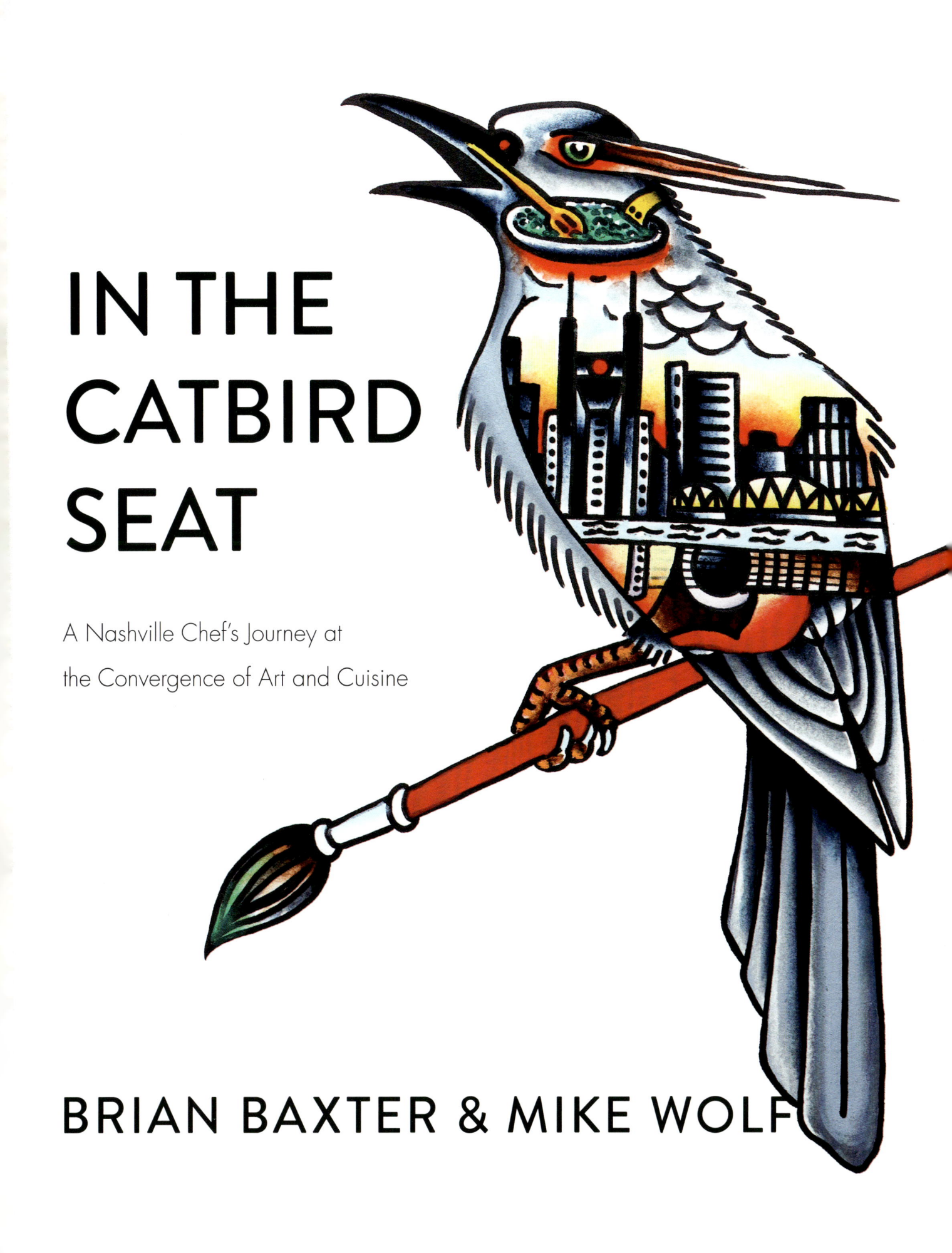

IN THE
CATBIRD
SEAT

A Nashville Chef's Journey at
the Convergence of Art and Cuisine

BRIAN BAXTER & MIKE WOLF

Turner Publishing Company
Nashville, Tennessee
www.turnerpublishing.com

Copyright © 2024 by Brian Baxter and Mike Wolf

In the Catbird Seat: A Nashville Chef's Journey at the Convergence of Art and Cuisine

No part of this publication may be reproduced, stored in a retrieval system, or transmitted in any form or by any means, electronic, mechanical, photocopying, recording, scanning, or otherwise, except as permitted under Sections 107 or 108 of the 1976 United States Copyright Act, without either the prior written permission of the Publisher, or authorization through payment of the appropriate per-copy fee to the Copyright Clearance Center, 222 Rosewood Drive, Danvers, MA 01923, (978) 750-8400, fax (978) 750-4744. Requests to the Publisher for permission should be addressed to Turner Publishing Company, 4507 Charlotte Avenue, Suite 100, Nashville, Tennessee, 37209, (615) 255-2665, fax (615) 255-5081, E-mail: admin@turnerpublishing.com.

Limit of Liability/Disclaimer of Warranty: While the publisher and the author have used their best efforts in preparing this book, they make no representations or warranties with respect to the accuracy or completeness of the contents of this book and specifically disclaim any implied warranties of merchantability or fitness for a particular purpose. No warranty may be created or extended by sales representatives or written sales materials. The advice and strategies contained herein may not be suitable for your situation. You should consult with a professional where appropriate. Neither the publisher nor the author shall be liable for any loss of profit or any other commercial damages, including but not limited to special, incidental, consequential, or other damages.

Cover Design by William Ruoto
Book Design by Anna B. Knighton; Adapted for Trade by Ashlyn Inman
Photography by Andrew Thomas Lee

Library of Congress Cataloging-in-Publication Data
    Names: Baxter, Brian (Chef), author. | Wolf, Mike (Bartender), author.
    Title: In The Catbird Seat : a Nashville chef's journey at the convergence of art and cuisine / Brian Baxter & Mike Wolf.
    Description: Nashville, Tennessee : Turner Publishing Company, [2024] | Includes index.
    Identifiers: LCCN 2024002503 | ISBN 9781684427079 (deluxe) | ISBN 9781684427086 (hardcover)
    Subjects: LCSH: Catbird Seat Restaurant | Cooking. | LCGFT: Cookbooks.
    Classification: LCC TX714 .B3842 2024 | DDC 641.5—dc23/eng/20240212
    LC record available at https://lccn.loc.gov/2024002503

Printed in Canada
1 2 3 4 5 6 7 8 9 10

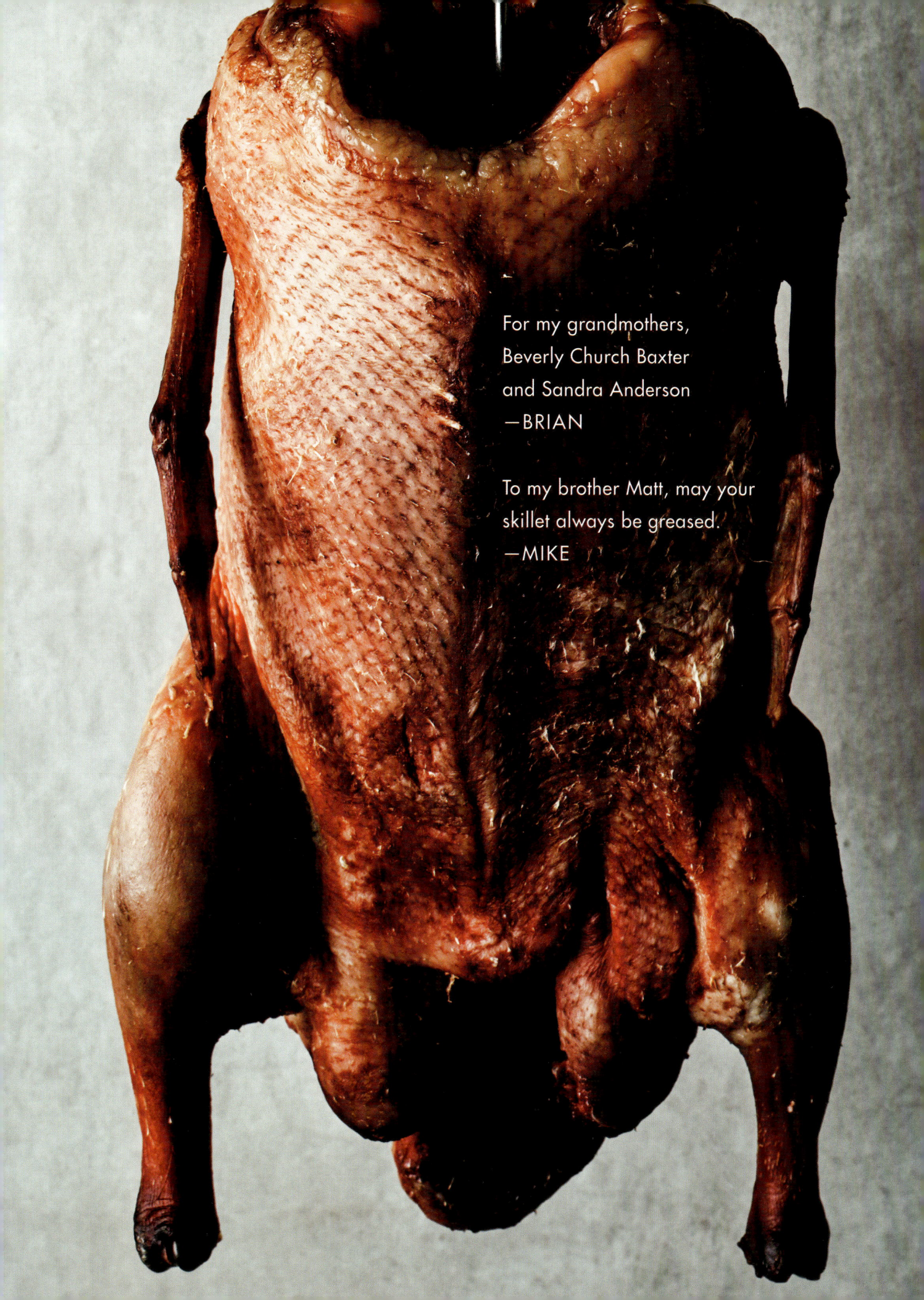

For my grandmothers,
Beverly Church Baxter
and Sandra Anderson
—BRIAN

To my brother Matt, may your
skillet always be greased.
—MIKE

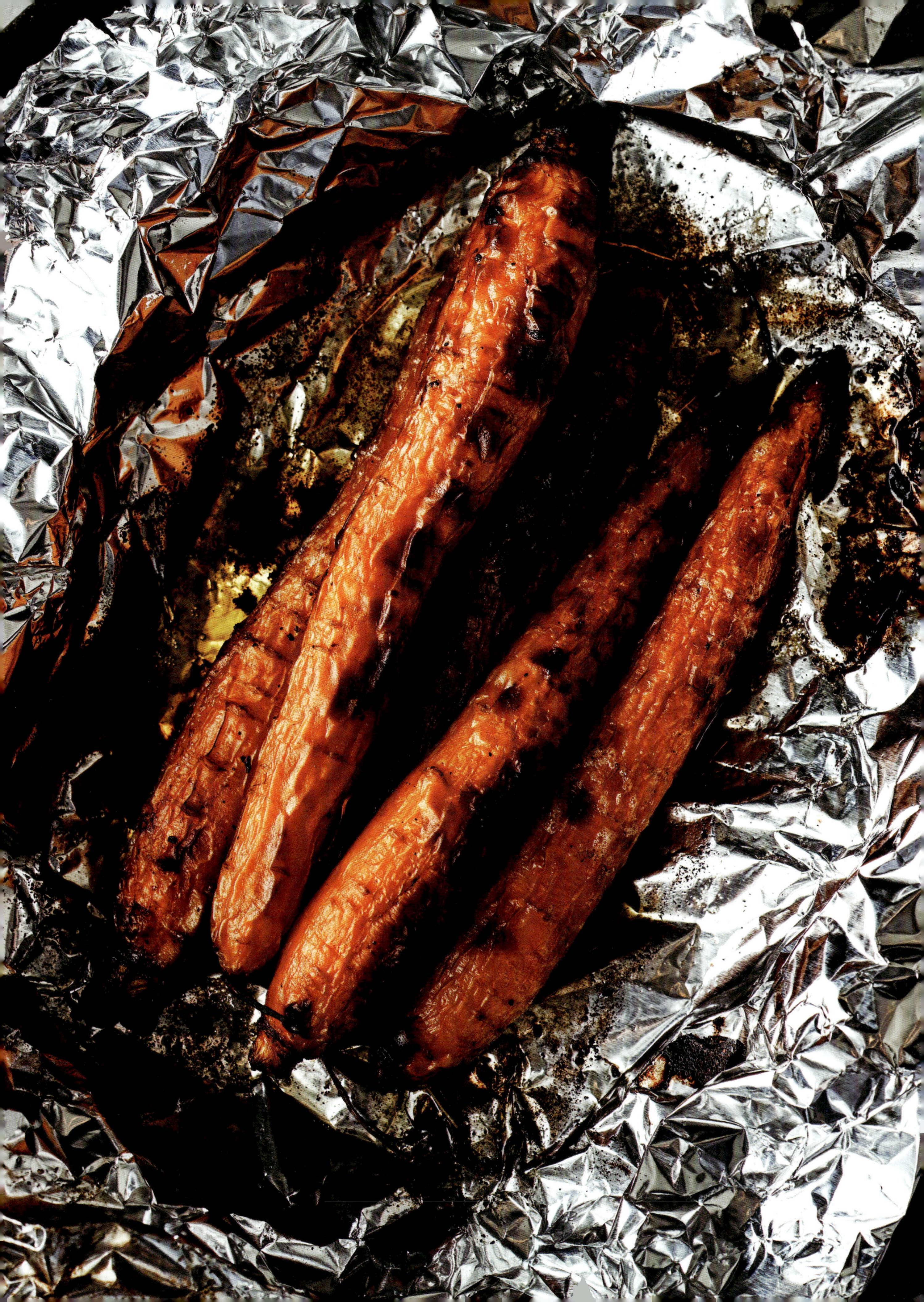

CONTENTS

foreword by pedro iglesias **viii**
introduction by josh habiger **x**
sitting in the catbird seat by mike wolf **xiii**
foundations & inspirations **xx**

my first year in the catbird seat: 2020 to 2021 **xxviii**

june 2020: the first month **2**

summer 2020 **6**
   menu **11**

reflection **37**

fall 2020 **38**
   menu **43**

winter 2020–2021 **70**
   menu **75**

spring 2021 **104**
   menu **109**

cooking with confidence: after the first four seasons **138**

my second year in the catbird seat: 2021 to 2022 **140**

summer 2021 **142**
   menu **147**

fall 2021 **172**
   menu **177**

winter 2021–2022 **202**
   menu **207**

spring 2022 **232**
   menu **237**

reflection **265**

base recipes **267**
cured, dried & fermented vegetables **269**
cured, dried & preserved seafood & meat **272**
stocks **274**
epilogue: new adventures by mike wolf **276**
acknowledgments **279**
index **282**

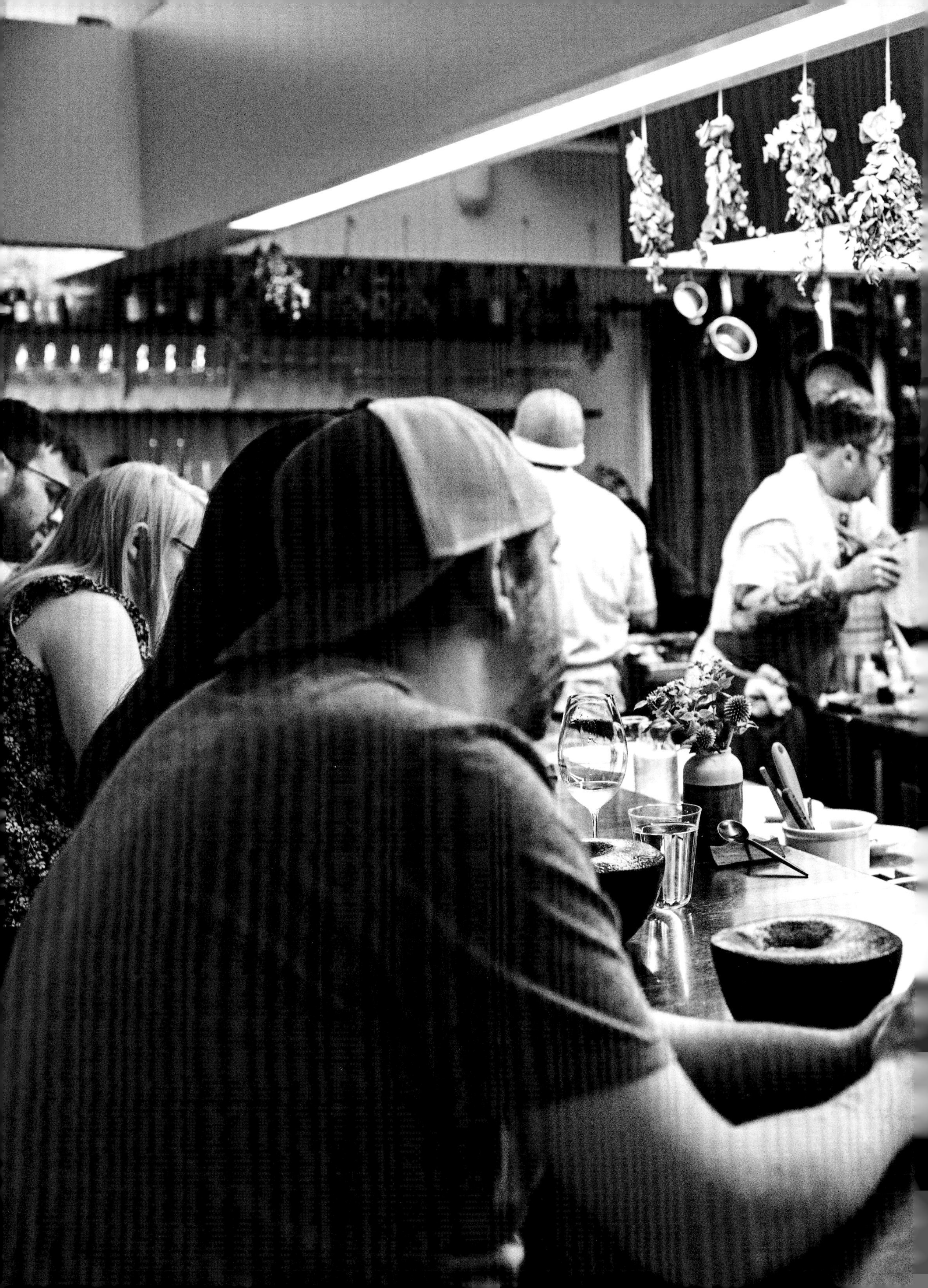

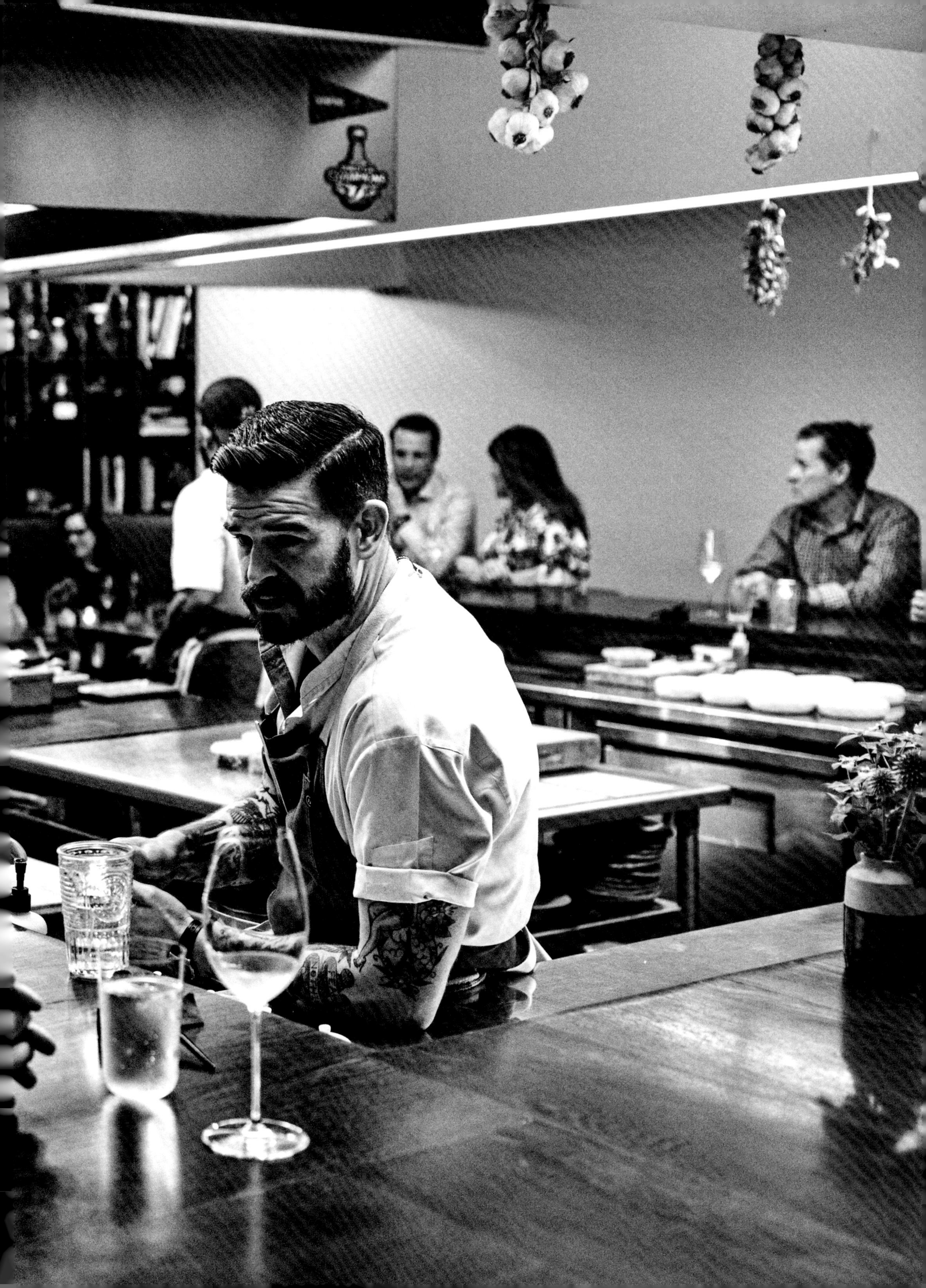

FOREWORD

Pedro Iglesias

When Chef Brian Baxter asked me to write the foreword for his upcoming book *In The Catbird Seat*, I couldn't have been more thrilled. As a gastronome with serious interest in both the art and science of good eating, and the different culinary customs and traditions around the world, compelling food continues to excite me in a powerful way.

This is remarkable: if you think that my first culinary trip was almost 35 years ago, and if you assume that all those years will make you immune to the seductive charms of cuisine, they do not. The nurturing power of food is high—and, in the case of great food, even higher.

Now, all that accumulated experience through several cycles of gastronomy in that time span developed my sensibility and gave me a unique perspective. This helps to build a discerning capability, directly connected to the compass that steers my gastronomic interest in the road of culinary proposals, which is very important in the continuous search for culture, deliciousness, and the special.

Enter Chef Brian Baxter, whom I formally met fortuitously in November 2021 at The Catbird Seat in Nashville, Tennessee, even though I'd had food prepared by him before in other restaurants that he used to work at, going as far back as Beacon in New York in 2006, a restaurant that Chef Waldy Malouf opened in 1999.

The occasion of our encounter was the 10 Year Anniversary Dinner (2011–2021) of The Catbird Seat, where he, as the current Executive Chef, welcomed his predecessors and inaugural chefs, Erik Anderson and Josh Habiger, to prepare a fantastic dinner that we enjoyed with Trevor Moran, a very talented chef and friend, who also preceded Chef Brian at the restaurant as Executive Chef.

The first bite served by Chef Brian at that dinner was "redneck sushi," and it made an impression: thinly sliced swordfish, cured and smoked like country ham (see page 12), painted with a nikiri sauce made with lady peas seasoned with a reduction of fermented tomato, over deep-fried grits smeared with preserved horseradish. Fantastic!

That dinner was a success. We were in the presence of great craft and talent, and they delivered in spades. But this dish and others from Chef Brian triggered an interest and friendship that led me to come back to The Catbird Seat solely to enjoy his food. It turned out that they were the tip of the iceberg of what I later discovered as a super-delicious and very special cuisine.

Chef Brian comes from Safety Harbor, Florida, and his heritage is beautifully reflected in his food, which is even more special as he is the fifth Executive Chef in the history of The Catbird Seat—which limits by choice the stints of their chefs to a two-year maximum, and he is the first chef with a Southern-cuisine background.

Classically trained at the Culinary Institute of America in Hyde Park, New York, he acquired the foundation that allowed him to sharpen his craft and develop his talent, working with such prestigious chefs as Todd English, Norman van Aken, David Bouley, and, above all, Sean Brock.

Consistency, perseverance, and great work ethic successfully converted into reality those initial dreams of becoming a chef, fueled by the cooking shows he used to watch in his youth, admiring the work of Chef Emeril Lagasse and Iron Chef Hiroyuki Sakai. Those were the times when he took his first steps in this industry, working as a busboy in The Wine Cellar, a restaurant located in North Redington Beach, Florida, that operated for 38 years and where he would later return as a chef.

His background, training, and work experience are reflected in his cuisine as expected. But, very clearly, he grew and developed his own voice—and boy, what a fantastic voice that is.

Powered by his great passion for gastronomy, his respect for the different culinary customs and traditions around the world, his high regard for the best product, his innate proclivity for hospitality, and his immense thirst and humility for learning, he became an excellent chef with an impressive arsenal of knowledge encompassing ingredients, products, procedures, and techniques.

I have been a firsthand witness of his passion for learning and for the relentless work he does until he masters the ingredient, product, procedure, or technique. Also, for his generosity in sharing this knowledge.

He has a commendable and sensible approach to cooking that avoids extremes, favoring local product and local farmers and producers when possible, but not limiting himself on what he can serve to his guests. He is also very committed to avoiding waste. He cleverly puts this to use, many times adding surprising nuances to the same ingredient or other ingredients in the dish.

Chef Brian uses all these tools in his cuisine with great effectiveness, as reflected in his outstanding preparations, where you can appreciate his very broad range.

During our last visit, he dazzled our palate. Sauce poulette, nuanced by saffron, amchoor, and ground smoked mussels (see page 47), gave immense depth and persistence to blue mussels from Maine. Green short-spine sea urchin from Maine was incredibly complemented by the floral and fruity notes of loquat oil, fermented raspberry juice, rose water, and raspberry vinegar. Fermented guava, fresh guava, and fermented guava jam beautifully nuanced fresh spiny lobster from Florida. Cold and warm egg custards were a testament to his passion and respect for Japanese food, the first showcasing with elegance and finesse the clean flavors in dry-aged fish, with the second harboring a seamless combination of murasaki uni and pumpkin "ham."

The exhilarating aroma of beurre noisette was the prelude to pristine seared scallops from Maine, served with salsify barigoule, fermented white asparagus hollandaise, and Kaluga caviar. Comforting sea lettuce was braised in the fashion of collard greens, in a dashi that used the trimming and discarded parts of Pacific razor clams instead of the traditional ham hocks. The "fruitiness" of "almost raw" dry-aged ora king salmon was enhanced with kiwi and grated horseradish, plus grilled avocado and pistachio furikake: absolutely brilliant. And it continued in this fashion, on and on and on, until an unforgettable dessert consisting of burnt banana, black walnut toffee, and Siberian caviar, unmovable from the menu, which honors his grandmother.

During this experience, 31 sauces were used in the tasting menu, not counting any desserts or any of the shiro dashi, or any of the lacto-ferments they use to season their food, which amounted to 70 at that time.

This was not done to have bragging rights, as their use was judicious throughout the entire experience and they didn't take leadership in the preparations. Rather, they were integrated seamlessly as part of the dishes to make them more delicious, one of the goals of cooking, and something I always look for in a chef.

It was also very impressive how service was conducted: not one single yell, in a menu where almost all the dishes were cooked à la minute. Orders were given with gestures, signs, and whispers. Don't misunderstand me: this was a very serious kitchen, and that was evident from the authority, order, method, and excellent flow, plus the rhythm and timing of the brigade.

This is a captivating book about Chef Brian Baxter's time as Executive Chef of The Catbird Seat. In the very words of Chef Brian, which I make mine because I couldn't agree more, Catbird is "one of the most important and underrated restaurants in the United States."

The book tells a complete story of the challenges, failures, struggles, and victories that go along with opening and running a restaurant.

It also tells part of the personal history of one of the most brilliant American chefs of his generation.

A very inspiring story that fills us with hope for the future of American cuisine.

INTRODUCTION

Josh Habiger

I grew up in a small town in rural Minnesota and knew that I wanted to see so much more of the world. I spent my twenties working in kitchens in different cities (Chicago, New York, London, Vail), but always found myself back in Minneapolis. I had done my culinary school externship at an incredibly underrated little restaurant called Auriga for Chef Doug Flicker. Years later, I would end up working there again alongside my friends Erik Anderson and Jon Radle (RIP). When we were working in that kitchen together, we would talk about opening a restaurant with one another. We had this idea of finding a shuttered old diner (my first job was at a diner in St. Joseph, Minnesota) and doing a tasting menu at the diner counter. The ultimate juxtaposition of highbrow meets lowbrow: the counter would allow the guests to see what we were doing, allow us to interact directly with them, and the room itself would remove any stuffiness that fine dining often has.

I'll admit, it wasn't an entirely original idea. Joel Robuchon had L'Atelier that had a similar setup, but those were in Paris and Tokyo and we were in the American Midwest.

In 2008 I was back in Minneapolis again, this time as the CDC of a new hotel project that was opening. We had a top-notch team full of ambitious cooks (seriously, if I had a copy of the kitchen schedule it would read like the who's who of the Minneapolis dining scene years later), but in the end we were trying to do something different than what the hotel leadership wanted. I departed the hotel restaurant and found myself without a job and depressed. I remember sitting at a fancy cocktail bar and chatting with the bartender there, watching him work and thinking "I think I want to do that." He mentioned that the guys (Toby Maloney and Jason Cott) who opened The Violet Hour in Chicago were in town consulting on a new bar. I had a loose connection with them through my time at Alinea, so I thought I would give them a shout. For some reason they liked me and asked, "Have you ever thought about moving to Nashville?" and I am pretty sure I just said "nope." They said they wanted to hire a chef to be the head bartender, that chefs can "lead people, follow a recipe, and have low pay expectations." They were persistent and convinced me to at least take a trip down there to meet these two brothers that "were doing cool things down there." I figured I had nothing to lose and packed my car for a road trip to the South. I met with Benjamin and Max Goldberg and decided to take the leap. I knew very little about bartending but my proximity to Toby was like having a teacher's manual and I was keeping at least one lesson ahead of the rest of the class (we almost exclusively hired people without bartending experience on the opening team at The Patterson House).

Bartending was amazing. I was learning so much, I got to be creative in a new way, I had direct interaction with the guests, and at least one woman left me her phone number! Cocktails have history, stories, reasons behind why they exist. At the beginning I was kind of faking it, but eventually it became my life. My favorite part of it was that you could talk to a guest, ask them a few questions about their favorite drinks, and either steer them to something on the menu or create something just for them.

Then you got the opportunity to watch them interact with it. You slide the glass across the bar to them, twist a lemon peel over the top it, leaving tiny droplets of aromatic citrus oil on the surface of the drink. First, they smell it, then you watch them take their first sip. Immediately you will know if they like it or not, even if they tell you otherwise. This is something that I never really got to experience working in a restaurant kitchen. We would put the final garnish on a dish with a pair of tweezers and the food runner would whisk the plates through the swinging doors into the dining room and the cook/diner relationship was basically over. Every now and then a happy guest would pop their head into the kitchen to wave to the team and say thanks, but that's about it.

I was enjoying the bartending life but was starting to miss cooking. I asked Ben and Max if I could cook a tasting menu for Valentine's Day (which we did) and picked up a few catering gigs on the side, including a high-profile wedding in town. I am not sure if Ben and Max knew the extent of my cooking, but I think they were impressed. At one point they had asked if I ever wanted to do a restaurant and I told them that idea about the chef counter thing (at this point Momofuku Ko had opened in NYC with a very similar concept) but thought it was too crazy of an idea to work. At that time there was a salon operating in the space above The Patterson House and we found out that their lease was running out. The landlord asked Benjamin if they were interested in doing something up there and he asked me "what if we did that restaurant that you talked about up there?" My first reaction was "no, no, no, that would never work." He said he penciled some numbers and thought we could make it work, but who would we get to work in a restaurant like this?

I mentioned Erik Anderson, who I worked with in Minneapolis (he has family here in Nashville, too). Toby and Jason had recommended Jane Lopes, a bartender from The Violet Hour that was really into wine, to be the sommelier. She didn't have experience, but she had some wild ideas and was perfect for the job. I knew a young woman named Mayme Gretsch from Minneapolis that mentioned she'd be interested in moving for the job. Then, there was a really talented young guy cooking down in The Patterson House named Tom Bayless who rounded out the team. The five of us were the opening team of The Catbird Seat.

In the fine dining restaurants that I had worked in, I never really felt comfortable when I would go in to eat there. One of the important ideas that we had talked about was how to make the experience more comfortable, genuine, and approachable. We wanted to open a Nashville restaurant, not a New York or Napa restaurant in Nashville. What would a Nashville tasting menu restaurant be? It was 2009 and things like Food Network and Top Chef were going strong. All of a sudden, people were interested in food in a different way and they could watch us, like they were a judge on one of those food shows. But while they were watching us, we were able to watch them. We could see how people were interacting with our dishes. Are they pushing the garnish to the side with their fork instead of incorporating it into the dish? How can we plate it differently so they get every element in each bite? Are they not finishing the duck? Should we adjust the cooking time or cut it a different way? When the guest is directly in front of you, it really takes the ego out of your cooking and gives you a more objective lens to see things as they really are. It also becomes sort of a self-correcting tool for everyone cooking there. In a normal kitchen you might not take the time to check the seasoning because you are too weeded and fear the chef's wrath of a slow ticket time, but in this environment, you are going to look the guest in the eye when you hand them something that you made. Are you really going to serve them under-seasoned food? Or anything that you aren't proud of? It really makes you understand and appreciate the chef/guest transaction.

The tasting menu format is obviously different for different chefs. When we first opened Catbird, it was a little chaotic. I think of a band like Drive-By Truckers in their earlier days (everything I knew about The South before moving to Nashville was from their records). They'd have a Patterson Hood song, then a Mike Cooley song, then a Jason Isbell song; they were all great songwriters individually, yet somehow it all contributes to a cohesive whole. In those early days of Catbird, there would be Erik dishes, my dishes, and a few from Tom and Mayme that would all come together to create this menu that represented us at that time. It was probably a little disjointed at certain points, but it was genuine and natural and gave us the opportunity to not be locked into one "style" of cooking or cuisine. I think it was exactly what we needed to get our feet under us.

It was probably 18 months from when I stopped cooking at Catbird for me to be able to come back into the restaurant as a guest. Human emotions are weird. I guess it felt a little like seeing your ex-girlfriend out with a new guy. Luckily, Chef Trevor Moran was at the helm of the restaurant at that point and he was an absolute madman in the best way. I thought what he was doing there was so much better than what we were doing. It was aggressive yet refined, beautiful dishes without fussiness, and complex flavors that seemed simple. He only offered silverware for a few of the courses because he wanted everyone to use their hands; eliminate the middleman! The menu was like a concept album where there was a musical theme (Trevor was from Ireland and the theme was potato) and he kept coming back to that musical theme throughout the meal.

The idea to change chefs every few years started with those initial conversations about mental sustainability. Out of the gate we decided on four nights of service (Wednesday through Saturday) with a prep day on Tuesday. This would generally give everyone a full two-day weekend every week as long as we didn't have too many other things going on. Admittedly, we had way too many other things going on in those early days. Changing chefs would keep the restaurant fresh for guests and create sort of an incubator, ideally a place to develop your craft before you open your own spot.

When I first met Brian Baxter I was a little intimidated. He had a great résumé and came from this whole Sean Brock world of food and flavor and this big team of talented people. He also has an intensity to him that kind of fades away once you realize how great of a guy he is. I didn't know a lot about him, but I was looking for someone to come over to work at Bastion with me (years before he took over at Catbird). He fit in really well here and immediately began putting dishes on the menu. I was constantly impressed by his style and the kind of dishes he was coming up with. It's really interesting to see someone doing the same job as you but looking at it in a different way; it's inspiring. You start to question things like "How did he even come up with that?" There is one specific dish that I sometimes think about which involved chicken gizzards and tsiri spice. We hadn't put chicken gizzards on the menu, and I just assumed that it was something that nobody would order (Bastion's menu at the time was a choose-your-own-adventure tasting menu, so you had options for each course) but I figured I'd let him roll with it and find out for himself. Of course, we put it on the menu and everyone who ordered it absolutely loved it. This is just one of the many dishes that he made in his time at Bastion that I was blown away with. He had a knack for making those dishes that make other chefs mad because they didn't come up with the idea themselves.

I'm always impressed by the different ways that chefs come into the space at Catbird and make it their own. I think of it like when I used to snowboard in Vail, and we'd get a good snow day. If you wanted to hike the backcountry and explore new terrain, you'd take the lift as far as it would go, and you'd venture out into the mountains, see a good path forming, and then hike up a hill. If you were the first one, you'd get all this fresh snow, and you were the one stomping your footprints into the snow to make that trail. The people coming down after you had plenty of fresh snow to work with, but they were still following that trail that you had set out for them. And it made for a smoother hike up for the people who came after you. They got to benefit from the trail that you helped make, even though we all had to climb up that mountain to get there. That's how I look at the different chefs who have come through The Catbird Seat. Some of them have even stepped off to the side to blaze their own trail and find new ground, and that's been amazing to see as well. The last time I ate at Catbird was to experience what Chef Baxter and his crew were doing. From the quality of the food to the level of the execution, I was so impressed. I'd put what they're doing up against any restaurant in the world. It's that special.

SITTING IN THE CATBIRD SEAT

Mike Wolf

With the curtains drawn and the meticulously extensive preparation for that night's service done, before the first guest steps into the gleaming elevator at The Catbird Seat to be beamed up to a world of culinary delights, it's easy to forget the chaos that swirls around Division Street in Nashville on any given day. Just around the corner is Music Row—where some of the biggest hits of the last seventy-five years were cut, where Elvis and Dolly made history and where Kris Kristofferson walked around lonely, busted, and "wishing, Lord, that I was stoned," as he wrote "Sunday Mornin' Comin' Down" while walking these streets with that same scent of fried chicken hanging in the air like a leaf suspended by a strand of spiderweb. Now party buses careen down the streets filled with bachelorettes crushing White Claws, and Midtown bars two blocks down fill up fast with day drinkers just looking for an excuse (it's Thursday, or the sun is out) to get a buzz on before sunset, as construction crews put the finishing touch on the new boutique hotel down the street and the fiery smells of Hattie B's hot chicken mingle with the beer spilled on the sidewalk the night before.

But just as you step off the elevator, beyond the stylishly lit hallway, you enter a square box of a room with 22 seats surrounding a gang of highly skilled chefs who have trained all their young lives for the sole purpose of blowing your fucking mind using the best fish, produce, and meat they could buy—flown in from halfway around the world if the dish calls for it—all bolstered by a pantry that has taken weeks to methodically bring to fruition, and they're going to cook this food right in front of you and tell you all about it while your senses max out and the courses whiz by like wind on the water, making you realize you're not really in Nashville anymore. You don't know *where* you are, but that outside world of dreamers, schemers, and last of the true believers doesn't seem to matter at all. For three hours it's just this room, one of the best chefs in the country, a crack culinary team complete with a beverage specialist, and a journey through a menu that said chef has worked their whole career to prepare for.

The fact that a restaurant like The Catbird Seat just passed its ten-year anniversary during the writing of this book is impressive enough, but it's *how* they've managed to do it that makes it so unique. As an ever-evolving incubator and showcase for culinary talent from around the world, Catbird brings in a new chef every few years, shutting down the restaurant for a month or two as the new crew comes in, wipes the slate clean, and builds an entirely different experience, from the plateware to the artwork, from the music to the menu design. They develop a new pantry, with all its whizbang wizardry and fermenting, bubbling vinegars, as they undertake projects like drying beans above the range to develop umami-rich flavor compounds that will lead to shoyus, garums, and all the other weird shit that chefs—especially excellent ones—use to scale the mountains of flavor manipulation and explore new terrains of taste.

When local restaurateurs and brothers Ben and Max Goldberg opened Catbird in the spring of 2011, directly above their pioneering craft cocktail haven the Patterson House, Nashville had never seen anything like it. They enlisted the talents of now-multiple-Michelin-starred chef Erik Anderson and Josh Habiger, their uber-talented food and beverage specialist from the Patterson House (now a James Beard-nominated chef in his own right). Cut to months later, and one of their early iconic dishes—a full

full squab served with a maple leaf to one side and a leg complete with its claw intact to the other—graces the cover of *Bon Appetit* magazine. The early hype of restaurants like Catbird, City House, and Margot helped put Nashville on the map as a city not just to swill bottles of beer in neon nights with blaring Telecasters firing on all cylinders (though it still *is* that), but a city to eat in *now*. Soon, whispers of Chef Sean Brock coming to town, bringing with him some of his most talented teammates from the low-country Catbirdesque institution McCrady's (Brian Baxter among them), begat a restaurant revival in Music City. But not before Catbird would make a splashy move of its own, bringing in a chef from arguably the most famous and fawned-over restaurant in the world at that time, and the lodestar lighting the way for a new culinary revolution: Noma in Copenhagen.

Irish chef Trevor Moran came to helm The Catbird Seat all the way from Noma in 2013, carrying a refined yet wild and idiosyncratic style all his own, culminating in some of Catbird's most notable dishes from its early era: a salad comprised completely of wild herbs and greens from the verdant Tennessee countryside; a tomato dish that appeared as if you were eating a rose blossom petal by petal; and an oyster dish with Earl Grey tea—an unforgettable highlight of my own dining experience in 2014—not to mention the very-Irish-but-somehow-not "Potato Sushi." Moran's impact on the Nashville dining community at large seemed only to reinforce the idea that creative souls were drawn to Nashville, and it wasn't just a launchpad to something else. Sean Brock's Husk and Moran came to Nashville in the same year, and both remain there to this day, helming their own restaurants, with Moran's Locust rocketing onto "Best New Restaurant" lists and garnering him a James Beard nomination just as this book is going to press. When the New York Times in 2014 announced that Moran would be heading back to Copenhagen to run the new iteration of Noma, billed as "2.0" and complete with an onsite farm, this news (the only coverage the Nashville dining scene would receive in the periodical that year) seemed to suggest something about The Catbird Seat—now a worldwide top-tier talent incubator—and about Nashville itself: cool enough to come make some noise, but not cool enough to plant down roots. Until Moran changed course and decided to build his own restaurant just a few miles south of downtown Nashville.

When Moran's two-year-and-change tenure was up, Catbird looked to another globe-trotting wunderkind chef who had cut his teeth in the highly competitive, cutthroat Chicago restaurant scene: Ryan Poli. Fresh off tenures at highly respected restaurants Tavernita and Perennial, and with a pedigree that included time at Dan Barber's Blue Hill at Stone Barns, Thomas Keller's The French Laundry, and a short stint at the aforementioned Noma, Poli took Catbird's cuisine to another worldly level, bringing inspirations from travels as far-flung as Japan (a big influence on Chef Baxter's tenure, as you'll see in this book), Vietnam, and Spain. Poli's Catbird tenure was peppered with thoughtful vegetable presentations, Japanese-inspired seafood, and beautiful, handmade pastas. Nashville would prove its magnetic pull on Poli as well, as he still resides in the city and is opening a restaurant of his own, with his beverage-specialist brother Matt, called Iggy's, which opened in spring 2023.

If The Catbird Seat was a rock band and Ryan Poli and Trevor Moran represented the all-important second and third albums, where the band looks to build on what made them so special in the first place while forging ahead with new sounds and exciting collaborations, the next chefs to grace the stage represented the experimental fourth-album phase. You know, the one that can divide fans while making others cling to their fandom even more. Chefs Will Aghajanian and Liz Johnson came to Catbird in 2018, bringing the by-now-requisite résumé with time spent at Noma (where the pair met) with Aghajanian's modern sensibilities honed under chef Eric Ziebold at Cityzen in Washington, D.C. Johnson was fresh off a role as head chef at MIMI in New York City, while also coast-hopping to Los Angeles to open the buzzy Jewish diner Freedman's, where she received a nod as one of Food and Wine magazine's Best New Chefs. Their tenure at Catbird was marked by new design flourishes, from custom-made serving bowls that played into the plating of certain dishes to a laser-inflected, mist-spewing art installation gracing guests as they walked into the space. Though admirable and full of forward-thinking dishes like Bougainvillea flowers draped over frozen guava with seawater meringue, the pair would depart Catbird after a little over a year, after being named as co-nominees in the Rising Stars category for the James Beard Awards.

Then, the world basically ended for a while in March 2020.

But let's go back to that fateful time in Nashville food. It was 2013, Italian pasta haven Rolf and Daughters had opened to wide acclaim and slack-jawed locals, and Catbird was recruiting one of Noma's best chefs from halfway around the world while Sean Brock, the first big-time James Beard award-winning chef to come to Nashville to plant a flag in the name of better grits, was about to set up shop at Husk, bringing with him a team of culinarians from his vinegar-soaked, tobacco-flavored-Dippin'-Dots-havin' mad science lab at McCrady's in Charleston. Enter a new talent, one of Chef Brock's most promising protégés, and someone who would stay in the shadows during his first year in town: Brian Baxter, who would take the helm as chef de cuisine at Husk within a year. As bar manager there, I had a front-row seat as I watched Chef Baxter grow from a man with ideas and ambition to a culinary wizard who never seemed to run out of flavor combinations. I paid attention, and I learned a lot—like how adding a hint of black pepper to cinnamon makes it pop, and zesting citrus into fresh green apple juice before straining gives it an ineffable brightness, as if tasting the sun as it rises. I also learned about the complexities of chef dynamics, as Chef Brock's stature grew toward that of a national figure away from the kitchen, while Chef Baxter's food only got better and more interesting.

Continuing his chef journey, Baxter went to work with Catbird co-founder Josh Habiger (see page x) at his new restaurant Bastion—which lived up to its name early in the game—refining many of the Southern-meets-mad-scientist ideas Baxter had honed throughout his years at Husk. Taking over The Catbird Seat seemed the next logical step, though an opportunity with chef Kevin Gillespie's burgeoning restaurant empire in Atlanta beckoned Baxter to the BeltLine to open the restaurant Cold Beer. This role gave him creative freedom to explore the highs and lows of cuisine, cooking everything from technique-driven masterpieces like Duck Wellington with elderberry compote to impossibly umami'd-out chicken wings, a highlight of one of my last great meals out before COVID set in like a long, strange winter of the soul. What's interesting about Baxter's tenure at Cold Beer—switched off like a light in the night as restaurants all over the country shut down—was that it was such a *Nashville* approach to food. I think of

Nashville as this potent mix of high- and low-brow culture: a Picasso exhibit at the Frist Museum opens as hundreds of honky-tonk bands wail away into the wee hours of the night merely three blocks away. Educational institutions like Vanderbilt and Belmont abound, buddying up to legendary dive bars like Springwater and Santa's Pub. (Where else would Santa Claus own a fucking bar?) Which inevitably brings us to why this book, why now?

Usually, chefs do a book much later down the line, when they're mostly out of the kitchen and can look back with cloudy recollections and take credit for dishes they may not have even made in the first place. As Baxter came back to Nashville to finally helm and reopen The Catbird Seat in one of the strangest times in world history, I saw a chef entering his prime at the perfect time. If the times hadn't been so damn strange, that is. This is the kind of showcase a chef works his whole career for, and I'd watched Baxter take creative leaps as well as the "one step forward, two steps back" we all endure along the way. But this was his LeBron to the Heat moment, his Steph Curry can't miss period, this was Tom Brady lining up with two minutes to go and the whole game on the line. Whichever sports metaphor you opt for, this was the big stage, a culmination of every dish he'd ever contributed to, at a time when the entire restaurant world was completely upside-down. How would a culinary and creative, incubating juggernaut cross the threshold of its ten-year anniversary, with eyes on a new location, as long as the world didn't implode? No pressure, Bax.

Welcome to Brian Baxter's time in The Catbird Seat.

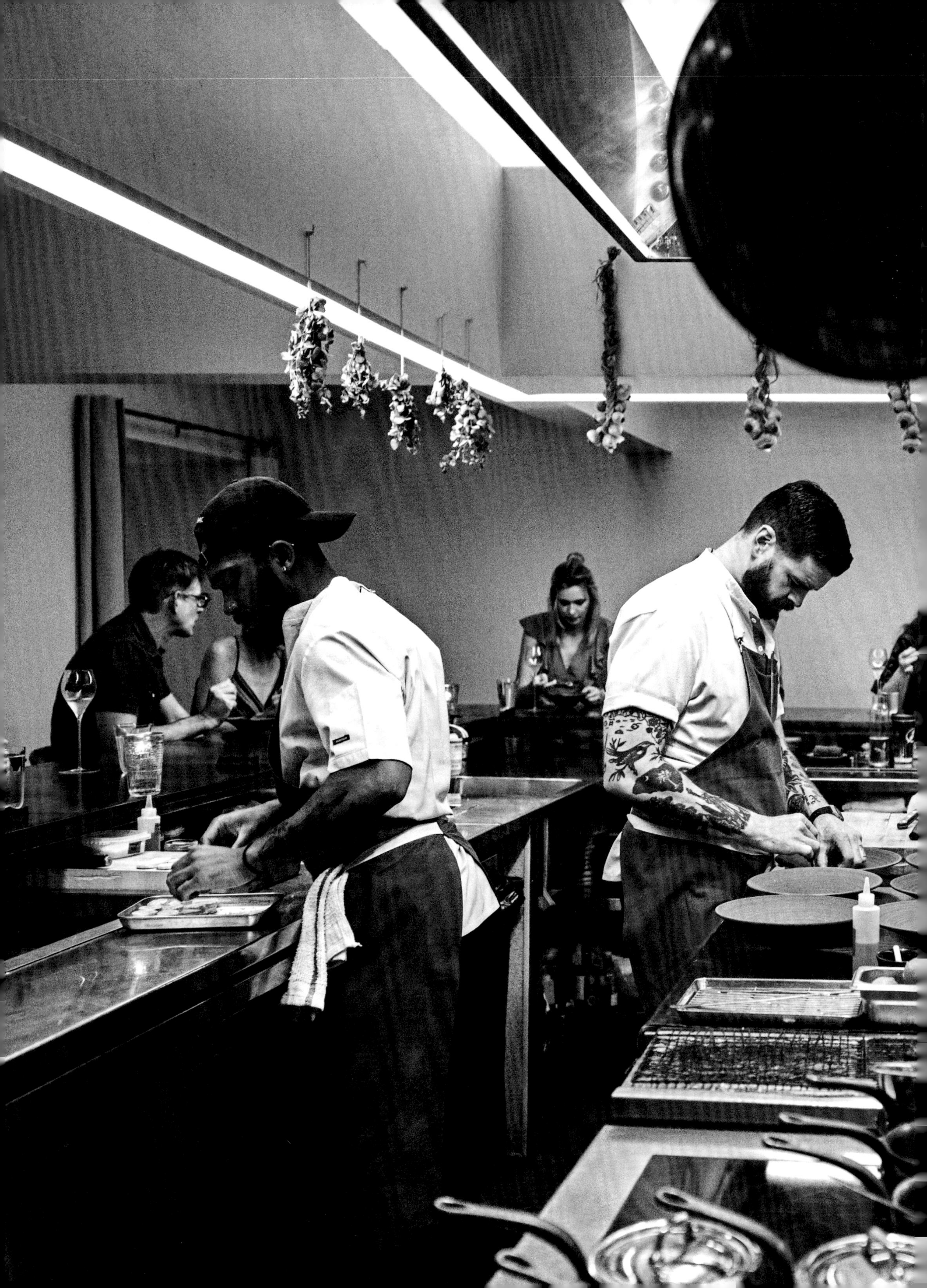

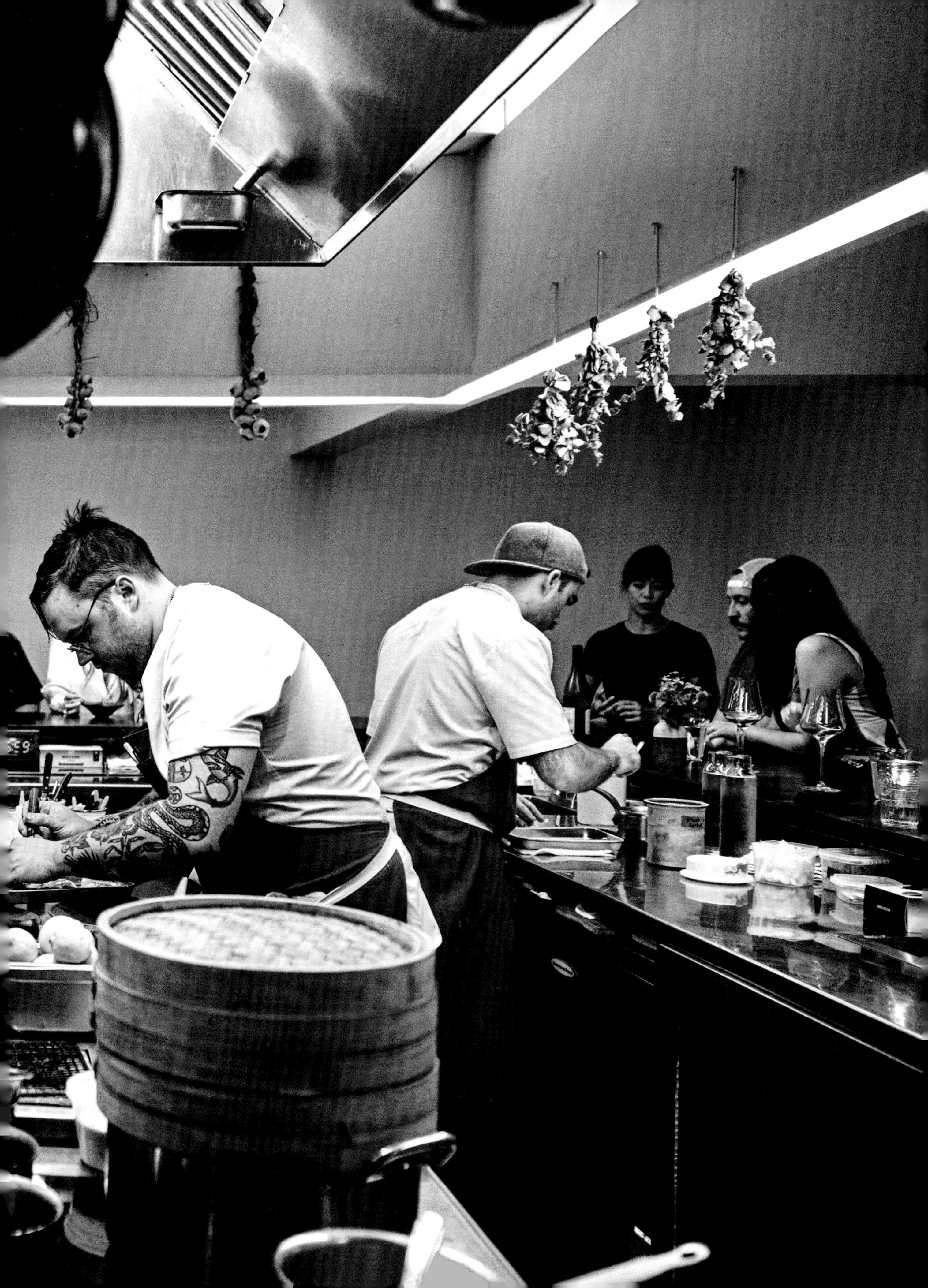

FOUNDATIONS & INSPIRATIONS

"What destruction have I been blessed by?" —A.R. Ammons

A New Beginning

After I was furloughed from my job on March 17, 2020, my wife and I were pretty nervous. We had moved to a new state the year before to help Kevin Gillespie open Cold Beer, his newest restaurant off of Atlanta's BeltLine. Two weeks prior to that move, she had given birth to our first child, my son Noah. We were now a few hours away from most of our friends and our families, and I was without a job. The world around us was slowly starting to see the effects of the pandemic, and seemed like it was ending. We sat down and had a conversation about money, our plan, and how to stay safe. Most importantly, how to keep our ten-month-old safe. We didn't know much about COVID-19 at that point. My wife and I both missed Nashville and everything we'd left behind. My mother-in-law was driving anywhere from 3.5 to 5 hours, depending on traffic, every week to watch our son. To be honest, I just didn't feel like I fit into Atlanta like I'd thought I would. I was depressed, stressed, and trying to figure out how to make the restaurant work. Guests weren't flocking in the way we had thought they would, and I don't think they could comprehend what we were trying to do. And now I didn't even have a restaurant for people to come to. I continued to try to fight my feelings in the gym—now my garage—and on constant walks around our neighborhood. I was slowly starting to go crazy being locked up inside, and I no longer had a creative outlet as a release. Of course, I started painting again, but it had been a year since I'd picked up a brush, so I was constantly angry and unhappy with everything I tried to create. I was starting to get a little worried about my sanity.

Thankfully, I had already been in contact with Josh Habiger and Max Goldberg about taking a position at The Catbird Seat in Nashville, Tennessee. They were planning on reopening in June and would need me to come much sooner than originally planned. I was torn, since I wanted to give Kevin as close to two years as possible in my role at Cold Beer.

However, given the current state of the world and the changes that would be made to the restaurant in order for it to reopen, I decided it was time to head back to Nashville and accepted the position. I had always dreamed about running a restaurant like The Catbird Seat, and years prior, while still in Nashville, had even mentioned to my wife, Michaela, that I would love to run it one day. I had a really good conversation with Kevin about the opportunity and told him that I was very grateful for everything he had done for me in the past year. He was completely understanding and very supportive. I think he'd felt worse about having to furlough me after having moved my family down to Atlanta, but no one could've predicted that this would happen. Nor could they have predicted that it is still something we are having to worry about a year and a half later as I'm writing this book.

So, needless to say, in the midst of a pandemic when many were dealing with strife and grief, I got my dream job. For that, I will be forever grateful. I told myself "I will not squander this opportunity." First, I had to figure out how I could take all that I'd learned over the years and combine it with the recent inspirations that had helped me get through adversity, to forge a new future for my cooking career.

Philosophy

When I decided to make the move back to Nashville and take over The Catbird Seat, I knew that I was going to cook with the seasons, only using ingredients that were at their peak. I was going to focus on working with local purveyors as much as possible, and I wanted to highlight the food I enjoyed eating and the flavors that inspired me. I wouldn't consider the food I cook any specific type of cuisine; however, I knew that the foundational techniques would be French and that most of the ingredients would be coming from the southeastern United States. Finally, I wanted to be as sustainable as possible. When I began, I didn't really know how to classify my cuisine, but I knew that I would find out a lot about myself over the next few months. I was going to approach my two-year tenure as eight separate seasons to show the diners and future investors what I could do. Of course I wanted diners and investors to be impressed, but I also felt the need to support the people and farmers I had built close relationships with over the past seven years.

With restaurants being closed due to COVID-19, farms were not able to sell their products. They not only lost products but money and staff, and some were even forced to close their farms. I felt a responsibility to help make up for the loss due to the shutdown of restaurants during the 2020 lockdown. I was going to buy up as much produce as I could, whether I could use it then or not. I figured it would force me to figure out what to do with it. We would find a way to serve it to the guests or the staff or preserve it for a future menu. This led us to do some things we ended up establishing as base preparations for multiple ingredients. We also found that this helped us to easily create flavorful, vegetable-forward dishes. We would often end up scratching the protein altogether. I love to showcase a different ingredient that we may have an abundance of, and use it multiple times throughout a menu. I feel like this forces you to be even more creative as you strive to make it more interesting and exciting, so the guest doesn't feel like they are eating the same thing repeatedly. A guest said to me the other night, "You guys really like your pumpkins." I told him "There were about ten different varieties available to me from the local farmers, so I was going to try to find a way to highlight them. Did any of the dishes taste the same?" I asked. He said "No. Not at all." I just responded "Okay, then."

In Japan there is a word, *shibui*, that refers to an aesthetic of drawing upon silent, subtle, and unobtrusive qualities of an object, performance, or person. The objects may appear to be simple, but they include subtle details that balance simplicity with intricacy and complexity. I now try to relate this to my food. Something can appear to be very simple or unassuming, but I try to load it with flavor and complexity. A good example is a dish that was on one of the late-summer menus: "Marinated Eggplant with Shiso." More on that dish later.

When I approach a dish, I want to make it as flavorful as possible. I figure out what the main ingredient and flavor profile are. The ingredient will tell you what you need to serve with it. A fruit, grain, vegetable, or protein—although relatively the same—will have small nuances that change from year to year, like wine. Taste it first, and mentally record what flavors stand out to you. Maybe a habanada pepper is sweeter and less bitter and tastes more like passion fruit one year, or a tomato is more savory and umami-forward and less sweet than the previous season. They may even change from farm to farm, or if there has been rain before being picked. Doing this allows you to build a flavor library in your brain, and over time it will make it easy for you to taste or smell something and know what you want to pair it with.

Once you choose the ingredient, you will need to figure out how you want to cook it. Will it need a sauce? A purée? Something for texture? Next, I think about what flavors will complement it and how many ways you can use the main ingredient in the dish. I also will try to hit all five of the basic tastes in every dish: sweet, salty, sour, bitter, and umami. This includes desserts too. The important thing is how to balance each dish while subtly touching each taste.

I also take temperature into account. An example from our most recent spring menu was dry-aged shima aji (Japanese horse mackerel) with a vinaigrette made from fermented pineapple and aji limo chilies, grilled avocado, and coconut. We served a nitrogen-frozen mousse of grilled avocado and coconut to help "cool down" the heat from the aji limo chilies. I consider both the temperature and fat from the mousse.

I also like to think about how the guest will eat the dish. Can I trust them to eat it properly and get every single flavor I intended to be in each bite? If the food is scattered all over the plate, how will they know to get every component on their spoon at the right time? I build each dish in layers. I layer them first in the order I want the flavors to hit your mouth. Then I focus on temperature and, finally, texture. This ensures that—unless they try really hard—the guest will taste the dish the way it was meant to be tasted. If I do serve it with separate components or have them separated on the plate, I always instruct the guest to eat it in the order it is meant to be eaten. However, people don't always listen very well and can still manage to mess this up.

Now, back to the eggplant. I knew I wanted to use eggplant, as it was perfectly in season. I knew I wanted it to be very flavorful, because I would only have four to five bites to showcase it. I knew I wanted it to be sweet to balance the bitterness. I also envisioned it as salty, smoky, rich, and full of umami. I wanted it to have a custardy texture but also to have some crunch. I wanted the brightness that citrus brings to a dish, but without the acidity. This is what I came up with. I was inspired by eggplant agebitashi—a Japanese word meaning deep-fried and soaked—where Japanese eggplant is scored and blanched in a fryer. This deep-frying technique doesn't use any breading. This process helps pull the bitterness out of the eggplant and makes it easier to peel. We fry it long enough that the eggplant begins to soften and turn golden brown. It is then peeled and marinated in a mixture of sake, mirin, and soy sauce that's been infused with different aromatics. I knew I wanted the flavor of bonito in there, but I wanted to keep the dish vegetarian. So, in exchange for bonito, we decided to cure, smoke, and dry eggplant like katsuobushi and infuse it into the vin blanc (a classic French white-wine cream sauce). To add some creamy texture, there is a smoked eggplant cream in the bottom of the bowl, and it is finished with shiso oil, furikake, and fresh green yuzu zest. It arrives in a warm bowl with just a hint of eggplant and crispy furikake peeking through the smoky, umami-rich cream sauce. It doesn't look like much, but it packs a ton of flavor.

eggplant vin blanc

shallot	312g
kombu, rinsed	15g
sake	700mL
mirin	400mL
cream	1890mL
cured eggplant, shaved thin (see base recipes, page 269)	50g

Bring the shallot, kombu, sake, and mirin to a simmer over medium heat. Cook until all the alcohol has evaporated. Add the cream and shaved eggplant, bring to a simmer, and cook for an additional 20 minutes. Remove from the heat, cover, and let steep for 30 minutes. Pass through a fine-mesh strainer and cool. Before using, season to taste with salt.

This is a great example of many of the recipes you'll find throughout this book.

A Note on Recipes

The reason I record all of my recipes is for consistency. If I make the recipe while developing a dish, but I don't make it every time, how can I ensure that someone makes it the same way I would? I record everything in metric measurements, make it together with my staff the first time they make it for the menu, and check it every single time after that. We still have to take what nature gives us and be able to adapt. You also must use your knowledge, experience, and senses to make adjustments. Maybe a piece of meat is leaner than when we wrote the recipe, or an onion is tasting sweeter. Maybe the garlic is a little more pungent later in the season, or the hakurei turnip is much larger than the petite ones we were getting three weeks earlier. Recipes are just guidelines, but, if you have a solid foundation for those guidelines, you're off to a good start.

However, to cook and thrive in a high-pressure situation like The Catbird Seat requires both building on those foundations *and* finding inspiration anywhere you can. Even if a painting doesn't influence a dish, it can put me in the right frame of mind to forge ahead with a new idea and see it through.

FOUNDATIONS & INSPIRATIONS

Credit: Todd Saal

Watercolor Inspirations

In 2017, I had surgery on my ankle to remove a cyst that had formed in the bone. I ended up being off my feet for three months. That whole time, I was in either a hard cast or a walking boot, so I was completely unable to work. During that time, I was in such pain and so uncomfortable that I had a hard time sleeping. I didn't take many pain meds after the first week or so and just relied on Tylenol and ibuprofen for the duration of my recovery. The only thing that could help me fall asleep was watching hours of Bob Ross's *The Joy of Painting* shows from the '70s and '80s.

Once I eventually got my cast off and was able to balance on crutches, I took Bob's word for it that anyone could paint. I had plenty of time on my hands, so I went to an art store, bought a mixed-medium art set, and promptly set up in the living room and painted. I quickly realized how messy the oils were. I eventually started painting on the porch and would watch Bob's instructions through the open doorway and try to paint along. However, as the temperature began to drop, painting outside was less pleasant, so I decided to play with the media in the set I had bought. I ended up falling in love with watercolor (with a dash of love/hate in there as well). Even though I was terrible at using them, I couldn't stop painting. I wanted to get better.

Fast-forward to 2018, and my buddy Chad Koeplinger showed me an artist on Instagram by the name of Todd Saal. Todd was a local impressionistic watercolor artist who did mostly plein air, and he happened to be extremely good at it. I reached out to him to see if he ever did workshops, and I was in luck. So we decided to meet out at Bear Creek Farm, a special place for me as it was the first farm I'd visited when I came to Nashville to work at Husk, a place where I had been accepted as part of LeeAnn and Bill Cherry's extended family, and where I got married in 2018. We started from the very basics: different types of brushes, the relationship between the pigment and water, and how to mix them on your palette. We also started chatting about our careers and found that we had more in common than just painting. Todd was born and raised in New York and used to be a musician who cooked in restaurants when he came home from touring. Over the next couple of years, we continued to paint together and became good friends. We chatted about living in New York, cooking, eating, and of course painting, as he would continue to give me tips and become a mentor.

During quarantine, I started painting again and would talk to Todd about my frustrations.

Credit: Todd Saal

He recommended we do a couple lessons via Zoom to try to get me back on the right track. Once I found out that I was going to be moving back to Nashville, I told him that I wanted to integrate watercolor into the space and incorporate it throughout the menu. I decided to turn the entryway into "the gallery," where his artwork would hang, as well as floral arrangements that would change seasonally. I also asked if he would paint an image for each season's menu. We started with paintings of ingredients that we planned to highlight throughout the season; by the second year, we featured scenes of a farmer in each season. I wanted to get to the point where I could eventually take over the artwork myself. However, I knew I had a very long way to go. But just like in cooking, I knew I was on the right path to becoming a more complete person, which in turn would make me a more complete leader in my role as chef. And getting in the right headspace to be creative is just as important as taking time away from the kitchen to find inspiration in other things too.

Staying Refreshed by Foraging

When I was working at McCrady's in Charleston, South Carolina, Jeremiah Langhorne—now of The Dabney in D.C.—was our chef de cuisine. He drew a lot of inspiration for the menu not only from what was in season from farmers and purveyors, but also from what was available to us in the wild. Living on the coast provides you the opportunity to use a plethora of unique ingredients available right outside your back door. Between Folly Beach and Sullivan's Island, we would find wild onions, sheep sorrel, samphire (also known as sea beans or beach asparagus), red bay leaves, sweetgrass mussels, cattails, sea rocket (similar to arugula), salt bush, and green briar shoots. If we headed twenty minutes inland, we could find chanterelles, scuppernong grapes, wood violet, spruce tips, and Virginia Pine. I enjoyed my mornings foraging with Jeremiah. It was like we were kids again. We would pretend to be knights with our Excaliburs and fight giant dragons (really just banana spiders, because Jeremiah is afraid of spiders) or that we were in a war and throwing hand grenades. It was fun, but it really put us behind for the day, and it was always a push to be ready for service. However, I realize now that the time I spent outside was necessary and, even though I didn't know it at the time, important for my mental health and staying inspired. It was a way to forget about the stress of the restaurant, and for those few hours in the

FOUNDATIONS & INSPIRATIONS

morning it was just us, the sound of nature, and pine-cone grenades. Foraging—even something as simple as walking a nature trail and looking for dandelion or violet blossoms—can be a great way for a chef to find inspiration and clear their head. Being mindful of mental health has become essential in the restaurant business.

A Note on Mental Health

I didn't realize it until now, but I am writing this on Mental Health Day, October 10, 2022. Self-care and mental health have become increasingly important topics in our industry, and I want to discuss it quickly for the benefit of all the young aspiring chefs out there.

In October 2015 I decided to become straight-edge. I quit putting anything into my body that I felt clouded my mind and kept me from being the best version of myself. I wanted to focus on being a better chef, partner, friend, and mentor and felt that I was unable to do that if I was not thinking clearly because of substance abuse. I have always struggled with patience and anger (still do) but would never have been able to grow as a person, chef, or parent if I hadn't learned to practice patience and control my temper. I realize that everyone needs a release or distraction to deal with their stresses. This is how

I have chosen to focus on my own mental and physical health. I also now realize that plein air painting gives me the same stress relief that foraging in the mornings with Jeremiah did, as well as a creative outlet that allows me to create without being overconsumed by the restaurant.

When I was off my feet for those three months after my ankle surgery, I enjoyed my time finally getting to attend weekly sporting events, eating all the concessions, and eating at friends' restaurants since they had usually been closed on my days off. Though this did come with a price: unnecessary weight gain. I gained over forty pounds during that time. Since then, I have made it a goal to get my health under control and to establish a solid routine of exercise (indoor and outdoor) and focus on a healthy diet. This has also helped with issues that I had sleeping, breathing, and relieving the added stress to my ankle and body. Most importantly, I feel that it has helped with mental clarity and allowed me another outlet to release negative emotions, instead of keeping them bottled up and taking it out on others.

Cooking is a very stressful vocation. The restaurant industry is demanding, and I don't see that changing as soon as we would like. The hours are long, the kitchen is hot, and your mind must be sharp constantly or you will make mistakes. So I recommend for any young culinarian to find a healthy outlet for creativity and try to focus on their mental and physical health. Many companies offer reasonably priced mental-health resources, mental-health professionals, and life coaches. If you need to talk to someone, do not be afraid or embarrassed to find the support you need. Sometimes just talking to someone about your feelings, not over a beer at the bar, will help more than you think. Another thing that helped me along the way was to keep a journal and write down thoughts, ideas, problems, and anything else that came to mind. Journaling can help crystallize your thoughts and allow you the opportunity to go back to them to see how you've grown, how the kernel of an idea began, and it gives you a timeline to go back and measure your growth. I kept a journal throughout my time at Catbird and will share some of those entries in this book to provide some context on where my head was at. At first it was swimming with ideas, stress, and possibilities.

This book was written to tell the stories and the inspirations behind the menu. To talk about the struggles, failures, and victories that go along with opening a restaurant that reopens every two years with a new chef and making it your own. The book is broken up into seasons to reflect how we went about changing the menu and how we tried to get the most out of every season. This is my story about the time I spent—from emerging out of the COVID doldrums of early summer 2020 to the spring of 2023—in what I think is one of the most important and underrated restaurants in the United States, from where it started to where it is now, and my journey in being a part of its history. It's about what it took for me to gain confidence in myself and realize my potential. I had to learn how to just trust myself and my team and cook food that I believe is delicious and keeps people coming back, and to build relationships with those people. If I make something that someone finds inspirational or cool along the way, then great. If not, then that's okay too. Remember to cook what you love, love what you cook, and always try to be a good person.

"The world abounds with different aspects of beauty. The lovely, the powerful, the gay, the smart—all belong to the beautiful. Each person, according to his disposition and environment, will feel a special affinity to one or another aspect. But when his taste grows more refined, he will necessarily arrive at a beauty which is shibui. Many a term serves to denote the secret of beauty, but this is the final word."
—Yanagi Soetsu (1889–1961)

MY FIRST YEAR IN THE CATBIRD SEAT
2020 to 2021

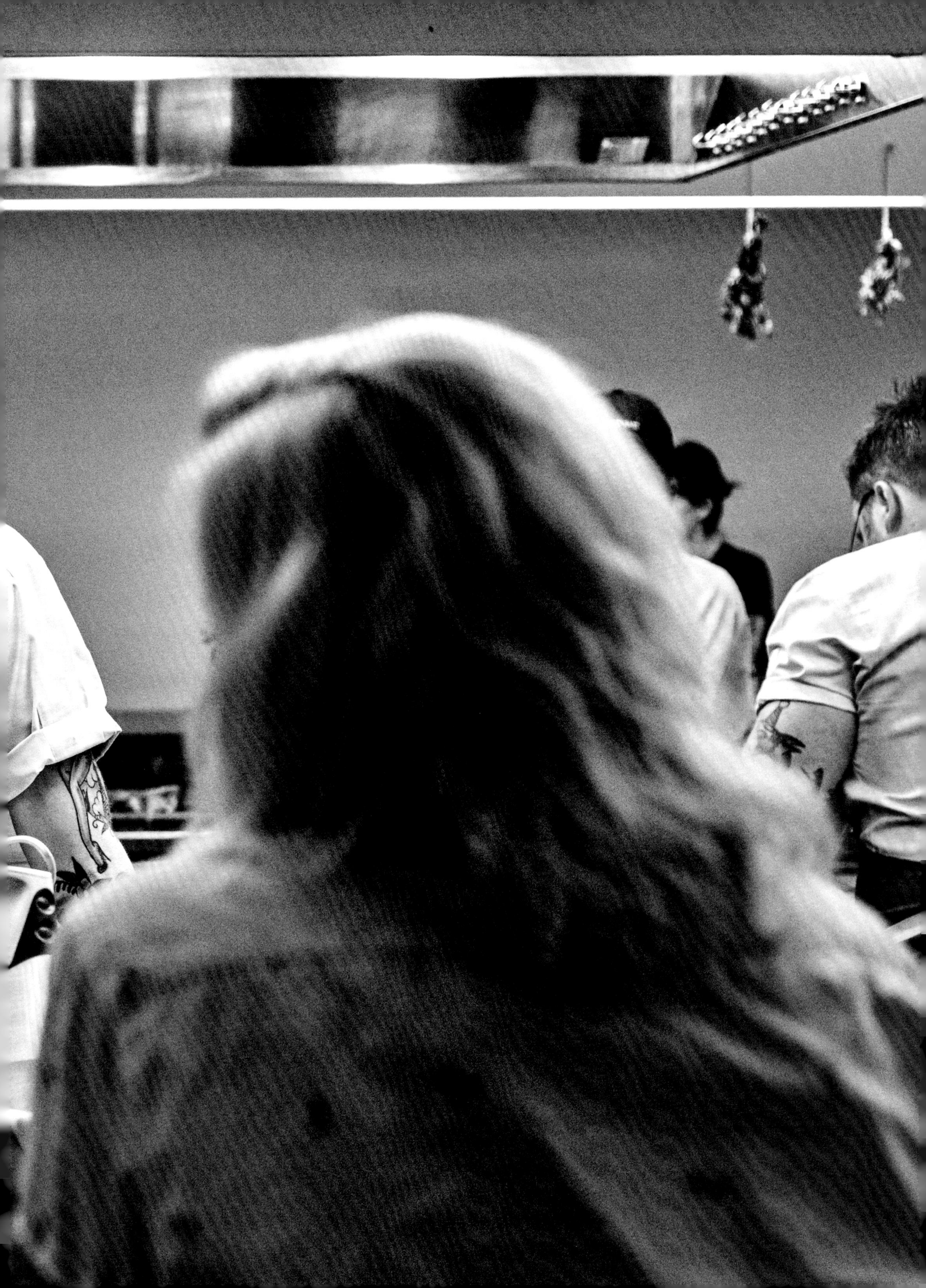

JUNE 2020
THE FIRST MONTH

"Struggle is nature's way of strengthening it." —Dwayne "The Rock" Johnson

To begin my tenure at Catbird, I couldn't have picked a better month on the calendar, as far as ingredients go. June in Middle Tennessee is a lively month in terms of produce. If you think of a growing cycle lasting between fifty-five and seventy-five days and consider that much of the bounty of Tennessee summer produce is planted in late March/early April, I knew I'd have plenty of beautiful local vegetables and herbs to play with. Tomatoes start coming in, peppers are plentiful, and summer staples like corn and watermelon are on the horizon. Since the first menu of a new tenure can really help set the tone for how things will go, I placed a lot of importance on making it special. Here I was, in the spot I'd wanted to be for some time, and I was driven to make the most of the resources at my disposal. What follows are journal entries from that fateful first month as we dove in on research and development, honing a menu we could be proud of before the first night of service. And remember, this was June 2020, a time when many restaurants were closed, and plenty would never even open again.

Day 1   Today is the first day in the kitchen. I am excited, nervous, and full of ideas. I hope I can create an environment where the team feels inspired and proud of the menu we come up with. I have a handful of ideas but want to talk through them as a team. I am confident in the staff I have put together. We will see what we come up with. At least I know the products we will be working with are going to be great. We just need to find the best way to highlight them.

Opening-menu ideas I'm thinking about:

tomato
- tomato sandwich: sauce gribiche, fresh tomato, milk bread, caviar
- tomato pie: candied tomato, cheese fat tart, sauce choron, cheese, oregano
- tomato nduja: fermented potato bread, tomato nduja, Maldon

oyster, cucumber, geranium
- Dukes of Topsail Sound oysters, oyster dashi gelee, cucumber-geranium granita, buttermilk-wasabi pearls, Maldon sea salt

peppers, grilled bread, swordfish ham
- grilled bread rouille, pickled and grilled peppers, fermented banana pepper emulsion, swordfish ham dressed in "escabeche," chives, smoked paprika oil, Maldon sea salt

sourdough crepe, escargot, spring onion
- sourdough crepe, escargot-oyster mushroom ragout, herb butter, fermented ramp powder, 25% ramp pickle, fines herbes

raw beef & tuna, watermelon dashi
- cured tuna dressed in tosazu, pickled watermelon rind, tomato
- 'boshi,' furikake, shiso, shaved short rib, sesame oil, watermelon dashi, Maldon

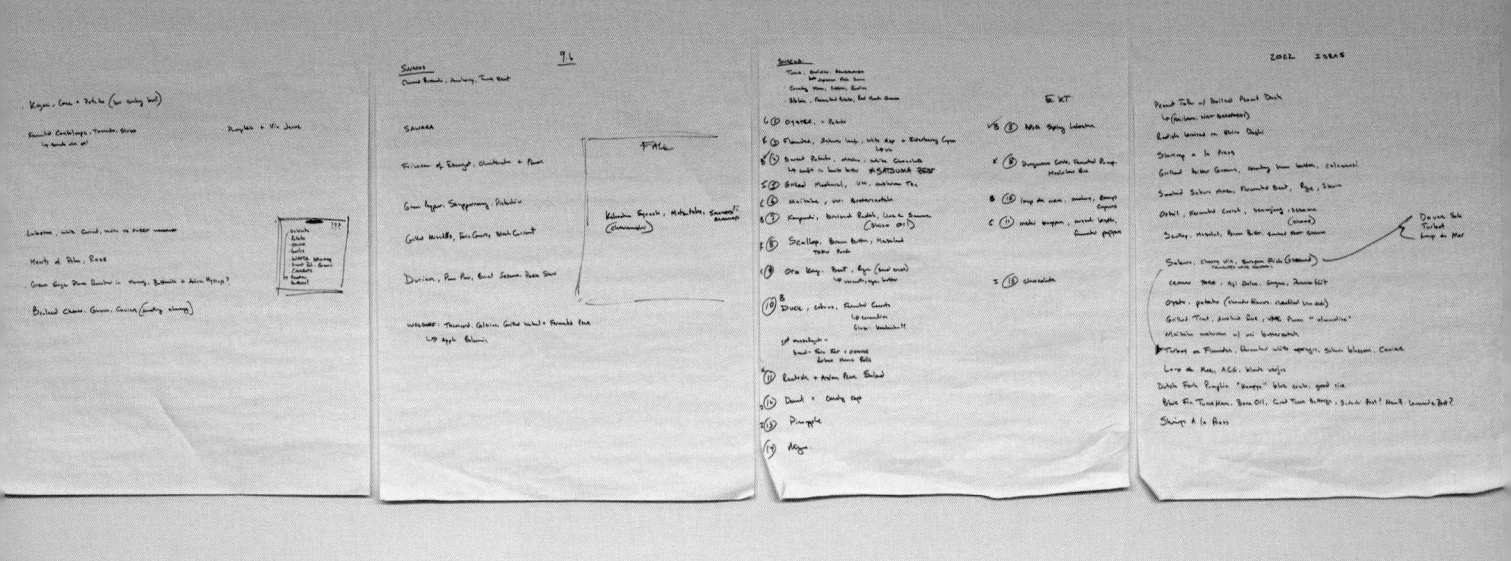

crab & courgette
— sunflower miso, chives, shaved courgette dressed in olive oil and lime zest, crab cooked in bonito butter seasoned w/Japanese curry and lime juice
— squash blossom, tempura battered, season w/Japanese 7 spice, garlic mayo, lemon wedge

steamed flounder, fermented green tomato butter
— flounder steamed in corn husk w/herbs, roasted garlic puree, fermented green tomato beurre blanc seasoned w/dill oil and lemon juice, grilled fava beans, lemon oil

dry-aged beef, corn and summer truffle
— spinalis w/sauce perigueux, charred corn puree
— corn chawanmushi, smoked marrow bones, truffle dashi
— corn fritter, cured beef belly, truffle catsup
— soured cornbread, truffle butter

tomato salad, lovage, pickled cucumber seeds
— brined and dried tomato dressed in tomato gazpacho, lovage ice cream, pickled cucumber seed, tomato vine oil, lemon oil, herb salad

yeast donut, foie gras pastry cream, strawberry
— yeast donut, foie pastry cream w/preserved strawberry, strawberry glaze seasoned w/elderberry cordial, elderflower

rhubarb, strawberry, angelica
— macerated strawberries, vanilla oil, angelica frozen buttermilk, poached rhubarb, Maldon salt, strawberry tuile

almond gelato, sour cherry, rose
— raw almond gelato, sour cherry dressed in rose kombucha, rose oil, rose milk meringue

mignardises
— beef fat butterscotch
— mint chocolate

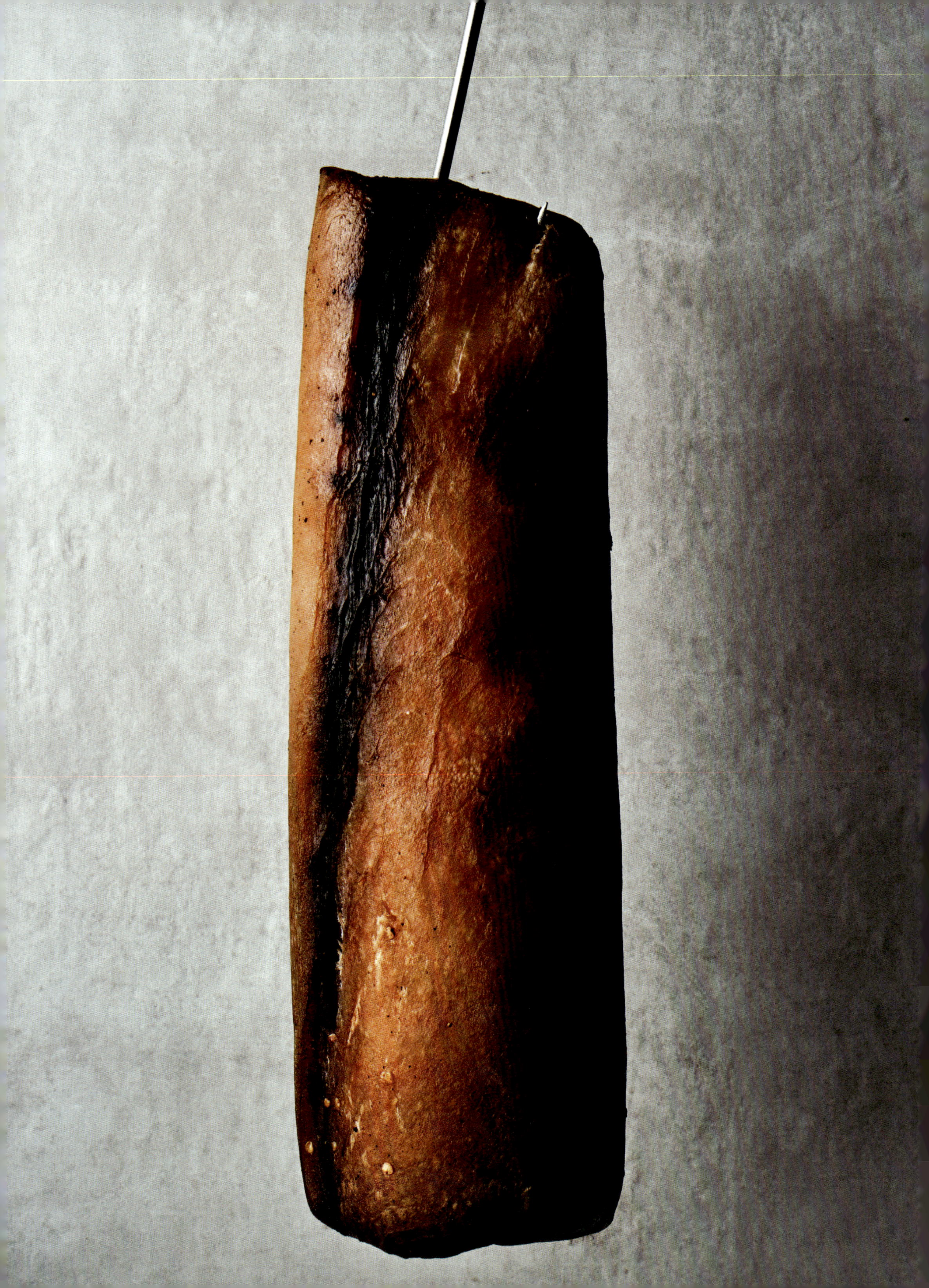

Day 8   This week leading up to the first service is a time of much uncertainty. Between COVID-19 and the protests for racial justice ongoing in downtown Nashville, we're still not sure how people will respond to our reopening, not to mention that we still have a ton of prep to do before opening night and are still trying to source all the products we need to open. I don't usually get anxious, but this is a big opportunity. My brain feels clouded, and I have a pounding headache. This is The Catbird Seat. All the chefs who have worked here in the past have incredible résumés and cook incredible food. It has been on lists of all kinds from *GQ* and *Bon Appetit*'s Best New Restaurant to *OAD*'s (*Opinionated About Dining*) top 100 and even a semifinalist for Best New Restaurant from the James Beard Awards. What if I don't keep up with the tradition and rise to the challenge? I continue to tell myself "None of that matters. You're not afraid. It's good to be nervous, but you're not afraid. It's just cooking. You've been working the last fifteen years for this moment. A restaurant's name or its past doesn't define you. It's what you make of it that will define you. Cook to the best of your abilities, let the products speak for themselves, make delicious food, and make the guests feel welcomed and comfortable. Try to be the best that you can every single day, and the rest will come."

Day 11   It's a few days before what is supposed to be our first night of friends and family, and we still haven't moved into the next phase of restrictions from COVID-19. We were originally supposed to cook for a couple close friends on Thursday and then have a small group of friends, regulars, and investors come in Friday and Saturday who would pay 50 percent of the normal menu price (to help with the loss of the closure from the last few months). As I am expressing my concern to my wife, I realize I'll already need to rewrite some of the menu, as we had just found out that she is pregnant with our second child (our daughter Ella) and will not be able to eat a number of the dishes. The last restaurant I helped open (Cold Beer, with Kevin Gillespie in Atlanta) was a time when our first son was merely two weeks old. Sleep wasn't something that either of us got much of back then, but at least I was able to help with him. Now I'm not only at work most of the day, but there is nothing I can do to help her feel better physically. So the least I can do is make sure she is able to eat a good meal. We spent our anniversary at Miller's Ale House, for crying out loud, but at least it was better than our first at The Varsity in Atlanta (I had to finish her food and drive her through Chick-fil-A on the way home). The least I could do is feed her one good meal after being quarantined for months and making her join me for a zinger mountain melt. I told her "Next year we're flying somewhere and having a nice meal . . . if we can get a sitter."

Day 16   It's the first seating on the first night of service, and we somehow miss all our greeting and service steps that we literally just went over fifteen minutes prior. I'm thinking in my head, "How's everyone feeling? Well, we shouldn't be nervous anymore. The first guests are down. Now's the time to wake up. The time to be nervous has come and gone. Act like you've done this before, because I know we all have."

Day 19   Driving home from the last night of the first week of service, I have a mixture of feelings. I'm exhausted, but I also have a ton of ideas running through my head. It was a good finish to the first week, but we have such a long way to go. I can't tell if people are really enjoying the food or just being courteous, because it would be too awkward to say "Eh, it's okay." I know we need to raise the service standards, but maybe that will come once everyone gets comfortable with having to cook and serve at the same time. I also don't understand how some of the stuff we ordered isn't quite available yet. We're three weeks into June already, and it's hot as hell outside. Any bit of spring that existed is over. I really don't want to have to rewrite the menu after all the work we did the last week and a half.

SUMMER 2020

#	Dietaries	Visit Notes	Guest Notes
		2 Birthdays	
4	1x Pescatarian (Lillian) 1x No Fish & No Scallops (Andromache) 1x No Scallops (Amanda)	1x Birthday (Andromache)	20+ Visit, Last in 7.13.22 - **Charlotte, NC; Interpreter / translator at Self Employed** - comes with someone new all the time - she drinks still water- Sometimes gets N/As
2			**Celebrating living in Nashville for a year** - No Tock History
2			In TN - No Tock History - **Senior Manager, Restaurant Excellence/Ops Support with CKE Restaurants, Inc. OR Records Analyst with Tennessee Secretary of State**
2			From Denver, CO, Now in Nashville - 2nd Visit, Last in 3.20.21 - **CDP @ Audrey**
2			From Atlanta - 3rd Visit, Last in 4.21.22 - **Celebrating Friendship; Drinks Still water** - Pairs - **Partners name is Adam (He likes his drinks to the left of him; college thing)**
2	1x Shellfish Allergy -All (Daughter)		Mississippi - No Tock History - **Research Hydraulic Engineer at USDA-ARS**
2		1x Birthday (Wife)	Arkansas - No Tock History - **commercial and architectural photographer**
2			California - No Tock History - **Owner of Gundersen Properties**
2			Nashville, TN - No Tock History - **Either Pharmacist or Co-Owner of Children's Corner Store**
4	1x Tree Nut Allergy		In TN - 2nd Visit, Last in 4.1.21 - **girlfriends name is Sarah, had a good time**
2			$$$ NEEDS TO PAY - No Tock History - **Reservation was made under Porter Allison; Stopping In Nashville for one night - Moving from Virginia to California**
2			Arkansas - No Tock History - **She's a foodie**
2			Atlanta, Georgia - No Tock History - **US Customs Broker** - Bringing their service dog
4	1x Peanut Allergy		$$$ NEEDS TO PAY - 8th Visit, Last in 7.14.22 - **Drinks Sparkling - Bunch of his friends coming from all over**

$$$ NEEDS TO PAY						$$$ NEEDS TO PAY			
Evan Long		Brooke Williams		Joe Valles		Ron Egan		Jackson Zeitlin	
8:15	2	8:15	2	8:15	2	8:45	4	8:15	4
46,45		44,43		42,41		32,31,26,25		BOOTH	
	2	SNACKS	2	SNACKS	2	SNACKS	4	SNACKS	4	SNACKS
INAMA (ZW)	2	OYSTER	INAMA (ZW)	2	OYSTER	INAMA (ZW)	2	OYSTER	INAMA (ZW)	4	OYSTER	INAMA (ZW)	4	OYSTER
	2	BUTTERFISH		2	BUTTERFISH		2	BUTTERFISH		4	BUTTERFISH		4	BUTTERFISH
	2	CLAM		2	CLAM		2	CLAM		4	CLAM		4	CLAM
SAKE	2	SALMON	SAKE	2	SALMON	SAKE	2	SALMON	SAKE	4	SALMON	SAKE	3	SALMON 1 TREE NUT
VOLTA (LF)	2	SQUASH	VOLTA (LF)	2	SQUASH	VOLTA (LF)	2	SQUASH	VOLTA (LF)	4	SQUASH	VOLTA (LF)	4	SQUASH
	2	WATERMELLON		2	WATERMELLON		2	WATERMELLON		4	WATERMELLON		4	WATERMELLON
GRUNER (ZW)	2	BEANS	GRUNER (ZW)	2	BEANS	GRUNER (ZW)	2	BEANS	GRUNER (ZW)	4	BEANS	GRUNER (ZW)	4	BEANS
	2	PRAWN		2	PRAWN		2	PRAWN		4	PRAWN		4	PRAWN
RED (G)	2	SEA BASS	RED (G)	2	SEA BASS	RED (G)	2	SEA BASS	RED (G)	4	SEA BASS	RED (G)	4	SEA BASS
CHABLIS (G)	2	ONAGA	CHABLIS (G)	2	ONAGA	CHABLIS (G)	2	ONAGA	CHABLIS (G)	4	ONAGA	CHABLIS (G)	3	ONAGA 1 TREE NUT
	2	BRAIN		2	BRAIN		2	BRAIN		4	BRAIN		4	BRAIN
	2	PLOUT		2	PLOUT		2	PLOUT		4	PLOUT		4	PLOUT
RIVESALT (ZW)	2	CHEESE	RIVESALT (ZW)	2	CHEESE	RIVESALT (ZW)	2	CHEESE	RIVESALT (ZW)	4	CHEESE	RIVESALT (ZW)	4	CHEESE
	2	BANANA		2	BANANA		2	BANANA		4	BANANA		3	BANANA 1 TREE NUT
	2	FIG		2	FIG		2	FIG		4	FIG		4	FIG
CHAMP (ZW)	2	DONUT	CHAMP (ZW)	2	DONUT	CHAMP (ZW)	2	DONUT	CHAMP (ZW)	4	DONUT	CHAMP (ZW)	4	DONUT
	2	CORN		2	CORN		2	CORN		4	CORN		4	CORN
	2	MIGN		2	MIGN		2	MIGN		4	MIGN		4	MIGN
									1x Peanut Allergy			1x Tree Nut Allergy		

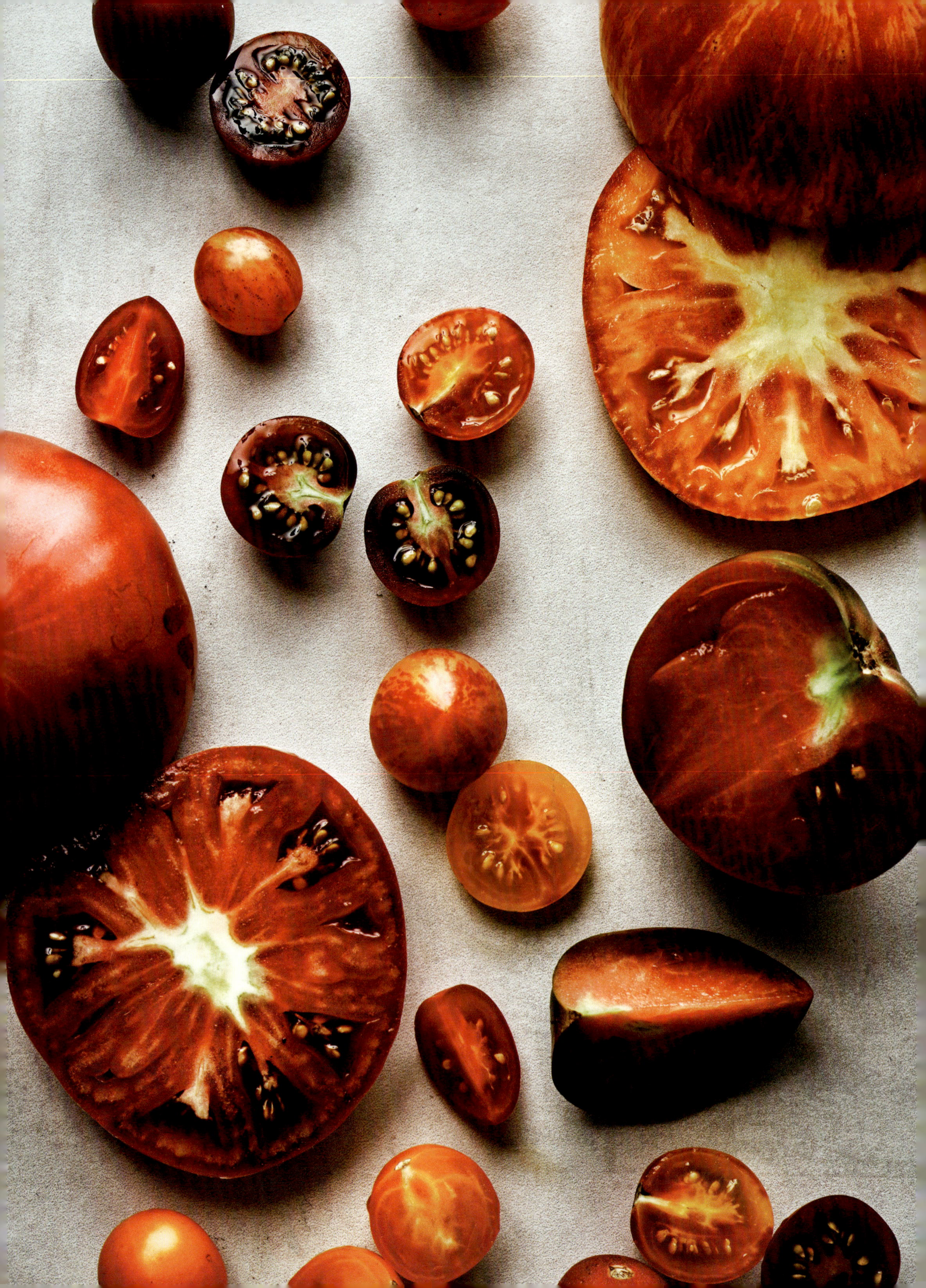

Now we can see how those initial ideas, fleshed out, became our first menu in our first season, summer. With all the tomato ideas floating around, I decided to have a "feast of tomatoes" toward the end of the meal to highlight the incredible flavor punch of Tennessee tomatoes at their peak of deliciousness. While I wanted to work with country ham—and did, as you'll see in the unexpected combination of melon, elderflower, and country ham—I was also inspired to use cured and smoked swordfish for the redneck sushi bite, treating it in much the same way as you would smoked country ham.

Summer never goes by without my thinking about the freshness of cucumber and melons, which I love to pair with another summer staple: elderflower. We also made use of a bounty of filet green beans, something that would make my aunt Beth proud, as she was the person who actually got me to eat them in the first place. Her secret, like many cooks before her, was bacon. I went with a lighter touch.

Some other fun combinations I highlighted in this inaugural menu were Alabama Blue Crab (which has a painfully short season) and summer squash, sunflower and curry, and corn made into a custard-like chawanmushi with winter truffle dashi. It didn't take us long to hit our stride, and I was very proud of the first menu.

Credit: Todd Saal

SUMMER 2020 MENU

"redneck sushi" crispy grits, swordfish ham, fermented tomato **12**

cucumber & melon salad, salted buttermilk, country ham gelee **15**

filet beans with smoked clams & leather britches tea **16**

alabama blue crab & courgette **19**

corn chawanmushi, 24-month aged ham, winter truffle dashi **20**

———————

A FEAST OF TOMATOES

beefsteak tomato roasted in dry-aged beef fat, porcini,
sauce marchand de vin **24**

sungold tomatoes oscar **27**

green garlic fry bread with fermented tomato
& aged sheep's milk cheese **28**

tiny tomato pie **31**

tomato salad with pineapple & litchi blossom **32**

———————

cantaloupe sherbet with sake & elderflower **35**

"REDNECK SUSHI" CRISPY GRITS, SWORDFISH HAM, FERMENTED TOMATO

Redneck sushi is a bite that has been on our menu from the beginning and has evolved a bit with each season, depending on what's available or what we may have cured from a previous season. It's built like a bite of nigiri using mostly Southern ingredients—a great way to utilize any extra grits remaining from a batch. Our first version was swordfish loin that was cured, smoked, and aged like country ham, served over the top of crispy grits with preserved horseradish and brushed with a smoked soy sauce. We also did a version with a glaze made from Spam garum and fresh wasabi. Here it is served in its original form: crispy grits seasoned like sushi rice, preserved horseradish, swordfish "ham," and smoked and fermented tomato.

---

sushi grits

cooked grits	850g	Mix until well combined. Allow to cool. Quenelle and reserve in the freezer.
mirin	15g	
brown rice vinegar	20g	
salt	2g	
glutinous rice flour	30g	

smoked tomato nikiri

smoked tomato reduction (see page 269)	150g	Whisk together until incorporated. Reserve chilled until needed.
yeast emulsion	2g	
benne seed oil	6g	
okra seed oil	10g	

swordfish ham

swordfish loin	1kg	Rub the swordfish loin in half of the cure and cover for 5 days. After 5 days, rub with the remaining cure, cover again for another 5 days. After day 10, rinse the swordfish loin and place on a rack in the reach-in to form a pellicle overnight. Cold-smoke for 8 days and place in a curing chamber. Continue to dry until 30 percent weight loss has been achieved. Trim away any of the fish that is too dry, portion into manageable blocks, freeze, and slice on a meat slicer to desired consistency.
country ham cure (see page 273)	985g	

additional ingredients & to finish

preserved horseradish	Fry the grit quenelles at 350°F until golden brown and hot all the way through. Top with desired amount of preserved horseradish and a slice of the swordfish ham, and brush with the smoked tomato nikiri.
Maldon sea salt	

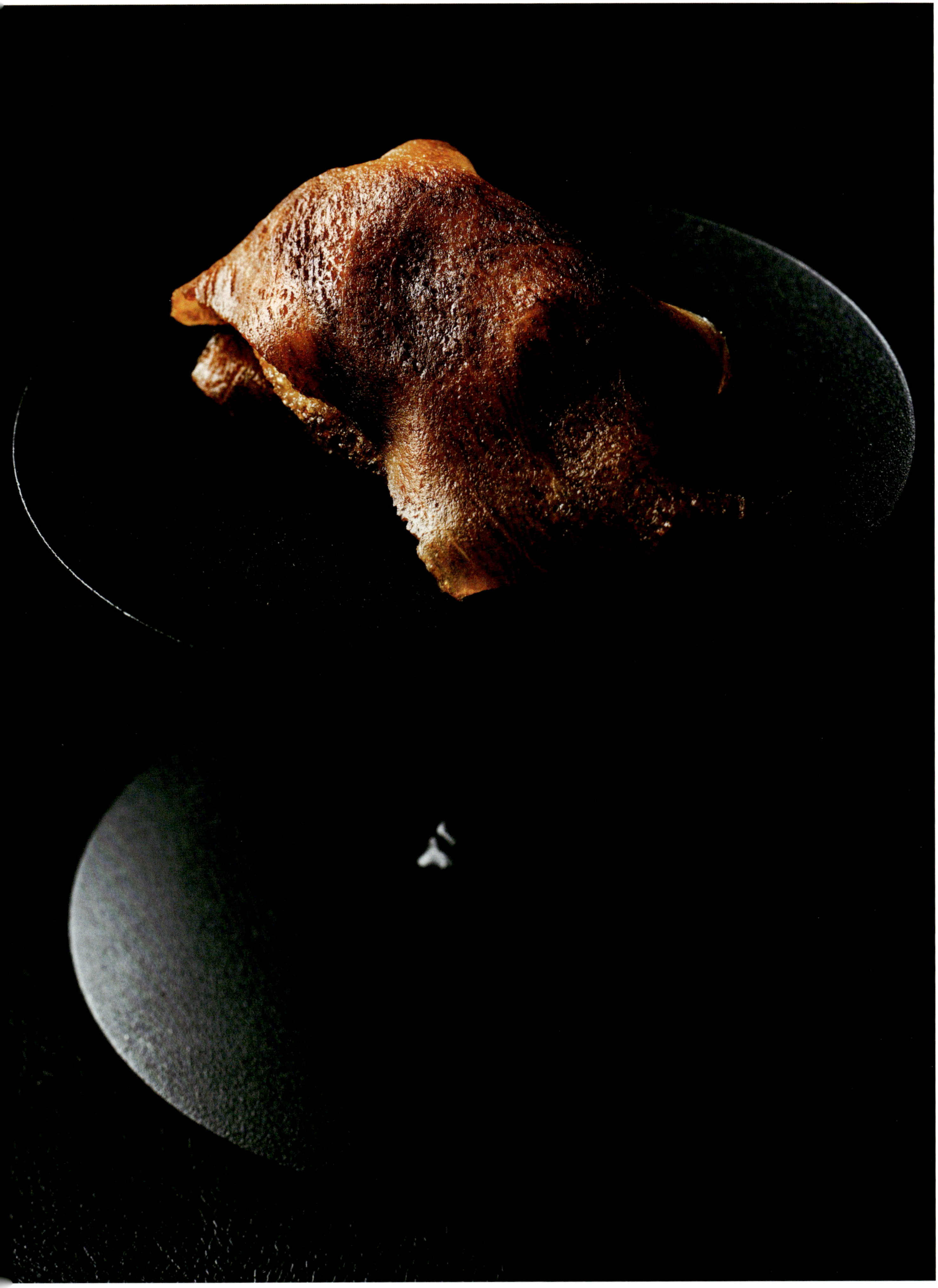

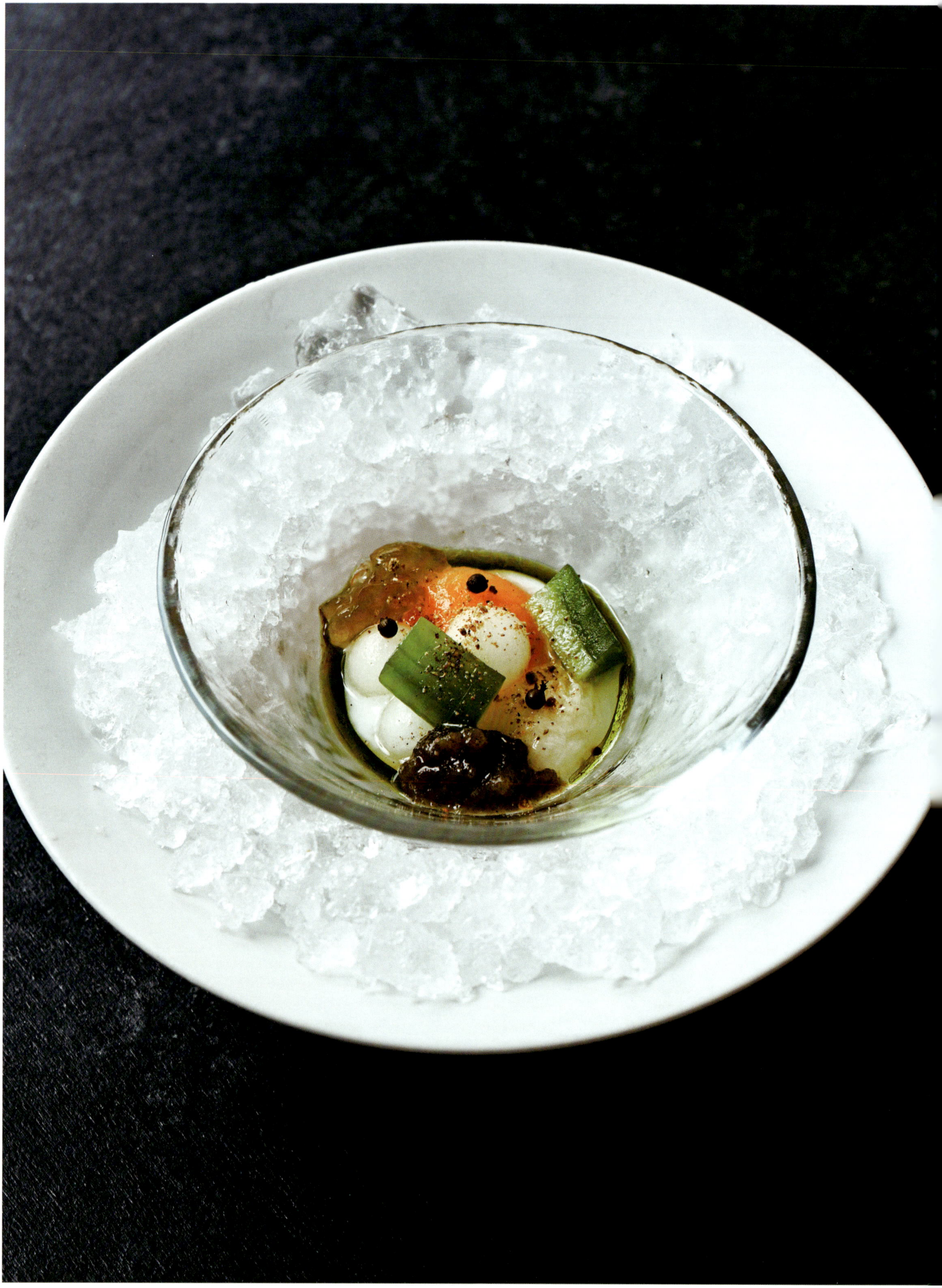

CUCUMBER & MELON SALAD, SALTED BUTTERMILK, COUNTRY HAM GELEE

For this dish, I wanted to play with the classic pairing of melon and prosciutto while using a Southern ham. Since we were already using Middle Tennessee's legendary butcher Bob Woods's "Tenniscuitto" in one of our other dishes, we decided to use the poaching liquid from his holiday hams. It already has a lot of gelatin and salinity to it because of its concentration from poaching the cured hams, so we didn't do much but add a small percentage of gelatin to tighten it up a bit. We also added a gelee made from burnt cucumber to add a bit of smoke flavor. We left the melons to be at their absolute peak ripeness and scooped them out to order, which can be a bit messy, but the flavor doesn't get any better. We served it all over buttermilk that had been lightly soured with a kosho made from coriander berries, topped with some capered coriander berries from our garden, and seasoned with a mixture of different toasted peppercorns.

---

salted buttermilk

kosher salt	20g
buttermilk	1L
green yuzu kosho	20g

Mix salt and buttermilk and ferment at room temperature for 5 to 7 days. Add yuzu kosho and allow to steep overnight or for a minimum of 12 hours at room temperature. Strain through a fine-mesh strainer and chill.

oyster gelee

smoked oyster shiro dashi	100g
smoked and dried oysters	25g
yuzu juice	50g
mirin	20g
kombu	2g
agar-agar	1g
gelatin, bloomed in ice water	1.5g

Bring shiro dashi, smoked oysters, yuzu juice, mirin, and kombu to a simmer and allow to infuse for 30 minutes. Strain and shear in the agar-agar. Bring to a boil for one minute, add the gelatin, and chill in a shallow pan until completely cool and set. Use a fork to bust up into a rough jelly texture.

charred cucumber gelee

slicing cucumber	450g
agar-agar	1g
gelatin, bloomed in ice water	1.7g

Lightly oil the cucumbers. Burn them until charred but before they begin to split and lose too much water. Juice the charred cucumbers, strain the juice, and reduce to 200g. Add the agar-agar and bring back to a boil for one minute. Add the gelatin and chill in a shallow pan until completely cool and set. Use a fork to bust up into a rough jelly texture.

compressed cucumber

slicing cucumber, deseeded and cut into 4" batonnets	1 ea
lemon verbena oil (see below)	25g

Season the cut side of the cucumber lightly with kosher salt. Place in a Cryovac bag, add the lemon verbena oil, and seal on full pressure. After 10 minutes, remove from the bag and reserve in the oil until needed.

lemon verbena, dried	200g
grapeseed oil	500g

Place all ingredients in a Vitamix and blend on high until the oil reaches 62°C. Allow to strain overnight through a coffee-filter-lined mesh strainer.

peppercorn spice

bee pollen	15g
black Lampong peppercorn	25g
red Sichuan peppercorn	5g
kampot long peppercorn	10g
red kampot peppercorn berries	10g
fennel pollen	5g

Toast all the peppercorns over medium heat until aromatic. Allow to cool and grind until a coarse texture is achieved. Mix with the pollens and store in an airtight container.

additional ingredients & to finish

country ham stock
coriander capers
charentais melon
piel de sapo melon
canary melon

Place a few drops of the lemon verbena oil in the bottom of the bowl. Spoon 2 tablespoons of the salted buttermilk into the center of the oil. On top, scoop 2 balls of each of the melons and scatter around the buttermilk, followed by 2 slices of the compressed cucumber. Place a teaspoon-sized scoop of each of the jellied ham stock, oyster gelee, and cucumber gelee. Spread 3 coriander capers around the melon, and finish by seasoning with the peppercorn.

FILET BEANS WITH SMOKED CLAMS & LEATHER BRITCHES TEA

I have a similar feeling about green beans as I do zucchini—I don't like when they are overcooked and the texture is soft. However, thanks to my great aunt Beth, I will still devour green beans that have been stewing away with a good bit of bacon and ham in them. This dish was another favorite of most of the guests, as it was quite unassuming because of its simplistic presentation. A pile of lightly charred, almost raw filet beans dressed in a vinaigrette made from cured and smoked littleneck clams with a chilled tea made from leather britches (dried greasy beans, an heirloom variety of bean grown in the South) that had been steeped in the clam juices and seasoned with fermented green gooseberry juice. The meatiness of the broth from the beans was quite a surprise.

---

clam & leather britches tea

sake	750mL	Cook sake, shallot, kombu, and leather britches until all the alcohol has burned off. Add the clam stock and reduce at a slow simmer to 650ml. Season with the fermented gooseberry juice and strain through a fine-mesh strainer.
shallot	170g	
kombu	5g	
leather britches	50g	
clam stock (see page 274)	1L	
fermented green gooseberry juice	100g	

smoked clam vinaigrette

grapeseed oil	100g	Place the shiro dashi, clams, sugar, and vinegar in a small pot and bring to a simmer. Remove from the heat and cover for 30 minutes. Transfer to a Vitamix and blend until smooth. Slowly emulsify in the oils.
toasted sesame oil	50g	
smoked and dried clams	45g	
seasoned rice vinegar	65g	
granulated sugar	5g	
smoked clam shiro dashi	65g	

leather britches oil

smoked and dried pea shells	30g	Blend on high for 5 minutes. Strain through a coffee filter and reserve.
leather britches	30g	
grapeseed oil	255g	

clam furikake

Seto Fumi Furikake Rice Seasoning	45g	Mix together until well combined. Store in an airtight container until needed.
smoked and dried clams, ground as fine as possible	10g	

additional ingredients & to finish

green beans, trimmed of stems		Quickly grill the green beans on one side until charred and just beginning to warm through. Slice them to order on the bias and dress in the smoked clam vinaigrette. Season with leather britches oil and furikake. Pour the warm tea right before serving.

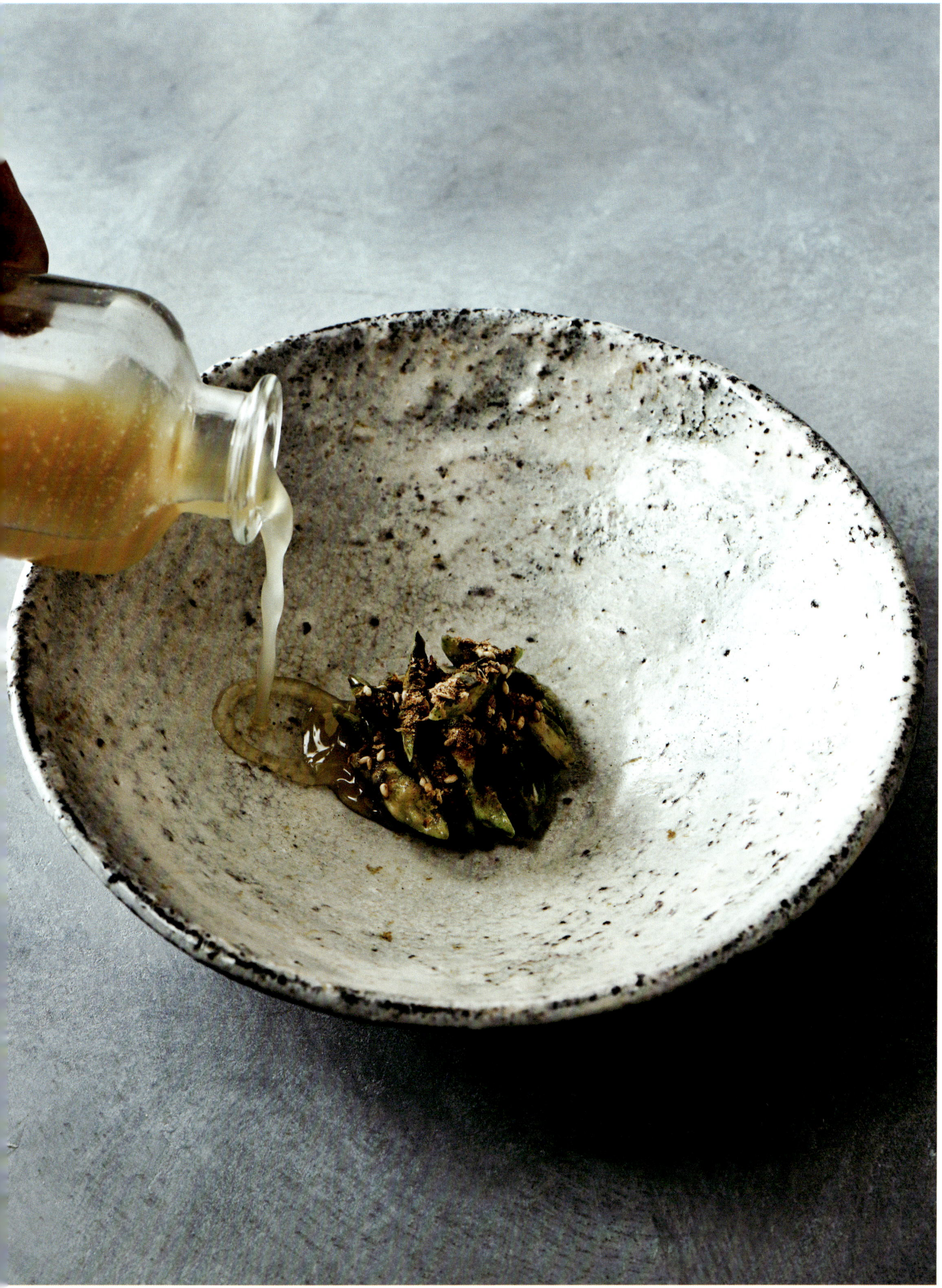

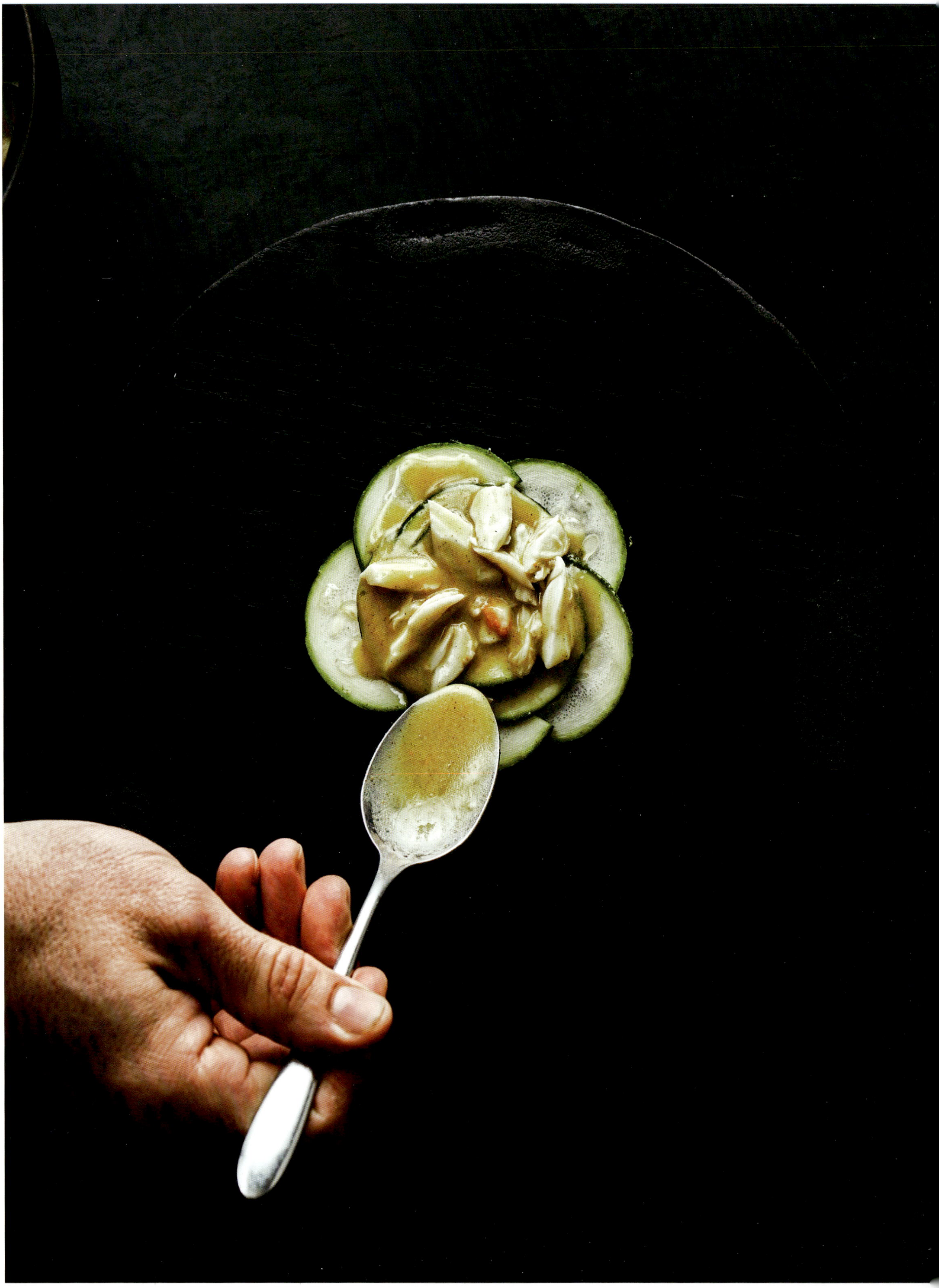

ALABAMA BLUE CRAB & COURGETTE

I love zucchini. This dish was one with which I really wanted to try to showcase the texture and flavor of zucchini when it's just picked in the field. I like the almost-nuttiness it has and the crisp texture. I can't stand when zucchini is served overcooked. It becomes soft and leaches a ton of water. I decided to just cut the zucchini to order and dress in some olive oil, sea salt, and lime zest. We hid a sunflower seed and miso puree underneath. I would then pour a warm crab butter sauce over it, which would just warm the zucchini but allow it to maintain its crisp texture. We finished the butter sauce with our version of a Japanese curry spice and served it with a tempura fried zucchini blossom—to soak up any extra sauce—that had been seasoned with Japanese seven spice and crab powder.

---

sunflower-miso puree

sunflower seeds	222g
butter	225g
filtered water	450mL
white miso	70g
sugar	6g
white shoyu	48g
mirin	16g
sake	16g

Slowly toast the sunflower seeds in the butter until golden brown. Strain off the butter and reserve in a warm place. Add the water and toasted seeds to a pressure cooker on high for 45 minutes. Strain off the water and reserve. Add all the remaining ingredients with the sunflower seeds, and puree until smooth. Add some of the water, if needed to adjust the consistency of the puree. It should be smooth and the texture of peanut butter. Finish the puree by adding 50g of the reserved brown butter.

curry butter

shallot, sliced thin	30g
lacto-fermented whey	100g
crab butter base	150g
bonito	10g
Japanese curry spice	20g
butter, cubed and chilled	220g

Reduce the shallot, whey, crab butter, and bonito over low heat to a volume of 150g. Place in the Vitamix with the curry spice and blend on high. Slowly emulsify in the cold butter. Pass through a fine-mesh strainer and reserve in a warm place until needed.

crab butter base

carrots, small dice	25g
fennel, small dice	45g
onion, small dice	30g
butter	20g
sweet vermouth	300mL
crab juice, reserved from cooling and cleaning	700mL

Sweat the aromatics in the butter over medium heat until soft and translucent. Add the vermouth and reduce until all the alcohol has evaporated. Add the crab juice and reduce until only 400g remains. Pass through a fine-mesh strainer and cool.

additional ingredients & to finish

zucchini, washed and dried
picked crab meat
olive oil
lime zest
lime juice
Pacific sea salt

Slice the zucchini into ¼" half-moon shapes. Dress them in olive oil, sea salt, and lime zest. Place a small spoonful of the sunflower-miso puree in the center of a plate and shingle the zucchini over the top. Gently warm the crab in the curry butter, season to taste with fresh lime juice, and pour the warm sauce over the top of the zucchini.

CORN CHAWANMUSHI, 24-MONTH AGED HAM, WINTER TRUFFLE DASHI

Chawanmushi is a Japanese egg custard that uses dashi as the base. Steaming it very gently leaves you with a silky, umami-rich custard. I thought we could get a little more creative with it if we made a dashi from a particular vegetable juice instead of just filtered water. For this version, we used corn juice infused with kombu and cured, smoked, and dried corn cobs. We cooked it in a sous vide bag, then strained and seasoned it like a traditional chawanmushi base. Once steamed, we dressed it in a dashi made from country ham scraps, fermented winter truffles, and diced ham from Bob Woods. We finished it with rendered ham fat and shaved Australian winter truffles. These are often considered some of the best truffles in the world, and we are very lucky that they are in season during our summer months. We often had a version of chawanmushi on the menu, but I think this one is my favorite.

---

country ham dashi

filtered water	1.1L
kombu, rinsed	25g
dry shiitake	50g
Benton's ham, sliced thin	30g

Place all ingredients in a Cryovac bag sealed on full pressure. Cook in a water bath at 60°C for 45 minutes. Remove from the water bath and allow to steep an additional hour. Strain through a fine-mesh strainer and reserve.

seasoned dashi base

country ham dashi	660g
mirin	200mL
white shoyu	200mL
kuzu starch	15g
cold water	28g
black truffle paste	15g

Bring the country ham dashi, mirin, and shoyu to a simmer. Mix the kuzu starch and cold water, and slowly whisk into the dashi base. Bring back to a simmer and allow to simmer for 2 minutes. Pass through a fine-mesh strainer. Stir in the truffle paste, and cool.

corn dashi

fresh corn juice, strained	1L
kombu	25g
cured, smoked, and dried corn cobs	50g

Process the same as the country ham dashi. Strain immediately after cooking, and cool.

corn chawanmushi base

corn dashi	500g
egg yolks	185g
sake	10mL
white shoyu	20mL
mirin	20mL

Mix well and reserve until needed.

additional ingredients & to finish

Benton's ham, brunoised
Australian winter truffles

Divide 15g of the base into separate bowls. Cover with plastic wrap. Steam at 82°C for 8 minutes or until just set through, but allowing the custard to have a slight jiggle to it. Add the diced ham to the seasoned-ham dashi base and bring to a simmer. Add desired amount of dashi to each bowl, and top with freshly shaved truffles.

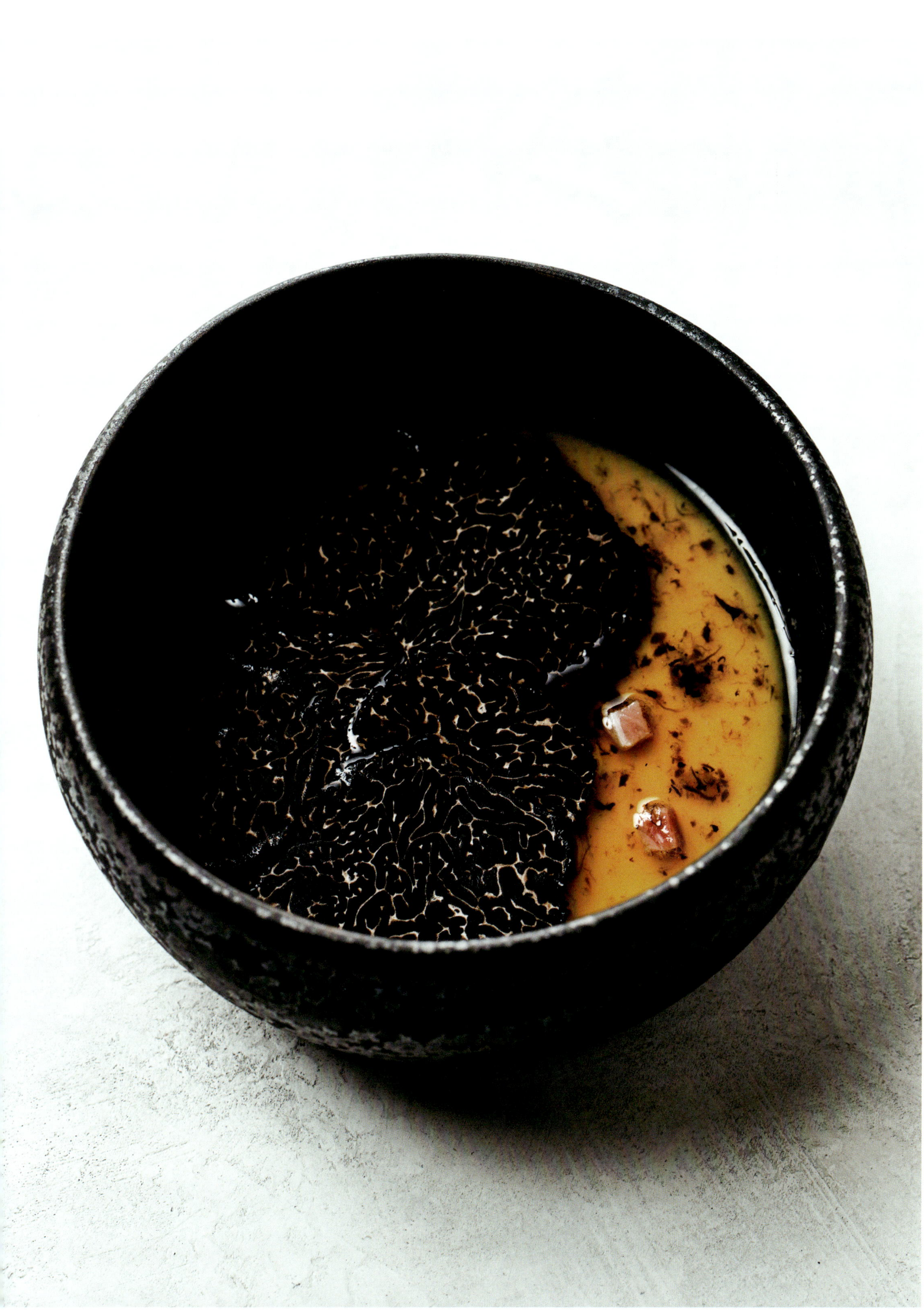

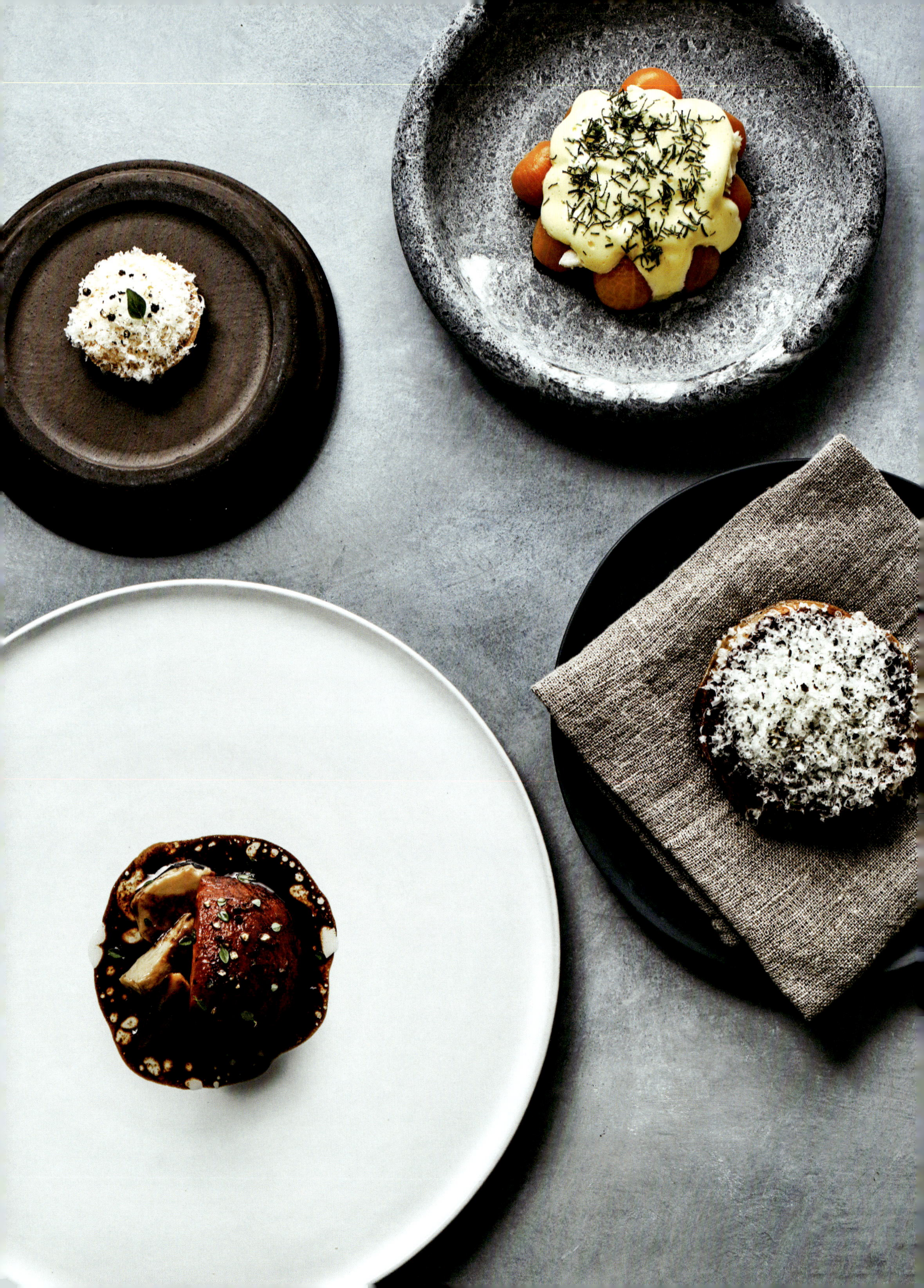

a feast of tomatoes

BEEFSTEAK TOMATO ROASTED IN DRY-AGED BEEF FAT, PORCINI, SAUCE MARCHAND DE VIN

I love highlighting ingredients when they are at their peak as much as possible in a menu. There are so many varieties of tomato that it is usually one of the easiest components to use multiple times without seeming redundant. For our main course, we took whole beefsteak tomatoes that were peeled, cured, and sun-dried for a few hours until a good bit of the moisture had left the fruit. This not only helps concentrate the flavor, but it also makes them easier to roast in the hot fat. To order, the tomatoes are roasted in a mixture of beef fat, butter, garlic, and thyme, and basted until dark and almost crisp on the outside. They are sliced and served with porcini mushrooms that have been confited in beef fat and seasoned with porcini mushroom garum. I then made a quick pan sauce with some of the remaining brown butter and finished the dish with lemon thyme from our garden.

---

confited porcini

porcini mushrooms, cleaned and quartered	1kg
kosher salt	10g
rendered dry-aged beef fat (tallow)	1kg
bay leaves	2ea
thyme sprigs	5ea

Toss the mushrooms in the salt and let sit for 30 minutes. Cryovac all the ingredients at full pressure. Cook at 85°C for 12 minutes. Allow to cool to room temperature. Transfer to an ice bath until completely cooled.

sauce marchand de vin

beef tallow	100g
shallot, sliced thin	300g
mushroom stems, sliced	120g
dried mushroom such as maitake or morel	60g
black peppercorns	12g
dry red wine, such as tempranillo, pinot noir, or cabernet sauvignon	750mL
bay leaf	1ea
thyme sprigs	5g
demi-glace	3500g
porcini garum (see page 271)	t.t.

Melt the beef tallow. Once hot, add shallot and mushrooms and cook until a deep golden brown. Add the black peppercorns and cook until aromatic, about 3 to 4 minutes. Next, add the red wine, bay leaf, and thyme. Cook on medium heat until reduced by ¾ of its original volume. Add the veal stock and reduce to 1L. Strain through a fine-mesh strainer, season to taste with the porcini garum, and reserve.

beefsteak tomatoes

beefsteak tomatoes	4ea
kosher salt by weight	10%
sugar by weight	2%

Peel the tomatoes and weigh them. Season with the proper weight of the salt and sugar (multiply by .10 for the salt and .02 for the sugar). Place a layer of cheesecloth on a sheet pan lined with a roasting rack. Arrange the tomatoes on the rack, making sure they do not touch. Cover in cheesecloth and dry in the sun or a dehydrator set to 115°F until they begin to shrivel and the outer layer begins to dry out, 3 to 4 hours.

additional ingredients & to finish

rendered beef fat
butter, cubed
thyme sprigs
garlic cloves, peeled
lemon juice
lemon thyme leaves
black peppercorn
Maldon sea salt

Place a cast iron over medium-high heat. Add a couple of tablespoons of beef fat and a couple of tablespoons of butter. Once the butter begins to foam, add the tomatoes stem-side down. Slowly start basting the tomato in the warm butter. After a couple of minutes, add 2 smashed garlic cloves and the thyme sprigs. Continue to roast in the butter until the tomato begins to turn a dark brown color on the outside and is warm all the way through. Remove the tomato from the pan and drain off all but a tablespoon of the butter. Squeeze in a little lemon juice, add 3 oz of the marchand de vin sauce, and reduce by ⅓. Slice the tomato, serve with a couple of pieces of confited porcini, and dress with the pan sauce. Finish with Maldon salt, freshly cracked black peppercorn, and lemon thyme leaves.

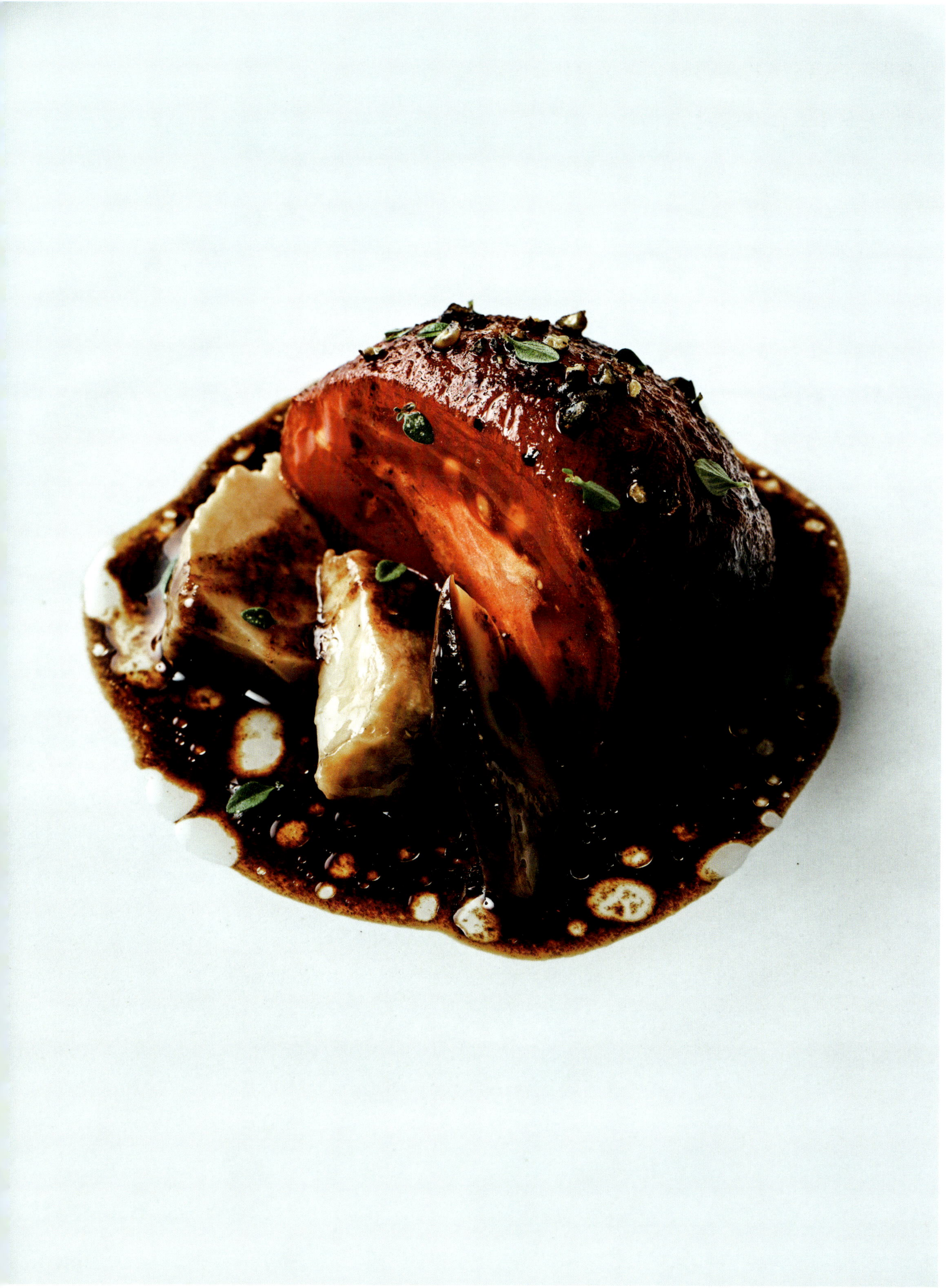

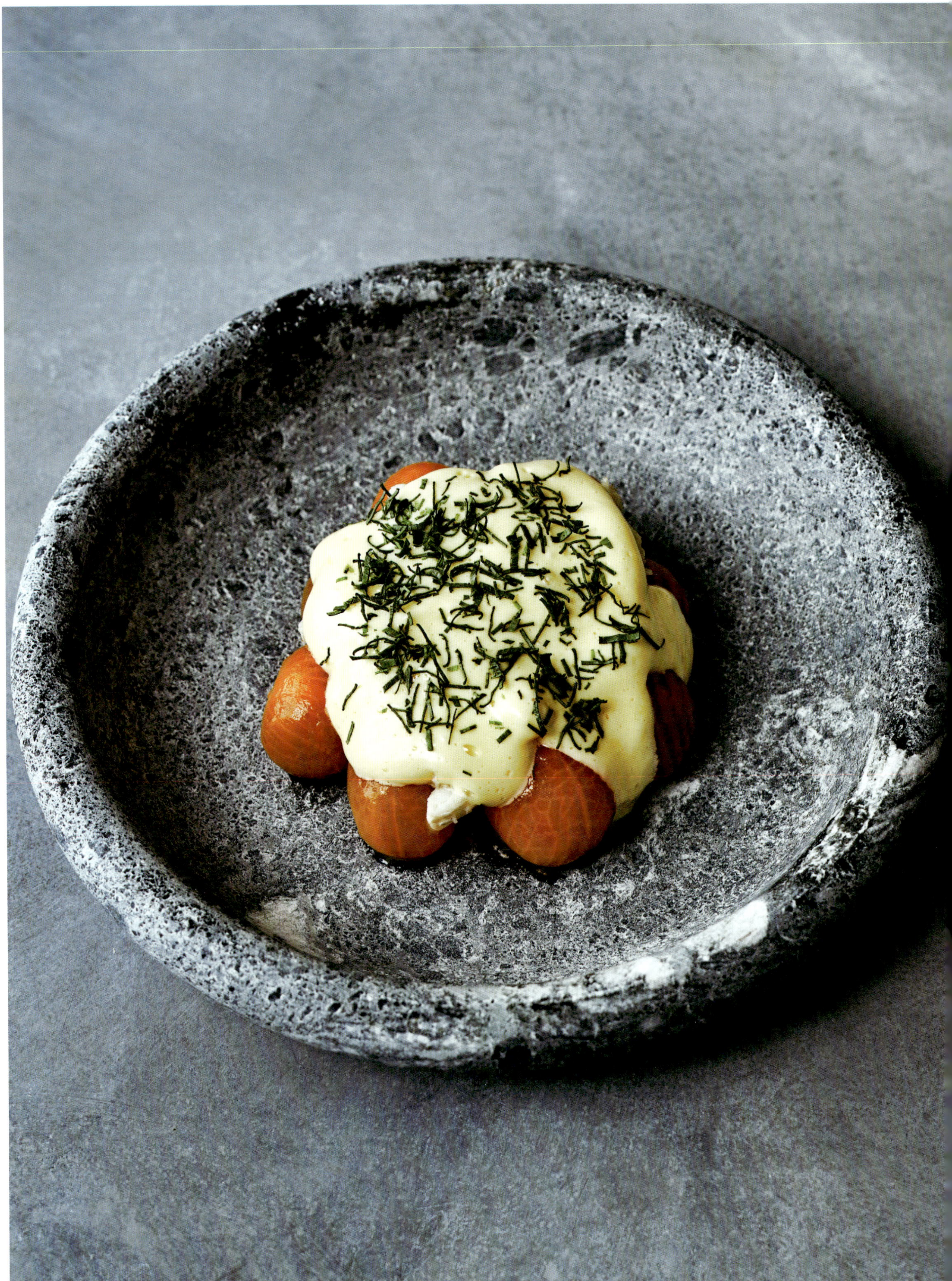

SUNGOLD TOMATOES OSCAR

To continue with the steak theme, I decided to serve something simple here: fresh-peeled Sungold tomatoes with Hokkaido hairy crab warmed in butter and dressed in a white asparagus bearnaise. I have loved bearnaise since the first time I tried it at The Wine Cellar, my first restaurant job in Indian Rocks Beach, Florida. It was there that I first saw dishes carved or finished tableside, such as chateaubriand, rack of lamb, Dover sole, and baked Alaska to name a few. The restaurant has since closed, but I'm glad I was able to work somewhere that still cooked so many classic dishes. This is a tribute to the classic edition of Oscar; however, we've used the asparagus in the sauce.

---

tarragon vinegar

shallot, brunoised	25g
tarragon leaves, minced	35g
seaweed vinegar	350g
black Lampong peppercorn	1g

Reduce on low heat by 50 percent. Allow to cool to room temperature, and steep overnight.

fermented white asparagus bearnaise

egg yolks, cooked at 65°C for 45 minutes	160g
tarragon vinegar	15g
fermented white asparagus (see page 269)	40g
fermented white asparagus juice (reserved from above)	45g
lemon juice	10g
butter, melted	454g
salt	t.t.

Puree the cooked egg yolks with the vinegar, the white asparagus and its juice, and the lemon juice. Slowly emulsify in the melted butter. Season to taste with salt. Reserve in a warm area.

sungold tomatoes

Sungold tomatoes	1 pint
kosher salt	3%
granulated sugar	1.5%

Blanch and peel the tomatoes. Save the skins for another use (we ferment and dry to steep in oils and sauces). Weigh the tomatoes, and season with proper amounts of salt and sugar. Let cure for 30 minutes. Rinse gently in cold water and pat dry. Sun-dry for 4 to 5 hours until the tomatoes start to lose some of their moisture and the flavor begins to concentrate. Alternatively, dry at 110°F.

additional ingredients & to finish

picked hairy crab meat
tarragon leaves
yuzu juice

Arrange 7 or 8 of the tomatoes on a plate. Dress the crab with yuzu juice and spoon over the tomatoes. Completely cover in the bearnaise and garnish with freshly minced tarragon.

GREEN GARLIC FRY BREAD WITH FERMENTED TOMATO & AGED SHEEP'S MILK CHEESE

This was my sous chef Ian's recipe for bread that we have used on a few different sets. It is rolled super-thin, brushed with an infused butter of preserved green garlic, and rolled before being proofed. When fried, you are left with a super-airy, light, and flaky bread. We brushed it with a jam made from fermented and smoked tomatoes, fresh thyme, pecorino cheese, smoked sea salt, and freshly cracked peppercorns. He described it as "the best garlic knot you've ever had."

---

green garlic butter

butter, softened	450g
green garlic bulbs, minced thin	30g
green garlic tops, grilled and minced fine	25g
pickled ramp, brunoised	10g
salt	t.t.

Mix together in a robot coupe or mixer set with a paddle attachment.

garlic fry bread

egg	1ea
sweetened condensed milk	30g
salt	8g
filtered water	288g
high-gluten flour	520g

Combine all ingredients and mix with a dough hook on low speed for 10 minutes. Let the dough rest for 10 minutes, then mix for an additional 5 minutes. Portion into 100g balls. Place on a lightly oiled plastic- or Silpat-lined tray. Coat the dough balls in the oil, wrap in plastic, and proof for one hour. After one hour, take one of the portioned balls and roll paper-thin on a flat surface. Spread a thin layer of garlic butter to cover the dough. Starting with the end closest to you, slowly roll the dough over itself toward the top of the dough. Take one and coil the bread around tightly. Transfer to another lightly oiled plastic- or Silpat-lined tray. Repeat with the additional portions. Wrap in plastic and proof an additional 30 minutes. After the second proofing, roll out to ¼" thickness, and sear in a cast iron over medium heat until deep golden brown, crispy, and cooked all the way through.

fermented tomato reduction

lacto-fermented tomato juice	1L
granulated sugar	70g

Slowly reduce over low heat until a syrupy consistency is achieved. Reserve until needed.

fermented tomato jam

smoked and lacto-fermented tomatoes	900g
Omed cider vinegar	480g
Worcestershire	60g
brown sugar	215g
allspice berries	2ea
salt	t.t.

Slowly reduce all the ingredients except the salt until most of the moisture has evaporated and a jam consistency is achieved. Season to taste with salt, remove the allspice berries, cool, and reserve in an airtight container.

additional ingredients & to finish

lemon thyme leaves
pecorino cheese
black peppercorns

Brush a piece of the warm fried bread with the tomato reduction. Top with a thin layer of tomato jam and fresh thyme leaves and cover with shaved pecorino. Finish with freshly cracked black peppercorns.

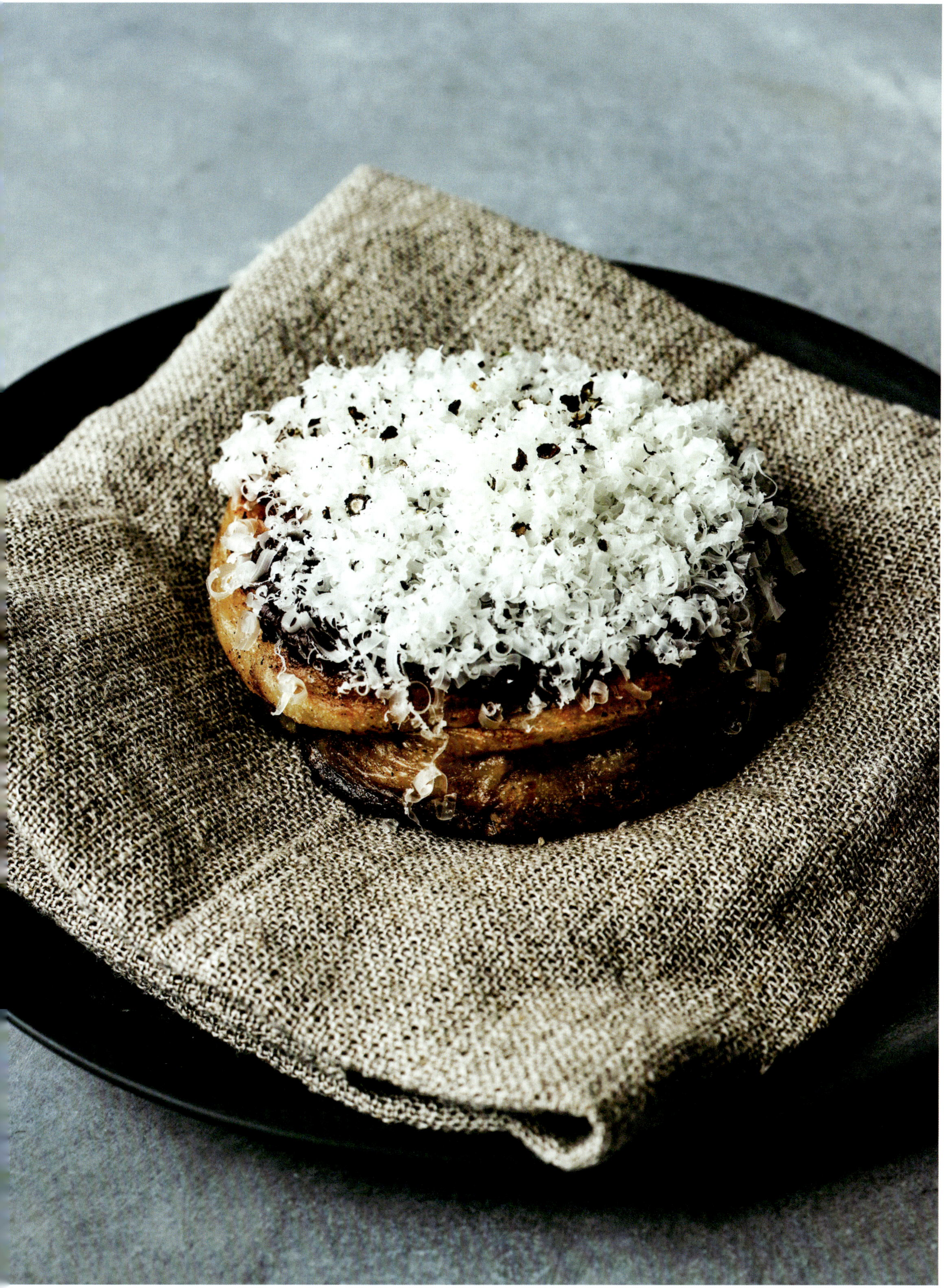

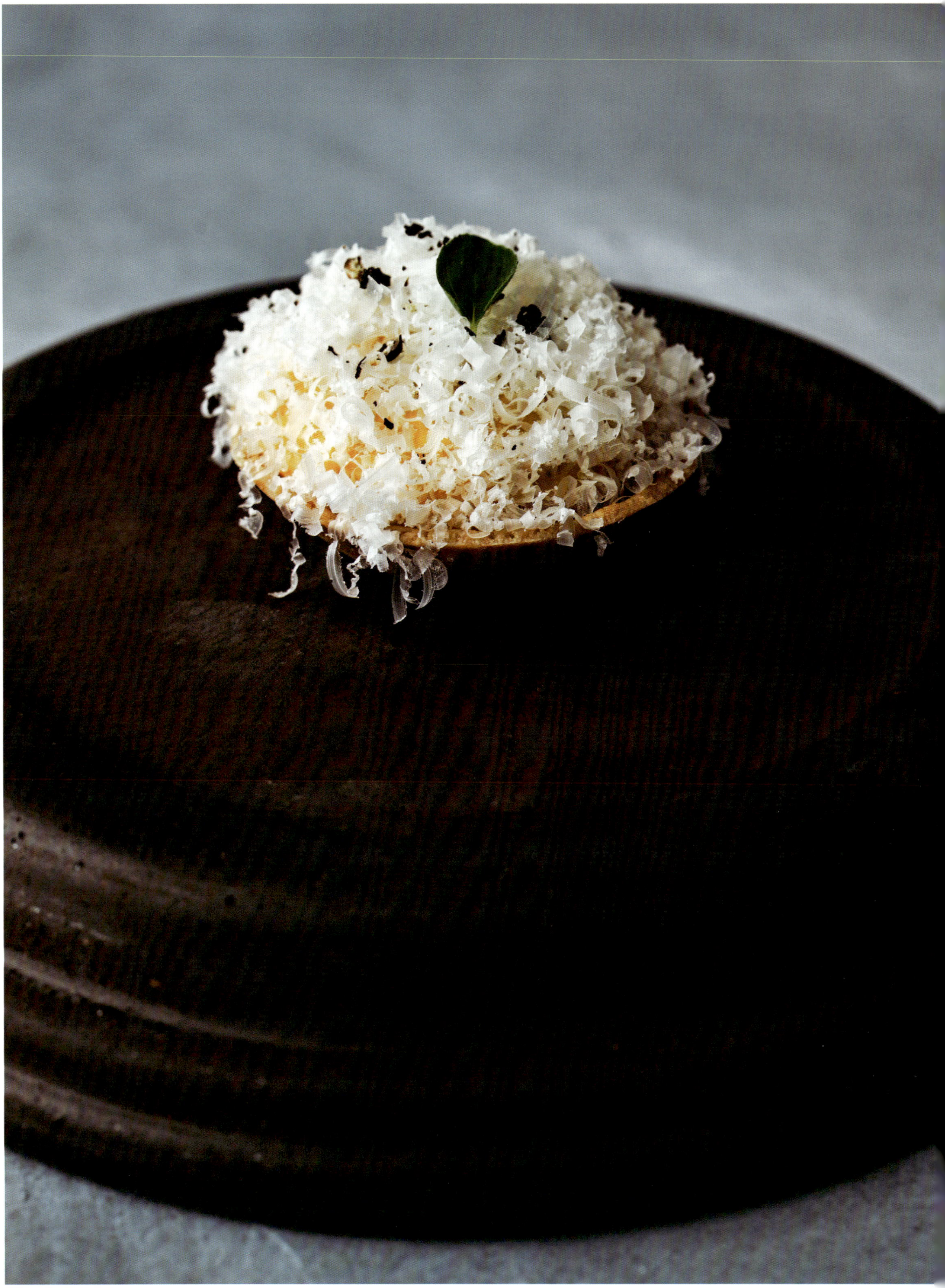

TINY TOMATO PIE

The finishing bite of the feast is the smallest, but also ended up being most people's favorite. What looks like a tartlette with only 3 ingredients actually has the most ingredients on this course. We used a few different tomatoes throughout the season, but Sungold is definitely our favorite for this. The Sungolds are peeled, cured in salt and sugar, smoked, and then dehydrated until they have the texture of a rehydrated raisin and concentrated tomato flavor. They are then tossed in a vinaigrette made with a reduction of fermented tomato juice, tomato-leaf oil, and rendered pecorino-cheese fat. They are served in a pie crust made with pecorino-cheese fat, filled with a small spoonful of tomato nduja and fresh herbs, and finished with a sauce chorón made from a fermented tomato paste, made similarly to making a bouillon paste. The herbs in this changed, based on availability; but lemon thyme, wild marjoram, and pineapple sage flower were our favorites.

---

tart dough

AP flour	450g
kosher salt	7g
rendered cheese fat, chilled	100g
olive oil	125g
ice water	120g

In a robot coupe, mix the dry ingredients. Pulse in the cheese fat, followed by the olive oil. Do not overmix. The dough should be a sandy texture. Lastly, pulse in the ice water, remove from the robot coupe, and quickly knead into a smooth dough. Do not let the dough get too warm. Wrap in plastic and cool overnight.

sauce chorón

tomato bouillon (see page 270)	55g
butter	200g
egg yolks	65g
tomato vinegar	10g
filtered water	10g

Melt the tomato bouillon and butter over low heat. Place the egg yolks in a Vitamix. Bring the water and tomato vinegar to a simmer, pour over the eggs, and puree until smooth. Slowly emulsify in the butter mixture. Season to taste with salt and place in an ISI charger with one charge of N2O. Hold in a water bath set to 45°C.

tomato vinaigrette

fermented tomato reduction	50g
yeast emulsion	2g
tomato vine oil	6g
burnt cheese fat	10g

Mix together and reserve warm in a small sauce pot.

cured tomatoes

cherry tomatoes	1pt
salt	3%
granulated sugar	1.5%

Blanch and peel the tomatoes. Save the skins for another use (we ferment and dry to steep in oils and sauces). Weigh the tomatoes and season with proper amounts of salt and sugar. Let cure for 30 minutes. Rinse gently in cold water and pat dry. Cold-smoke for 30 minutes, and dry in a dehydrator set to 120°F until almost the texture of raisin but still slightly plump. Place in the tomato vinaigrette and reserve warm until ready to plate.

tomato nduja

tomato pulp (left over from juicing)	1kg
rice koji	50g
smoked paprika	38g
cayenne	1g
chipotle Morita powder	4g
garlic, microplaned	10g
kosher salt	24g
grapeseed oil	100g

Mix all the ingredients except the oil together and puree in a Vitamix. Cold-smoke for 4 hours. Cool, place in a Cryovac bag, and seal on full pressure. Allow to ferment in a warm place for at least 1 week. Once desired sourness is achieved, puree in a Vitamix on high speed with the grapeseed oil. Cool and reserve in an airtight container.

additional ingredients & to finish

pecorino
marjoram or oregano
black pepper

Place a teaspoon of the nduja in the center of a tart shell. Add one or two of the cured tomatoes, depending on the size, and top with a small dollop of the sauce chorón. Finish with the shaved pecorino, freshly cracked black peppercorns, and a marjoram leaf.

TOMATO SALAD WITH PINEAPPLE & LITCHI BLOSSOM

We always finish our savory dishes with a salad, as a nod to Auguste Escoffier. This was a simple salad of fresh tomatoes dressed in a tea made from clarified tomato water that was frozen and allowed to drip in our Kyoto cold-brew coffee maker over a mixture of litchi blossom, tomato vine, and dried herbs. It is finished with a granita made from pineapple and fresh herbs from our garden.

---

pineapple granita

glucose	150g
fresh pineapple juice	1L
fermented pineapple reduction	10g
gelatin, bloomed	2g
white verjus	100g
citric acid	1g

Warm the glucose, 200g of the fresh pineapple juice, and the fermented pineapple reduction over medium heat. Melt in the gelatin and mix with the remaining ingredients, stirring well to combine. Freeze in a shallow third pan.

tomato tea

Emperor's litchi blossoms, broken apart	2ea
dried lemon verbena	10g
dried lemon balm	5g
dried lemon thyme	5g
dried anise hyssop	5g
vanilla bean, not scraped	2g
clarified tomato water, frozen in ice cube trays	1L

Place the aromatics in the middle beaker of the cold brewer. Place the frozen tomato water in the top beaker and adjust the brass fitting to slowly drip over the herbs overnight. Chill immediately and reserve.

additional ingredients & to finish

fresh heirloom tomatoes

fresh herbs such as anise hyssop flowers, lemon verbena, fennel flower, tangerine lace or marigold leaves, cilantro flowers, etc.

Maldon sea salt

Cut the tomatoes to order into different bite-size shapes. Place in the center of the bowl, and season with a pinch of Maldon. Dress with the chilled tomato tea and a few shavings of the pineapple granita. Garnish with a few herbs and serve immediately.

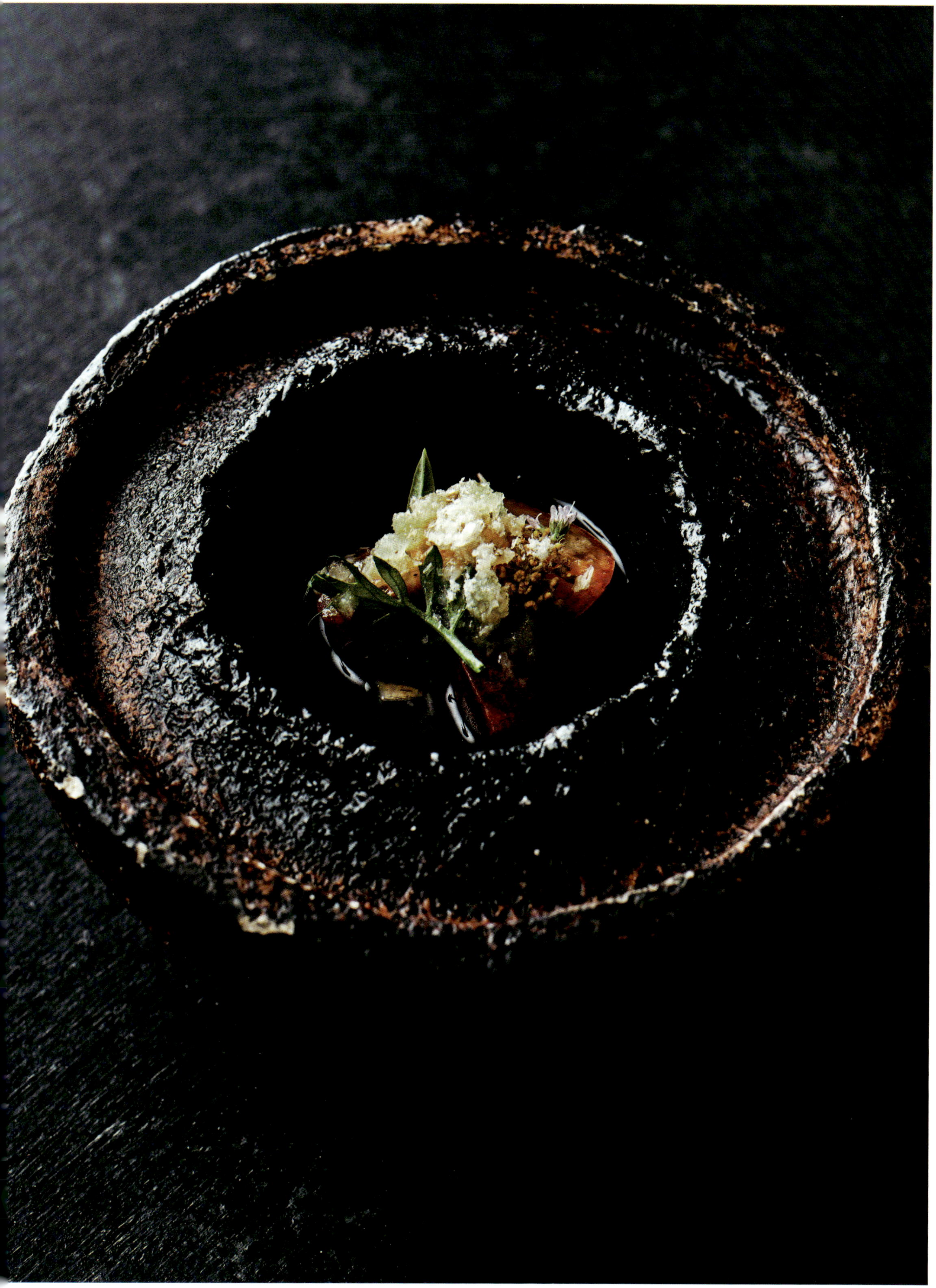

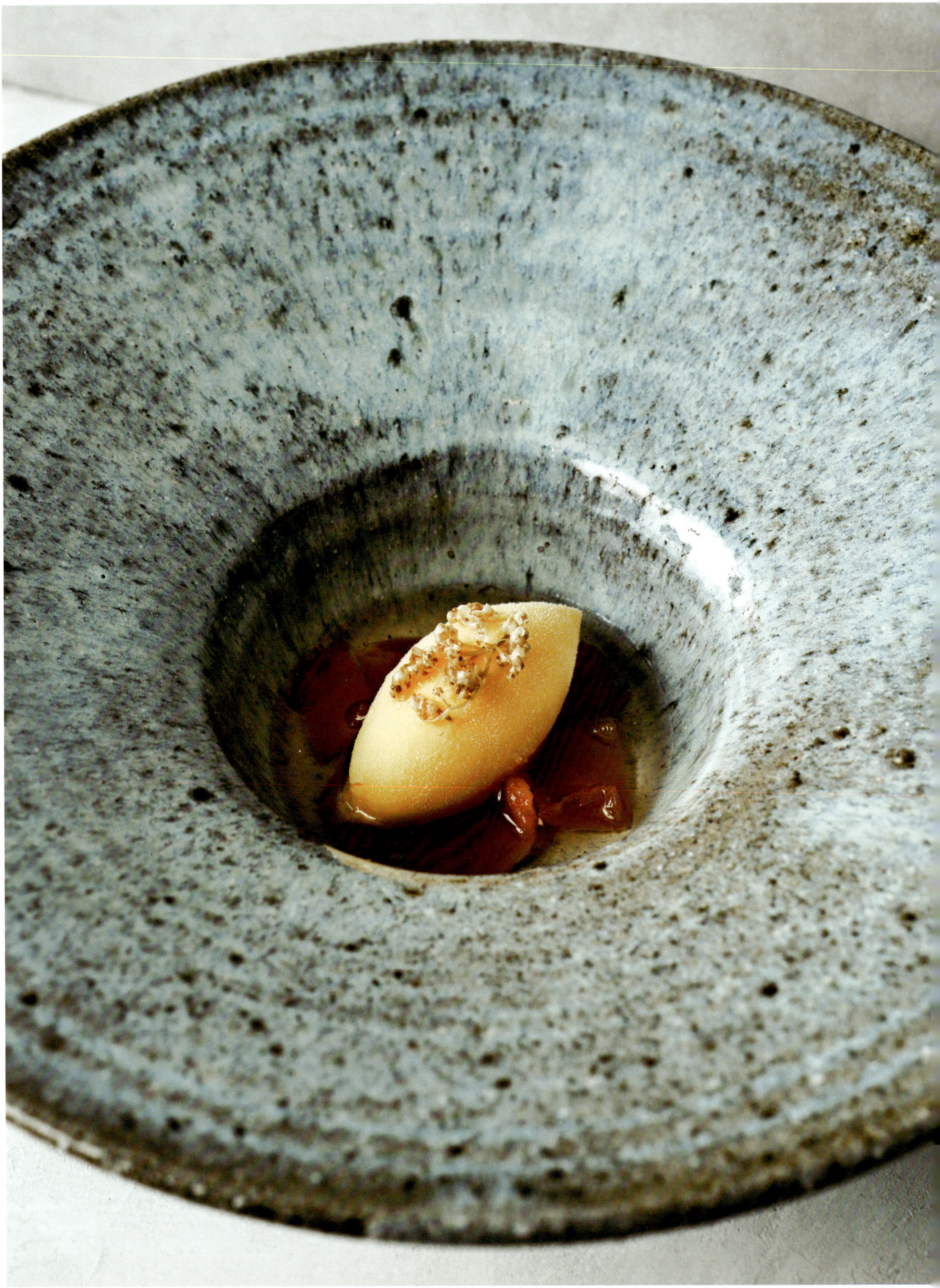

CANTALOUPE SHERBET WITH SAKE & ELDERFLOWER

My sous chef Ian and I developed this dish at the beginning of the summer. I give a lot of credit to his working under Geo Salas at Smyth in Chicago for his ability to take my ideas for desserts and make them a reality. For this, we took cantaloupe juice and turned it into a classic sherbet. He then proposed cooking the melon in a syrup made from St-Germain Elderflower Liqueur, pickled elderflower, and sake, and then dehydrating it to create a concentrated, chewy bite of cantaloupe. The chilled, reduced syrup is poured over the chewy cantaloupe, and the sherbet is topped with pickled elderflower.

---

cantaloupe sherbet

heavy cream	240mL
corn syrup	360g
granulated sugar	100g
kosher salt	1.5g
cantaloupe juice	480mL

Bring the cream, corn syrup, sugar, and salt to a simmer. Once dissolved, remove from the heat, and stir in the melon juice. Pour into Paco canisters and freeze. Spin 30 minutes before using.

pickled elderflower

fresh elderflowers, picked of larger stems	1pt
Omed cider vinegar	300mL
St-Germain Elderflower Liqueur	200mL
sugar	100g

Bring the cider vinegar, sugar, and St-Germain to a boil for one minute. Pour over the flowers and allow to cool at room temperature. Store in the refrigerator for at least 5 days before using.

candied cantaloupe

cantaloupe, deseeded and cut into 1" × 3" × 1/8"-thick slices	850g
granulated sugar	450g
filtered water	250mL
sake, alcohol burned off	200mL

Mix all the ingredients together and cook over a double boiler until the cantaloupe is tender but still holds its shape. Remove the cantaloupe ribbons, gently draining off as much of the liquid as possible. Dry at 120°F until chewy but not dry. Reserve the liquid for the cantaloupe syrup.

cantaloupe syrup

reserved candied cantaloupe liquid	800g
citric acid	4g

Mix until the citric acid is dissolved. Reserve chilled.

additional ingredients & to finish

Maldon sea salt	

Place a spoonful of the chilled cantaloupe syrup in the bottom of a bowl. Cut a cantaloupe ribbon into 3 equal pieces and add to the syrup. Place a quenelle of the cantaloupe sherbet in the bowl, and finish with a few pickled elderflowers and a pinch of Maldon.

reflection

We made it through our first season of service, and I couldn't have been happier with the team. We'd been grinding sixty-five to seventy-five hours a week, and people seemed to be responding well to what we were doing. I still wasn't convinced that we were hitting the high level of service required of a place of this stature and wanted the service to reflect the food we were producing. I'd started to worry that maybe we weren't living up to the guests' expectations, hoping I wasn't in over my head, and knowing I couldn't show to the staff that I was doubting what we were doing. I constantly wondered if the food tasted good enough, was interesting enough, looked good enough. I never want to be a dick to someone when they make a mistake, but I wasn't sure the whole team understood that if something wasn't right, the guest wouldn't simply say "Well, Tommy was tired and just wasn't focused today. Guess we'll have to come back and spend another $600 next week." That's not how it works. And if a reviewer came in and said "Chef Baxter actually doesn't make very good food, he overcooks his fish, he serves scrambled custards, he doesn't have attention to detail, and he doesn't season his food well enough. . . ." But I caught myself. Screw that. I said when I was reopening this restaurant that I wasn't going to care what a blogger, food writer, or someone who reviews food for *Eater* said. This was my food, and this was how I thought it was meant to be eaten.

FALL 2020

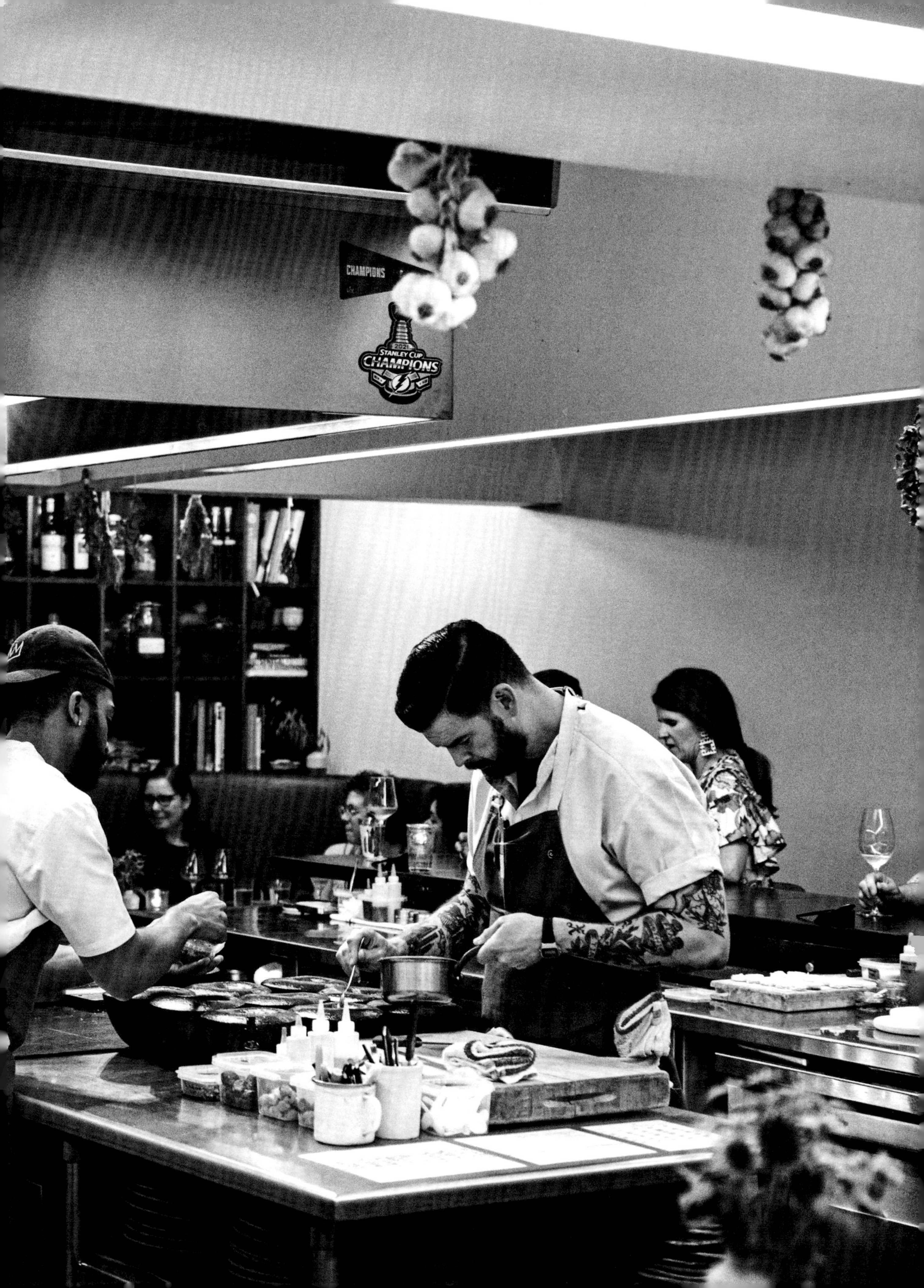
CHAMPIONS
2021
STANLEY CUP
CHAMPIONS

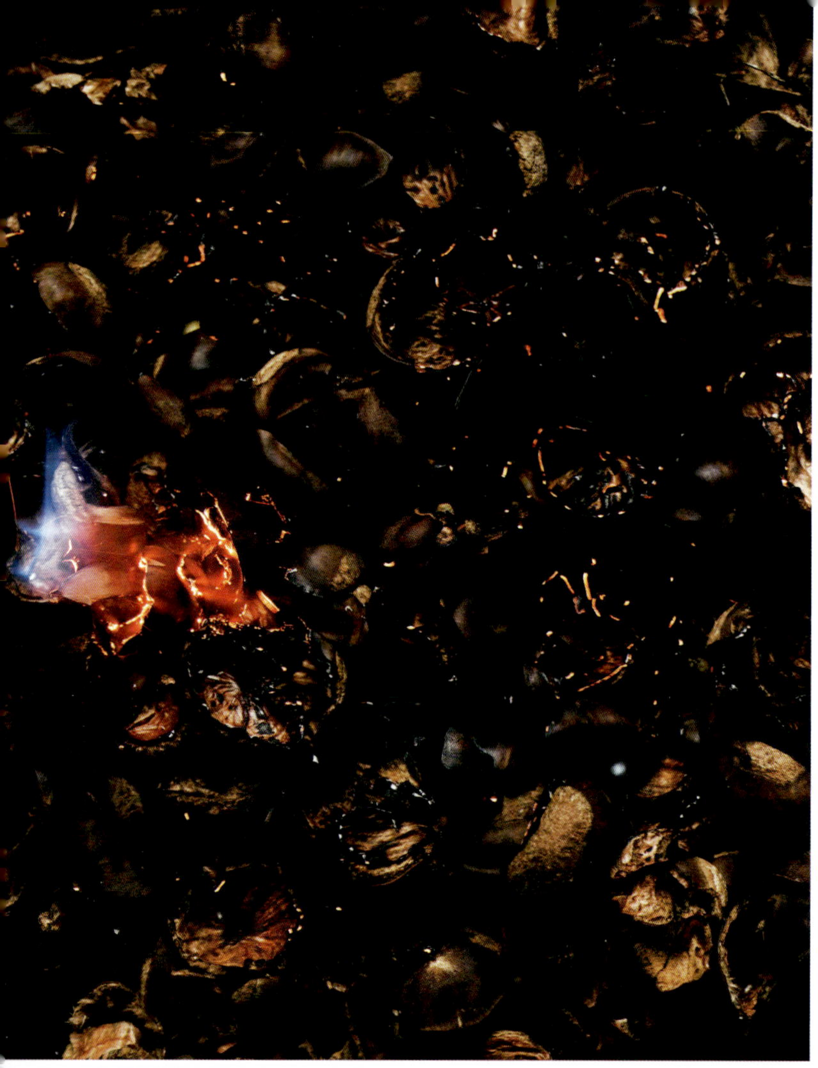
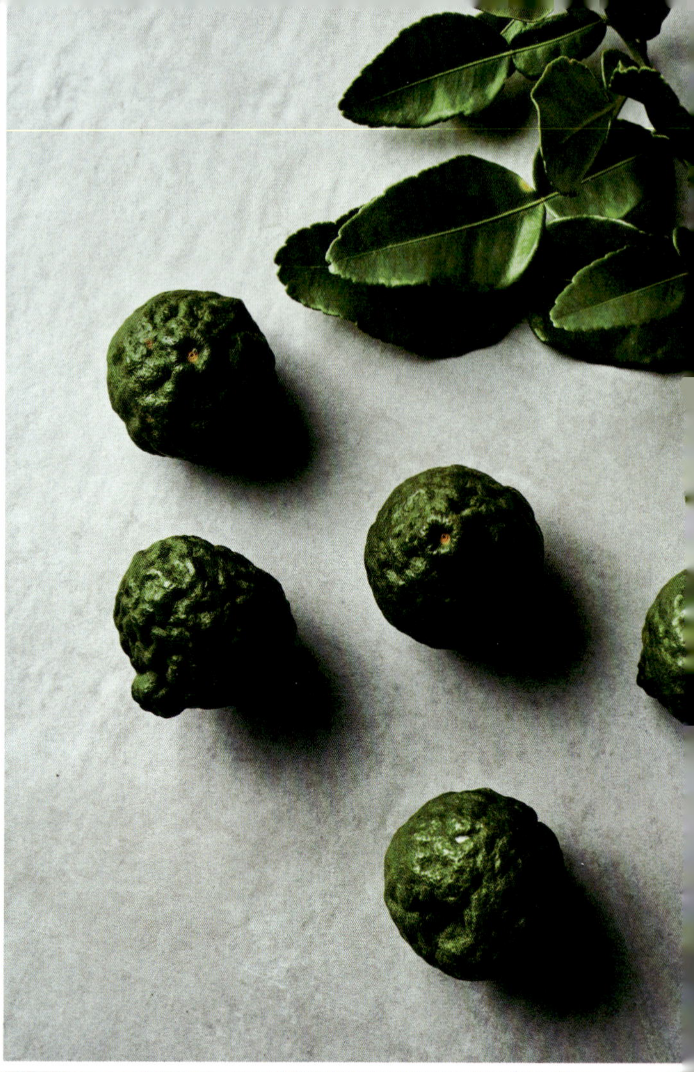
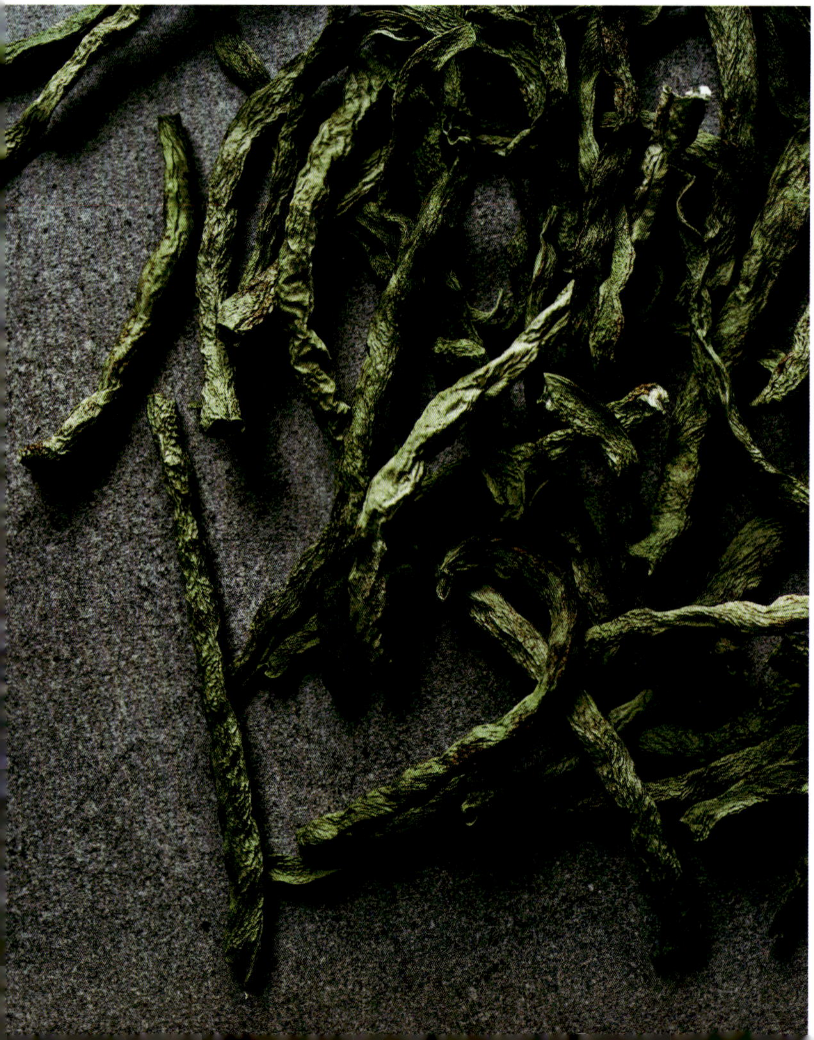
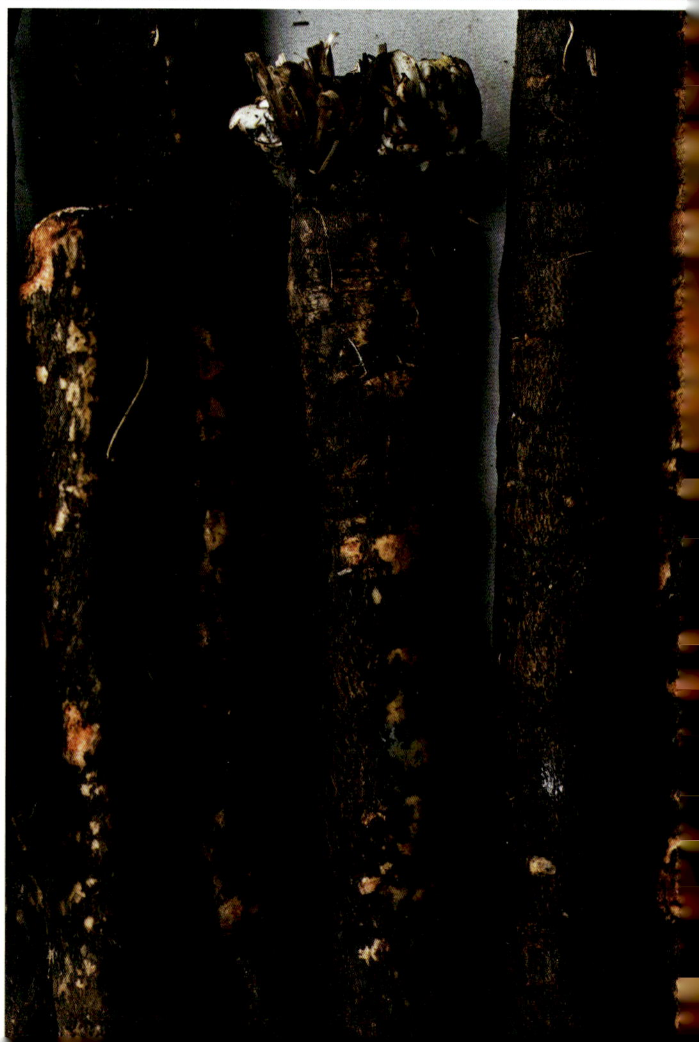

Transitioning into fall can be bittersweet. While it's tough to see the bounty of tomatoes go, and the multitude of dishes that we did with them, fall brings a completely new set of ingredients and ideas to dive into. It also allows us a chance to get creative with some of the summer ingredients we've held on to and preserved in different forms. While we used cayenne peppers (one of the key elements of Nashville's famous hot chicken) occasionally during the summer, we've let plenty of them dry and will use that intensity of flavor and deep earthiness from the drying process to provide bursts of flavor in some of the new fall dishes. The green beans we cooked with during the summer? Now they'd been dried for weeks and turned into "leather britches," an Appalachian technique where beans are strung up, dried, and used later to provide umami and meaty flavor (without meat!) to stocks, broths, and sauces. The summery, tropical flavor of pineapple has been fermenting to make a powerful barbecue-inspired sauce.

The transition from summer to fall early during that first year made me a little nervous, as some of the new dishes may have been a little too progressive—or just flat-out weird—for some of the guests. Though we started to see a lot of repeat diners and were getting plenty of positive feedback, I really felt the need to keep pushing and getting better. I always told the team "The only option is to get a little better every day."

I faced some adversity early in the fall season as my wife came down with COVID-19, forcing me to spend ten days away from the restaurant during a very crucial stretch. To make matters even worse and worrying, my wife was pregnant, and we had a 17-month-old child at home. To further complicate things, we had lost one of our strongest opening kitchen members, who definitely could have helped ride out the storm while I was away. While I wasn't necessarily worried about my own health or the prospect of catching the virus, I was very concerned for my wife and our baby. She began to get worse, and I had a sinking feeling in my stomach. I couldn't leave the house: I couldn't go to the restaurant, and I couldn't even go to the gym to get any stress out. I was worried about my family *and* worried that the restaurant wasn't living up to my high standards while I was away. I decided to take some quiet time while I had it to read and keep writing the new menu. Luckily, my wife slowly began to feel better, and neither I nor the baby had any COVID-related problems. While I felt immense stress about the whole situation at home, I'm sure the team at the restaurant was also stressed at having to fill in for me while I was gone. It turned into a proud moment for me, as I was very impressed with the team's ability to soldier on without too many major hiccups, and we continued getting great feedback from guests throughout the time I was away.

One ingredient I really sat and thought about a lot while I was quarantining at home was salsify, something I've always enjoyed cooking with and exploring. You've probably seen it on long drives through the country, growing by the roadside. Salsify, also known as "oyster root," is like a cousin to dandelions with a similar lion's-mane flower head but with a long, sturdy stem. Some have even dried out the stem and cured it like a vegetarian "beef jerky." The flavor is nutty, similar to artichoke, and has a flavor profile akin to oysters, hence the alternative name. This got me thinking about oyster stews in the Low Country and conjured up memories of clam chowder in St. Pete (see below).

Some other ingredients I really enjoyed from this fall season were the unique pumpkins we got to cook with: Long Island Cheese Pumpkin and Fairytale Pumpkin. While the Long Island variety was much more earthy and intense than a traditional pie pumpkin, the Fairytale variety had a buttery mouthfeel and was sweeter to taste, lending itself to a dessert preparation (page 58). I was also blown away by the complexity of fermented butternut squash juice and the acidic tang of pickled huckleberries from the summer.

What follows are recipes from the first fall of my tenure at The Catbird Seat.

Credit: Todd Saal

FALL 2020 MENU

oyster root stew, matsutake mushroom, dried chilies **44**

hay smoked mussels with sauce poulette **47**

littleneck clams, leather britches & chicken fat **48**

barbecued spiny lobster, fermented pineapple, burnt fresno chilies **51**

long island cheese pumpkin, makrut lime, red curry **54**

warm salad of hakurei turnips, lovage & smoked bucksnort trout **57**

maine scallops, fairytale pumpkin & preserved ground cherries **58**

dry-aged tennessee duck with wild mushrooms & preserved summer berries **61**

lettuces dressed with fermented cranberries, walnuts & goat-milk kefir **65**

_____

yeast donut, foie gras, black apple **66**

an ice cream sundae of beets preserved like luxardo cherries with shio koji caramel **68**

OYSTER ROOT STEW, MATSUTAKE MUSHROOM, DRIED CHILIES

With this dish, I wanted to serve something to the guest that was warm and satisfying as the temperatures outside began to cool. Something that was familiar but a little different. When I was a kid, my mom used to love the clam chowder at this restaurant in St. Petersburg called Johnny Leverock's. I remember going many Sundays after church, growing up as a kid. I can still smell the dining room. My mom always got the clam chowder. This recipe is inspired by those flavors but using oyster root—or salsify— with confited matsutake mushrooms and fried gulf oysters dusted with a powder made from dried chilies from the summer.

---

oyster root stew

celery, small dice	75g
onion, small dice	80g
salsify, peeled and diced small	600g
butter	125g
matsutake dashi (see below)	800L
kosher salt	t.t.

Sweat the celery, onion, and salsify in the butter over medium-low heat. Do not allow to get any color. Once the salsify is beginning to soften, cover in the dashi and top with a cartouche. Cook until the vegetables are completely soft. Puree until smooth and season to taste with salt. Pass through a fine-mesh strainer and reserve.

matsutake dashi

filtered water	1.1L
kombu, rinsed	25g
dried matsutake	100g

Place in a sous vide bag under full pressure and cook at 60°C for 45 minutes. Allow to steep for 1 hour and strain through a fine-mesh strainer. Reserve until needed.

poached matsutakes

matsutake mushrooms, cleaned	200g
matsutake dashi	100mL
matsutake shoyu	5mL
butter, cubed and chilled	10g

Place all ingredients except butter in a sous vide bag under full pressure and cook at 82°C for 5 minutes or until just cooked through. Strain and reduce liquid by half. Slowly whisk in the butter until emulsified and reserve in a warm place.

dried chile powder

dried cayenne, ground as fine as possible	100g
smoked paprika	50g
kosher salt	10g

Mix until well combined. Store in an airtight container until needed.

additional ingredients & to finish

saltine crackers, ground fine
AP flour
whole eggs, whipped
oysters, shucked and reserved in their liquor

Heat some of the stew in a small pot. Meanwhile, grill the poached matsutakes, cut into desirable size, and glaze in the reserved butter. Dredge the oyster in the flour, followed by the egg, and lastly the ground saltines. Fry at 325°F until golden brown and crispy. Dust with the chile spice. Place 2 oz of stew in a bowl, followed by the grilled mushrooms and the oyster.

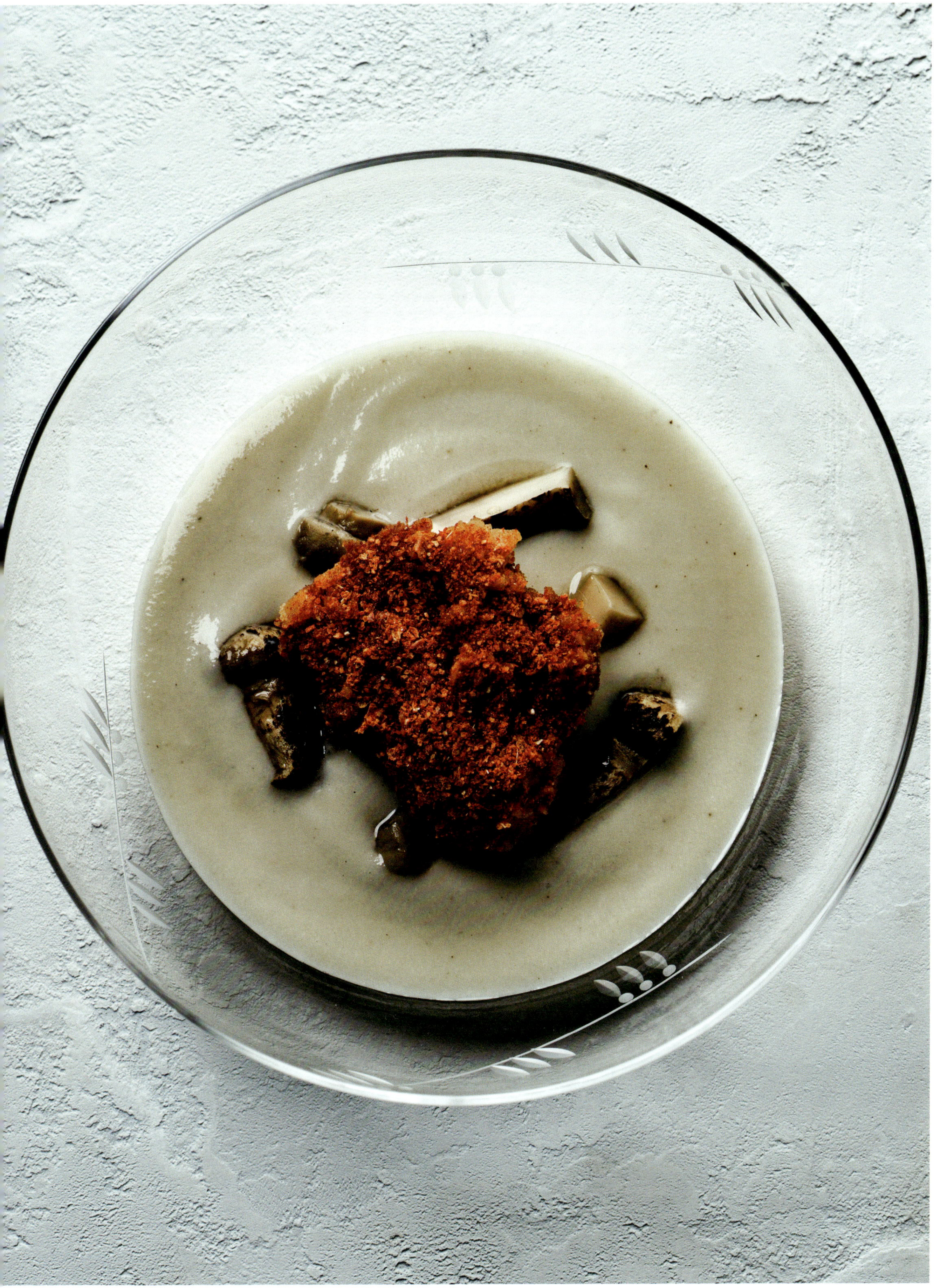

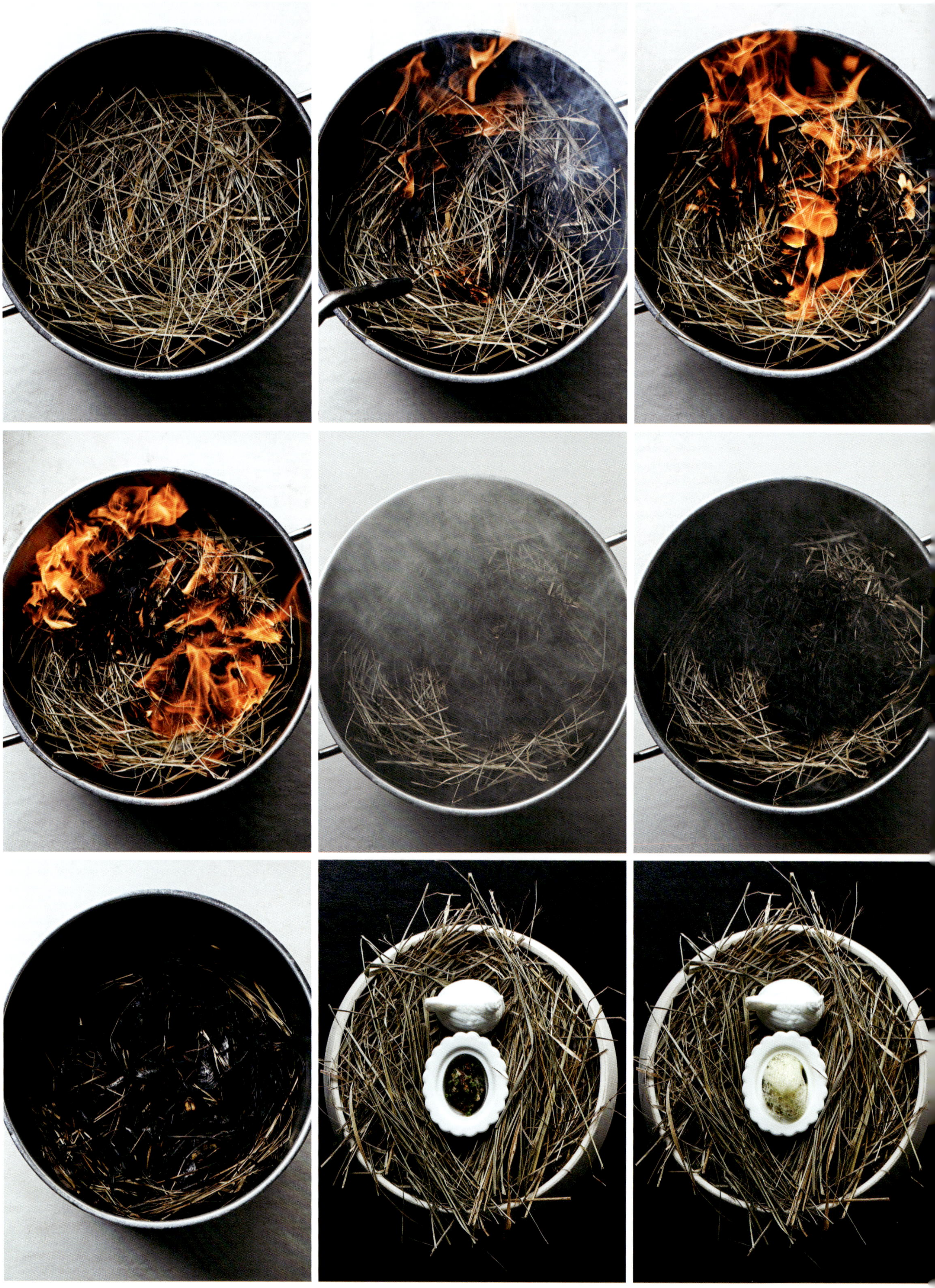

HAY-SMOKED MUSSELS WITH SAUCE POULETTE

This little bite came from wanting to tweak a classic French dish, Moules Poulette. The mussels are steamed with garlic, shallot, saffron, and sweet vermouth. Once opened, they are covered in hay. The hay is then lit on fire, the pot is covered, and the hay is allowed to smolder, slowly smoking the clams and the cooking liquid. Since it was such a small bite, I tried to layer as much flavor in there as possible. The mussels are served under a fudge made from mussel garum lees, seasoned with a spice made from amchoor or green mango powder, saffron, smoked mussel powder, turmeric, and espelette pepper. Lastly, finished with a sauce made from the reduced cooking liquid that had been clarified, seasoned with saffron, and emulsified with egg yolks that were cured in the garum and cold-smoked.

---

hay-smoked mussels

mussels, washed	2lb
sweet vermouth	500mL
shallots, sliced thin	200g
garlic, sliced thin	20g
saffron threads	1g
gelatin, bloomed	3g

Place all ingredients except the gelatin in a pot and cover well. Bring to a simmer on medium-high heat and cook until all the mussels have opened. Cover with hay, light the hay on fire, and cover with a tight-fitting lid until completely burnt out. Keep covered for 20 minutes. Remove the mussels, cool them, remove from the shells, and debeard them. Reduce the liquid over medium heat to 300mL. Add the gelatin and stir until melted and well combined. Strain through a fine-mesh strainer. Freeze in a shallow tray. Once frozen, place over a mesh strainer lined with cheesecloth, and allow to defrost completely. Reserve the clarified liquid until needed.

poulette sauce

egg yolk	30g
mussel garum	100g
clarified mussel stock (see page 275)	275mL
kombu vinegar	5g

Cryovac the egg yolk in mussel garum for 12 hours or overnight. Carefully strain off the mussel garum and cold-smoke for 1 hour. Puree the smoked egg yolk, mussel stock, and kombu vinegar until smooth. Pass through a chinois and reserve.

poulette spice

cured, smoked, and dried mussel powder	1g
saffron	1g
turmeric	.5g
amchoor, green mango powder	5g
espellete, French chile spice	1g

Mix well and store in an airtight container.

cured egg yolk

egg yolk	1ea
mussel garum	50g

Fully submerge the egg yolk in the mussel garum and allow to cure for a minimum of 12 hours. Be careful not to break the yolk. The next day, strain the egg yolk and cold-smoke it for 30 minutes.

mussel fudge

cured egg yolk	1ea
dried mussel garum solids, ground fine	25g
Minus 8 Ice Wine Vidal Vinegar	35g
hot water	10g
burnt hay oil (see page 271)	50g
grapeseed oil	70g
kosher salt	t.t.

Place egg yolk, mussel garum solids, ice wine vinegar, and water in a robot coupe. Blend until frothy, and slowly emulsify in the burnt hay oil, followed by the grapeseed oil. Season to taste with salt, place in a piping bag, and reserve in the refrigerator until needed.

mussel butter

mussel shiro dashi	25mL
saffron powder	.5g
butter, cubed	75g

Warm the mussel shiro and saffron powder in a small sauce pot over medium heat. Slowly whisk in the butter until emulsified. Reserve in a warm place until needed.

additional ingredients & to finish

chives, minced fine	
lemon juice	

Lightly dress the mussels in grapeseed oil and grill until just beginning to caramelize. Toss the mussels in the mussel butter, and season to taste with lemon juice. Place a small amount of mussel fudge in the bottom of a bowl or plate, and top with the mussels, poulette spice, and chives. Gently warm the poulette sauce, whisking constantly to incorporate some air and to prevent scorching. Dress the mussels in a few spoonfuls of the sauce.

LITTLENECK CLAMS, LEATHER BRITCHES & CHICKEN FAT

I first learned about leather britches working for Sean Brock at Husk here in Nashville. The greasy beans are strung up in a fashion reminiscent of something Rambo would've worn in First Blood, but less deadly, and dried slowly. The depth of flavor they take on through the process is like no other. We pressure-cooked them, fortified the pot liquor, and served them with grilled clams from Florida that were dressed in schmaltz, or rendered chicken fat, and topped with lemon thyme from our garden, which added a nice bright herbaceous finish.

---

leather britches oil

smoked and dried pea shells	30g
leather britches	30g
grapeseed oil	255g

Cryovac all the ingredients, and seal at full pressure. Place the bag in boiling water, and boil for 4 hours. Cool and allow to infuse overnight. The next morning, place in a coffee-filter-lined fine-mesh strainer and allow to strain. Reserve until needed.

leather britches

olive oil	30g
medium onion, peeled and cut through its center	½ ea
Blackberry Farms Leather Britches Porter	475mL
kombu	7g
cured and smoked fish bones	45g
leather britches	200g
filtered water	5L

Set an electric pressure cooker to sauté and add the olive oil. Once hot, add the halved onion and cook until golden brown and caramelized on the cut side. Add the porter, kombu, fish bones, and leather britches and cook until the alcohol has cooked out of the beer, 5 to 10 minutes. Add the filtered water, place the lid on, and switch to high pressure. Cook for 45 minutes. Release the pressure, remove the lid, and carefully remove the bones and kombu. Remove the onion half and fish bones. Strain the liquid and chop the beans into ¼" pieces. Add back to the liquid and reserve warm until ready to serve.

clams

Process the clams the same way as the mussels on page 47, omitting the saffron threads.

schmaltz (chicken fat)

filtered water	50g
chicken skins and fat	454g
garlic cloves, smashed	25g
sprigs lemon thyme	8-10 ea

Place all ingredients in a small pot and cook over medium-low heat until all the moisture has evaporated and all the fat has rendered from the skins. Be sure to stir often, especially early on, to prevent the skins from sticking and burning. Pass through a fine-mesh strainer and reserve in a warm place until needed.

additional ingredients & to finish

lemon juice
lemon thyme leaves, picked

Brush the clams with chicken fat and grill them until warm and beginning to caramelize. Dress the clams in more chicken fat and lemon juice to taste. Season the leather britches with salt to desired taste. Place about a cup's worth of leather britches and their pot liquor in a bowl, add the clams and chicken fat-lemon mixture, and finish with lemon thyme leaves.

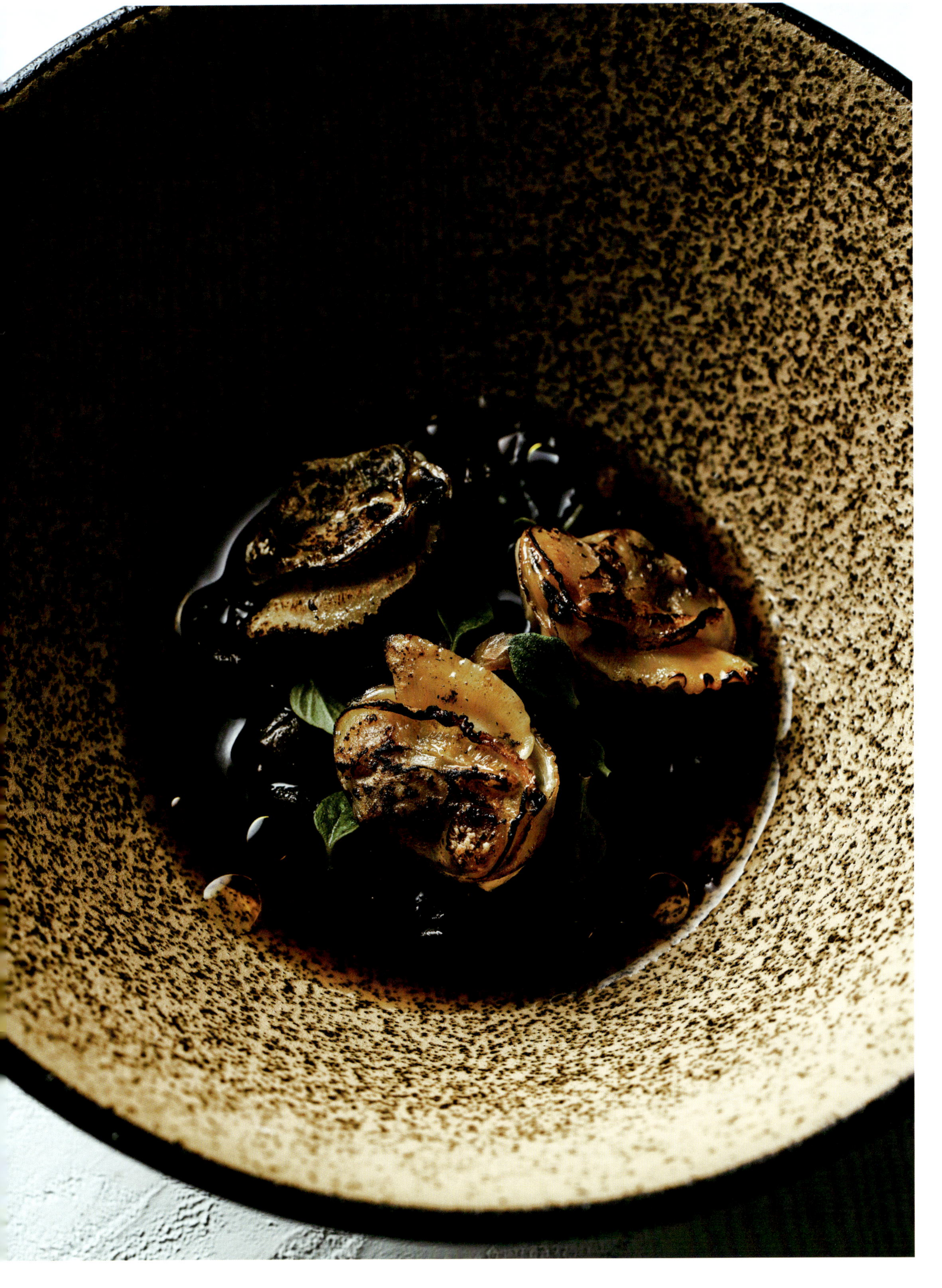

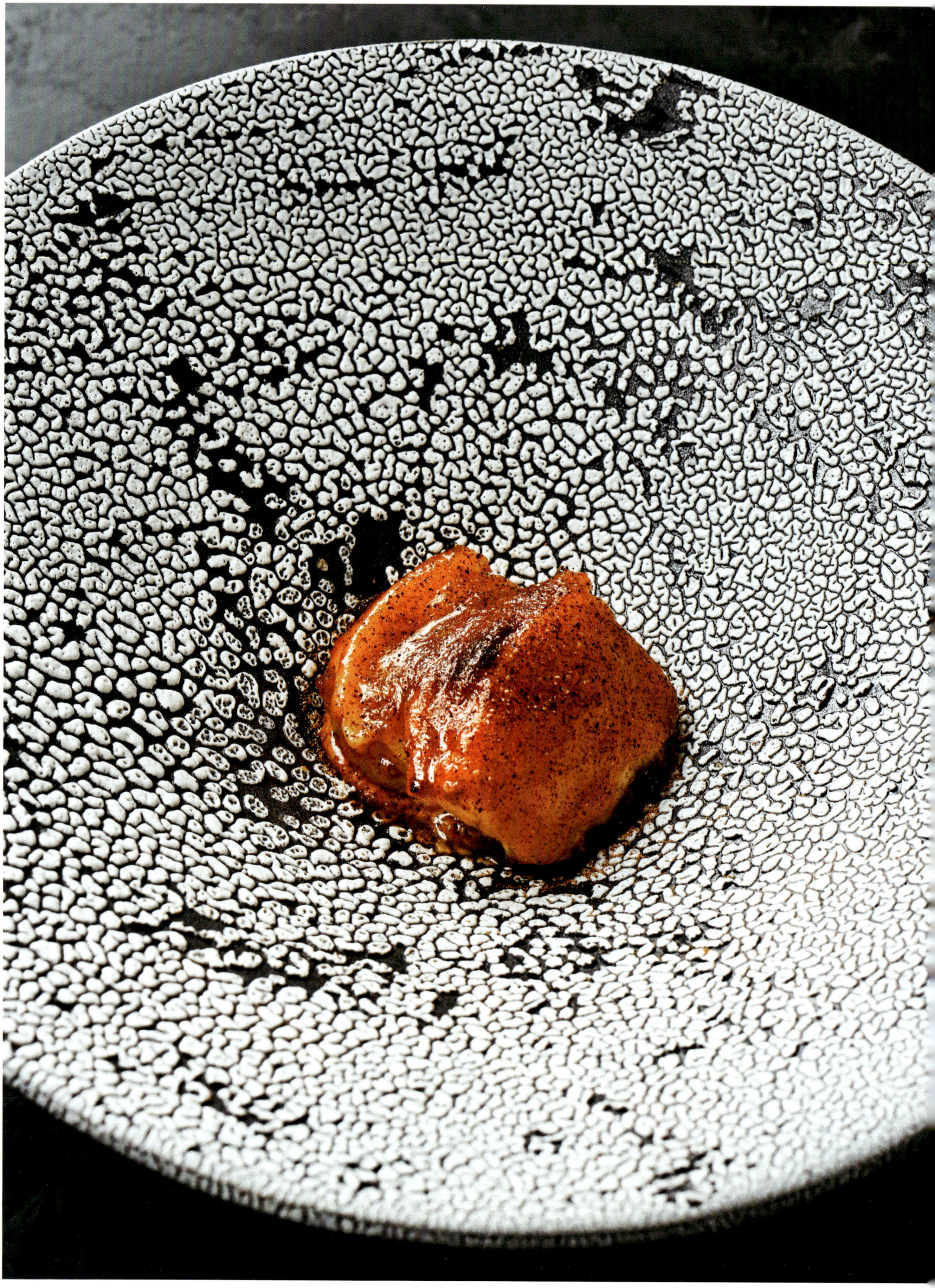

BARBECUED SPINY LOBSTER, FERMENTED PINEAPPLE, BURNT FRESNO CHILIES

I didn't intend this dish to come across this way at first, but everyone related it to al pastor. I like spiny lobster with tropical fruits (especially served raw like a ceviche or crudo). We had fermented a bunch of pineapple, keeping the juice and pulp separate. We then made a catsup from the pineapple pulp, reduced the juice with 7 percent sugar, and mixed those with a reduction of saffron and fresh pineapple juice. Slowly grilled spiny lobster was constantly lacquered with this pineapple "barbecue" sauce. We seasoned with house-made tajin and served over a mayonnaise made from achiote and burnt Fresno chilies from the summer.

---

burnt chile mayo

Duke's mayo	500g	Mix all ingredients together until well combined. Reserve until needed.
achiote paste	50g	
fresno chile ash	5g	
Tapatio hot sauce	8g	

pineapple bbq

pineapple catsup	180g	Mix all ingredients together until well combined. Reserve until needed.
pineapple reduction (see below)	110g	
fermented pineapple reduction (see page 270)	210g	

pineapple reduction

pineapple juice	240g	Reduce over low heat to 110g. So that the sugars will not begin to caramelize, be sure that the mixture never comes above a lazy simmer.
saffron	.5g	

pineapple catsup

fermented pineapple pulp	2,100g	Combine the fermented pineapple, onion, garlic, and water in a large stainless steel pot and bring to a simmer over medium heat. Simmer for 10 minutes, stirring occasionally. Add the brown sugar, vinegars, and spices. Bring back to a simmer and cook, stirring occasionally, until reduced by two-thirds, about 45 minutes. Puree the mixture in a Vitamix in batches, using a small pinch of xanthan gum to help smooth. Pass through a fine-mesh strainer and cool.
sweet onion, diced	200g	
garlic cloves, chopped	3ea	
water	180mL	
brown sugar	300g	
white vinegar	120mL	
cider vinegar	120mL	
kosher salt	30g	
black pepper, finely ground	1.25ea	
dry yellow mustard powder	4.5g	
clove, ground	1g	
allspice, ground	1g	
chipotle powder	1g	
xanthan gum	pinch	

chile lime salt

espelette	49g	Mix until well combined. Store in an airtight container until needed.
chile powder	49g	
smoked Maldon	49g	
lime powder	100g	

additional ingredients & to finish

spiny lobster, cleaned and brined in 3% salt for 20 minutes	Slowly grill the spiny lobster while constantly brushing with the pineapple BBQ. Once it begins to caramelize and is cooked to medium on the inside, remove from the grill and allow to rest for one minute. Place a small amount of the burnt chile mayo on a plate. Slice the lobster, and brush with more pineapple BBQ to glaze. Place the lobster on top of the mayo, and season with the chile lime salt.

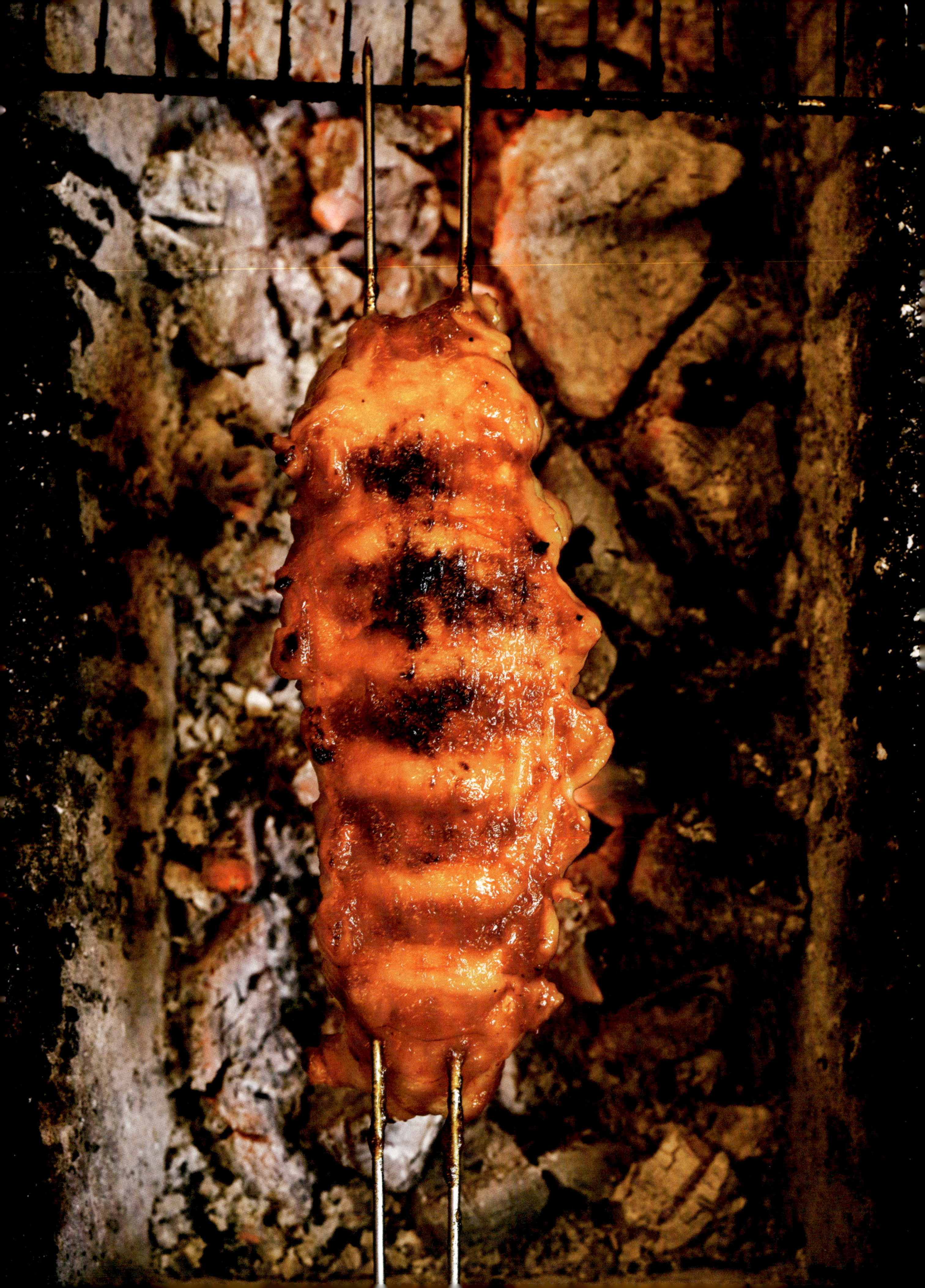

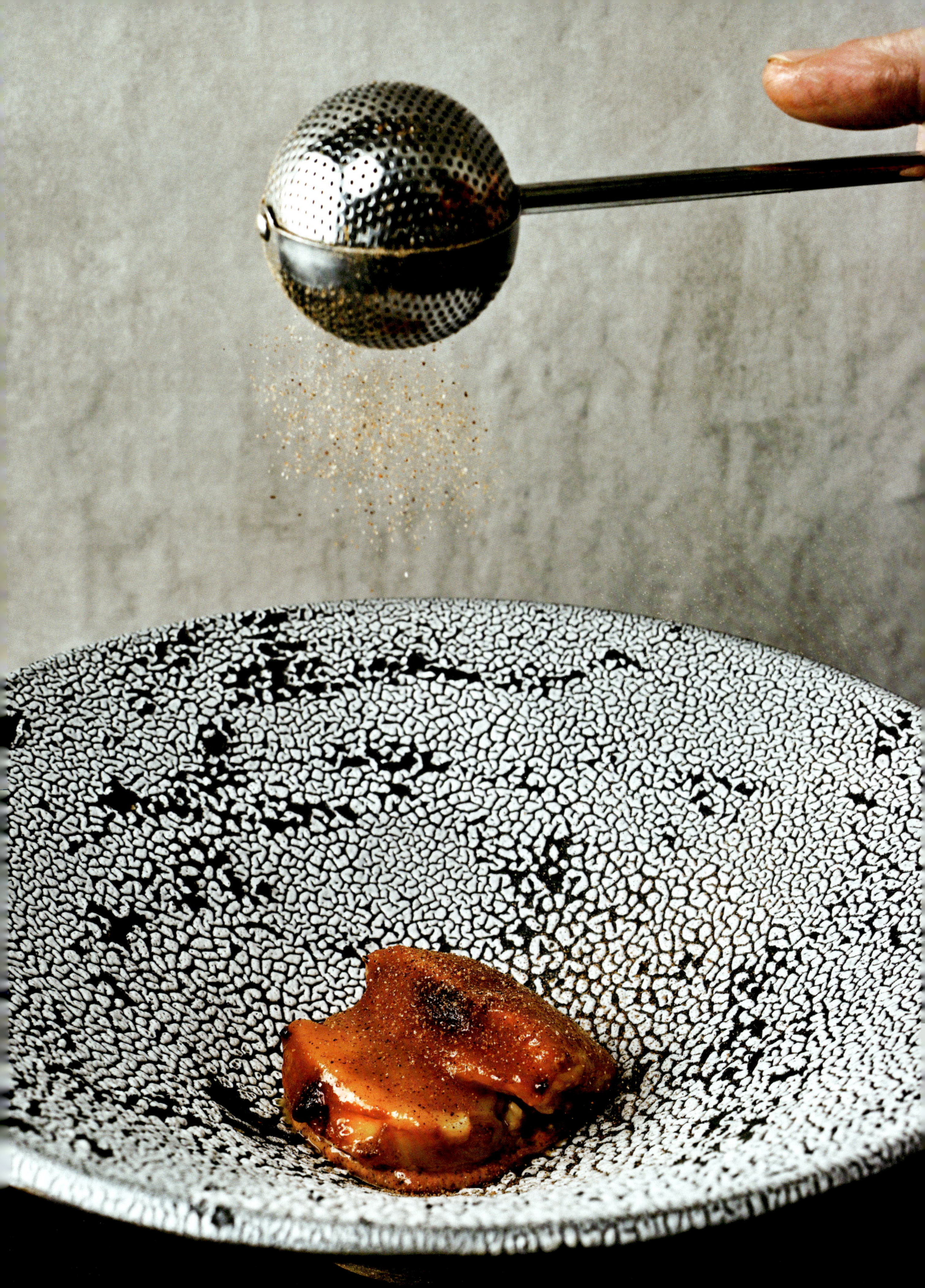

LONG ISLAND CHEESE PUMPKIN, MAKRUT LIME, RED CURRY

This dish came about from cross-utilization of the lobster shells/heads from the previous dish. We try to be as sustainable as possible and eliminate waste as often as we can. We had an abundance of lobster stock made from the shells, which we cooked down with a red curry paste and served alongside Long Island cheese pumpkin, which has an earthier flavor than some of the sweeter pumpkins often used in baking. The pumpkins were cooked to order in their own juice and glazed with butter and an oil made from leaves of our makrut lime tree, fresh makrut juice, and zest. We finished with puffed wild rice that was tossed in fermented chile, which we dried and pulverized to a fine powder. The warmth of the broth and kick of the spice makes it a nice dish to serve later in the fall as the temperature begins to drop outside.

---

spiny lobster stock

spiny lobster heads, split	12ea
white miso	200g
spiny lobster tail shells	12ea
cream sherry	750mL
bay leaves	6ea
filtered water	4L

Rub the inside of the split lobster heads with the miso and roast on a rack-lined sheet tray at 425°F for 15 minutes or until caramelized. Place heads and remaining shells in a rondeau, and cover with sherry and bay leaves. Cook on medium-high heat until the sherry has reduced by ¾. Cover with the filtered water and continue to reduce, skimming any impurities that rise to the top, until the liquid volume has reduced to 1,320 mL. Strain and reserve.

spiny lobster red curry

shallot, sliced thin	50g
garlic, sliced thin	5g
grapeseed oil, as needed	
red curry paste	105g
cream sherry	260mL
makrut lime leaf	1ea
spiny lobster stock	1,320mL
kombu	5g

Sweat shallot and garlic in a small amount of grapeseed oil on medium heat until soft and beginning to caramelize. Add the red curry paste and toast until aromatic. Add the cream sherry, making sure to scrape all the fond that has formed on the bottom of the pot with a wooden spoon. Reduce on medium-high heat until the alcohol has burned off. Add the lime leaf, kombu, and lobster stock. Reduce by ¾. Strain through a fine-mesh strainer and reserve.

fermented butternut squash butter

shallot	50g
fermented butternut squash juice	300g
xanthan gum	.05g
butter, cubed	265g

Reduce shallot and butternut squash juice to a weight of 180g. Add to a Vitamix, puree on high, add xanthan gum, and slowly emulsify in the butter.

lime leaf oil

makrut lime leaf	120g
parsley leaves, picked and washed	50g
grapeseed oil	500g

Place all ingredients in a Vitamix and blend on high until the oil reaches 62°C. Allow to strain overnight through a coffee-filter-lined mesh strainer.

additional ingredients & to finish

butternut squash, Parisienne scooped
puffed rice
makrut lime juice
makrut lime zest

In a small pot, add the balls of butternut squash and enough of the fermented butternut squash butter to cover. Slowly simmer until butternut begins to just cook through but still has some texture to it. Zest and season with the makrut lime juice. In a separate pot, warm the red curry sauce. Froth with a bamix or a stick blender. Add the pumpkin balls to a small bowl, top with the puffed rice, and finish with the lime leaf oil and a spoonful of the curry sauce.

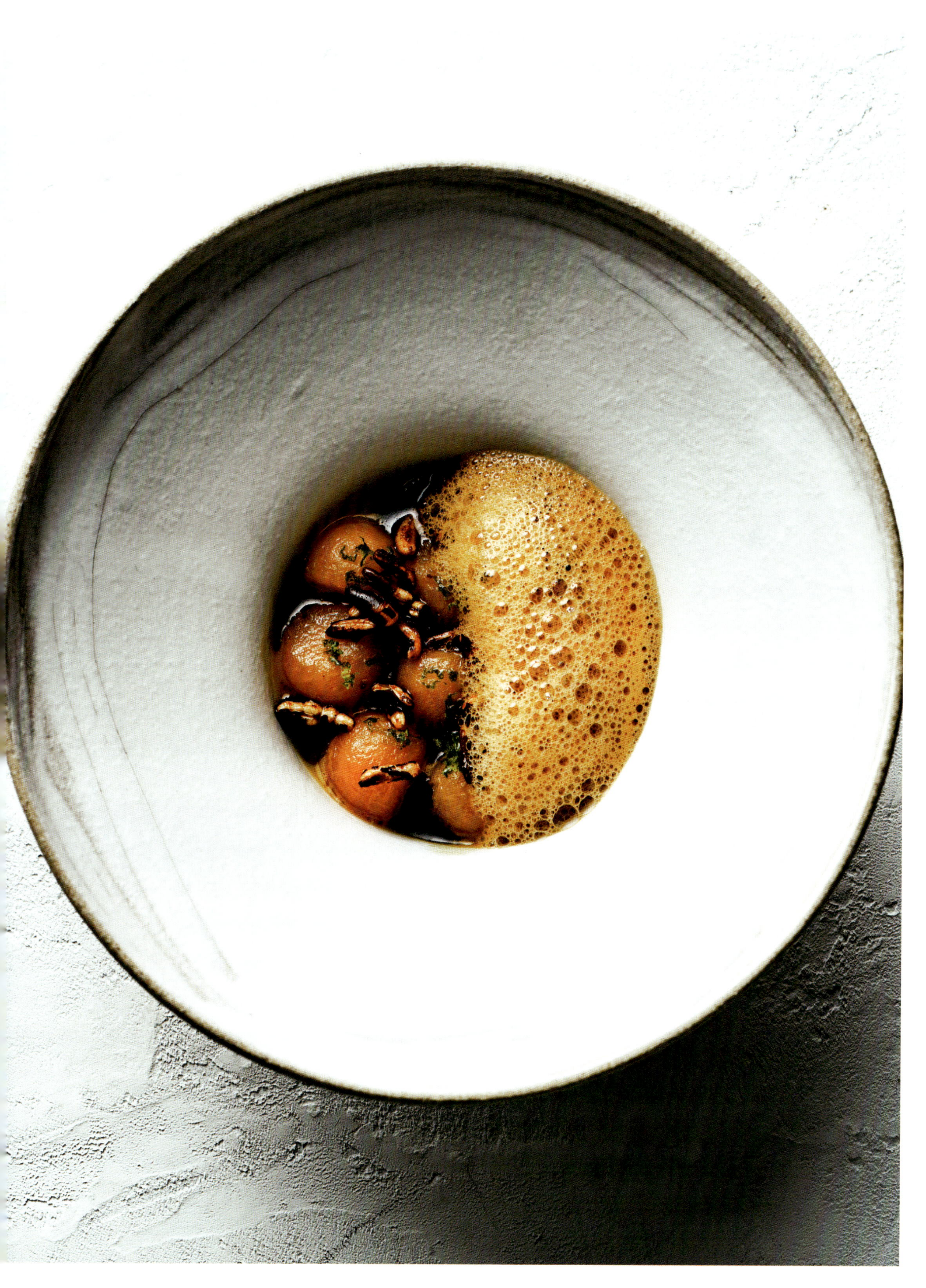

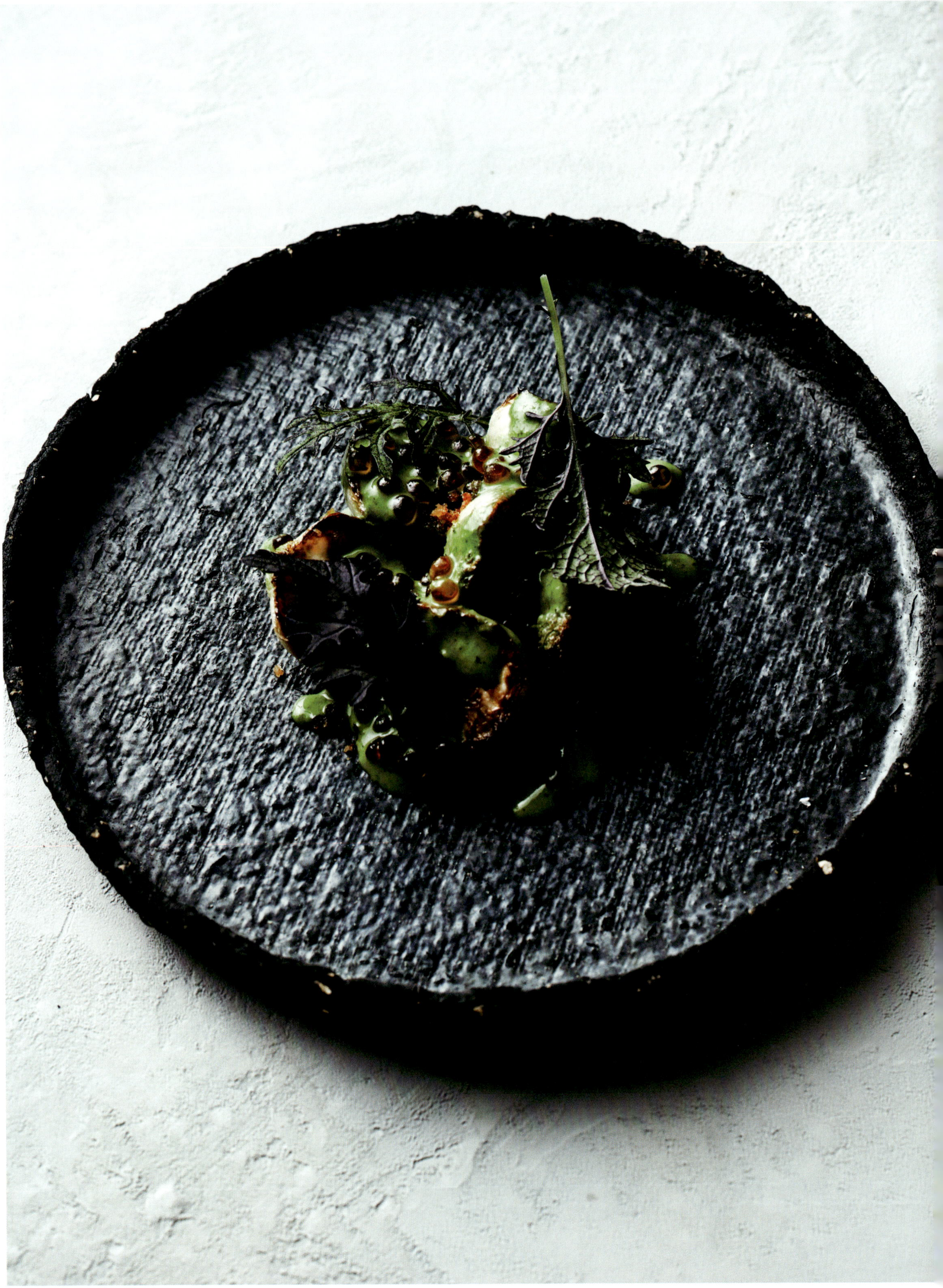

WARM SALAD OF HAKUREI TURNIPS, LOVAGE & SMOKED BUCKSNORT TROUT

I love the sweetness of hakurei turnips when they are young. We would cut them to order, salt them, and let the juice that was pulled out of them slowly caramelize on the cut side, just barely warming them but retaining the nice crunch of biting into a raw one. We then dressed them in fermented turnip juice and a green goddess dressing made from lovage from our garden, and served them over smoked Bucksnort trout.

---

smoked trout dip

smoked trout	500g
kosher salt	t.t.
granulated sugar	t.t.
cream cheese	225g
buttermilk or more if needed	75g
lemon juice	t.t.
aji-no-moto	t.t.
salt	t.t.

Season the trout liberally with a 50/50 mix of kosher salt and granulated sugar. Hot-smoke until fully cooked but not overcooked. Puree the trout, cream cheese, and buttermilk in a robot coupe until smooth. Season to taste with the lemon juice, aji-no-moto, and salt. Cool and reserve until needed.

turnip top dressing

turnip tops, blanched and shocked	330g
lovage leaves, picked and washed	85g
parsley leaves, picked and washed	45g
basil leaves, picked and washed	40g
scallion tops, chopped	25g
tarragon leaves, picked and washed	15g
garlic, sliced thin	4g
anchovy	20g
Duke's mayonnaise	500g
buttermilk	330g

Puree all ingredients until smooth. Do not strain.

fried bread

loaf good sourdough, crust removed	1ea
butter	400g
thyme sprigs	4-5ea
garlic cloves, crushed	5ea

Remove the crust from the sourdough and reserve for a miso or other use. Dice the sourdough into ¼" pieces. Add the butter to a pot and cook over medium heat until melted. Add the diced bread, thyme, and garlic and slowly cook in the butter. Be sure to constantly stir with a rubber spatula to ensure even cooking. Once a nice golden-brown color is achieved, remove from the butter and drain on paper towels. Reserve the brown butter for another use. Once all the butter has drained from the croutons, season them with salt, and reserve in a dehydrator or airtight container.

additional ingredients & to finish

fermented turnip juice (see page 269)
mustard greens
smoked trout roe
hakurei turnips, scrubbed and washed
lemon zest
lemon juice

Halve the turnips, season the cut side with salt, and allow to sit for a few minutes. Place cut-side down in a nonstick pan and slowly cook until the turnip begins to caramelize. Deglaze with the fermented turnip juice and drain on a paper towel. Season with lemon juice. Place a small amount of the smoked trout on a plate. Place the cooked turnips on top of the smoked trout, dress with the turnip-top dressing, smoke trout roe, fried croutons, and mustard greens. Finish with lemon zest.

MAINE SCALLOPS, FAIRYTALE PUMPKIN & PRESERVED GROUND CHERRIES

I often like to highlight the same vegetable or a different varietal throughout a meal to showcase the versatility. Sometimes I'll use it to bridge two dishes back-to-back; other times I'll serve it raw or even as a dessert. This dish combines multiple varieties of winter squash and fairytale pumpkins, which have a silky, buttery mouthfeel and sweeter flavor than the Long Island cheese pumpkins. We roasted scallops and allowed them to rest. We took the juice from the scallop and emulsified with a reduction of lacto-fermented apple cider and pumpkin seed oil. For pops of acid and sweetness, we finished with pickled ramps and ground cherries that had been fermented with tarragon, dehydrated, and then pressure-canned in a simple syrup infused with tarragon.

---

pumpkin butter

fresh pumpkin juice	720g
bonito	15g
xanthan gum	.15g
quatre epices	.5g
whole butter, cubed and chilled	65g
brown butter, cubed and chilled	65g
kosher salt	t.t.

Reduce pumpkin juice and bonito over medium-high heat to a total weight of 330g. Strain into a Vitamix, and, while on low, slowly add the xanthan gum and quatre epices. Turn the blender to high and emulsify in the whole butter, followed by the brown butter. Season to taste with kosher salt.

preserved ground cherries

ground cherries, husks removed and washed well	1,000g
salt	30g
tarragon, washed and dried	50g
granulated sugar	250g
filtered water	250g

Prick each ground cherry with a cake tester and toss with the salt and 20 grams of the tarragon leaves/stems. Cryovac and ferment 14 days or until it no longer smells of alcohol. Dry them in the sun or in a low dehydrator, around 90°F to 100°F, until the texture of a golden raisin. When ready to can, bring the sugar, water, and remaining tarragon to a boil. Place the ground cherries into sanitized Mason jars and pour the boiling syrup over the top until ¼" under the rim. Wipe the rim with a warm wet cloth followed by a clean dry cloth. Gently add the lid and twist with one hand until it catches and the jar begins to move with it. Steam in a Rational or boil for 45 minutes. Carefully remove and place upside down on a flat surface lined with a kitchen towel. Allow to cool completely, preferably overnight. The next morning, fully twist the lids as tight as they will go, and reserve until needed.

fermented apple cider
(see page 270)

additional ingredients & to finish

pickled ramps, cut into rings (see page 270)
pickled ramp brine
pumpkin seed oil
lemon juice
scallops, confited and patted dry

Slowly roast a scallop in brown butter until warmed through. Let rest on a tray for 1 minute. Meanwhile, heat the pumpkin butter in a tall, narrow sauce pot. Dress with a good bit of lemon juice, and then place the scallop on the serving piece. Using the back of a spoon, emulsify in the pumpkin seed oil, pickled ramp brine, and some of the roasting butter. Season to taste with salt and dress the scallop in a spoonful of the vinaigrette, sliced pickled ramp rings, and three halves of preserved ground cherries. Aerate the pumpkin butter using a bamix or stick blender and add a small spoonful over the top of the scallop. Serve immediately.

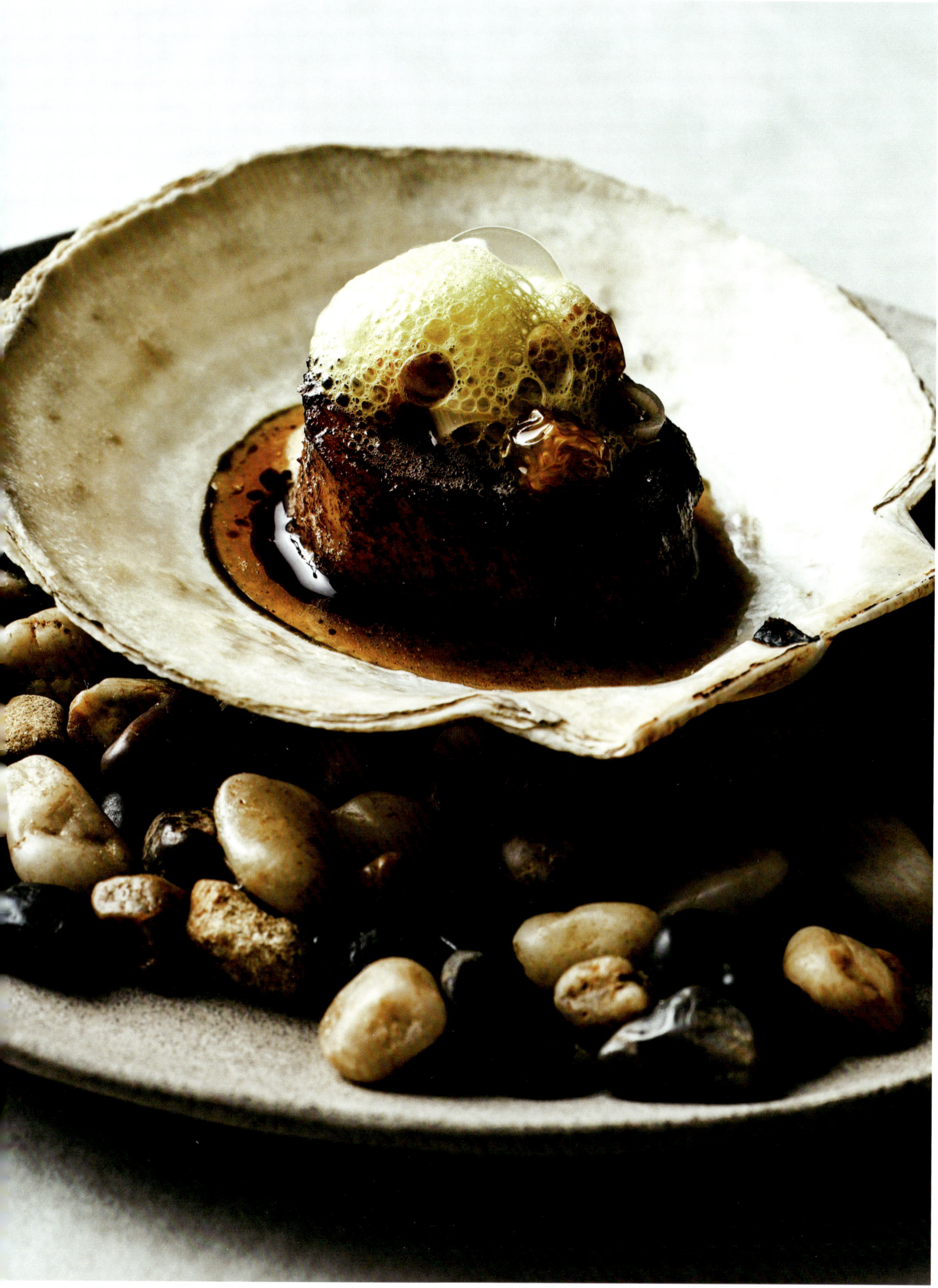

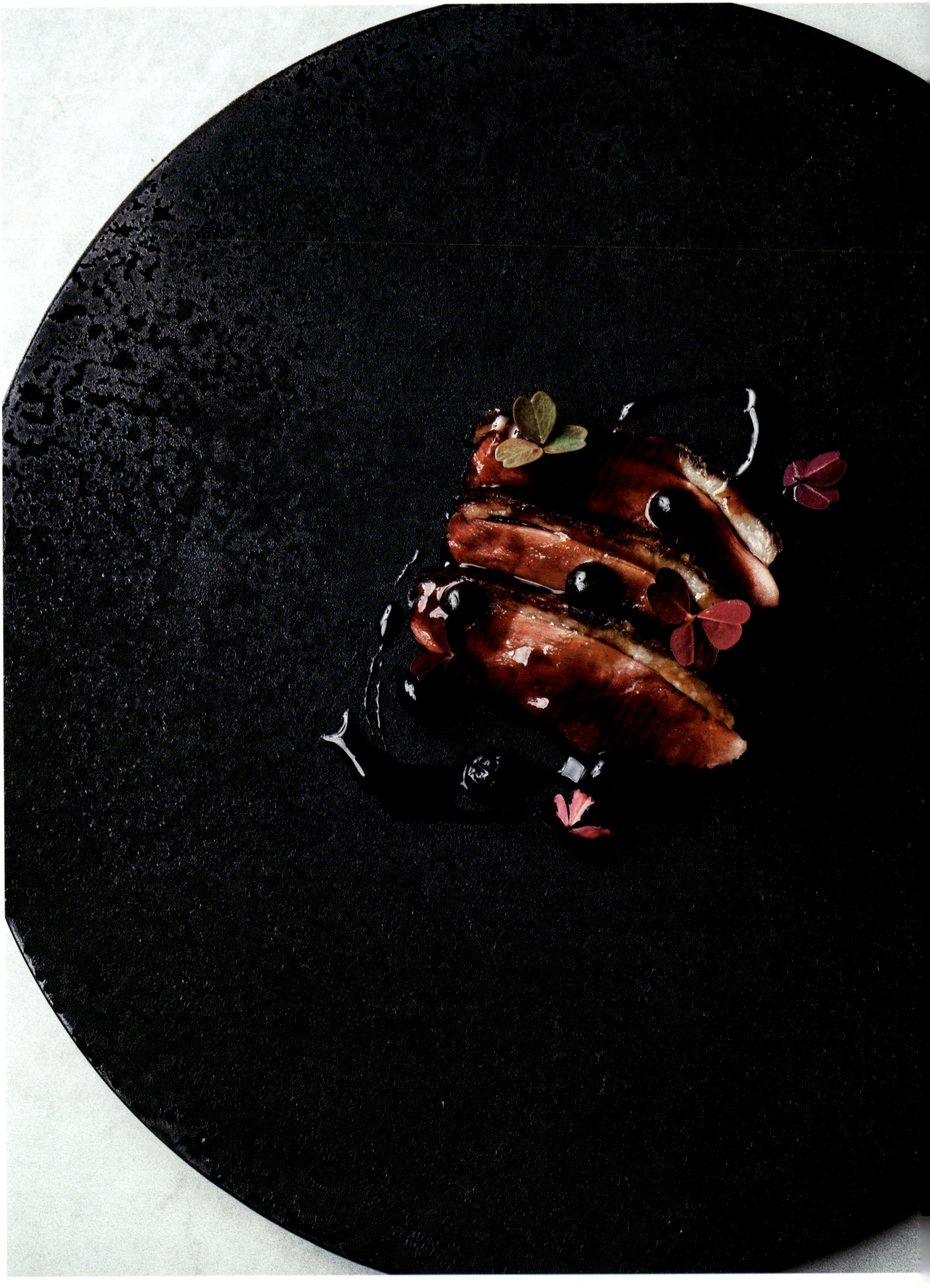

DRY-AGED TENNESSEE DUCK WITH WILD MUSHROOMS & PRESERVED SUMMER BERRIES

This dish was inspired by a more classical preparation of duck, highlighting Muscovy duck from Giving Thanks Farm here in Tennessee. The birds were aged for two weeks and then served as the breast and legs side-by-side in two different preparations. The first featured the breast cold-smoked, slowly roasted on the bone, and carved to order, dressed with a rich chevreuil sauce, pickled berries, and pinot sorrel. The legs were cured, confited, and dressed in bordelaise, fermented black truffle paste, and an umami-packed mushroom duxelles. We then baked the mixture between layers of puff pastry and served as a pithivier. The pithivier was dressed in a sauce rouennaise: foie gras parfait mounted into a bordelaise just before serving. For a bit of contrast from the richness, we served it with a black pepper-currant jam.

---

duck confit cure

kosher salt	540g	Combine and process in a robot coupe until the salt is green and the herbs have been incorporated. Reserve in an airtight container in the refrigerator.
black peppercorns, coarsely ground	20g	
tarragon leaves, roughly chopped	25g	
parsley leaves, roughly chopped	40g	
bay leaves, roughly chopped	6ea	

cured foie gras

rouge foie gras, sliced 1" thick and frozen	1kg	Season liberally with the country ham cure. Place into a vacuum bag and place in the freezer. Once frozen, seal at full pressure. Cook in a water bath at 60°C for 30 minutes. Chill and allow to mature in the refrigerator for 3 days. Dice into 1½" × 1½" squares and keep cold.
country ham cure	t.t.	

duck confit

duck legs	8ea	Season the duck legs liberally with the duck confit cure. Be sure to rub it in well. Cryovac and store in the refrigerator for 12 hours. Rinse well and pat dry. Place in a deep hotel pan. Cover in oil or melted duck fat, wrap in plastic and then aluminum foil, and cook in a Rational at full humidity 85°C for 10 hours. Once cooked and cool enough to handle, remove the skin from the legs, and chill. Pull the leg meat apart and reserve. Once the skin is cool, grind through the fine die of a meat grinder and reserve.
duck confit cure	t.t.	

duck presse jus

duck perigueux (make according to the sauce perigueux on page 222, substituting duck demi)	687g	Heat duck perigueux, truffle balsamic, and truffle paste over medium heat and stir in the bloomed gelatin until melted. Reserve in a warm place until needed.
truffle balsamic	15g	
truffle paste	500g	
gelatin, bloomed	3%	

pickled huckleberries

Omed rosé vinegar	185g	Bring the kombu, vinegar, sugar, and water to a boil. Add the huckleberries and remove from the heat. Allow to cool at room temperature. Reserve in the refrigerator until needed.
granulated sugar	75g	
filtered water	145g	
mountain huckleberries	225g	
kombu	10g	

foie parfait

shallot, sliced thin	100g	Reduce the shallot, garlic, aromatics, and alcohols until au sec. Add to a Vitamix with the foie gras and pink salt. Puree on high until smooth. Add the eggs one by one, being sure to fully incorporate after each addition. Slowly emulsify in the melted butter. Pass through a fine-mesh strainer, and chill immediately.
garlic, sliced thin	25g	
bay leaf	1ea	
thyme sprigs	2ea	
Madeira	125mL	
cream sherry	125mL	
calvados	125mL	
foie gras	225g	
TCM pink salt	.5g	
eggs	2ea	
butter, melted	225g	

Dry-Aged Tennessee Duck with Wild Mushrooms & Preserved Summer Berries continued

forming the pithivier

pulled duck meat
ground duck skin
duck presse jus
fines herbs, minced fine
kosher salt
ground black peppercorns
cubed foie gras pieces

Mix the duck meat and ground skin together and weigh. Add 25 percent of the weight of the ground duck confit/skin mixture of the duck presse jus. Season to taste with fines herbs, salt, and ground black pepper. Place in 3" cylinder silicone molds, place the foie pieces directly in the center, and allow to cool completely. Once set up, place between two sheets of puff pastry. Brush with egg wash to seal. Cut with an appropriate-size ring mold and crimp the cut sides with a fork or by folding together. Brush with egg wash and bake at 400°F for 18 minutes. Reserve in a warm place until needed.

currant-black pepper jam

blackcurrant	950g
granulated sugar	950g
blueberry vinegar	170mL
filtered water	450mL
citric acid	20g
black Lampong peppercorns, toasted and ground	10g

Cook the blackcurrants, sugar, vinegar, and water over medium-high heat until the temperature reaches 220°F. Remove from the heat and stir in the citric acid and black pepper. Allow to cool, and reserve.

porcini puree

foie fat	40g
shallot	45g
fresh porcini, cleaned and sliced thin	450g
cream	400mL
cream cheese	25g
foie gras	25g
salt	t.t.

Warm the foie fat over medium heat. Sweat the shallot and porcini until the porcini begin to soften and become gold brown. Cover with the cream and cartouche. Cook until the mushrooms are completely tender. Strain the liquid and reserve. Puree in Vitamix on high, adding the reserved cream if needed. Mount the cream cheese, followed by the foie gras. Season to taste with salt, pass through a fine-mesh strainer, and reserve.

duck chevreuil

duck fat	30g
shallot	7g
garlic	6g
black peppercorn	1g
juniper	1g
clove	1ea
sprigs fresh thyme	2ea
bay leaf	1ea
port	330mL
Madeira	125mL
stock	1,785mL
dried currant	45g
78 percent chocolate	75g
crème de cassis	55g
kosher salt	t.t.

Warm the duck fat over medium heat. Sweat the shallot and garlic until soft and translucent. Add the black peppercorns, juniper, and clove, and toast in the pot 2 to 3 minutes until aromatic. Add the thyme, bay leaf, port, and Madeira. Reduce by ¾. Add the stock and dried currants. Continue to simmer, skimming constantly. Reduce by half. Once reduced, whisk in the chocolate and crème de cassis. Pass through a fine-mesh strainer, season to taste with salt, and cool until needed.

to finish

For the breast Slowly roast the duck on the bone until desired doneness. Meanwhile, warm the porcini puree and chevreuil sauce. Slice the duck and serve with the puree and pickled huckleberries, and dress with the chevreuil sauce.

For the pithivier Place a spoonful of the currant jam in the center of a plate. Place the warm pithivier on top. Warm a small amount of chevreuil sauce over medium heat. Once it's to a simmer, whisk in a few spoonfuls of the foie parfait, whisking constantly. Return to a simmer, remove from the heat, and season to taste with kosher salt and quince vinegar. Dress the pithivier in desired amount of sauce.

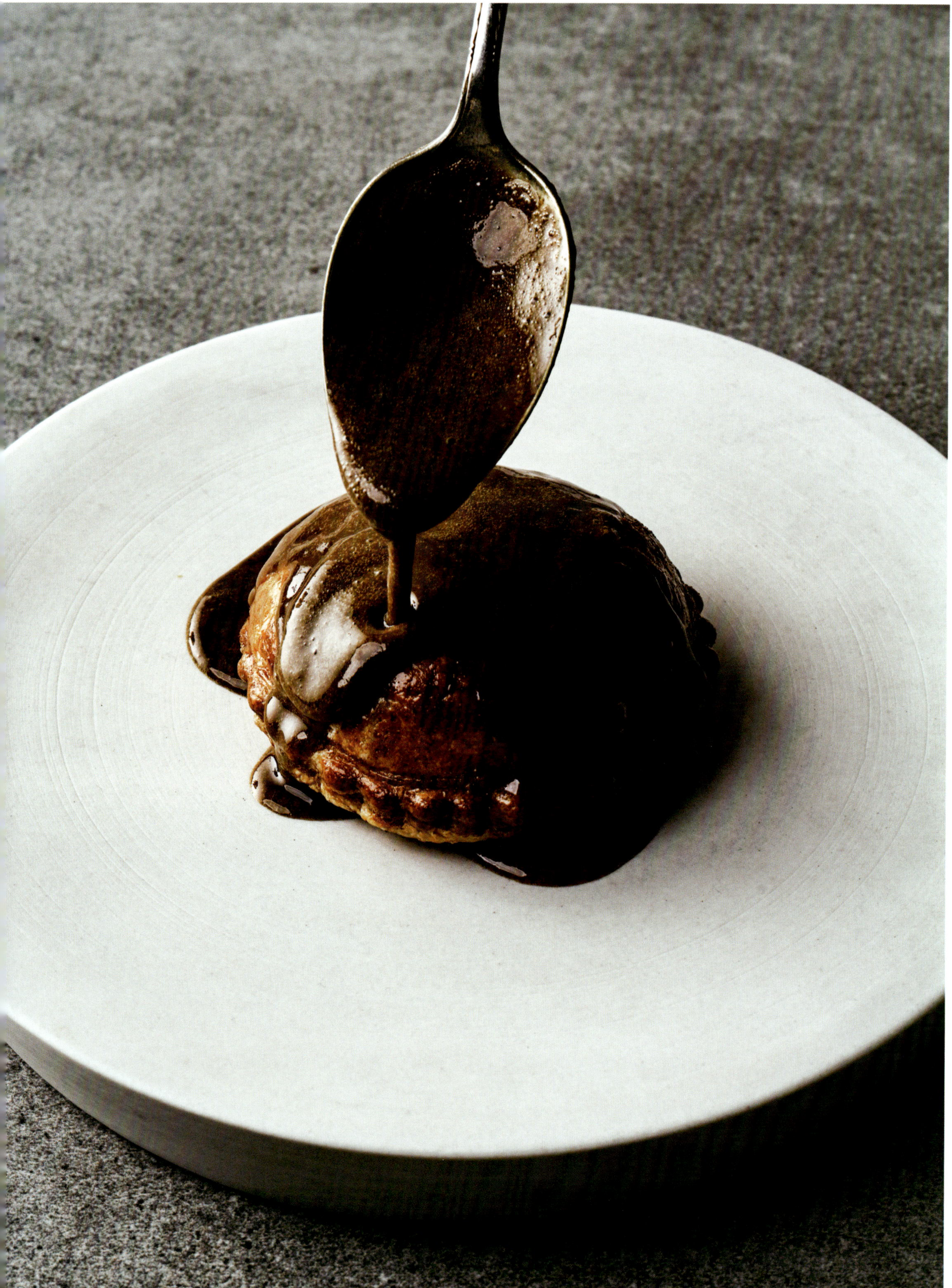

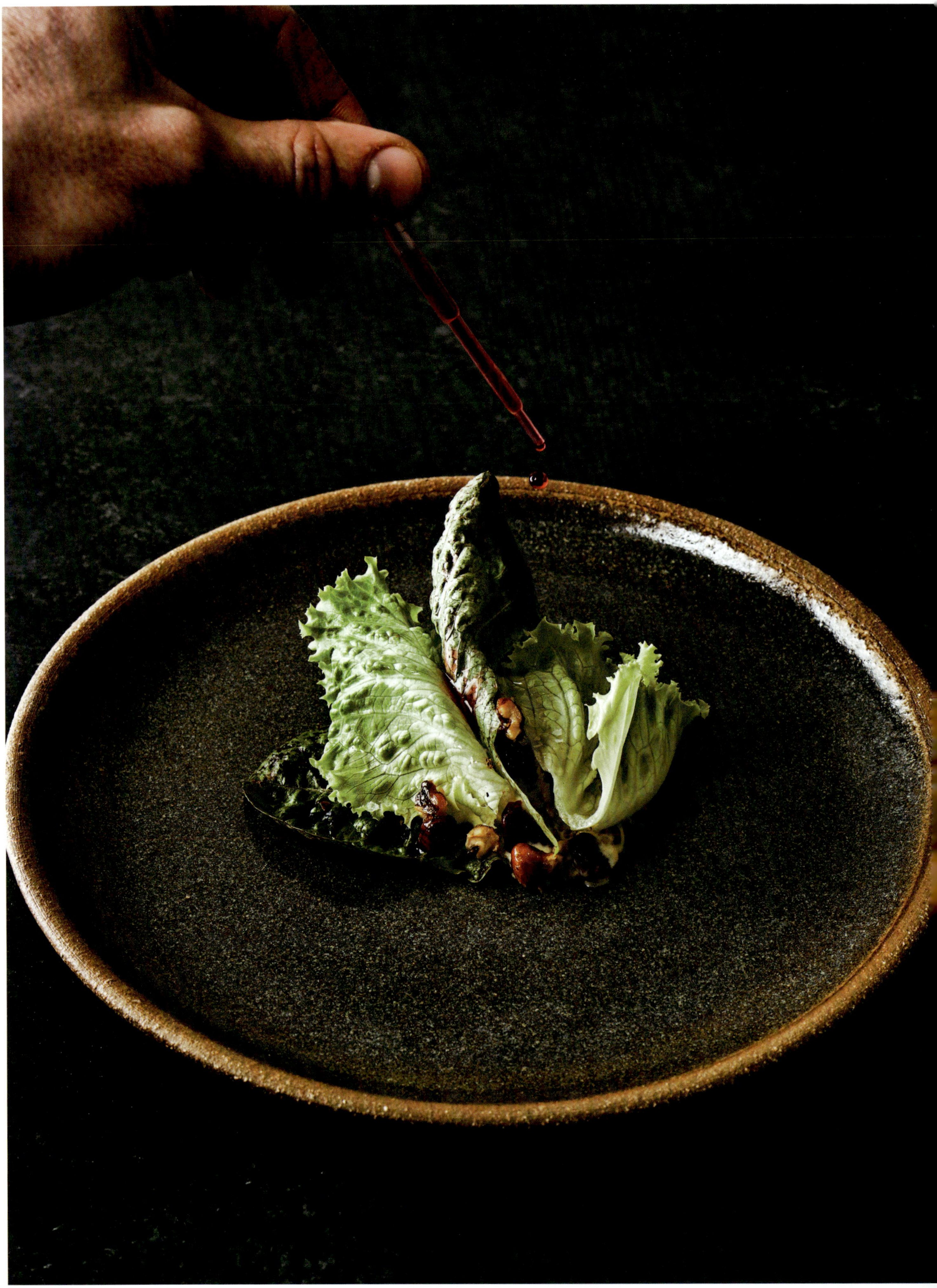

LETTUCES DRESSED WITH FERMENTED CRANBERRIES, WALNUTS & GOAT-MILK KEFIR

My favorite condiment at Thanksgiving is cranberry relish. I personally think it unfairly gets a bad rap, so I wanted to highlight it in this dish. We created a simple salad of lettuces from Bloomsbury Farms, dressed with a reduction of fermented cranberries and candied walnuts and filled with an ice cream made from goat-milk kefir infused with rosemary from our garden. We asked the guests to pick up the salad and eat it with their hands.

---

fermented cranberries

fresh cranberries	200g	Cryovac in a bag on full pressure. Ferment for 14 days, burping and sealing in a new bag as needed. Once ready, strain and reserve any liquid that comes off the cranberries. Dry the cranberries in the sun until they achieve texture of raisins. Reserve in an airtight container.
kosher salt	2g	

goat-milk kefir ice cream

fresh rosemary branches (split 25g/15g)	40g	Steep 25g rosemary in the kefir for 12 hours. Strain and place in a sauce pot with the honey and trimoline over medium heat. Once dissolved, whisk in the salt and sodium hexametaphosphate. Bring to 120°F and quickly whisk in the egg yolks. Bring to 180°F, whisking constantly. Remove from the heat, add the remaining rosemary, and cover for 5 minutes. Pass through a fine-mesh strainer and freeze in a Paco canister. Spin before using.
goat milk kefir	1L	
wildflower honey	100g	
trimoline	140g	
kosher salt	1g	
sodium hexametaphosphate	10g	
egg yolks, whisked together well	260g	

caramelized walnuts

walnuts	150g	Combine ingredients. Bring to a simmer and cover with a cartouche. Cook until the walnuts are tender and most of the liquid has evaporated. Drain well. Fry at 300°F until golden brown. Allow to cool on a rack so they can drain. Place on a c-fold-lined tray to absorb any additional oil. Pulse in a robot coupe. Season to taste with kosher salt. Roughly chop and reserve in an airtight container.
dry curacao	150g	
sugar	150g	
filtered water	150g	
orange peel	5g	
salt	t.t.	

additional ingredients & to finish

walnut oil	Place a small amount of the kefir ice cream inside the lettuce. Dress with the walnut oil, fermented cranberry juice, dried cranberries, and candied walnuts. Season with kosher salt and serve immediately.
fermented cranberry juice	
kosher salt	
small heads of lettuce, washed well	

YEAST DONUT, FOIE GRAS, BLACK APPLE

The only thing that has never left the menu since I reopened the restaurant is the donut: a yeast-risen donut, fried and stuffed with a foie gras pastry cream. The glazes change seasonally and have varied between sweet and savory. This version highlights apples. First the glaze takes apples that were treated like black garlic and cooked down into an apple butter. We also took apples that we had dried back in August, reconstituted them in water, and fried them in butter with brown sugar and spices. We then folded them into the pastry cream before piping into the warm donuts.

---

donut dough

milk	180mL
granulated sugar	114g
buttermilk	300mL
active dry yeast	10g
bread flour	910g
kosher salt	10g
whole eggs	2ea
butter, softened	114g

Bring the milk, sugar, buttermilk, and yeast to 105°F. Place the flour and salt in a stand mixer set with a dough hook attachment. On low speed, add the warm milk mixture. Once fully combined, add the eggs one at a time, being sure each is fully incorporated before adding the next. Add the butter and continue to mix until completely combined and a smooth dough is formed. Place in a bowl covered tightly with plastic wrap, and proof until doubled in volume. Punch the dough down, transfer to a clean work surface, and roll to ½" thickness. Place on a Silpat-lined tray sprayed lightly with nonstick spray. Wrap and place in the refrigerator to rest for 3-4 hours. Punch the donuts into desired shape and let proof for 30 minutes. Fry at 325°F until golden brown and cooked through.

black apple butter

black apples	400g
brown sugar	100g
quatre epices	5g

Slowly cook until sugar is melted and apples are completely soft. Puree until smooth and pass through a fine-mesh strainer.

black apple glaze

black apple butter	60g
10x sugar	125g
bourbon barrel-aged vanilla paste	2g
activated charcoal	t.t.

Mix the apple butter, sugar, and vanilla paste until smooth. Add activated charcoal until desired color is achieved.

fried apples

dried apples	285g
filtered water	500mL
butter	50g
brown sugar	60g
cinnamon	1.5g
black apple butter	50g
kosher salt	t.t.

Rehydrate dried apples in the 500mL water with a cartouche. Once soft, strain and reserve 100mL of the cooking water. Dice the apples into ¼" pieces. In a large sauté pan, add the butter over medium-high heat. Once it begins to foam, add the apples and sauté for 2-3 minutes. Add the brown sugar, cinnamon, and black apple butter. Cook until it begins to bubble. Add the reserved water and continue to cook over medium-high heat until most of the water has evaporated and a glaze consistency is achieved. Season to taste with salt, and cool. Reserve until needed.

foie pastry cream

kosher salt	4g
cornstarch	20g
egg yolks	80g
milk	200g
foie gras, deveined and cut into small cubes	240g

Mix the salt and cornstarch together. In a medium-size sauce pot, bring the milk to a simmer. Whisk the salt and cornstarch into the eggs, and temper in the milk. Add back to the pot and stir vigorously with a whisk until the mixture comes to a boil for one minute. Emulsify in the foie gras until completely combined. Season with more salt as needed. Pass through a fine-mesh strainer. Place in a shallow container covered directly with plastic wrap to prevent from forming a skin. Cool immediately. Before using, whip with a whisk until airy, transfer to a piping bag, and reserve.

additional ingredients & to finish

Maldon sea salt	

Make a small hole in the side of the donut and fill with the pastry cream. Glaze the top of the donut and season with the sea salt. Finish with crushed freeze-dried apples.

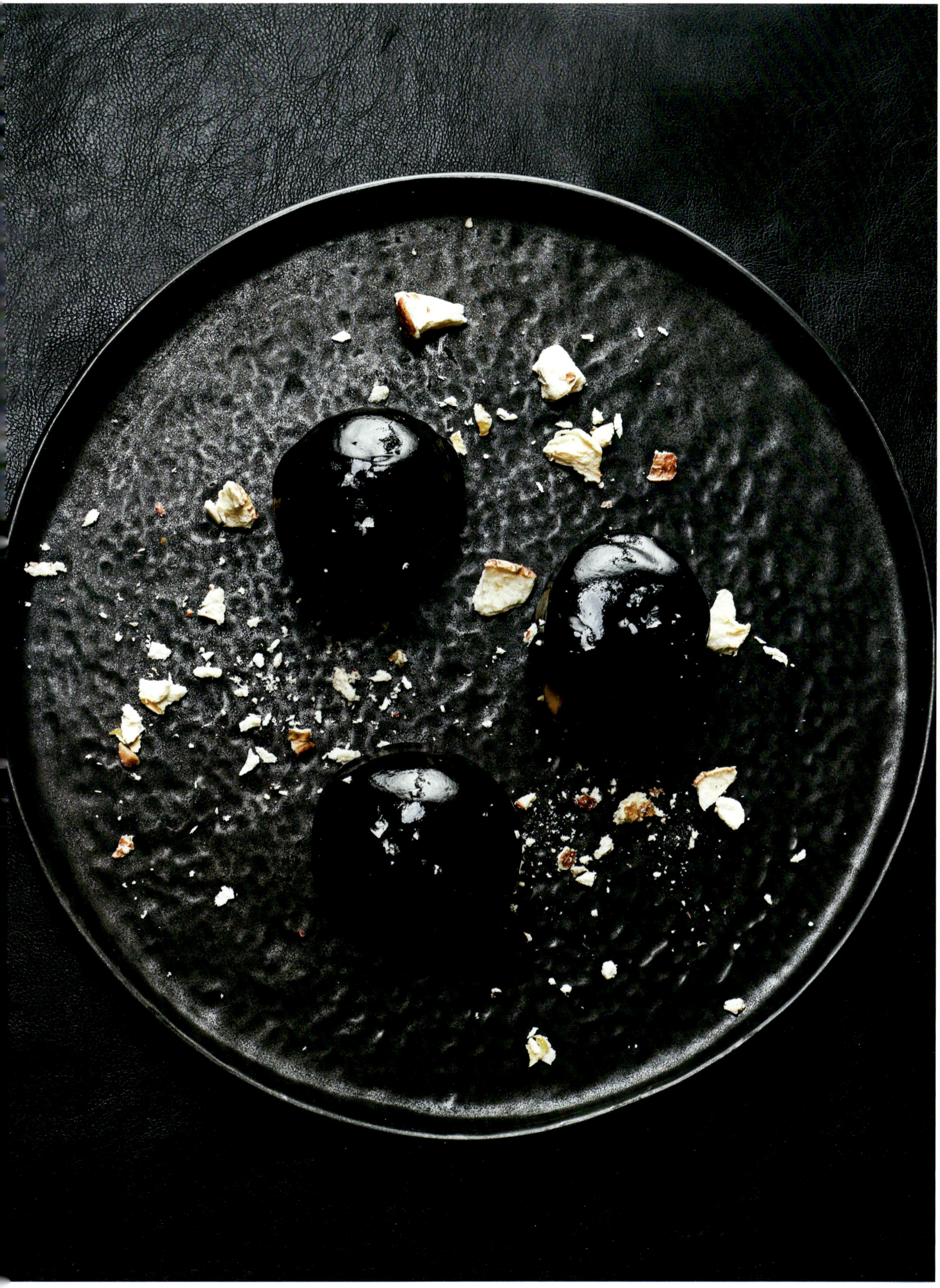

AN ICE CREAM SUNDAE OF BEETS PRESERVED LIKE LUXARDO CHERRIES WITH SHIO KOJI CARAMEL

I always enjoyed the pairing of beets with red fruit, especially cherries. I bought an abundance of red beets from my friend Chris at Southland Farms but didn't have any place for them on the menu, so I decided to treat them like Luxardo cherries and preserve them for a future use. They were removed using a Parisienne scoop to be the size of a cherry and cooked in a juice made from the scraps, Luxardo maraschino liqueur, and sugar. We dried them until chewy and then packed them back into the reduced cooking liquid. We then served them over an ice cream made from burnt pompona vanilla, black trumpet shortbread, and preserved strawberries. We finished it with a warm caramel made from sorghum and shio koji.

---

shio koji caramel

heavy cream	940mL
vanilla paste	2g
sorghum syrup	225g
light brown sugar	450g
shio koji (see base recipes)	225g

Bring all the ingredients to a boil in a heavy-gauged sauce pot. Cook until the mixture reads 225°F on a sugar thermometer. Set aside to cool.

to finish

For every 200g caramel, stir in 150g birch syrup.

burnt vanilla ice cream

sugar	15g
Uno ice cream stabilizer	.75g
nonfat dry milk solids	30g
kosher salt	.5g
milk	750mL
heavy cream	395mL
glucose	45g
trimoline	6g
pompona vanilla, charred over hardwood embers, halved, and scraped	10g
Luxardo cherry syrup	100g

Mix sugar, ice cream stabilizer, dry milk solids, and kosher salt together and set aside. In a medium-sized sauce pot, bring the milk, cream, glucose, trimoline, and vanilla bean to a simmer. Whisk in the dry ingredients; be sure there are no clumps and that it is completely combined. Whisk in the cherry syrup, and bring to a boil for one minute, whisking constantly. Pass through a fine-mesh strainer into Paco canisters and freeze. Spin 1 hour before serving.

black trumpet shortbread

AP flour	325g
butter	250g
sugar	150g
malt syrup	50g
salt	7g
black cocoa	25g
black trumpet mushrooms, dried	100g

Soak black trumpets in hot water and reserve. While soaking, mix dry ingredients in a robot coupe. Pulse in butter a little at a time until a sandy texture is formed. Mix in malt syrup very quickly. Do not let the dough come together. Drain the trumpet mushrooms and press out all liquid (reserve for another use). Split onto two Silpat-lined half sheet pans, scatter the drained mushrooms over the shortbread, and bake at 325°F, stirring every 6 to 7 minutes with a bowl scraper, until toasted and smelling nutty (approximately 15 minutes). Allow to cool completely, then process in a robot coupe until a fine crumb is formed.

beet syrup

beet juice, strained	1L
sugar	1kg
Luxardo liqueur	375g
Luxardo cherry syrup	200g

Bring to a simmer over medium heat and cook until the sugar is completely dissolved.

luxardo beets

beets, scooped with a 22mm Parisienne scoop	500g

Cook the beets in the beet syrup over medium heat until tender but still holding their shape. Drain the beets and dehydrate at 115°F until most of the moisture has evaporated and they are chewy. Meanwhile, reduce the beet syrup by half of its original volume. Pour the hot syrup over the beets and let cool to room temperature. Store in the refrigerator for a minimum of 48 hours before using.

preserved strawberries

strawberries, washed and halved	450g
granulated sugar	225g
St-Germain Elderflower Liqueur	50g

Cook over a double boiler until the strawberries are completely tender but still hold their shape. Drain and reserve the syrup for another use. Dry the strawberries at 110°F until most of the moisture has evaporated and they have the texture of a raisin.

to finish

Place a small spoonful of the shortbread in the center of a plate. Top with a piece of preserved strawberry and a quenelle of the ice cream. Drizzle with desired amount of caramel, a pinch of Maldon sea salt, and a spoonful of the beets and their syrup.

WINTER 2020-2021

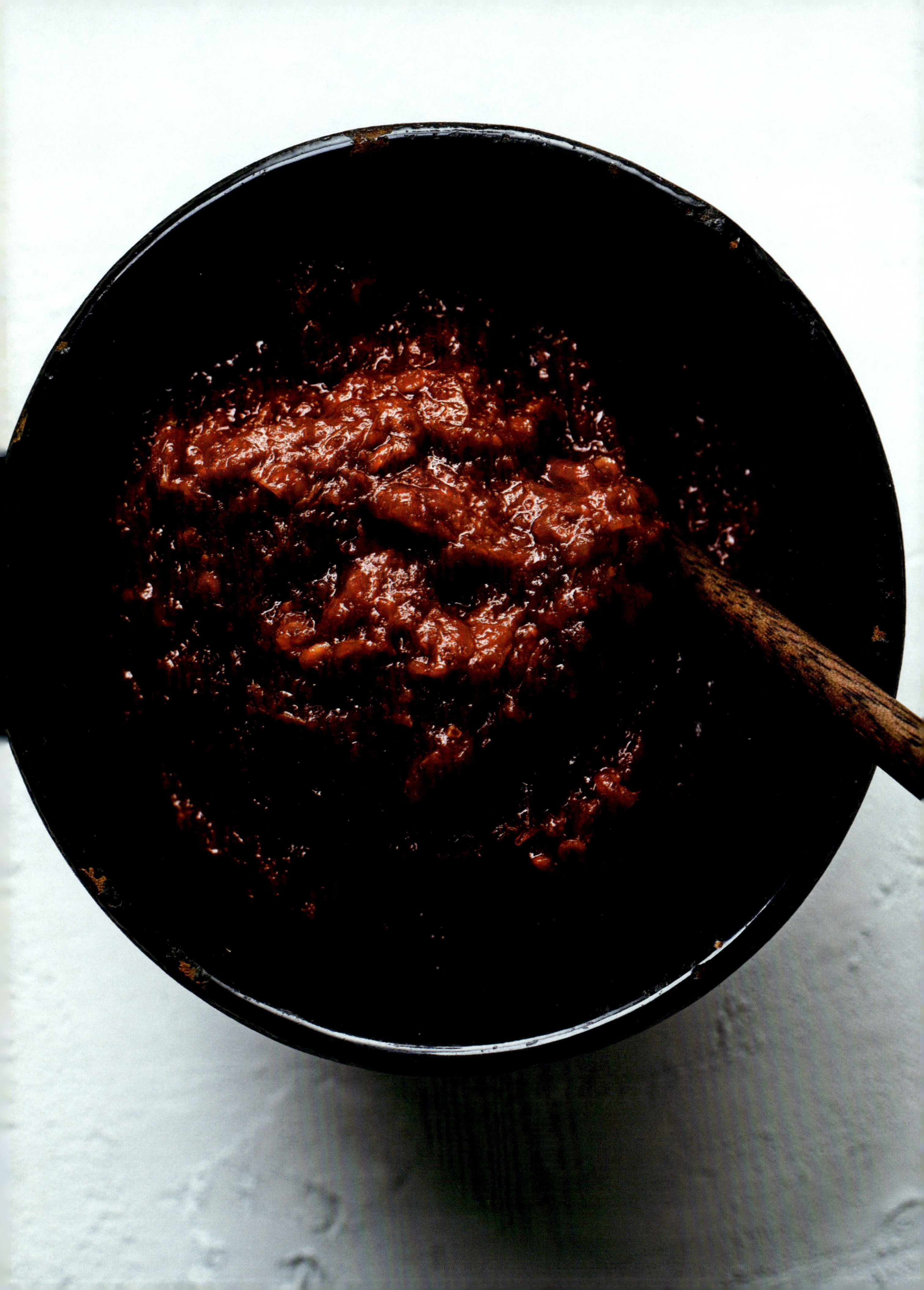

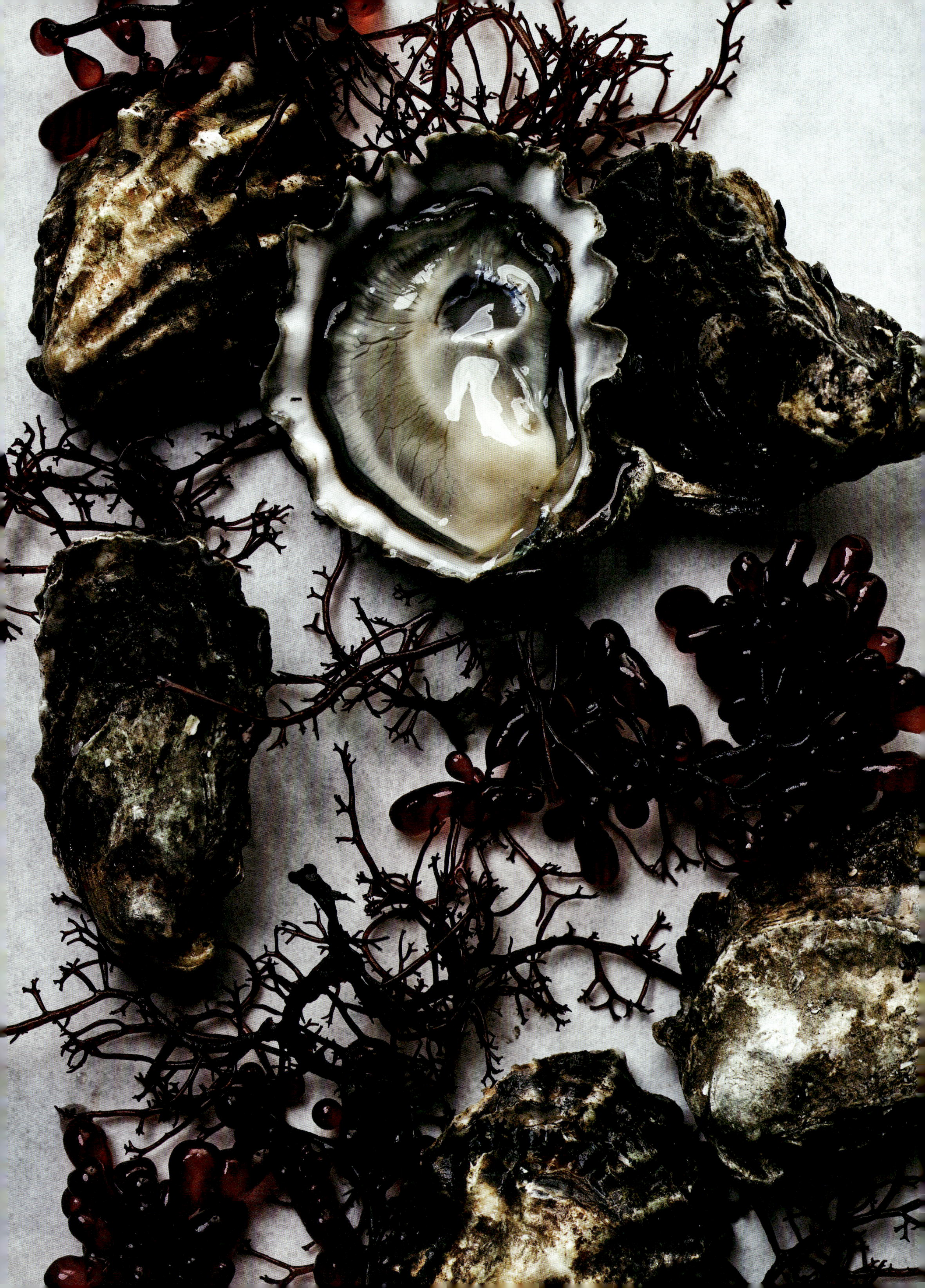

While fall in Tennessee can be long, languid, and unseasonably warm, winter often rears its head as a cold, gray beast that hangs around, blotting out the sun for two or three months. Working with seafood—the food I came to appreciate as I grew up in Florida and became exposed to a new kind of fish every year—has been continually inspiring throughout my tenure at Catbird. This winter was a great time for me to double down on the amazing quality of fish I had at my disposal, thanks to some dedicated purveyors bringing in delicate and delicious species of fish at lightning-fast speeds. For this particular season, I focused on king crab, one of my favorite food memories as a boy (page 83), and beautifully buttery scallops from the coast of Maine. I was proud of a halibut dish I knew would have to be great, as it was to be part of the tenth-anniversary dinner at Catbird, which saw the immensely talented opening chef team come back to recreate some of their classic dishes.

Another aspect of this menu I really enjoyed was a "Pork and Clams" succession of dishes that unfolded like a four-act play (page 91). Pork and clams together isn't a new combination—it's rooted in Portuguese cuisine, as well as the Portuguese-influenced food of northern New England, all well documented—but I was inspired to play with different combinations utilizing ingredients both local and far-flung. Here in Tennessee, mustard greens, kale, and other brassicas were plentiful and perfectly in season. I added brightness, acid, and nuanced floral elements to the equation by using some incredible Meyer lemons from the coast of California, coriander capers that we'd preserved in late summer, and some house-cured pork fat, which added plenty of depth and flavor.

In addition to the fresh seafood, greens, clams, and delicious pork products from Tennessee's Bear Creek Farm, I experimented with umami-laden fats such as a wasabi-spiced buttermilk concoction, a foie gras fat that took the halibut dish into the stratosphere, and a memorable dessert comprised of beef fat and smoky, scotch-infused caramel. Finally, exotic ingredients from the coasts helped to add briny, oceanic complexity to the many seafood dishes. Things like foraged sea lettuce, alba, sea truffles, and the clean minerality of pink moon oysters from Prince Edward Island had the kitchen smelling like we were right next to the ocean at times—which made me feel very at home. These are the dishes of my first winter season at Catbird.

Credit: Todd Saal

WINTER 2020–2021 MENU

beef belly ham, kimchi & asian pear **76**

pink moon oysters with an ice of mountain rose apple & fresh wasabi **79**

dry-aged buri with granny smith apple, fermented green gooseberry & sea lettuce **80**

norwegian king crab, rose & horseradish **83**

koji bucatini, fermented kohlrabi & king crab butter **84**

maine scallop, fermented celery butter & alba truffle **87**

halibut confited in foie gras fat with a sea truffle dashi **88**

———————

BEAR CREEK FARM PORK COULOTTE, CLAMS & BRASSICAS

littleneck clams, cured pork fat & coriander capers **92**

sourdough flatbread, smoked clams & mustard greens **95**

dry-aged pork coulotte, razor-clam chimichurri & braised collards **96**

killed lettuces **99**

———————

parsnip, black trumpet shortbread, hickory **100**

beef fat & laphroaig sponge candies **103**

BEEF-BELLY HAM, KIMCHI & ASIAN PEAR

This first little bite came from my love of Korean food. When I was living in Atlanta, I loved this place in Duluth called 678 Korean BBQ. It was the first time I had the kimchi warmed by the grill. I always try to have something salty, something with spice, and something acidic on the opening bites. This one combines all three and packs a lot of flavor. Shinko pear dressed in a house-made kimchi, wrapped in dry-aged beef-belly ham, and grilled is salty, smoky, spicy, umami-forward with a nice sharpness from the lactic acid in the kimchi. One of my favorite bites.

---

beef-belly ham

beef belly	2.2kg
country ham cure	100g

Rub the belly in 50 percent of the ham cure. Cover in a non-reactive container for 2 weeks, flipping every day. On day 15, drain the brine, re-rub the belly with the remaining cure, and cover for another 14 days. Rinse the belly and allow to dry in front of a fan in the walk-in/refrigerator overnight. The next day, cold-smoke for 8 hours. Hang in a cool place for at least 6 months. Before slicing, cut down into 4" blocks and freeze. Once frozen, slice as thin as possible and layer on sheets of deli paper.

shinko pear kimchi

Shinko pear pulp (left over from juicing)	900g
garlic, minced	30g
ginger, minced	22g
Aleppo chile flake	12g
Fresno chile, roughly chopped	60g
green onion, minced	45g
fish sauce	20g
honey	15g
salt	22g

Puree all ingredients and seal in a Cryovac bag on full pressure. Allow to ferment in a warm place for a minimum of 14 days.

korean bbq glaze

soy sauce	500g
mirin	250g
clover honey	250g
pear trim (reserve Shinko pear)	200g
beef garum	45g
sesame oil	45g
ground black pepper	5g

Puree all ingredients until smooth. Pass through a fine-mesh strainer and reserve until needed.

additional ingredients & to finish

Shinko pear, cut into 1/8" × 2" allumette

Dress 5 or 6 pieces of the Shinko pear in the pear kimchi, wrap in a slice of beef belly, and grill until it begins to caramelize. Brush with the Korean BBQ glaze immediately before serving.

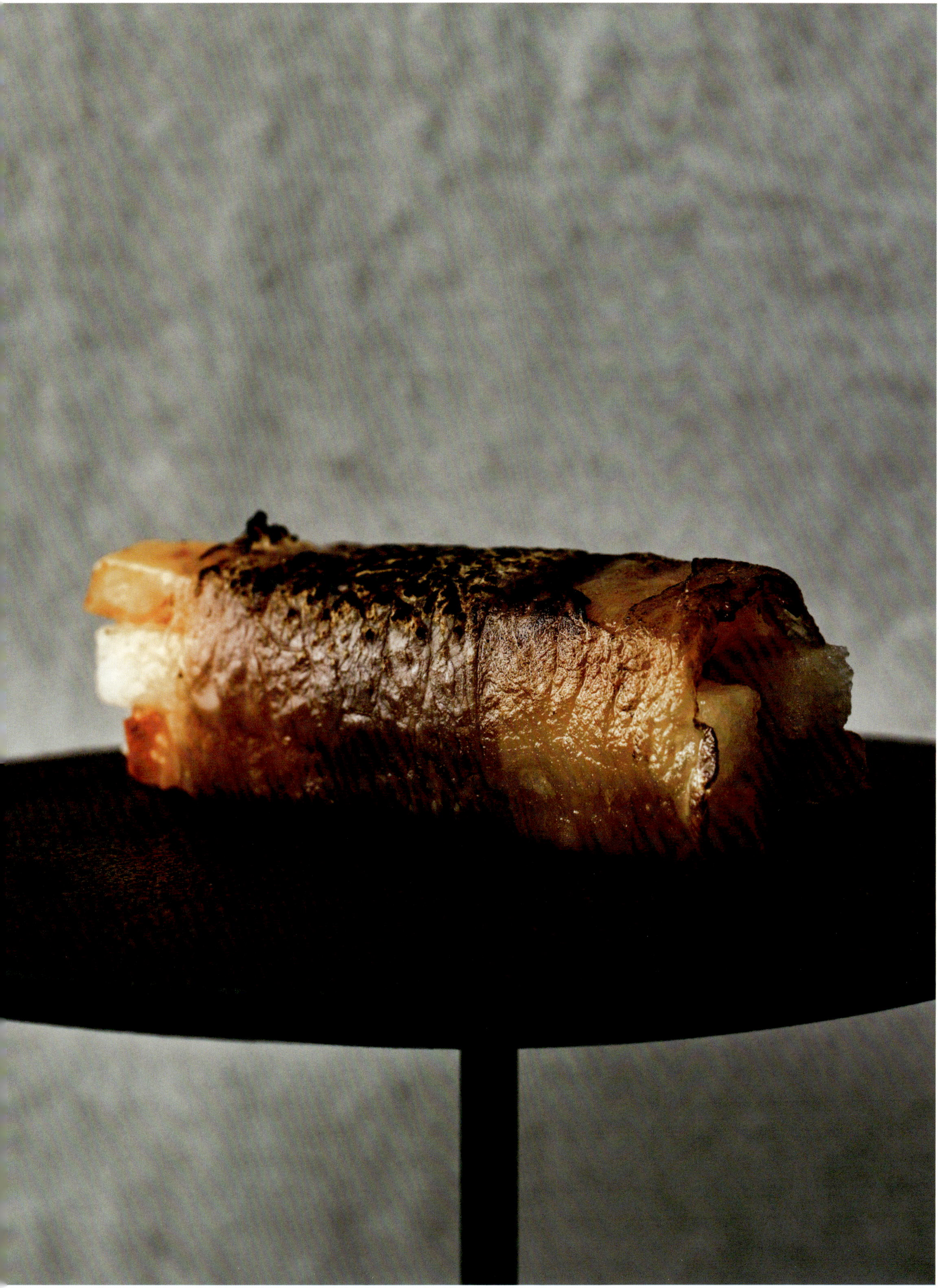

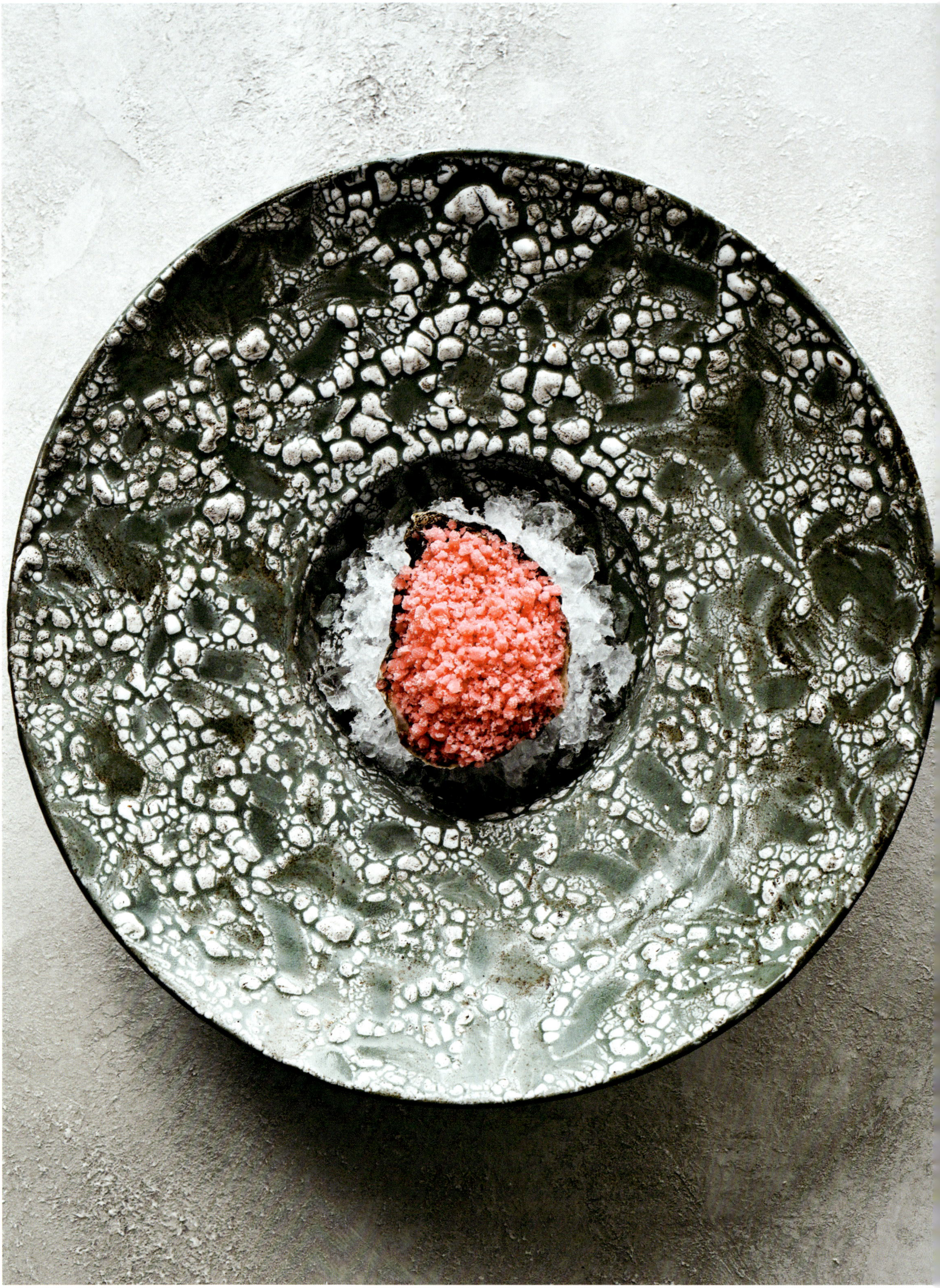

PINK MOON OYSTERS WITH AN ICE OF MOUNTAIN ROSE APPLE & FRESH WASABI

This was another nice bite that was salty, sweet, acidic, and spicy all at once. I figured pink apples and pink moon oysters had to work as a pairing. The creaminess of pink moon oysters works so well with the flavors that it allowed the cleanness and minerality of the oysters to be the star. It definitely takes your mouth on a wild ride. The oyster is dressed in salted buttermilk, allowed to ferment for a few days and then chilled, and served with a granita made from mountain rose apple and fresh wasabi from Japan.

wasabi buttermilk

good buttermilk	1L
fresh wasabi, grated on a microplane	15g
kosher salt	20g

Mix all the ingredients together well and allow to ferment at room temperature for 7 days. Pass through a fine-mesh strainer and chill.

mountain rose apple ice

mountain rose apple juice	900g
ascorbic acid	5g
dextrose	30g
cornstarch	10g
gelatin, bloomed	5g

Mix apple juice, ascorbic acid, dextrose, and cornstarch, and bring to a boil. Stir in bloomed gelatin. Allow to freeze in a shallow hotel pan. Once frozen, break up into small chunks and toss with liquid nitrogen. Process in a robot coupe or Thermomix until a fine snow is formed. Reserve in the freezer until needed.

to finish

Dress the oyster with the buttermilk followed by the shaved ice. Serve immediately.

DRY-AGED BURI WITH GRANNY SMITH APPLE, FERMENTED GREEN GOOSEBERRY & SEA LETTUCE

I love tilefish. It was one of my favorite types of fish to eat for a long time. Then I tried buri from my friend Liwei Liao, or Dry-Aged Fish Guy, owner of Joint Seafood in Los Angeles. Buri is a yellowtail, or amberjack, that can reach over 80 centimeters when fully grown. They migrate into the colder water around Japan, which makes their intramuscular fat content very high. Something about the flavor and mouthfeel of this fish, thanks to the fat content, just blew my mind. I love it both raw and quickly grilled. For this preparation, we served it with vinaigrette made from fermented green gooseberry juice, white shoyu, and an oil made from sea lettuce. We dressed it in a gelee made from Granny Smith apple and yuzu infused with jalapeno. For a little more sweetness and acidity, we added pickled sea lettuce. The freshness of the buri with the oceanic flavor of the sea lettuce reminded me of the clean ocean air when foraging for sea lettuce in Maine.

---

sea lettuce oil

sea lettuce	100g
2 percent apple pulp (see fermented apple cider recipe, page 270)	100g
grapeseed oil	200g

Cryovac all of the ingredients together and place the bag in a large pot of boiling water. Boil for 3 hours, shock in an ice bath and reserve in the bag overnight. The next day, strain through a coffee-filter-lined fine-mesh strainer. Reserve chilled in an airtight container until needed.

green gooseberry vin

fermented green gooseberry juice (see page 269)	1,335g
white soy (10 percent)	135g

Mix together well and chill.

granny smith gelee

Granny Smith apple juice	750g
silver leaf gelatin	24g
fresh yuzu juice	30g
jalapeno, deseeded and chopped fine	20g
malic acid	8g

Warm 200g of the apple juice and stir in the gelatin until melted. Mix in the remaining ingredients, and chill on a shallow tray. Once set, break up with a fork into small pieces.

pickled sea lettuce

seaweed vinegar	100g
water	50g
sugar	25g
sea lettuce	100g

Bring the vinegar, water, and sugar to a boil and pour over the sea lettuce.

to finish

buri loin, skin removed

Slice the buri as if you were preparing sashimi. Place in the center of a plate and make a quick vinaigrette by whisking a small amount of sea lettuce into the green gooseberry juice. Spoon over the slice of fish, and top with a small spoonful of the gelee and a few pieces of pickled sea lettuce.

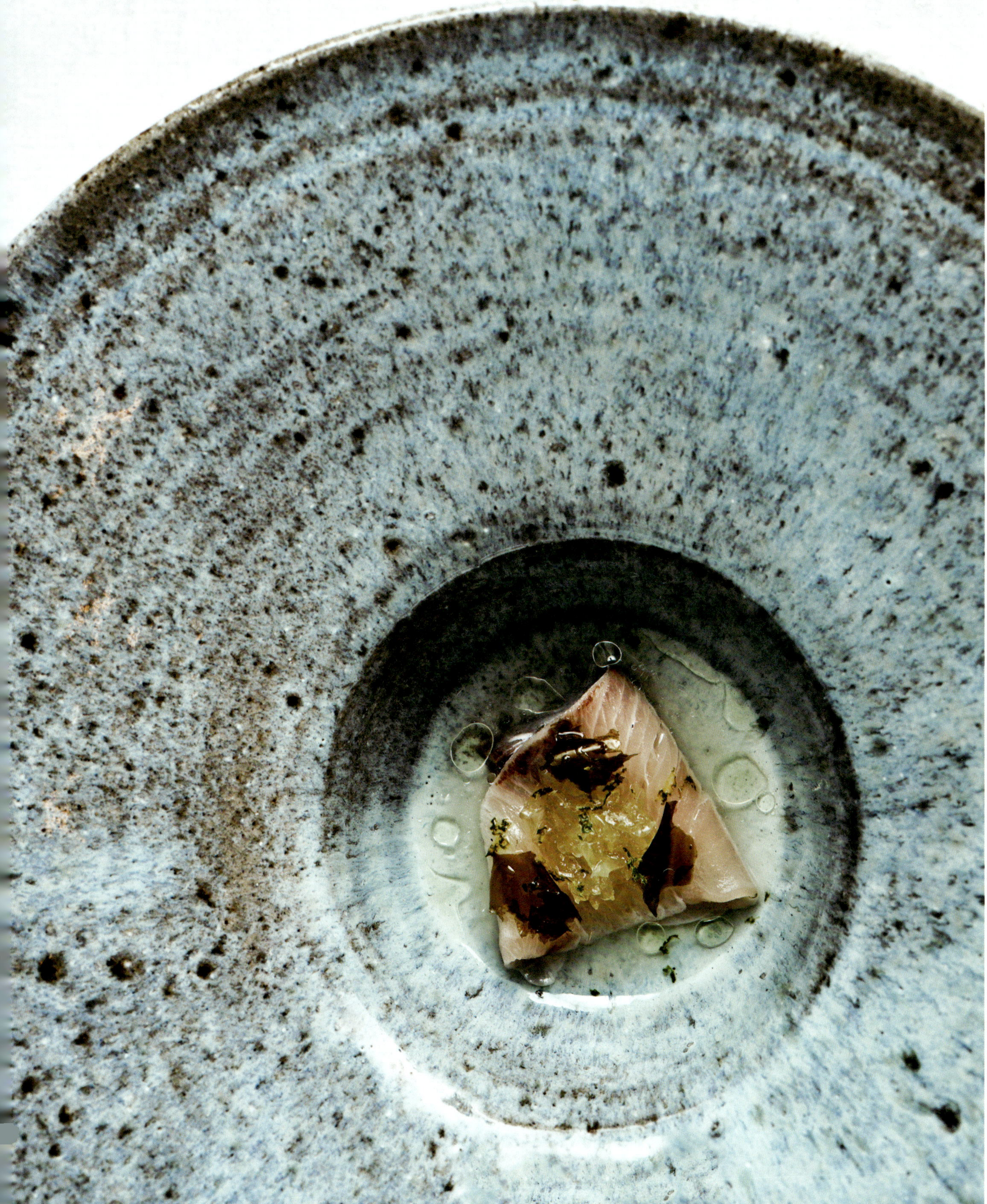

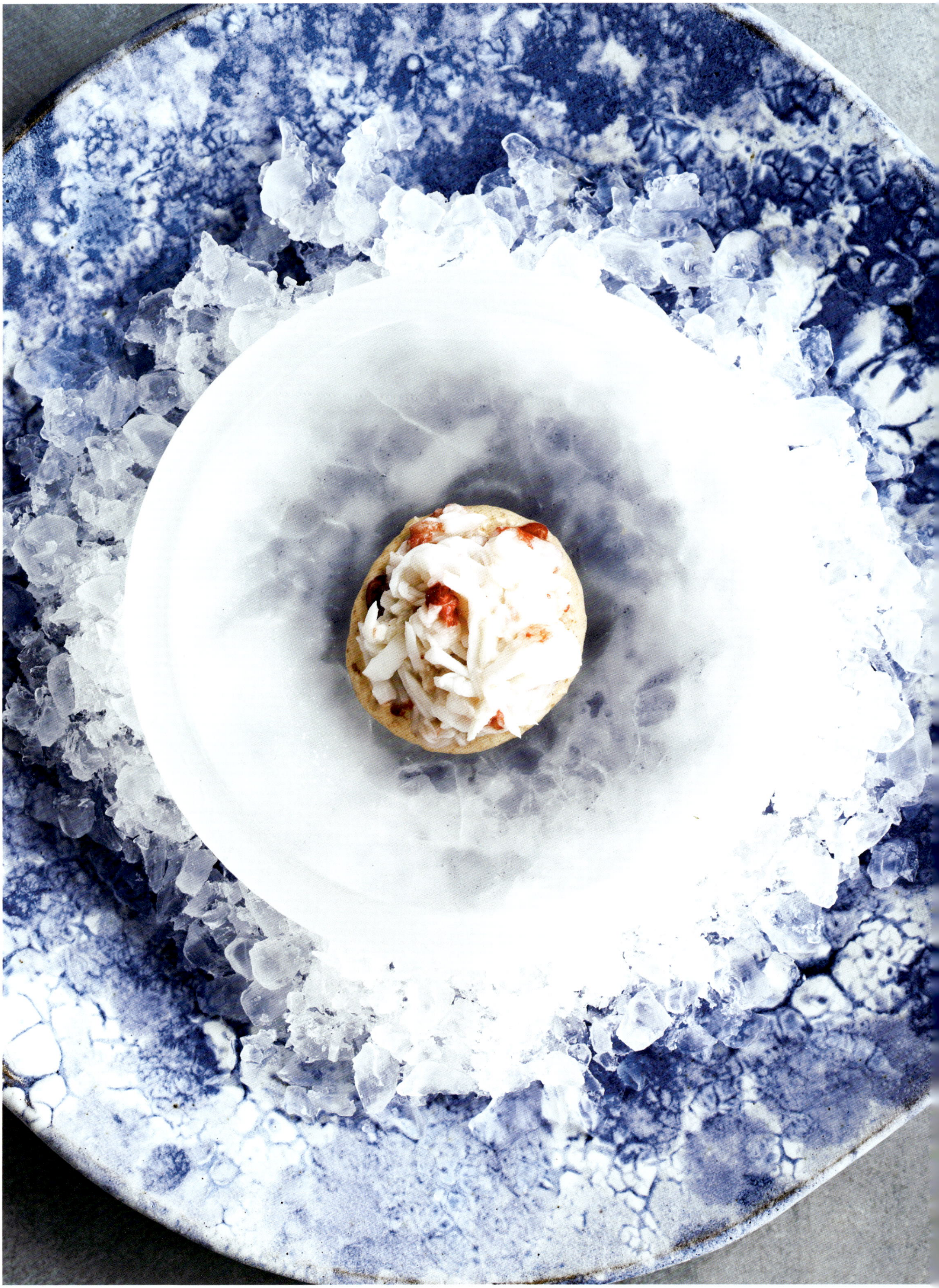

NORWEGIAN KING CRAB, ROSE & HORSERADISH

When you grow up in Florida, you eat a lot of seafood. I love it all—raw, fried, on the half shell, grilled, smoked, broiled, sauteed. One of my favorite things is cocktail sauce. It's good on the seafood, the fries, and even hush puppies (or maybe that's just me). I remember being very young and going to a crab house with our family for a celebration. My older cousin Chris ordered the whole steamed crab, so I decided to order one as well. I must have been nine or ten and had no idea what I was getting myself into. Needless to say, I loved it. It wasn't king crab, but it was my first taste of crab. I hammered it open, cracked every shell, and sucked every piece clean, doused in drawn butter and, of course, cocktail sauce left over from the fried shrimp. This dish is my way of trying to bring all of that into a couple of small bites. The richness and sweetness of the king crab were balanced by the saltiness and the spice of the dressing. It is very simple but hard to beat.

---

russian dressing

Kewpie mayo	300g
rose kosho (see page 271)	35g
tomato bouillon (see page 270)	30g
prepared horseradish	100g
chipotle powder	1g
yuzu juice	12g

Stir all ingredients together until well combined. Chill and reserve until needed.

king crab

Steam the king crab at 100°C for 20 to 25 minutes, depending on the size of the crabs. Allow to rest for 10 minutes at room temperature and then immediately cool in a refrigerator. Once cooled, remove all the meat from the shells, being sure to catch any juice that may release from the crab and reserving the shells for another use. Cut the crab into desired portions and reserve.

rose salt

rose petals	150g
Pacific sea salt	225g

Puree in a spice grinder until well combined. Slowly dry in a dehydrator or oven with a pilot light at 100°C until all of the moisture has evaporated.

to finish

Place a spoonful of the Russian dressing in a chilled serving bowl, add the portion of crab, and season with the rose salt..

KOJI BUCATINI, FERMENTED KOHLRABI & KING CRAB BUTTER

For this dish, we utilized the rest of the king crab—the inedible parts like the shells, mustards, and any juice reserved from the cleaning process. The bucatini was made by my friend Aaron Distler of Mr. Aarons Goods here in Nashville. We tossed the pasta in the butter sauce that had been emulsified with a vibrant herb oil and seasoned with more fermented kohlrabi juice. We finished the dish by grating some fresh sudachi zest and a bottarga made from crab roe.

---

crab butter base

carrots, small dice	25g
fennel, small dice	45g
onion, small dice	30g
butter	25g
crab shells	200g
crab juice, reserved from cooling and cleaning	700mL
Champagne, or other dry sparkling wine	300mL

Sweat carrots, fennel, and onion in the butter over medium heat. Add the crab shells, crab juice, and Champagne. Reduce by 50 percent. Strain through a fine-mesh strainer and cool.

crab butter

shallot, sliced thin	30g
2% kohlrabi juice (see page 269)	100g
crab-butter base	150g
butter	190g

Reduce the shallot, kohlrabi juice, and crab butter base until 120g remains. Place in a Vitamix and blend on high speed. Emulsify in the cubed butter. Pass through a fine-mesh strainer and reserve in a warm place.

herb oil

dill fronds	75g
parsley leaves	20g
chives	20g
grapeseed oil	275g

Puree in a Vitamix on high until blended well. Do not strain. Cool immediately.

additional ingredients & to finish

sudachi juice
sudachi zest
2% kohlrabi juice
crab roe bottarga
bucatini or pasta of choice

Bring a large pot of salted water to a boil. Cook the bucatini to desired doneness. While the pasta is cooking, emulsify a spoonful of the herb oil into a few ounces of the crab butter, whisking constantly. Season to taste with salt, the sudachi juice, and the kohlrabi juice. Drain the pasta, toss in the butter, and place in a bowl. Grate desired amount of bottarga and sudachi zest before serving.

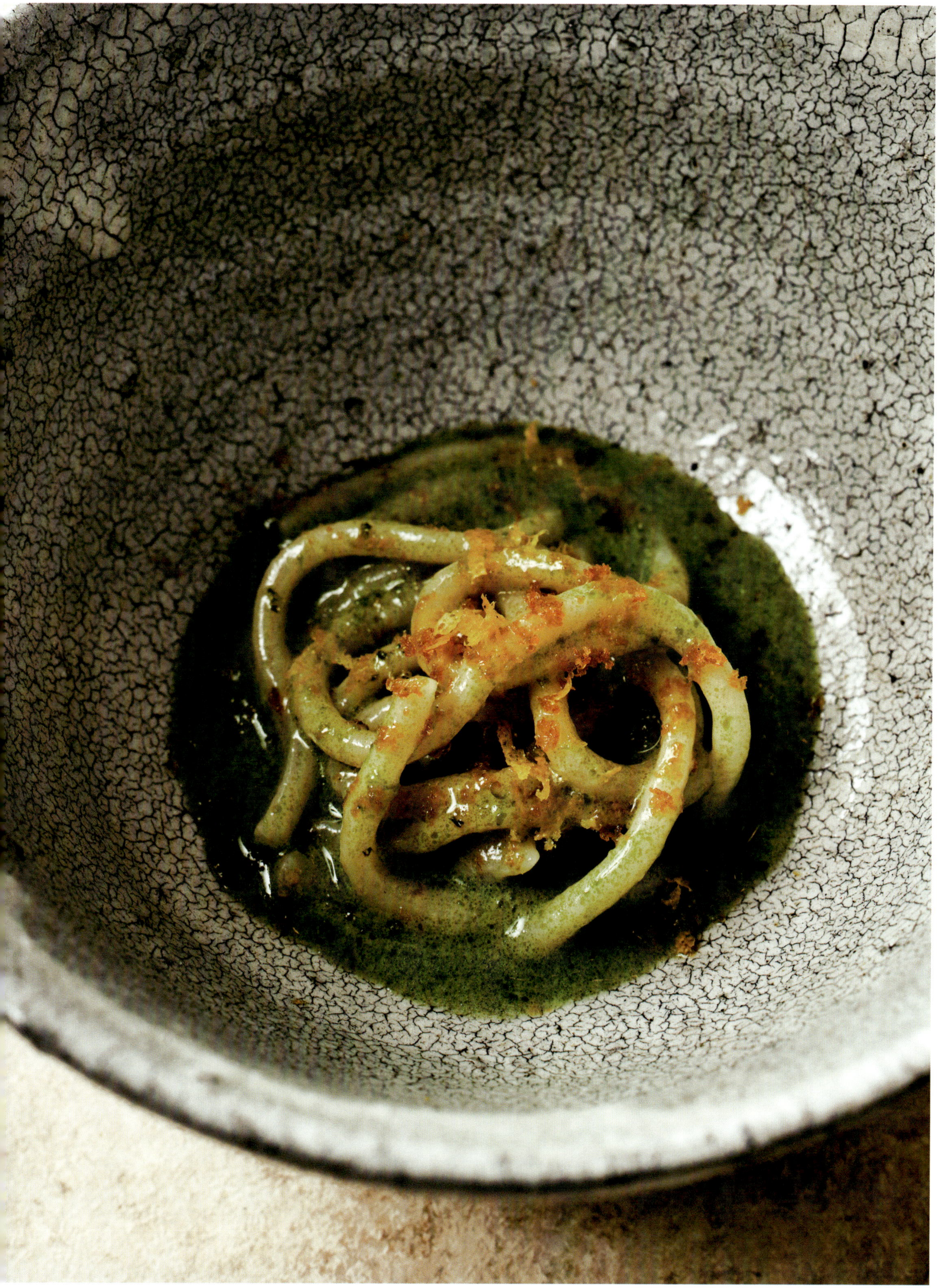

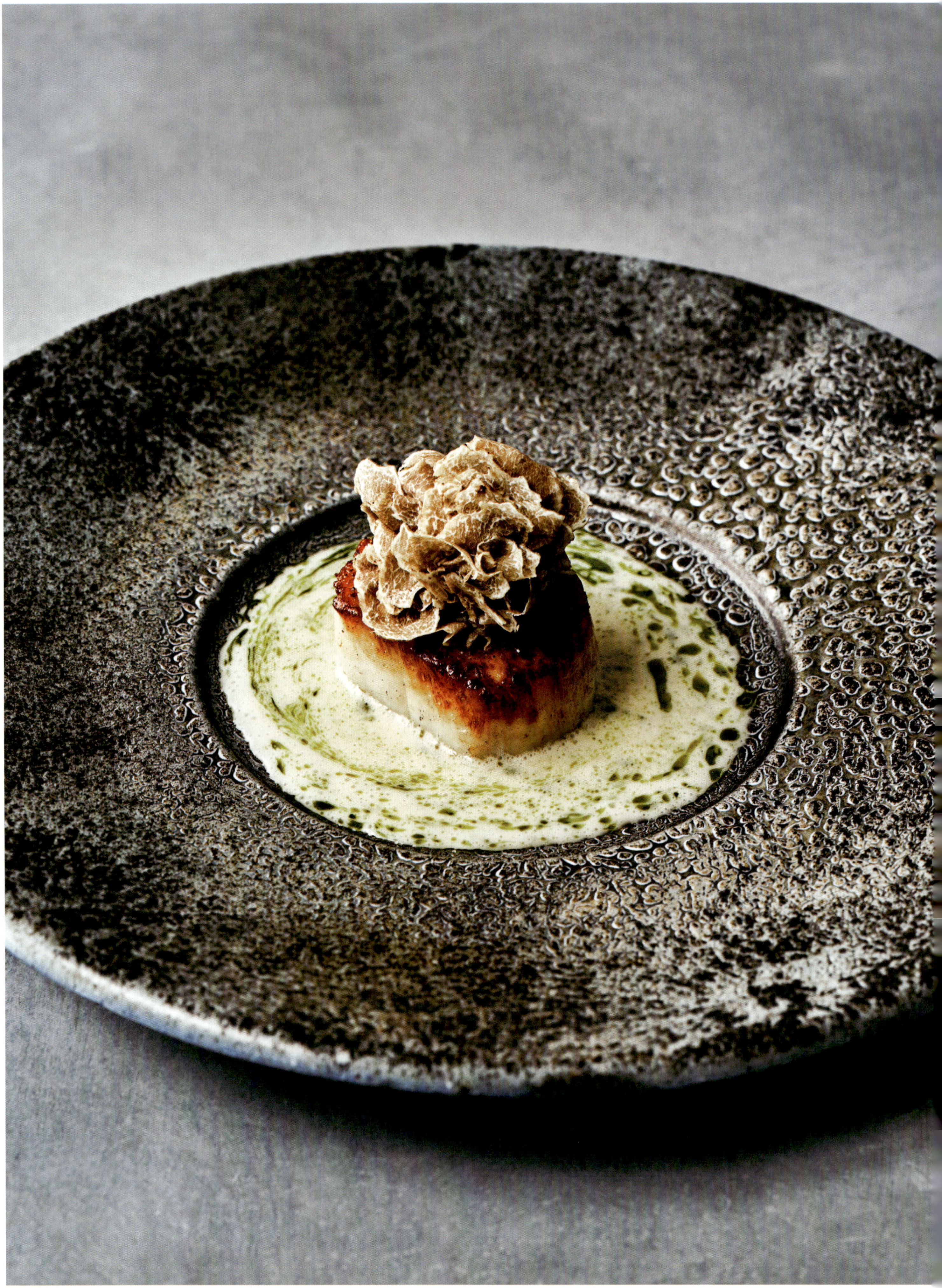

MAINE SCALLOP, FERMENTED CELERY BUTTER & ALBA TRUFFLE

For this dish, I wanted to highlight local celery we had purchased earlier in the year. Kelvin celery from Green Door Gourmet farm here in Nashville is a vibrant green with a sweet strong celery flavor and just a tiny bit of bitterness. We made an oil from the leaves and juiced and fermented the stalks with 2% salt. We eventually reduced the celery juice down with two different types of sherry into a flavorful butter sauce that we finished by folding the celery leaf oil into it. We served it with brown-butter-roasted scallops dressed in freshly squeezed lemon juice and fresh alba truffle. This dish appears very simple, but it's packed with flavor and still one of the favorites from this season.

fermented celery butter

shallot	25g
cream sherry	50g
oloroso sherry	50g
2% celery juice	200g
butter, cubed and chilled	200g

Reduce the shallot and sherries until all the alcohol has evaporated. Add the celery juice and reduce by ¾. Place in a Vitamix and blend on high speed. Emulsify in the cubed butter, pass through a fine-mesh strainer, and reserve in a warm place.

celery-leaf oil

celery leaf	105g
grapeseed oil	275g

Place in a Vitamix and blend on high speed until it reaches 64°C. Pass through a coffee-filter-lined fine-mesh strainer. Cool and reserve.

additional ingredients & to finish

confited scallops (see page 189)
fresh alba truffles

Roast the scallops in brown butter until desired doneness. Allow to rest on a c-fold-lined tray. Bring some of the celery butter back to a simmer and stir in a few spoonfuls of the celery-leaf oil. Season to taste with lemon juice. Spoon onto a plate, add the scallop, and top with desired amount of shaved truffles.

HALIBUT CONFITED IN FOIE GRAS FAT WITH A SEA-TRUFFLE DASHI

I did this dish for the ten-year anniversary dinner with opening chefs Josh Habiger and Erik Anderson. It had begun to cool down in October, and I just wanted a fish dish that was rich and unctuous. The guests enjoyed it so much that I decided to keep it around on the regular menu. Beautiful halibut from Maine was poached to order in rendered foie gras fat and dressed in a warm dashi made from sea truffle or truffle seaweed, a red algae that grows off of the stems of knotted wrack or bladder wrack. This was another very simple presentation that was just as aromatic as it was flavorful.

---

sea-truffle oil

sea truffle	100g	Place in a Vitamix and blend on high speed until it reaches 64°C. Pass through a coffee-filter-lined fine-mesh strainer. Cool and reserve.
grapeseed oil	200g	

sea-truffle dashi

filtered water	1L	Cook the water, dulse, and kombu at 60°C for 45 minutes. Strain dashi over sea truffle, cover and steep for 15 minutes, then strain. Add bonito and bring to a simmer. Remove from heat, cover, and steep for 15 minutes, then pass through a fine-mesh strainer.
salted dulse, rinsed	50g	
kombu, rinsed	15g	
sea truffle	100g	
bonito	12g	

seasoned dashi

dashi	850g	Bring all the ingredients but the kuzu and water to a boil. Stir the kuzu and water together until well combined, then add this slurry to the boiling dashi, whisking constantly. Bring back to a simmer for one minute and remove from the heat. Salt to taste. Reserve until needed.
mirin	150g	
sake	150g	
white soy	150g	
kuzu	20g	
filtered water	50g	
salt	t.t.	

additional ingredients & to finish

halibut, brined for 20 minutes in 3% salt brine, portioned into 56g slices	Place the halibut in an appropriately sized vac bag, add a spoonful of foie gras fat, and poach at 40°C for 45 minutes. Drain onto a towel, season with Pacific sea salt, and place in a small bowl. Heat a couple of ounces of the seasoned dashi, fold in the chopped sea truffles, and spoon over the fish. Dress with a small amount of rendered foie fat and sea truffle oil. Serve immediately.
sea truffle, chopped fine	
rendered foie gras fat	
Pacific sea salt	

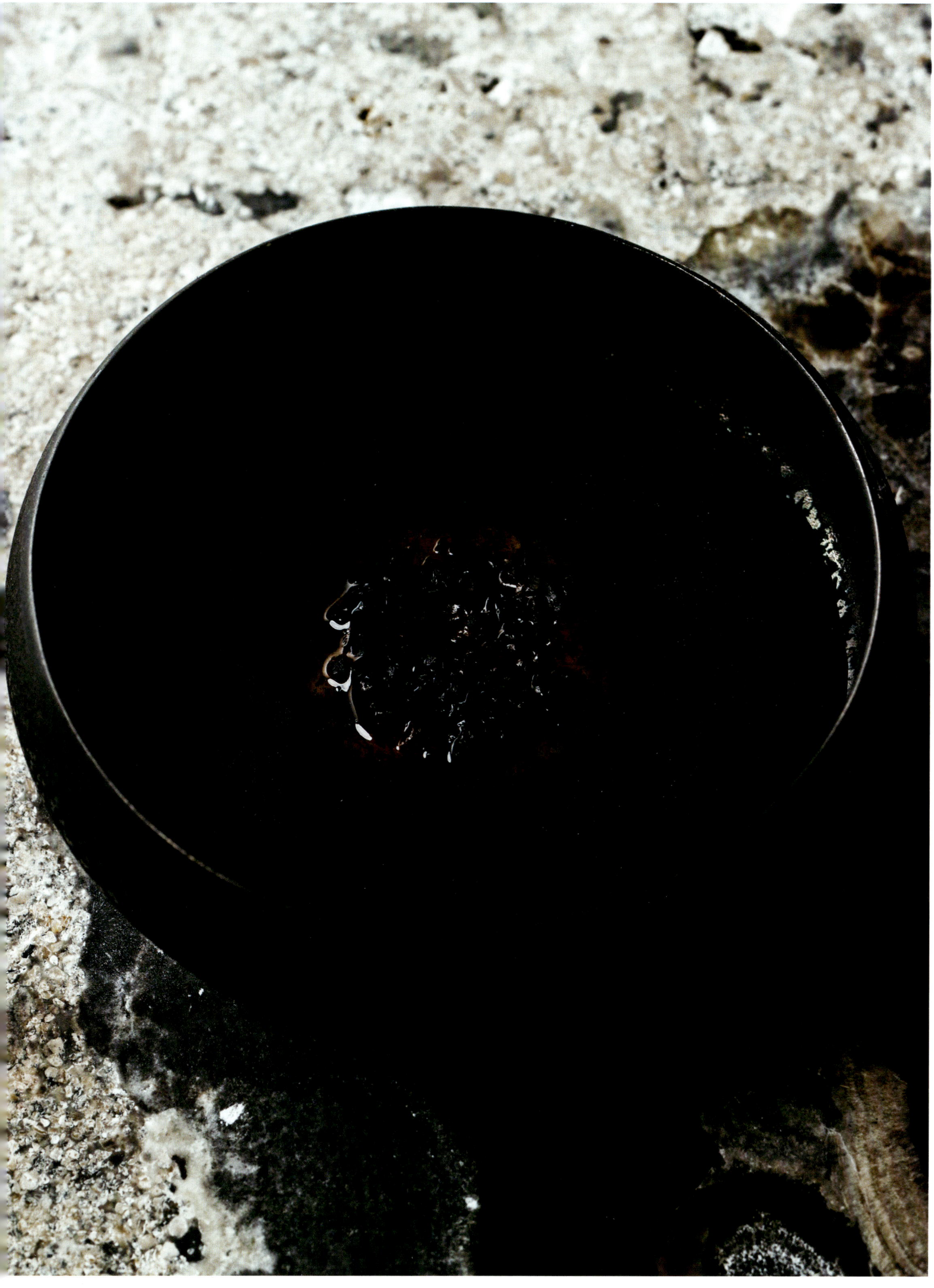

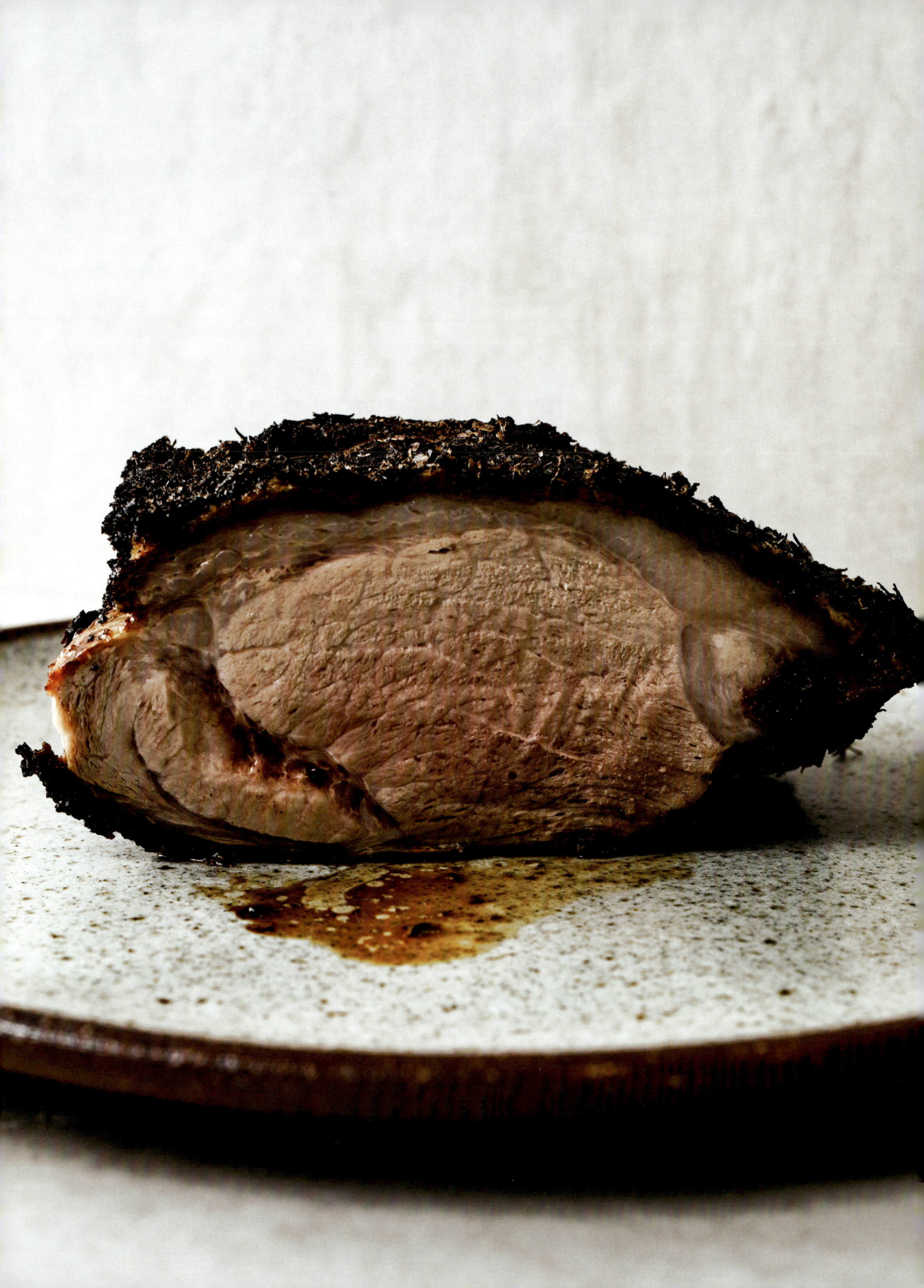

bear creek farm pork coulotte, clams & brassicas

I love how the brininess of the clams pairs with the richness and fattiness of the pork, especially after being aged. We wanted to highlight pork, clams, and brassicas throughout the progression of this course. We served this course in a succession of four parts, to highlight ingredients and exhibit the many different ways in which they work together. We started with a small bite of grilled littleneck clams and followed it with a version of clam pizza.

LITTLENECK CLAMS, CURED PORK FAT & CORIANDER CAPERS

For the first bite, we dressed littleneck clams in a country ham vinaigrette. Then we topped them with house-cured lardo and grilled them until the lardo just began to soften. We finished it by adding preserved Meyer lemon and coriander berries from our garden that we'd preserved like capers.

---

country ham vinaigrette

country ham stock	75g
filtered water	50g
calamansi vinegar	10g
rendered ham fat, warm	40g
grapeseed oil	40g

Warm the ham stock and filtered water over medium-high heat. Once it is hot, transfer to a Vitamix, add the calamansi vinegar, and spin on high speed. Slowly emulsify in the rendered ham fat followed by the grapeseed oil. Reserve until needed.

cured pork fat (lardo)

kosher salt	1,730g
Cure #2	6g
ground black pepper	150g
garlic, smashed	150g
chili flake	35g
rosemary leaves, roughly chopped	40g
bay leaves, roughly chopped	40g
sage, roughly chopped	25g
fat back	2.25kg

Mix all the spices together and rub the fat back completely. Seal in a Cryovac bag on full pressure. Allow to cure for 6 months. Remove from bag and hang for a minimum of 4 weeks. When ready to use, trim the edges where any herbs may still adhere. Slice into portions the same size as the clams you are using. Reserve on deli paper until needed.

additional ingredients & to finish

coriander capers
(see base recipes on page 270)
preserved Meyer lemon, brunoised
(see base recipes on page 271)
clams

Place the vinaigrette followed by the lardo over the clams, and grill until it begins to bubble and the lardo begins to soften. Garnish each clam with 1 coriander caper and 1 piece of brunoised Meyer lemon.

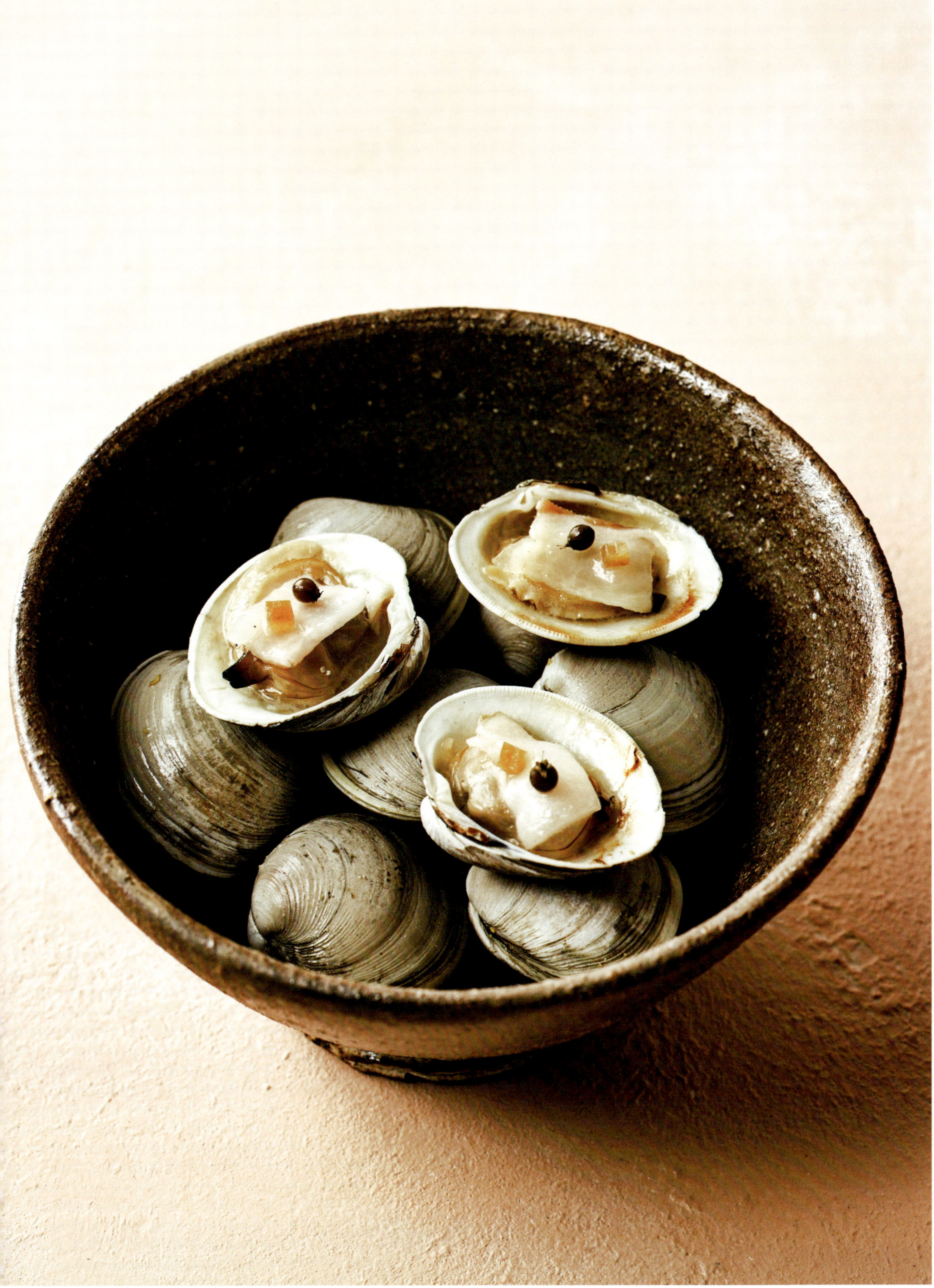

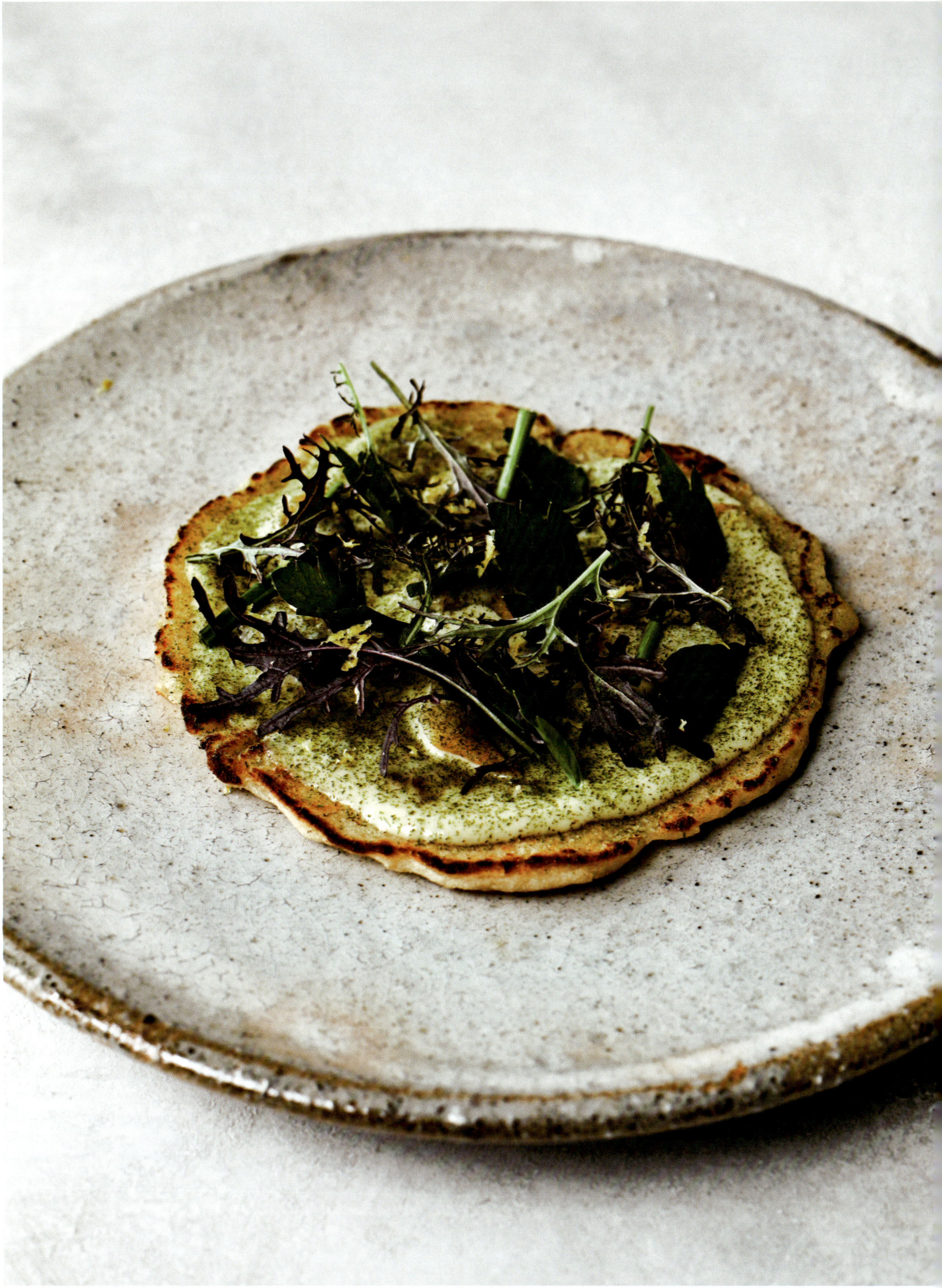

SOURDOUGH FLATBREAD, SMOKED CLAMS & MUSTARD GREENS

Second, we served our little take on a clam pizza: a grilled flatbread with an emulsion made from cured and smoked West Coast razor clams. We cured the chewier syphon and left the tender digger foot raw. The whole flatbread was grilled over hardwood charcoal and finished with tender mustard greens and dried, fermented ramp powder.

---

flatbread

bread flour	240g
sourdough starter	11g
dark honey	14g
olive oil	25g
kosher salt	15g

Place the bread flour and salt in a mixing bowl set with a dough hook attachment. Mix on low speed and add all the wet ingredients. Increase the speed to medium and continue to mix for 10 minutes. The dough should be smooth and spring back when pinched. Knead the dough to form into a ball and transfer to a lightly oiled mixing bowl. Cover with plastic wrap and place in a warm place to proof until doubled in size. Portion the dough into 40g portions.

clam mayo

smoked and dried clams (see page 272)	90g
egg yolk	1ea
garlic, microplaned	5g
seaweed vinegar	40g
lemon juice	30g
water	50g
grapeseed oil	320mL

fermented ramp powder

fermented ramp tops	100g

Dry in a dehydrator at 100°F until no moisture remains. Grind into a fine powder. Reserve in an airtight container.

smoked clam oil

cured, smoked, and dried clams	75g
grapeseed oil	225g

Seal the ingredients in a Cryovac bag on full pressure. Place in a pot of boiling water for a minimum of 4 hours. Cool and allow to steep in the bag overnight. Pass through a coffee-filter-lined fine-mesh strainer and reserve.

additional ingredients & to finish

olive oil
razor clams, removed from shells and sliced thin
mustard greens, washed and dried
parsley leaves, washed and dried
chives, cut into 1" batons
lemon juice
lemon zest

Roll the portioned dough into a circle of ¼" thickness. Brush with a small amount of olive oil and grill over hard wood. Once firm and golden brown, remove from the heat and dress with a thin layer of the clam mayo and some of the sliced razor clams. Return to the grill and cook until the emulsion and clams begin to warm, being sure not to burn. Remove from the heat. Dress the herbs and mustard greens with some of the clam oil and lemon juice. Scatter evenly across the flatbread. Finish with fresh lemon zest and ramp powder.

DRY-AGED PORK COULOTTE, RAZOR-CLAM CHIMICHURRI & BRAISED COLLARDS

The last serving was the coulotte from Bear Creek Farm that had been dry-aged for us. It was rubbed in a mixture of dried herbs and slowly roasted over the coals. We carved it to order and dressed it in a chimichurri made from East Coast razor clams, rosé vinegar, and the juice collected from the pork as it rested. Alongside that were some collards that had been braised with a mixture of the smoked clam syphons and Benton's bacon. One of my favorite things to eat are braised collard greens, but ones that haven't been cooked so long that they don't have a little bit of texture to them.

---

pork rub

dry oregano	15g	Mix together and store in an airtight container until needed.
dry thyme	15g	
dry basil	10g	
dry marjoram	6g	
dry parsley	18g	
granulated garlic	35g	
chipotle powder	10g	
smoked paprika	35g	
kosher salt	100g	
aji-no-moto	12g	

chimichurri base

Jean-Marc's Huilerie Beaujolaise calamansi vinegar	50g	Stir all ingredients together and reserve.
lemon juice	150g	
rosé vinegar	75g	
garlic, microplaned	5g	
shallot, minced	35g	
espellette	5g	
olive oil	75g	
lemon oil	50g	

to finish

pork coulotte		Rub the pork liberally in the pork rub and allow to come to room temperature. Slowly roast over the coals, being sure not to burn the herbs. Alternatively, you can grill the pork quickly and transfer to an oven to roast at 225°F until an internal temperature of 118°F. Remove from the heat, wrap in aluminum foil, and allow to rest for 30 minutes. Slice the pork to desired thickness and dress with the chimichurri.

braised collard greens

onion, small dice	150g	Render the bacon until it begins to turn golden. Add the onion and garlic and sweat until translucent. Add the diced clam syphon and render another minute. Next, add the collard greens and sweat until they begin to soften. Add the remaining liquids and cover with a cartouche. Simmer over medium heat until the collard greens are tender but still hold their shape. Season to taste with salt, hot sauce, and cayenne-pepper vinegar.
garlic, minced	10g	
Benton's bacon, small dice	125g	
clam syphon, smoked and dried, fine dice	75g	
lager-style beer	340mL	
pork stock	2L	
collards, washed well, stems removed, large dice	2qt	
salt	t.t.	
hot sauce, like crystal	t.t.	
cayenne-pepper vinegar	t.t.	

cayenne pepper vinegar

lacto-fermented cayenne peppers	450g	Cover the fermented cayenne and allow to steep for a minimum of 6 months.
white vinegar	1L	

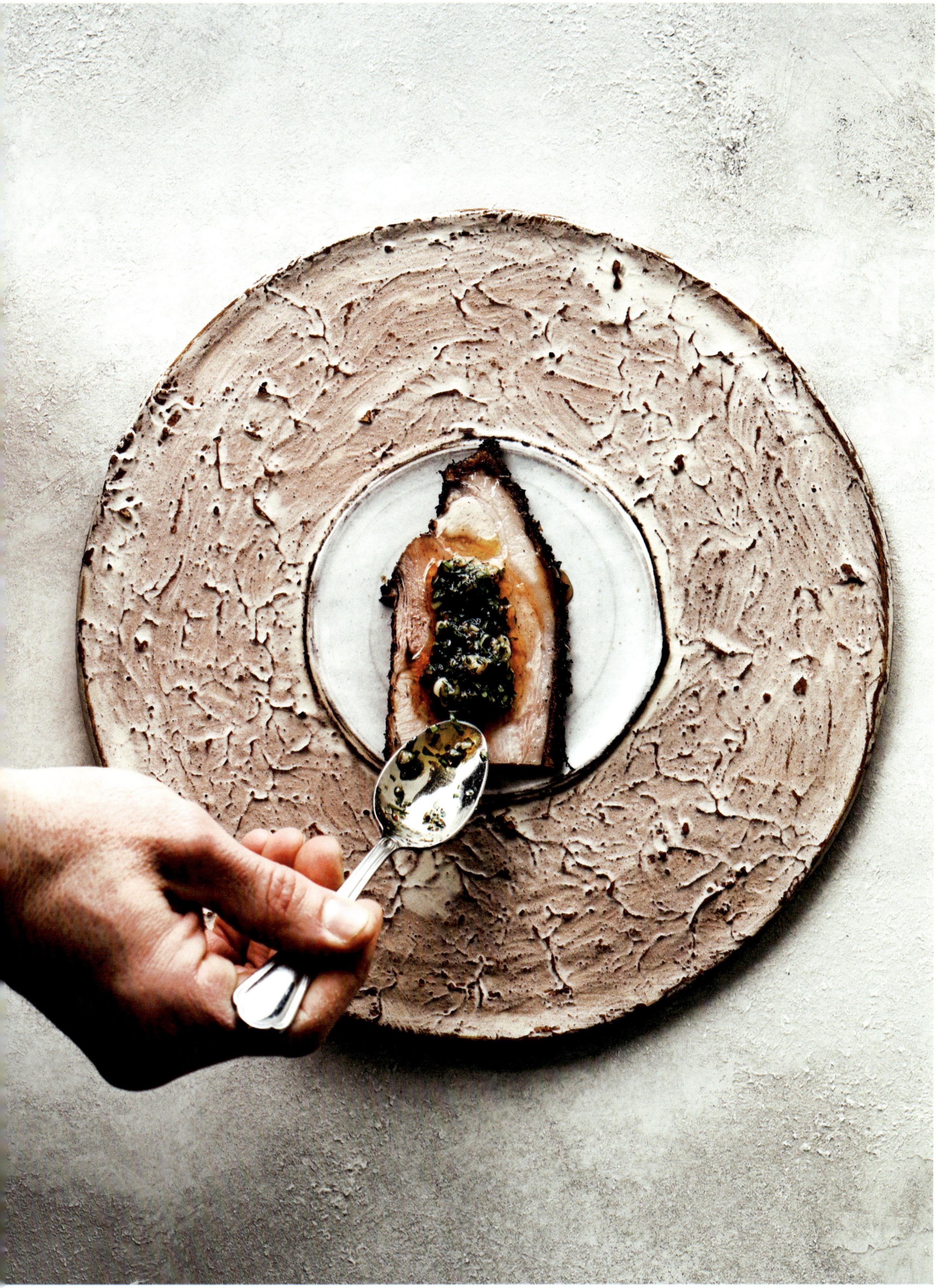

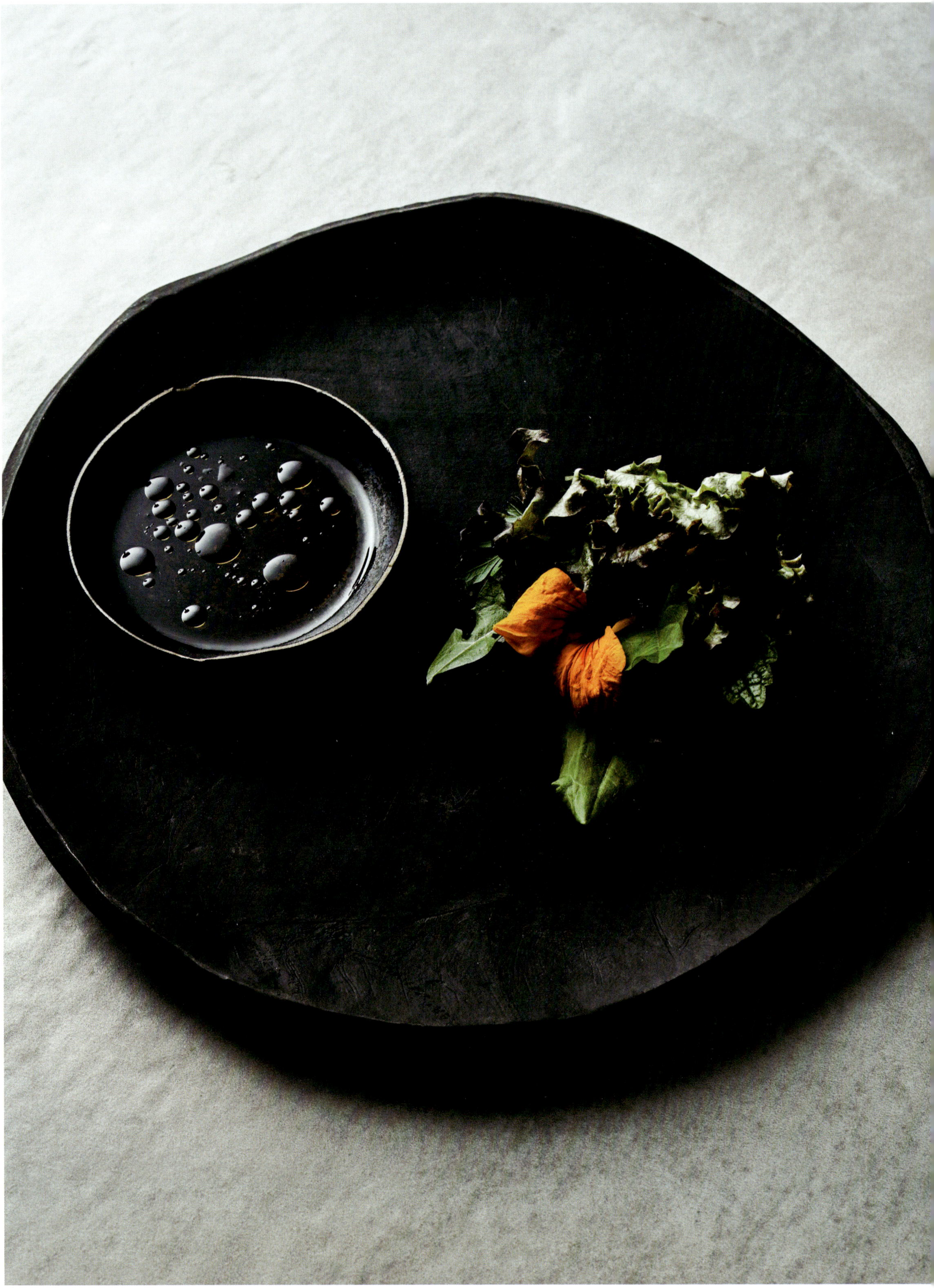

KILLED LETTUCES

I first learned about killed lettuces working for Sean Brock at Husk here in Nashville. These are lettuces that are wilted or "killed" by dressing with hot bacon fat. I wanted this one to act as a nice palate cleanser and transition into the sweeter dishes. Instead of dressing this one, we stuffed it with a tomato jam, lovage ice cream, and a mixture of herbs and flowers from our garden. We then instructed the guests to pick it up with their hands and dip it in the warm vinaigrette before eating it. Most people didn't have to be instructed to, but we did ask that you drink the rest of the vinaigrette after all the lettuce had been consumed.

---

sorghum vinaigrette

Benton's bacon fat, rendered	260g	Bring to a simmer, whisking constantly. Strain through a fine-mesh strainer and reserve until ready to serve.
sorghum	75g	
Omed cider vinegar	300g	

tomato jam

cured and smoked tomato (see page 31)	1,135g	Cook all ingredients over medium-low heat until most of the moisture has evaporated and jam consistency is achieved. Cool and reserve in a piping bag under refrigeration until needed.
granulated sugar	175g	
Omed cider vinegar	330g	

lovage ice cream

granulated sugar	498g	Beat 498g sugar and egg yolks until creamy. Puree the lovage and buttermilk until smooth. Pass through a fine-mesh strainer and reserve. Bring the 100g sugar, water, and stabilizer to a simmer. Whisk in the buttermilk and temper into the egg-yolk mixture. Cook until the mixture coats the back of a rubber spatula. Using a bamix or immersion blender, emulsify in the butter, followed by the mascarpone. Pass through a fine-mesh strainer into a Paco canister and chill immediately. Spin before using and place in a piping bag.
egg yolks	15ea	
buttermilk	425g	
lovage leaves, washed well	42g	
granulated sugar	100g	
water	138g	
Uno ice cream stabilizer	1.3g	
butter, cubed and chilled	175g	
mascarpone	300g	

additional ingredients & to finish

herbs		Bring 2 ounces of sorghum vinaigrette to a boil and place in a small bowl. Pipe a small amount of lovage ice cream and tomato jam into a small head of lettuce. Stuff in desired herbs or flowers. Serve immediately next to the vinaigrette.
flowers		

PARSNIP, BLACK TRUMPET SHORTBREAD, HICKORY

This dish came from revisiting an ice cream that I had done when I was the chef at Husk back in 2015. We used to drop whole burning logs of hickory into a pot of cream, would cover it and allow it to slowly smolder. Unfortunately, there is no space for that here at the restaurant, so I decided to slowly smoke the ice cream with hickory chips. It was served with a cake made from parsnips, a frozen shortbread made from black trumpet mushrooms, and a warm sauce made from burnt marshmallows. This dish reminds me of having s'mores while camping in the forest on a cool night in the fall.

---

hickory ice cream

milk	1,000g
heavy cream	200g
nonfat dry milk solids	100g
granulated sugar	200g
Uno ice cream stabilizer	2g
guar gum	2g

Combine milk and cream into a stainless-steel container. Place a burning log of hickory wood into the base and cover with a tight-fitting lid. Allow to steep for 20 minutes. If you don't have a live fire, you can wither smoke for 20 minutes or do the same process with burning wood chips. While the milk is smoking, mix all dry ingredients together until well combined. Once smoked, strain the milk into a clean pot and bring to a simmer over medium-high heat. Slowly whisk in the dry ingredients. Continue to whisk until the mixture returns to a simmer. Simmer for 3 minutes. Strain through a fine-mesh strainer. Freeze in a Paco container until needed.

parsnip cake

sugar	410g
grapeseed oil	290g
whole eggs	150g
salt	6g
AP flour	370g
ground cinnamon	5g
baking soda	7g
baking powder	3g
parsnip puree	480g

Preheat the oven to 350°F. Mix the salt, flour, cinnamon, baking soda, and baking powder together and sift. Set aside. Mix sugar and grapeseed oil in a mixer with a paddle attachment. Slowly add the eggs one at a time until well combined. Next, in thirds, slowly add the dry ingredients and parsnip puree, alternating between the dry and wet. Stop the mixer and scrape the sides between each addition. Be sure not to overmix. Spray 2 separate quarter-sheet pans, dust with flour, and shake off excess. Evenly divide the batter between the two cakes. Bake at 350°F for 20 minutes or until a cake tester comes out clean.

black trumpet shortbread

AP flour	325g
butter	250g
sugar	150g
malt syrup	50g
salt	7g
black cocoa	25g
black trumpet mushrooms, dried	100g
grapeseed oil	70g

Soak black trumpets in hot water and reserve. While that is soaking, mix dry ingredients in a robot coupe. Pulse in butter a little at a time until a sandy texture is formed. Mix in malt syrup very quickly. Do not let the dough come together. Drain the trumpet mushrooms and press out all liquid (reserve for another use). Split onto two Silpat-lined half sheet pans, scatter the drained mushrooms over the shortbread, and bake at 325°F, stirring every 6 to 7 minutes with a bowl scraper, until toasted and nutty-smelling, for approximately 15 minutes. Allow to cool completely, then blend in a Vitamix with the grapeseed oil. Freeze in 2" ninth pans and reserve in the freezer until service. Just before serving, shave into ribbons on a mandolin.

to finish

Punch the cake into 3" circles and brush with butter. Gently warm until caramelized on one side. Place in a serving bowl, top with a quenelle of the hickory ice cream, pinch of Maldon salt, and the shavings of black trumpet shortbread. Serve immediately.

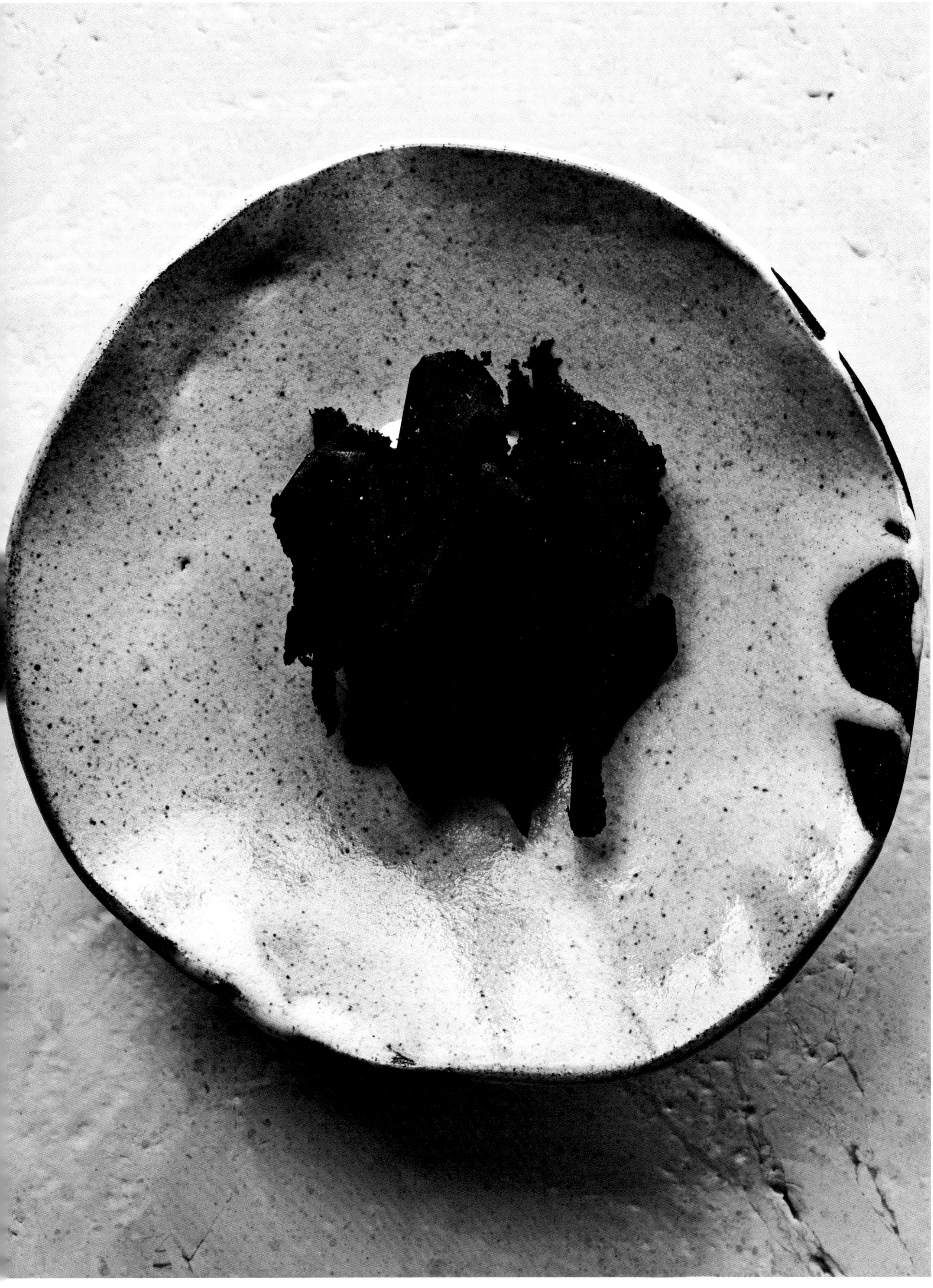

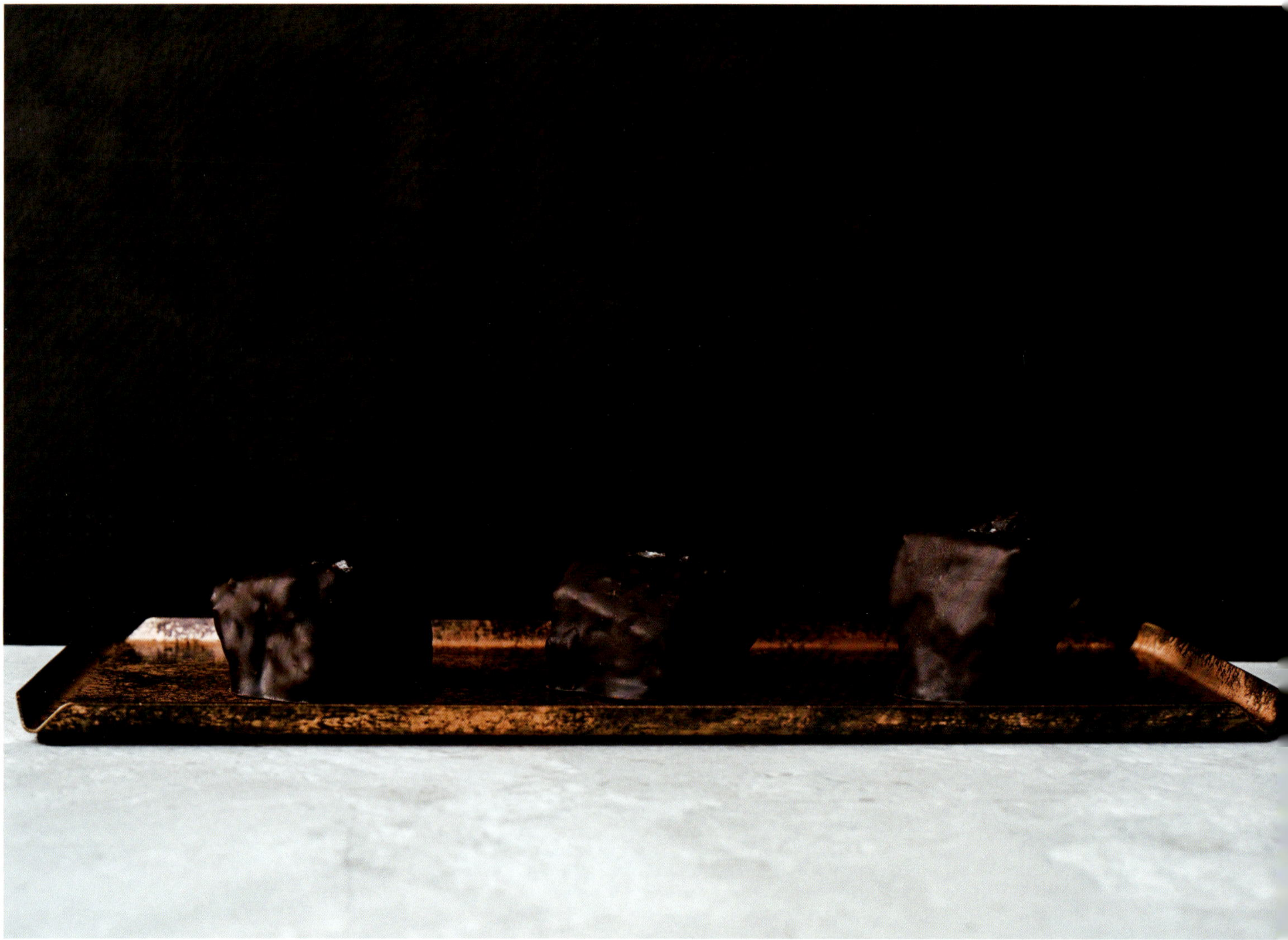

BEEF FAT & LAPHROAIG SPONGE CANDIES

My grandmother used to always have Werther's Originals in the house, and I wanted to create a butterscotch caramel that had a little bit of a twist and depth to it. This is where I came up with the beef fat and Laphroaig caramels. The peatiness of the scotch with the aged beef fat just made sense. I had gone home to visit my mom and she had some sponge candy that she had brought back home with her from Buffalo. I decided to combine the two ideas and thought this would be a good finish to a meal in the winter.

---

sponge candy

gelatin, bloomed	1.3g
granulated sugar	700g
filtered water	200g
corn syrup	290g
baking soda	28g
Laphroaig 10-year	36g

Line a 6" half hotel pan with parchment paper and spray with pan spray. Be sure the paper comes all the way up the sides. In a tall medium saucepan, mix the sugar, corn syrup, and water until dissolved. Bring to a boil and cook until the mixture reads 310°F on a candy thermometer. Remove the pot from heat and let sit for two minutes undisturbed. Carefully whisk in the gelatin and Laphroaig. This will cause the sugar to bubble up, so be mindful. Sprinkle the baking soda over the caramel and whisk vigorously. Return mixture to the heat and whisk for 30 seconds. The sugar mixture will begin to expand.

Quickly pour into the prepared hotel pan. It will begin to set, so work as quickly as possible. Do not spread the mixture; just let it settle into the pan. Allow the caramel to cool overnight. Using a serrated knife, cut into 2" × 2" squares. Dip the squares into the tempered chocolate (recipe to follow) and allow to cool on a Silpat-lined sheet tray. Reserve until needed.

tempered chocolate

chocolate couverture, Valrhona Guanaja 70%	1kg
cocoa butter	10g

Melt the chocolate in a ninth pan to 46°C in an immersion-circulated water bath. Be careful that you do not get any condensation on the chocolate, or it will seize. Remove the ninth pan from the water bath and allow the chocolate to cool to 35°C. Immediately stir in the cocoa butter until dissolved and completely emulsified. Meanwhile, adjust the temperature of your immersion circulator to 32°C and allow the water temperature to drop no lower than 31.5°C or rise higher than 32°C. At the same time, cool your chocolate mixture to 31.5°C. This is the working temperature you will want to maintain. Place the ninth pan in the water bath and hold.

to finish

rendered dry-aged beef fat

Take the reserved sponge candy and brush with rendered dry-aged beef fat and season with Maldon sea salt before serving.

SPRING 2021

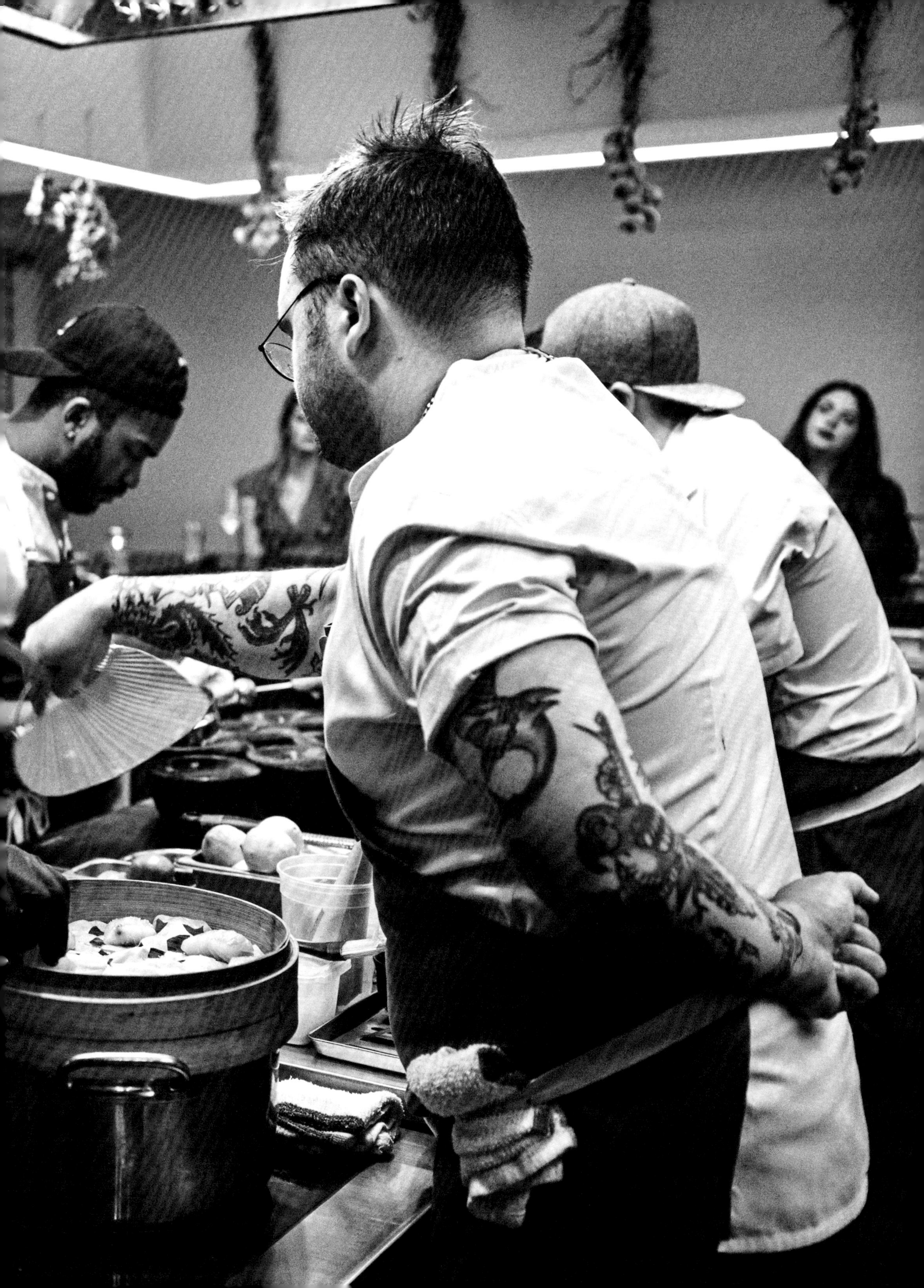

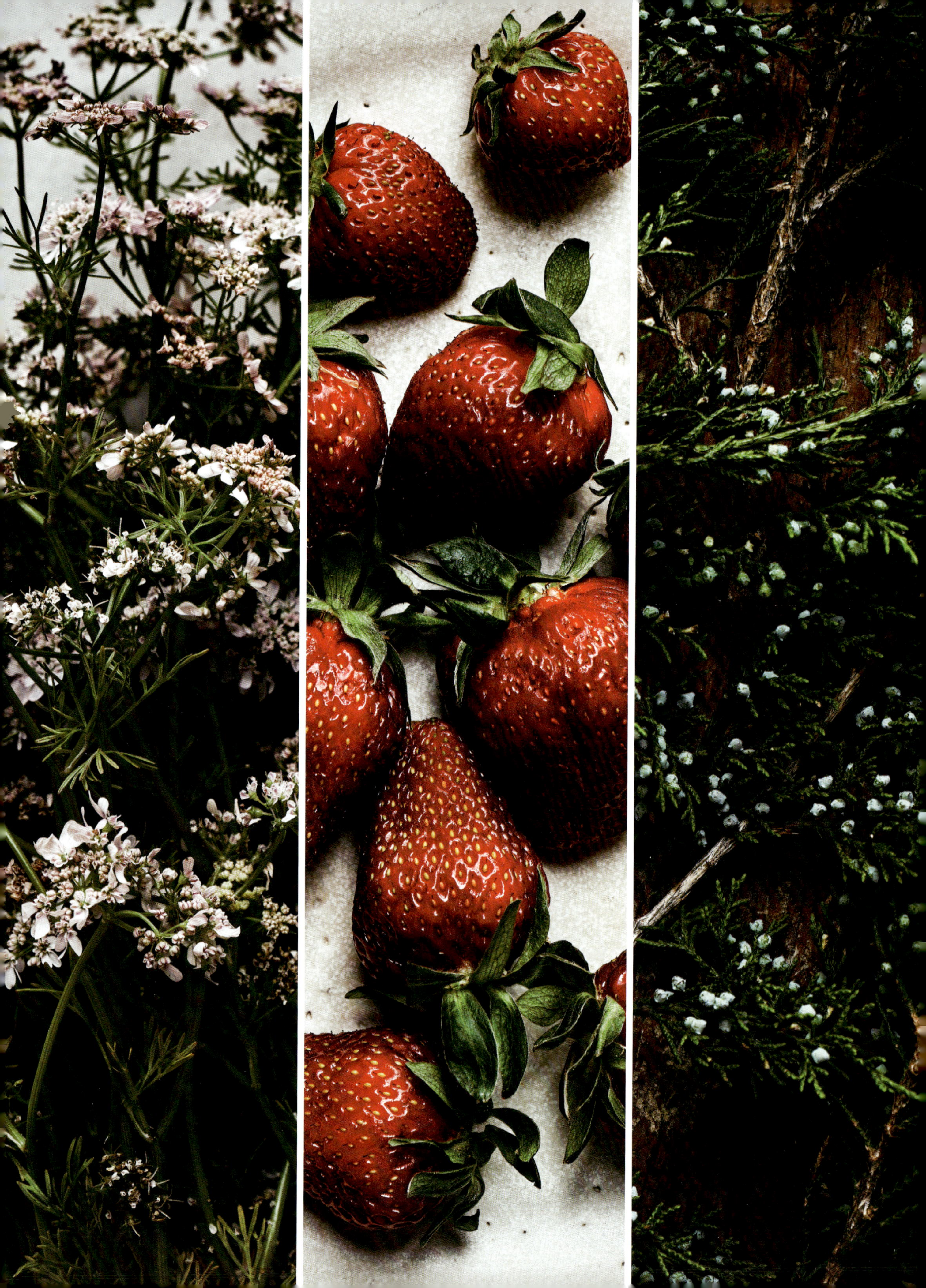

Every year when fall hits, I tell myself it's my favorite season. The weather begins to cool, the diverse canopy of trees in Nashville begins to change, the holidays are slowly approaching, and many of my favorite vegetables are coming into season. Then—and this happens without fail—I'm reminded of the Strawberry Festival that happened every year at the beginning of spring where I grew up near Plant City, Florida. It was one of my favorite times of the year growing up, as Plant City is the winter strawberry capital of the world. Biting into those first vibrant red strawberries of the season brought me some of my favorite food memories as a kid. It wasn't until I started working for chef Sean Brock at McCrady's in Charleston that I realized you can eat the unripe green strawberries as well. These green strawberries are now one of my favorite ingredients to pickle, giving intense tang to the unmistakably "spring" flavor. Even the tops have an herbaceous, complex flavor when used fresh or pickled (see page 135).

Another favorite spring ingredient perfect for pickling, and probably the most ubiquitous spring vegetable served in restaurants all over the world, is ramps. These wild alliums pop up every spring everywhere from Georgia, through Tennessee, and on up to New England and the upper Midwest. The flavor is similar to young wild garlic, with a much more intense onion flavor. They were practically put on this Earth to be used with pork, though I've also had much luck using them with local trout (see page 125). Another wild edible that I turn to every spring is the young tips of cedar trees, with a flavor and aroma reminiscent of freshly cut honeydew melon (see page 110). It sounds strange, but I think you'll find it inspiring. To play off the melon-flavor affinity, I used some of the watermelon rind we pickled from last summer, continuing the theme of past seasons and preservation giving birth to plenty of new ideas each season.

Some traditional spring ingredients were given rather non-traditional presentations as well. The asparagus-with-everything bagel spice was a hit (page 113), and strawberries were used once again to liven up and give fruity acidity to a play on the Chinese food takeout staple, General Tso's. Instead of chicken, we used crispy pig tails and fermented Jimmy Nardello peppers from the previous summer. Some Japanese influences showed up in this spring menu utilizing Sakura cherry blossoms (page 117), heirloom white sweet potatoes with bonito flakes (page 121), and smoked tofu. Here are the dishes from our spring 2021 menu.

Credit: Todd Saal

SPRING 2021 MENU

surf clam, cedar tips green curry & pickled watermelon rind **110**

asparagus glazed in a sauce of smoked trout bones with everything bagel spice **113**

crispy pig tail with general tso's sauce made from strawberry
& fermented jimmy nardello pepper **114**

scallop mi-cuit, fermented white asparagus, sakura blossom **117**

scallop xo cracker **118**

boniato, smoked tofu & a vin blanc of last year's cured & dried sweet potatoes **121**

english peas, louisiana crawfish, fermented green gooseberry juice **122**

grilled bucksnort trout, fermented green tomato butter & herbs from our garden **125**

kue grouper buried in embers, green garlic, fermented winter truffle **126**

bear creek farm lamb with swiss chard & cashew milk **130**

———————

PALATE CLEANSER

salad of english peas, green strawberries & green chartreuse **135**

———————

yeast donut, foie gras, strawberry & elderflower **136**

SURF CLAM, CEDAR TIPS GREEN CURRY & PICKLED WATERMELON RIND

Young cedar tips, when picked early in the spring, have this beautiful honeydew-melon smell and taste to them. I made a green curry paste, knowing that coconut and honeydew melon do well together, and cooked them down very quickly. I then dressed the raw surf clam in a fish sauce infused with smoked clams, a smoked-clam oil, some fresh lime juice, zest, and mint. For a little sweetness to contrast the bitterness of the cedar, I added some brunoised watermelon rind that had been pickled the previous summer.

---

cedar green curry paste

turmeric	3g
white peppercorn	.5g
cumin seed	.3g
mace	.1g
coriander seeds	.3g
lemongrass, sliced thin	105g
shallot, sliced thin	60g
garlic, sliced thin	30g
ginger, sliced thin	40g
jalapeno, deseeded and sliced thin	30g
palm sugar	6.5g
green cedar tips	50g
mussel garum lees (the paste reserved after straining)	15g
vitamin C powder	1.6g

Toast the turmeric, white peppercorn, cumin, mace, and coriander. Allow to cool, and grind as fine as possible using a mortar and pestle. Mix with the remaining ingredients in a Vitamix and blend on high until as smooth as possible. It will still be a coarse paste. Do not allow the paste to get warm.

cedar & coconut curry

cedar green curry paste (split 40g/10g)	50g
clam stock	80mL
coconut cream	330g
fish sauce	10mL

In a small sauce pot, toast 40g of the curry paste over medium heat until aromatic. Add the clam stock and coconut cream and bring to a simmer for 15 minutes. Remove from the heat and stir in the fish sauce and remaining 10g curry paste. Cover and steep for 15 minutes. Strain through a fine-mesh strainer and cool.

smoked clam oil

cured, smoked, and dried clams	75g
grapeseed oil	225g

Seal the ingredients in a Cryovac bag on full pressure. Place in a pot of boiling water for a minimum of four hours. Cool and allow to steep in the bag overnight. Pass through a coffee-filter-lined fine-mesh strainer and reserve.

pickled watermelon rind

watermelon rinds, washed and peeled, cut into 1" wide strips	1kg
filtered water	850mL
white vinegar	840mL
granulated sugar	600g
lemongrass stalks, bruised and cut into 3" pieces	1ea
ginger, 3" piece, peeled and sliced thin	1ea
mace	1g
allspice berries	3ea
cloves	3ea
cinnamon stick, 3" pieces	1ea
Thai long peppercorns	5ea

Mix ingredients together. Bring to a boil and pour over peeled watermelon rinds. Allow to cool at room temperature, and store in the refrigerator for at least 1 week.

additional ingredients & to finish

lime juice	
lime zest	
raw surf clam feet, cleaned	

Dice the raw clam feet and dress with the smoked clam oil. Gently warm a small amount of the curry, season to taste with fresh lime juice, and spoon it into the shell. Add the diced clam meat, and top with brunoised pickled watermelon rind and lime zest.

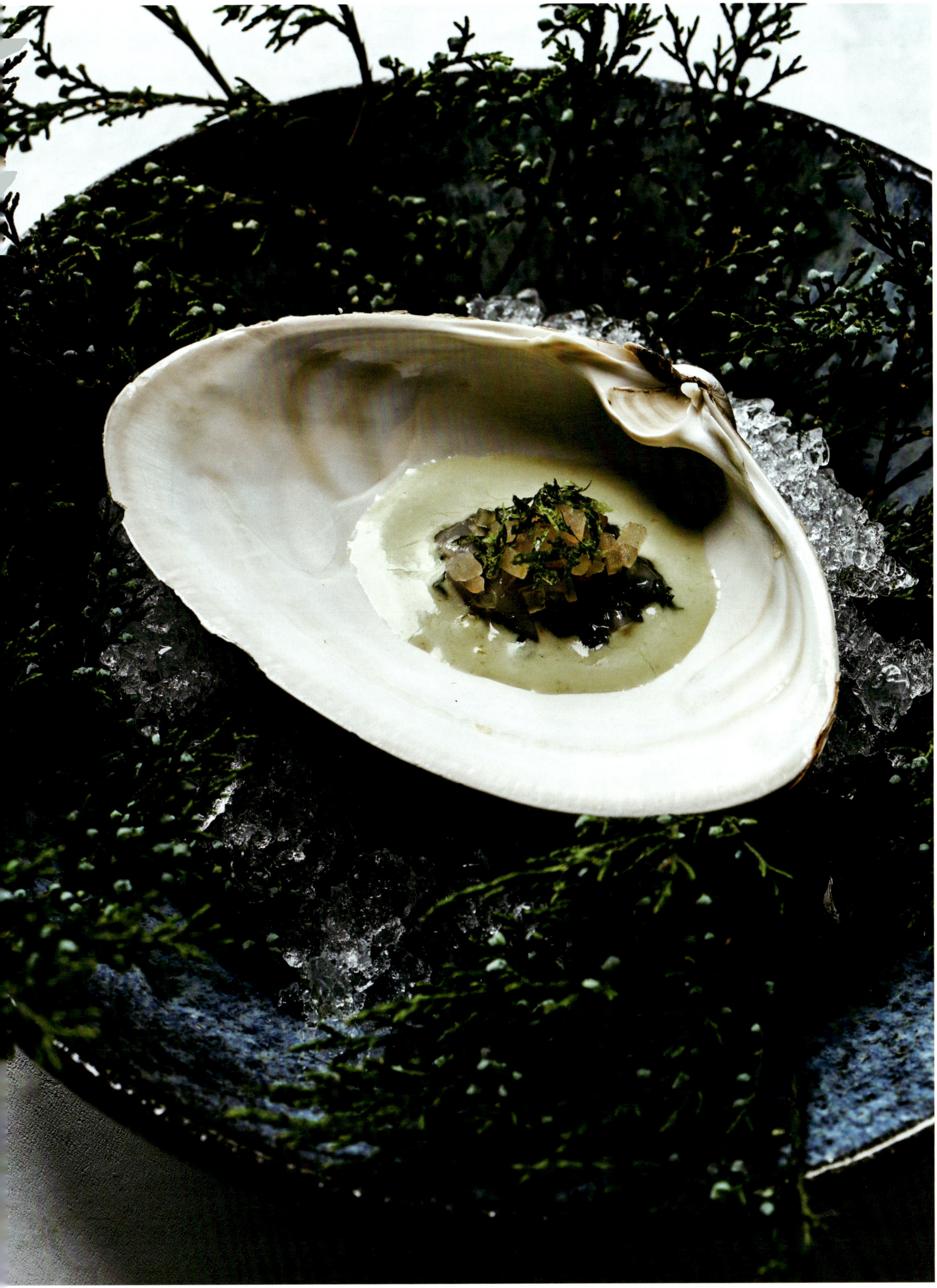

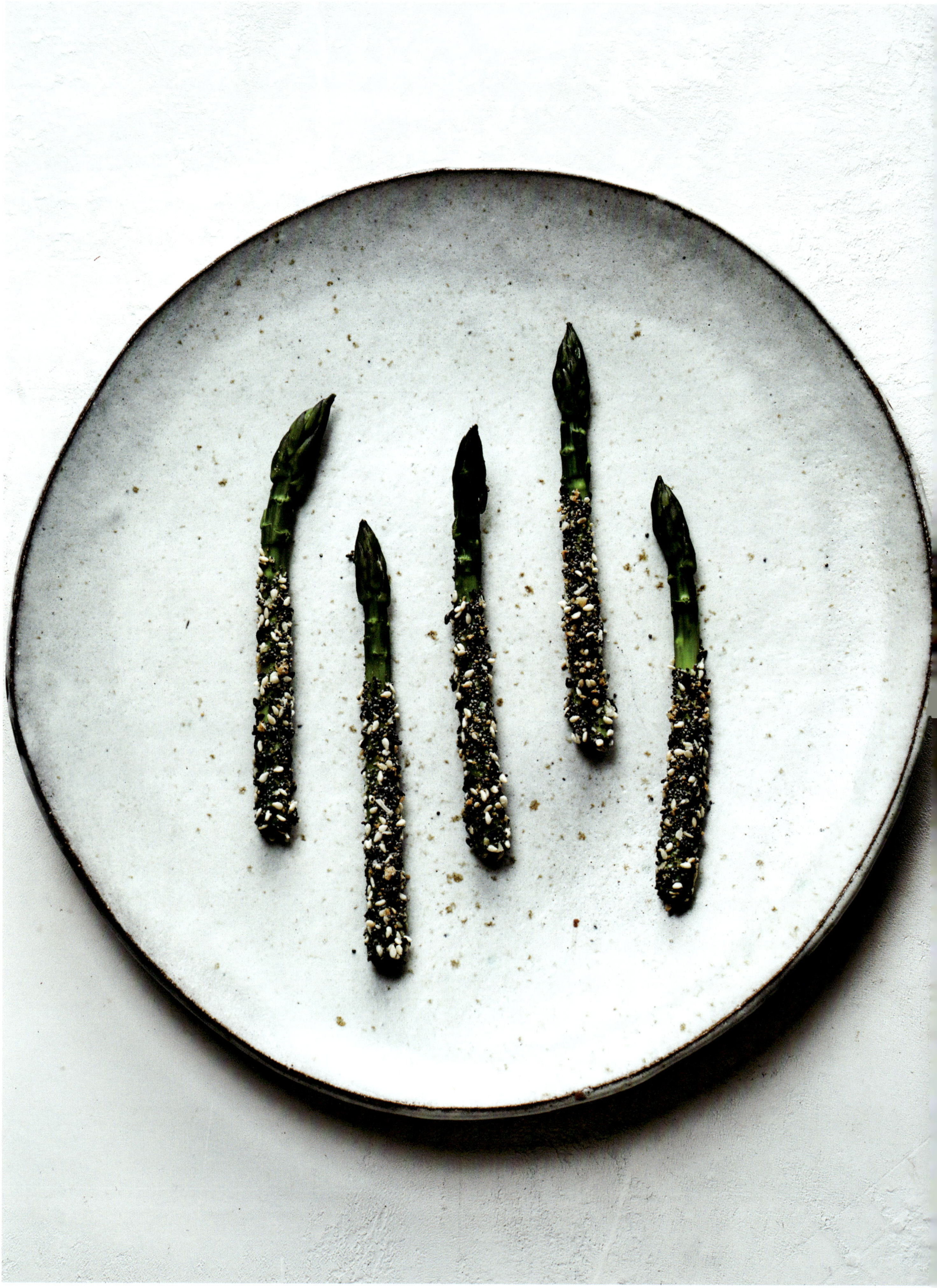

ASPARAGUS GLAZED IN A SAUCE OF SMOKED TROUT BONES WITH EVERYTHING BAGEL SPICE

This bite was created with one of my cooks, Jayce Knight, using a technique that we learned from my good friend Johnny Spero when he cooked with us for our first guest chef dinner. Trout bones that we had cured, grilled, and smoked were covered in a mixture of sake and mirin, then reduced to a sticky glaze. Young asparagus was peeled, lightly salted, and quickly charred in a hot pan over one side, gently warming the asparagus but maintaining the crunch you get when eating it raw. The asparagus was dipped in the bone glaze and crusted in an everything bagel spice made with hon dashi and a puffed cracker made from smoked trout stock.

---

everything spice

onion, sliced thin on mandolin	15g
garlic, sliced thin on mandolin	12g
black sesame seed	50g
white sesame seed	30g
poppy seeds	25g
trout cracker, crushed fine (see below)	50g
hon dashi	15g

Dehydrate the onion and garlic at 120°F until completely dry. Grind until a coarse powder is achieved. Toast the sesame seeds and poppy seeds. Allow to cool, and mix all the ingredients together. Reserve in an airtight container until needed.

smoked trout cracker

smoked trout	630g
tapioca flour	400g
hon dashi	10g
Pacific sea salt	20g

Puree all ingredients in a robot coupe until a smooth dough is formed. Divide the dough in half and place each half in desired shaped pans. Seal the pans on full pressure in an appropriately sized Cryovac bag. Steam at 100°C for 40 minutes. Transfer to a blast freezer or shock in an ice bath and then freeze completely. Once frozen, slice 1.5mm thickness on a meat slicer. Spread the slices onto a dehydrator tray and dry at 150°F for 40 minutes. Allow to finish drying at room temperature if needed. Fry at 375°F until golden brown and crispy. Drain on a paper towel and reserve in an airtight container.

trout bone glaze

trout bones	1kg
grapeseed oil	50g
mirin	1.5L
kombu stock (see page 275)	2L
mirin	75g
white shoyu	75g

Heat the oil over medium-high heat in a wide rondeau. Sear the bones until dark brown on each side. Add the 1.5L mirin and deglaze, being sure to scrape the fond off the bottom of the pan. Add the kombu stock and reduce until 500mL remains. Strain through a fine-mesh strainer. Season with the remaining mirin and shoyu, chill, and reserve.

additional ingredients & to finish

asparagus	

Peel the asparagus as close in time to cooking it as possible. Place a cast iron over high heat. Lightly season one side of the asparagus to begin to pull out moisture. Once the pan is smoking, place the asparagus in a single layer and cover with a meat weight. Cook until the asparagus just begins to char. Dip the base end of the asparagus in the chilled bone glaze and then roll in the everything bagel spice. Serve immediately.

CRISPY PIG TAIL WITH GENERAL TSO'S SAUCE MADE FROM STRAWBERRY & FERMENTED JIMMY NARDELLO PEPPER

I love Chinese food. I really love all Asian food, but there are certain things every kid wants to eat constantly while growing up, and for me General Tso's chicken is one of them. This version of the sauce was made with strawberries and fermented Jimmy Nardello pepper juice from the previous summer. In place of chicken, I substituted pig tails that had been braised, deboned, and rolled back together into their natural shape. We then deep-fried them and glazed them in the sauce.

strawberry general tso's

strawberries, diced	1,550g
fermented Jimmy Nardello pepper juice	1,700g
preserved strawberry syrup (see page 136)	500g
white shoyu	150mL
mirin	400mL
seasoned rice vinegar	270mL
Sambal chile paste	80g
kuzu	45g
filtered water	60mL

Bring all ingredients except the kuzu and cold water to a boil. Puree in batches in a Vitamix until smooth. Return to the pot. Mix the kuzu with the cold water and whisk into the warm sauce. Bring back to a boil for one minute. Pass through a fine-mesh strainer and reserve until needed.

pig tails

pig tails	8ea
filtered water	2L
kosher salt	200g

Mix the filtered water and kosher salt until the salt is dissolved. Brine the pig tails for 12 hours. Drain and pat dry. Cryovac on full pressure and cook in a circulator bath at 85°C for 12 hours. Remove from the bath and allow to cool until safe to handle but still warm. Make a slit lengthwise down one side of the tail, remove all the cartilage and bones, taking care to keep the meat as whole as possible. Place on a piece of plastic wrap and roll tightly to its original shape. Tie off each end by knotting the plastic wrap around itself, and drop in an ice bath until completely cool. Remove the plastic wrap and slice the pig tails into ½" rounds.

additional ingredients & to finish

toasted sesame seeds	
rice flour	

Toss the pig tails in the rice flour, and brush off any excess. Fry at 350°F until crispy and hot all the way through. Toss in the General Tso's sauce. Season with a pinch of the toasted sesame seeds.

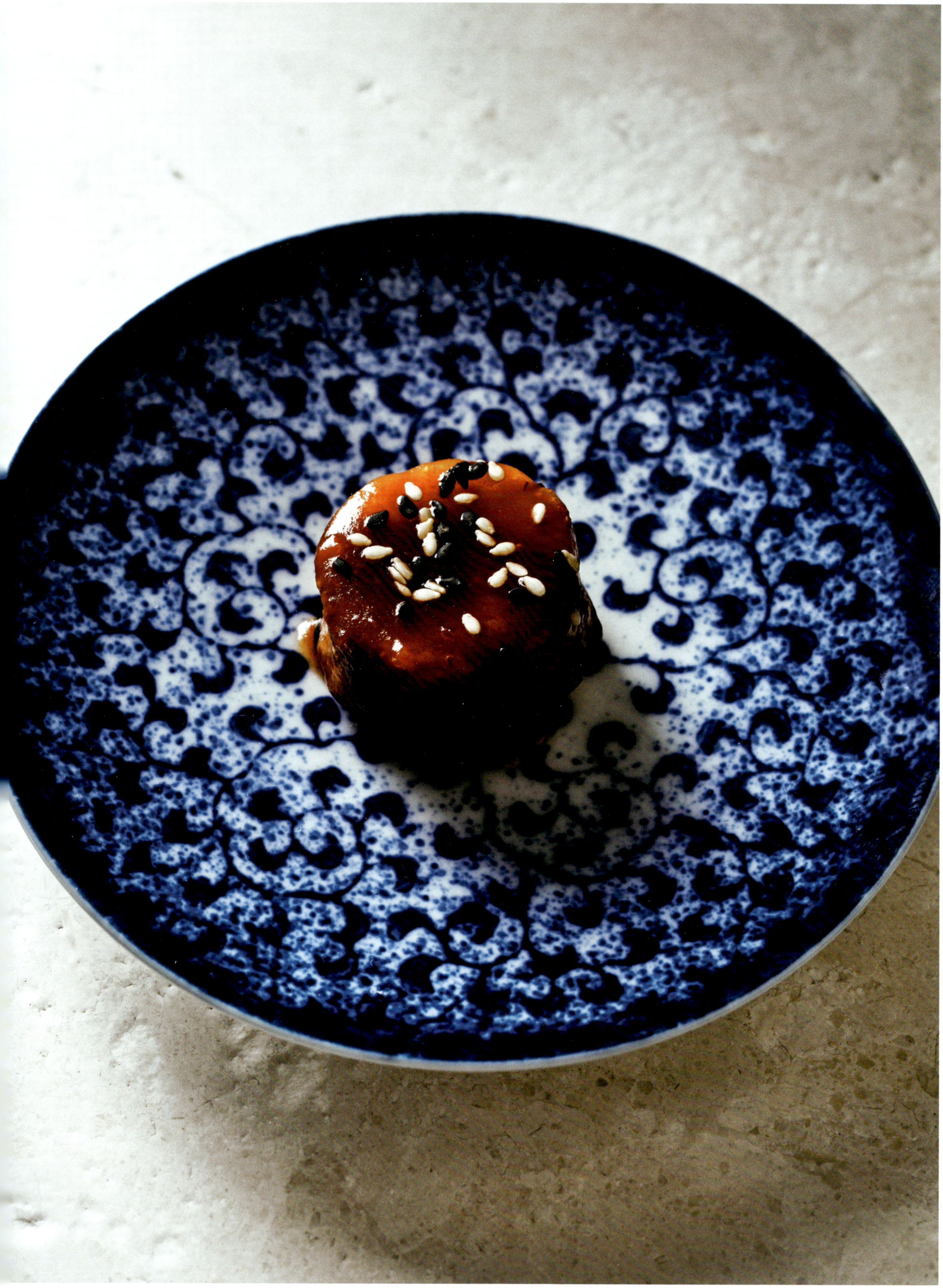

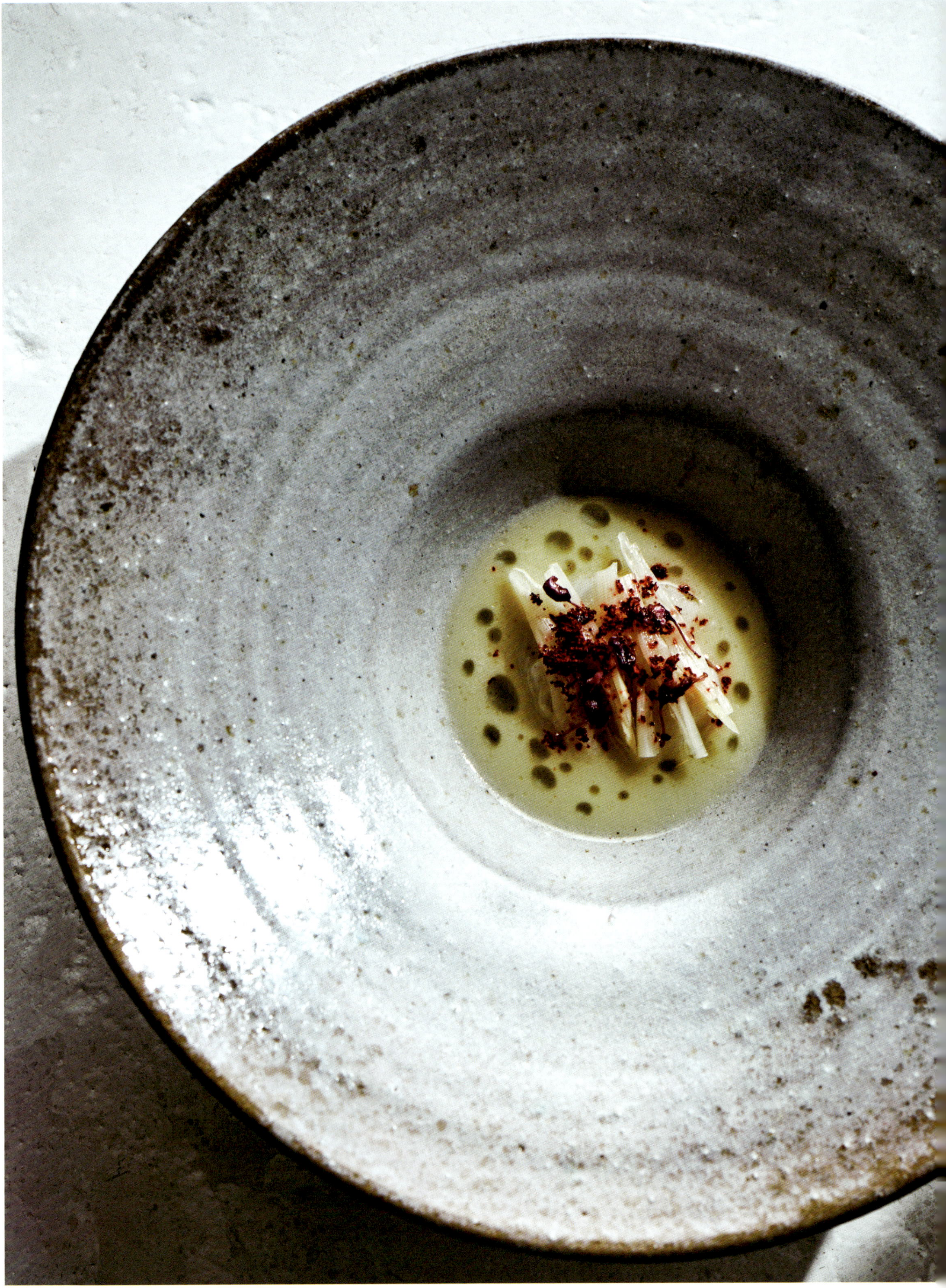

SCALLOP MI-CUIT, FERMENTED WHITE ASPARAGUS, SAKURA BLOSSOM

The first time I tasted fermented white asparagus, I thought it would pair well with something salty and floral. For this preparation I decided to use barely cooked scallops, slice them, and dress them in a warm butter made from fermented white asparagus juice that had been infused with Sakura, or preserved Japanese cherry blossoms. We finished it with an oil made from cherry wood and freeze-dried cherries for texture and acidity.

---

cherry wood oil

cherry wood	75g	Cryovac and boil for 6 hours. Allow to cool and store in the bag overnight. The next day, strain through a cheesecloth. Reserve until needed.
grapeseed oil	225g	

sakura blossom butter

cherry blossom	10g	Warm the cherry blossoms in the white asparagus juice. Slowly whisk in the butter and reserve. Strain immediately before using.
fermented white asparagus juice (see base recipes, page 269)	65g	
butter, cubed and chilled	120g	

additional ingredients & to finish

confited scallops (see page 189)
freeze-dried cherries
fermented white asparagus, julienned
Pacific sea salt

Temper the scallops for 10 minutes at 140°F. Slice, perpendicular to the cutting board, into ⅛" slices. Place in a bowl, top with desired amount of fermented white asparagus, and dress with a tablespoon of the warm butter. Finish with a pinch of Pacific sea salt, a few drops of the cherry wood oil, and a couple of crushed freeze-dried cherries.

SCALLOP XO CRACKER

This snack came about entirely from waste, as we used the foot or abductor muscle of the scallop. First, a dashi is made from the cured and smoked feet. It is reduced to a super-intense broth. Then, it is made into a dough that is portioned, steamed, frozen, sliced, dehydrated, and then fried, allowing it to puff like a chicharron. To finish it off, top it with an XO sauce made from cured, smoked, and dried scallop feet.

---

ramp root oil

washed and dried ramp roots	50g
grapeseed oil	250g

Seal the ingredients in a Cryovac bag on full pressure. Place in a pot of boiling water for a minimum of 4 hours. Cool and allow to steep in the bag overnight. Pass through a coffee-filter-lined fine-mesh strainer and reserve.

scallop xo

shallot, minced	100g
garlic, minced	35g
cream sherry	35g
bacon, ground through fine dye	40g
ramp root oil	225g
Korean chili flake	5g
maple sugar	15g
star anise pods	5g
vegetable bouillon paste	25g
scallop abductor muscles, cured, smoked, and dried	125g
scallop garum (see base recipes on page 272)	t.t.

Rehydrate the dried scallop in enough hot water to just cover for 30 minutes. Cook the shallots and garlic in the ramp root oil over medium heat until they begin to turn golden brown. Add the bacon and rehydrated scallops, reserving the rehydrating liquid. Continue to cook until the bacon has rendered and begins to crisp. Be sure not to let the mixture burn. Add the sugar, chili flake, star anise, sherry, vegetable bouillon, and reserved rehydrating liquid. Continue to cook over medium heat until most of the moisture has evaporated. Cool completely. Pulse in a robot coupe to desired consistency. Season to taste with the scallop garum.

scallop cracker

scallops, abductor muscles removed and reserved	630g
tapioca flour	400g
hon dashi	10g
Pacific sea salt	20g

Puree all ingredients in a robot coupe until a smooth dough is formed. Divide the dough in half and place each half in desired shaped pans. Seal the pans on full pressure in an appropriately sized Cryovac bag. Steam at 100°C for 40 minutes. Transfer to a blast freezer or shock in an ice bath and then freeze completely. Once frozen, slice 1.5mm thickness on a meat slicer. Spread the slices onto a dehydrator tray and dry at 150°F for 40 minutes. Allow to finish drying at room temperature if needed. Fry at 375°F until golden brown and crispy. Drain on a paper towel and reserve in an airtight container.

to finish

Cover the top of each cracker with a spoonful of the XO sauce.

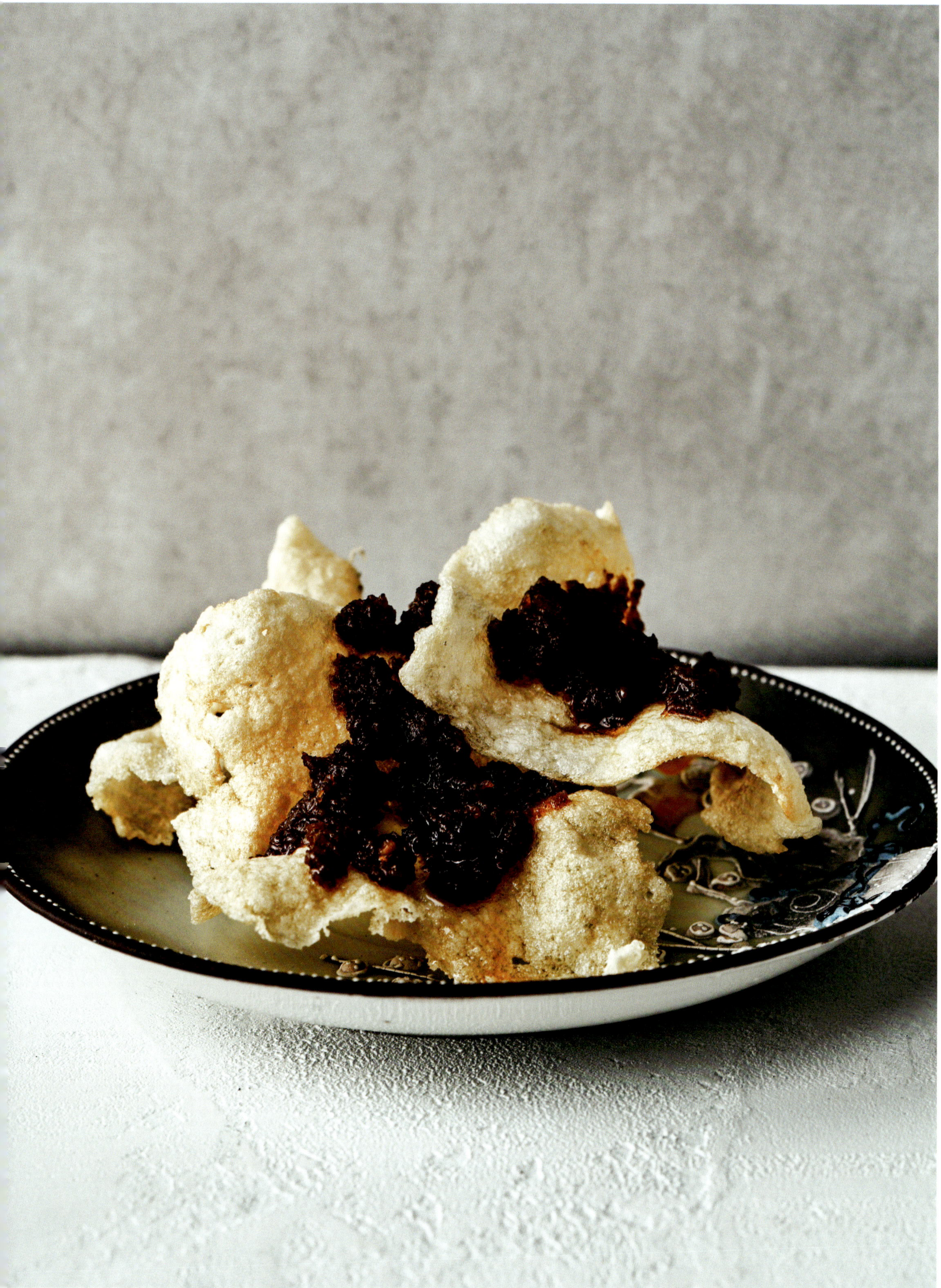

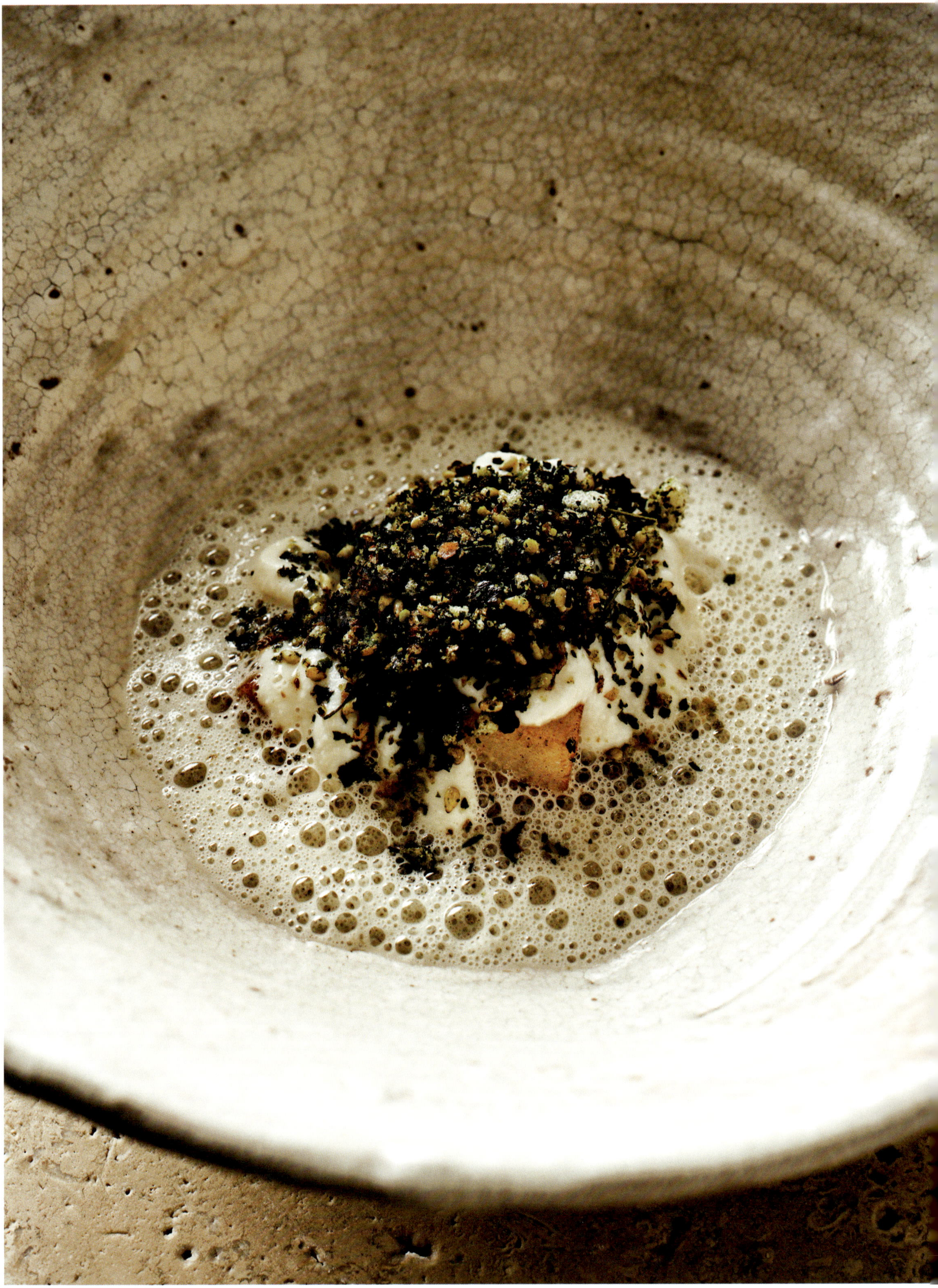

BONIATO, SMOKED TOFU & A VIN BLANC OF LAST YEAR'S CURED & DRIED SWEET POTATOES

Boniato is a white-fleshed sweet potato that is less sweet than your traditional orange-fleshed sweet potato. For this dish, I wanted to infuse as much flavor into them as possible, so I cooked them in a butter that had been infused with a ton of bonito (cured and dried tuna). We then roasted them to order in brown butter until golden brown and crispy and topped them with a rich puree made from smoked tofu, a furikake made with dried sweet potato leaves, and a vin blanc made with sweet vermouth and even more bonito. At one point, we had a lot of seafood and vegetarian restrictions, so I made it with sweet potatoes that we had processed like bonito. I ended up liking this depth of flavor more and the fact that it was vegetarian. We decided to keep the vin blanc this way. It turned out to be a favorite of our guests that season. People couldn't believe that it was a vegetarian sauce.

---

sweet potato furikake

dried sweet potato leaves, coarsely ground	20g
dashi cracker, coarsely chopped (see page 241)	14g
Seto Fumi furikake	14g
bonito flakes, coarsely ground	5g

Mix all ingredients until well combined. Store in an airtight container.

sweet potato "bushi" cream

shallot, sliced thin	125g
kombu, rinsed	6g
sake	425g
heavy cream	765g
hon dashi	12g
dried sweet potato shavings (see base recipes on page 269)	20g

Cook shallot, kombu, and sake until alcohol has burned off. Add cream, hon dashi, and sweet potato shavings. Bring to a simmer. Continue to simmer for 20 minutes. Allow to cool at room temperature for 15 minutes, strain through a fine-mesh strainer, and cool until needed.

smoked tofu

firm tofu	450g
shiro dashi	85g
mirin that has had alcohol burned off	50g
Omed cider vinegar	3g

Smoke tofu for 30 minutes. Puree all ingredients until smooth. Pass through a fine-mesh strainer and reserve until needed.

bonito butter

butter	4lbs
bonito shavings	105g

Bring the ingredients to a simmer over medium heat. Set aside to cool.

confit sweet potatoes

sweet potato, washed and quartered lengthwise	1kg
kosher salt	20g

Toss the sweet potatoes in the salt and let sit for 30 minutes. Place in a deep pan large enough to hold the potatoes, and cover with the warm bonito butter. Confit in a Rational set to full humidity and 85°C for 45 minutes to an hour, or until completely tender but still holding their shape. Allow to cool, remove from the butter, and cut into 1" pieces.

to finish

Roast the potatoes in butter, shaking the pan constantly so they roll and cook evenly on all sides. Once golden brown and beginning to crisp, remove from the pan, drain on a paper towel, and season with kosher salt. Place a heaping spoonful of tofu puree in the center of a plate. Place 5 or 6 of the potatoes on top and season with the sweet potato furikake. Rewarm the vin blanc, season with salt to taste, and aerate with a bamix or immersion blender. Spoon a couple of ounces around the sweet potatoes and serve immediately.

ENGLISH PEAS, LOUISIANA CRAWFISH, FERMENTED GREEN GOOSEBERRY JUICE

When I lived in Orlando, my buddy Logan and I used to love getting crawfish. There was a pub downtown that would get so busy on Fat Tuesday that you would have to call and order ahead however many pounds you were going to consume. It ended up having to be a group of people to ensure that we could get enough and get our table reserved.

For this dish, we served the crawfish along with the nage made of the poaching liquid with English peas. The sweetness of the English peas helped balance some of the spice. We gently warmed the crawfish in fermented green gooseberry juice for acidity and finished with an oil made from the smoked and dried pea shells for a little more depth of flavor.

---

crawfish boil

crawfish	2kg
potatoes, large dice	400g
onion, large dice	400g
garlic head, halved	1ea
smoked and dried corn cobs	100g
water	5L
seafood boil or blackening spice	25g

Bring all the ingredients except the crawfish to a boil for 5 minutes. Turn off the heat, add the crawfish, and cover with a lid for 5 minutes. Remove the crawfish and separate the tails from the heads. Allow to cool to room temperature and remove from the shells. Chill immediately. Strain the cooking liquid into another pot and add the heads and shells. Reduce the remaining liquid by half its original volume. Pass through a fine-mesh strainer, and crush all the heads with a ladle to push any remaining juices.

crawfish nage

grapeseed oil	28g
shallot, sliced thin	145g
smoked and dried English pea shells	40g
vermouth	220mL
crawfish boil reduction	375g
heavy cream	400mL
soy lecithin	.5%

Sweat shallot in the grapeseed oil over medium heat until translucent. Add the English pea shells and vermouth. Reduce over medium heat until all the alcohol from the vermouth has burned off. Add the crawfish reduction and heavy cream. Bring to a simmer, reduce the heat to medium-low, and cook at a lazy simmer for 25 minutes. Allow to cool at room temperature for 20 minutes, pass through a chinois, and reserve until needed. Before using, emulsify in the soy lecithin with a stick blender.

smoked pea shell oil

smoked and dried shells	55g
grapeseed oil	250g

Seal the ingredients in a Cryovac bag on full pressure. Place in a pot of boiling water for a minimum of 4 hours. Cool and allow to steep in the bag overnight. Pass through a coffee-filter-lined fine-mesh strainer and reserve.

english peas

Shuck and split by removing the outer skin.

additional ingredients & to finish

fermented gooseberry juice (see base recipes on page 269)
chives, minced
parsley, minced
mint, minced
lemon juice
lemon zest
lemon oil

Chop the crawfish tails into ½" pieces and dress with the herbs, lemon juice, lemon zest, and lemon oil to taste. Simmer the split peas in enough gooseberry juice to just cover them. Continue to cook until just tender. Spoon the peas and gooseberry juice into a bowl and top with the dressed crawfish. Season the nage with fresh lemon juice and salt to taste, rewarm, and aerate with a bamix or immersion blender. Spoon a couple of ounces over the peas and crawfish. Serve immediately.

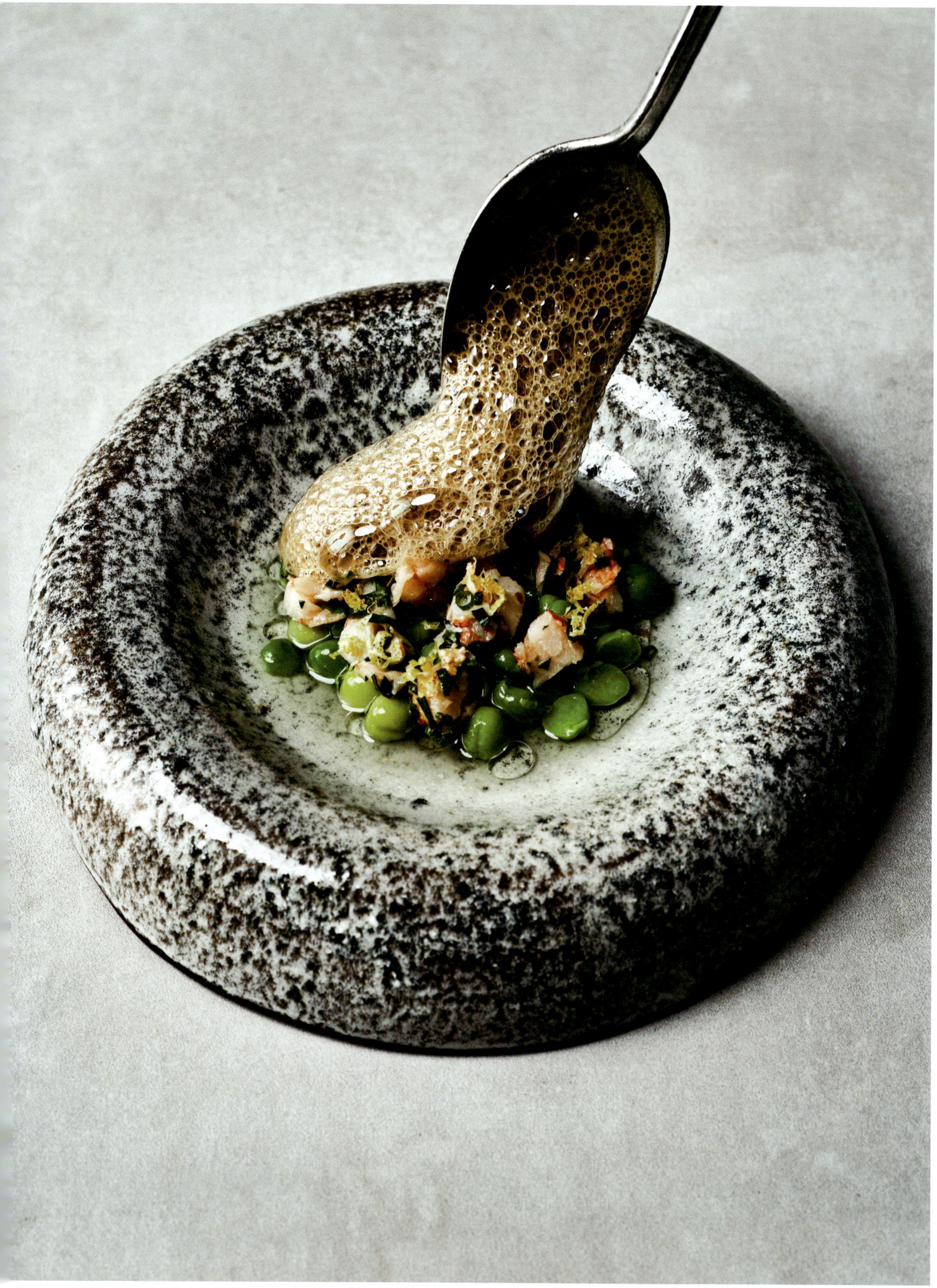

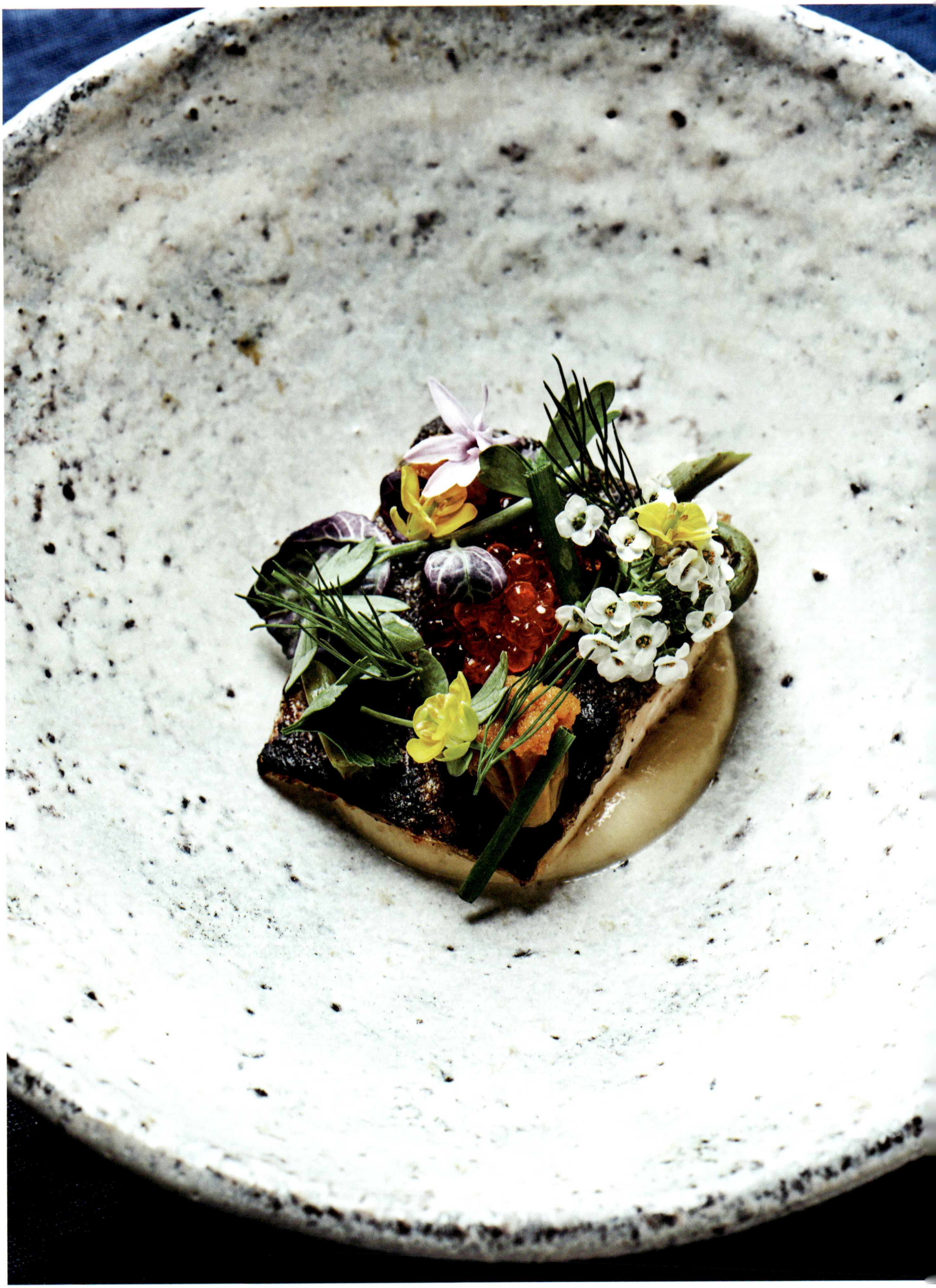

GRILLED BUCKSNORT TROUT, FERMENTED GREEN TOMATO BUTTER & HERBS FROM OUR GARDEN

When our larder grew full of several lacto-fermented fruit and vegetable juices, vinegars, and kombuchas, I started substituting some of the alcohol in traditional sauces with one of those ingredients. At one point, we even did a beurre rouge with a house-made verjus from local grapes. For this sauce, I wanted the flavor of the butter to have a familiarity associated with a classic beurre blanc but with that tart kick you get from a good kosher pickle. We reduced fermented green tomato juice with sweet vermouth and other aromatics, mounted it with butter, and broke it with dill oil right before serving. We poured this warm butter over all the herbs and flowers, which I thought helped bring more of their flavor out, almost as if they had just been picked and eaten right in the garden.

---

green tomato beurre blanc

shallot	105g
bay leaf	1ea
sweet vermouth	705mL
fermented green tomato juice	300g
butter, cubed and chilled	450g
xanthan gum	0.8%
fermented green tomato juice	t.t.

Reduce the shallot, bay leaf, and vermouth until all the alcohol has burned off. Add the green tomato juice and reduce by ¼. Add the mixture to a Vitamix with the xanthan gum and blend on high speed. Slowly emulsify in the cubed butter. Pass through a fine-mesh strainer and season to taste with additional fermented green tomato juice.

green garlic soubise

cultured butter	100g
spring onion, sliced thin and cold-smoked 30 minutes	200g
green garlic, tender white parts sliced thin	460g
fermented potato	125g

Melt the butter over medium heat. Put on two pairs of gloves, add the onions and green garlic, season with a pinch of salt, and massage the mixture into the warm butter. Continue to slowly sweat the spring onion and green garlic in the butter until they begin to soften. Cover with a cartouche and reduce the heat to low. Slowly cook until completely soft. Be sure not to get any color on the alliums. Transfer all the contents to a Vitamix and puree on high speed until completely smooth. Add the fermented potato and continue to blend until smooth. Pass through a chinois and reserve until needed.

herb oil

dill fronds	75g
parsley leaves	20g
chives	20g
grapeseed oil	275g

Puree in a Vitamix on high until blended well. Do not strain. Cool immediately.

green tomato mostarda

fermented green tomato pulp, cooked down with 7% sugar	375g
dry white wine	105mL
dry vermouth	205mL
white verjus	88mL
yellow mustard seed	60g
napé	50g
granulated sugar	50g
fermented green tomato juice	75g

Place all the ingredients in a sauce pot over medium heat. Cook slowly until all the moisture has evaporated, stirring constantly with a rubber spatula to prevent scorching.

additional ingredients & to finish

trout
herbs, any herb and flower in season
smoked trout roe
pickles, we used whatever was available: ramps, cauliflower, etc.
preserved dill stems (see page 271)
lemon juice
fish butter (see base recipes on page 272)

Season the trout with salt and gently grill on the skin side. Kiss the flesh side if needed. We cook our trout just to medium-rare, brush it with the fist butter, and finish with lemon juice. Place a spoonful of the soubise in the middle of a plate, add the fish, and top with a spoonful of smoked trout roe, a small amount of mostarda, pickles, and herbs. Bring the beurre blanc back to a simmer and gently fold in the herb oil. Spoon over the fish to wilt the herbs. Serve immediately.

KUE GROUPER BURIED IN EMBERS, GREEN GARLIC, FERMENTED WINTER TRUFFLE

This is another dish I did when Chef Johnny Spero was cooking with us. It took me the whole dinner to really figure out how exactly I wanted to cook it. Kue grouper was rubbed in a green garlic butter, wrapped in rehydrated kombu, and buried in embers. After slowly roasting, I flaked it apart and seasoned with a sauce made from a reduction of onion stock, charred green garlic, lovage stems, sweet aromatic soy sauce, smoked fish-bone oil, and a haché of fermented Australian winter truffle.

---

truffle puree

butter	50g
portobello mushrooms, small dice	225g
shallot	60g
preserved winter truffle, sliced	200g
dashi	815g
regalis black truffle oil	t.t.
regalis black truffle balsamic	t.t.
salt	t.t.

Melt the butter over medium heat, add the shallot, and cook until translucent. Add the mushroom and truffle, and cook until the mushrooms begin to soften and release some of their moisture. Cover with the dashi and a cartouche and simmer until everything is completely tender. Strain well, reserve the liquid, and add the solids to a Vitamix. Blend on high speed until completely smooth, adding any of the reserved liquid needed to help it spin. Emulsify in a small amount of the truffle oil. Season to taste with salt and black truffle balsamic. Pass through a fine-mesh strainer and reserve.

onion gravy

kuzu	7g
filtered cold water	16g
onion jus	375g
beef bouillon	30g
Worcestershire	5g

Mix the kuzu and water until smooth. Bring the onion jus, bouillon paste, and Worcestershire to a boil over medium-high heat. Quickly whisk in the kuzu slurry and bring to a simmer for one minute. Pass through a fine-mesh strainer and cool.

additional ingredients & to finish

green garlic, grilled and brunoised
lovage stems, minced fine
fermented black truffle, haché
smoked bone oil (see page 272)
sweet aromatic soy sauce
kombu, soaked in water until soft
grouper or other meaty fish, brined in 10% solution for 10 minutes

Cut the grouper into 6- to 8-ounce portions and wrap in the kombu. Place them in a pile of embers and shovel some more over the top of the kombu. Cook until a cake tester can easily pierce the flesh, but the flesh is still moist. Meanwhile, warm a couple of ounces of onion gravy. Season to taste with the sweet aromatic soy sauce, bone oil, haché truffle, green garlic, and lovage stems. Remove from the heat and allow to rest for 2 minutes. Place a small spoonful of truffle puree in a bowl, open the kombu, and slowly flake apart the fish. Spoon a few ounces of fish over the puree and dress with the warm sauce.

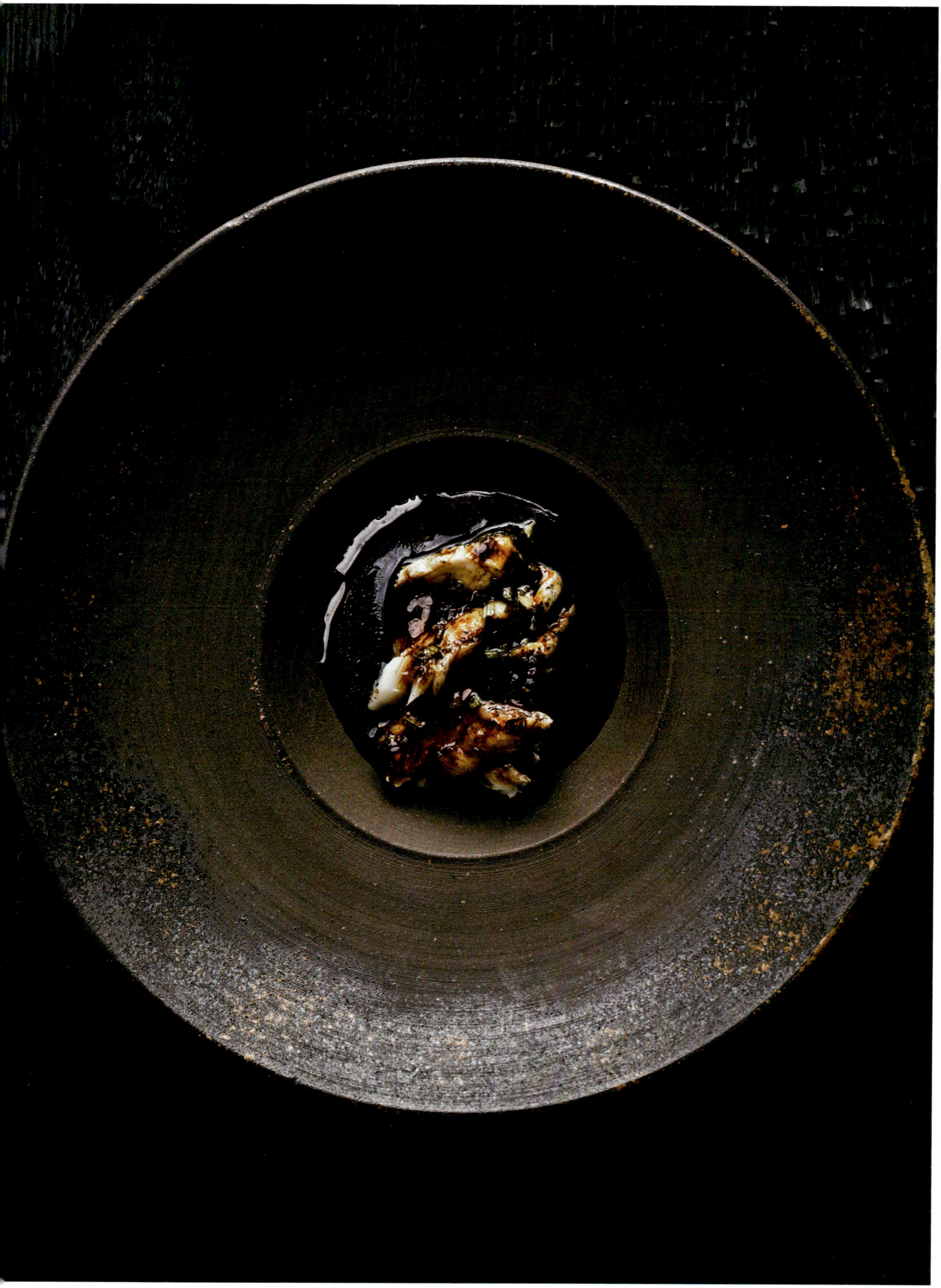

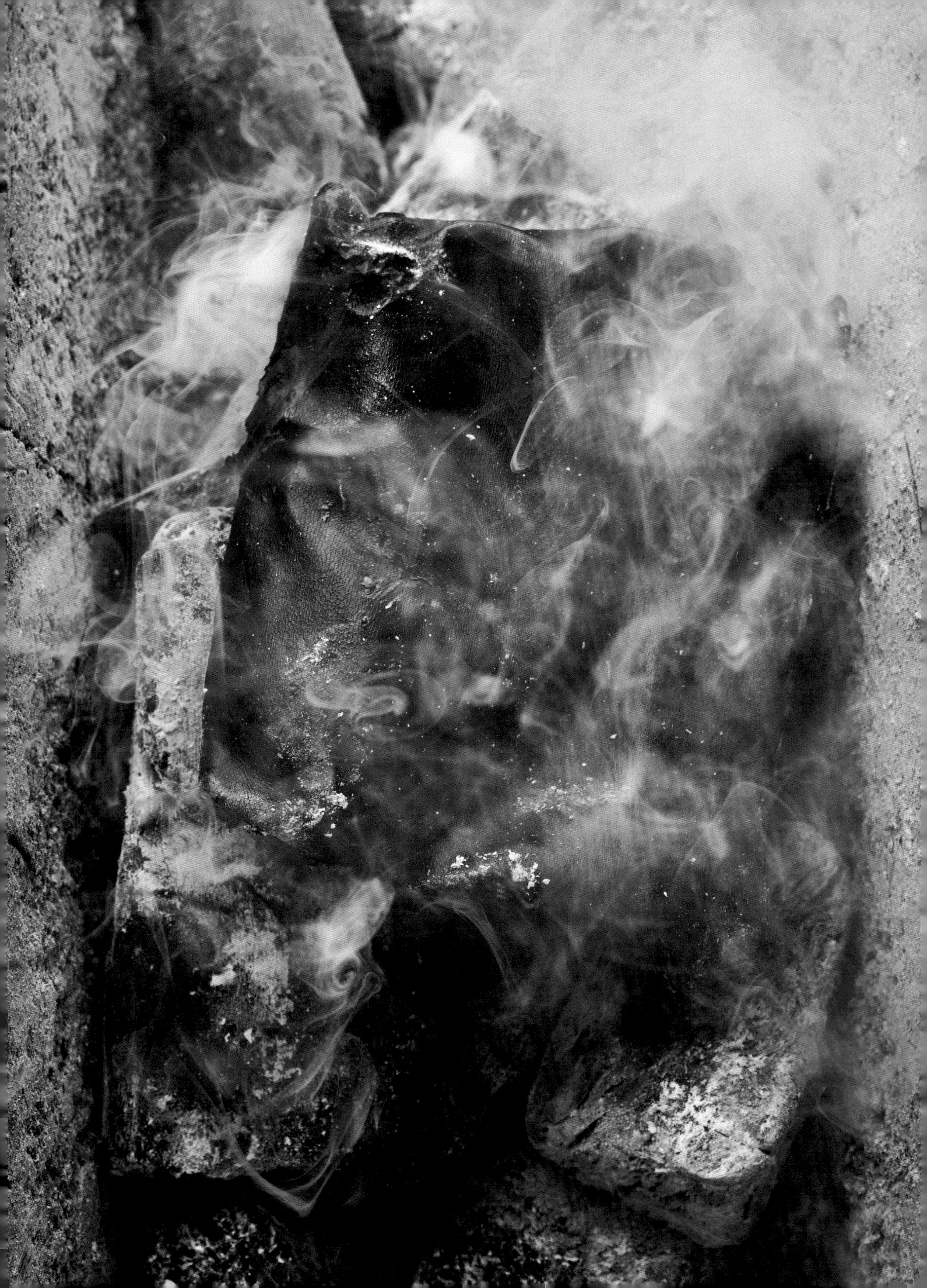

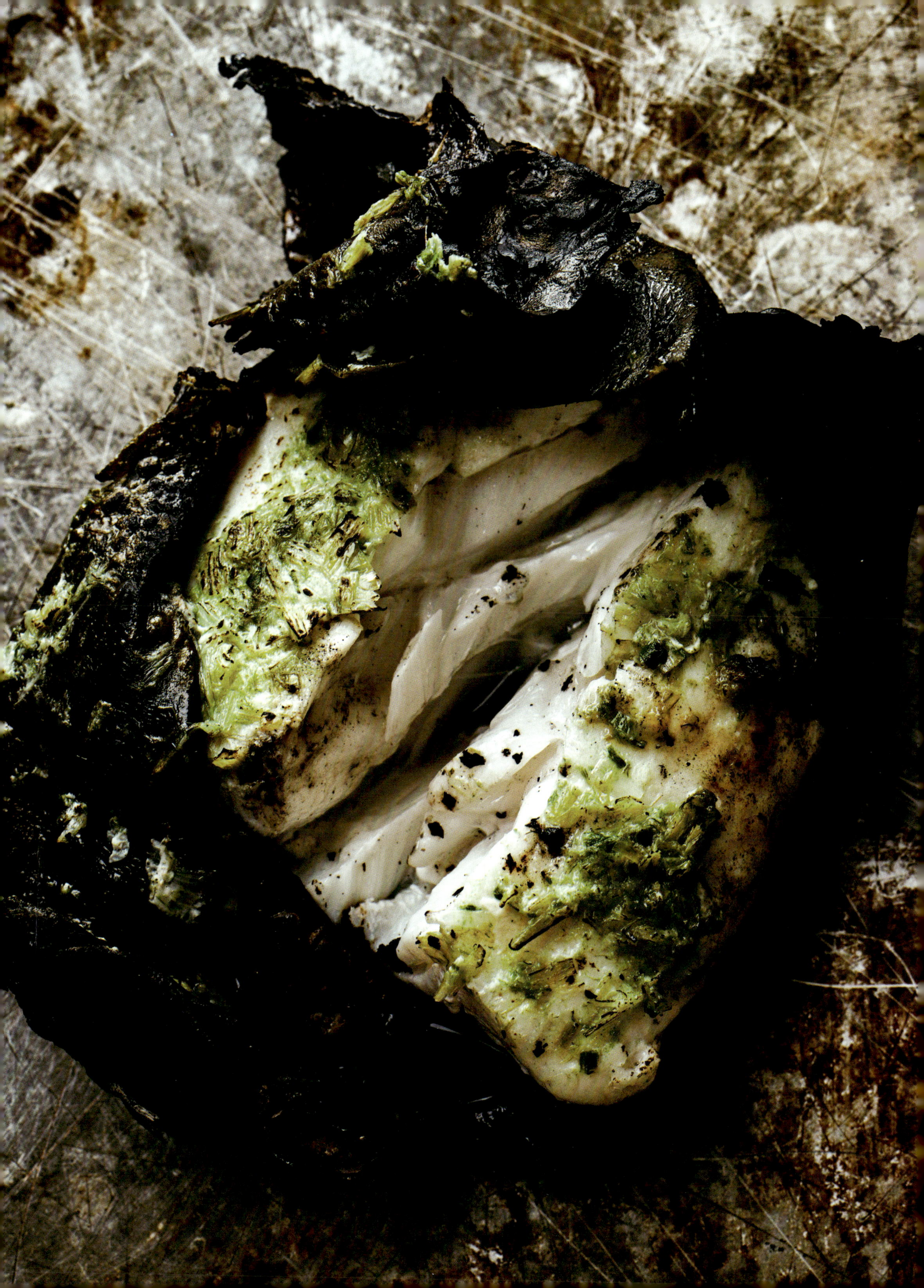

BEAR CREEK FARM LAMB WITH SWISS CHARD & CASHEW MILK

I always look forward to text messages each year from LeeAnn Cherry at Bear Creek Farm, saying she has 4H lamb coming in. She ages them whole for us, and we will either break them down and use different cuts, or she will cut and send broken-down in primals. For this dish, we'll highlight the T-bone that has been aged an additional 14 days. We also highlight the rib portion and a dolma filled with a farce made of the ground leg and shoulder. This dish is inspired by my love for lamb vindaloo, though I would not consider it Indian or in the style of vindaloo. It is probably closer to a korma, but even that is a stretch. It is served with a yogurt made from cashew milk; Swiss chard leaves that we cured like grape leaves and stuffed with ground lamb; and a chutney made from Swiss chard stems. Lastly, we presented a warm flaky flat bread to soak up any sauces that may be left.

---

cashew milk

sparkling water	1.5L
raw cashews	675g

Pulse the water and cashews in a Vitamix to roughly chop the cashews. Store under refrigeration for 48 hours. Puree until completely smooth and pass through a cheesecloth-lined fine-mesh strainer.

cashew curry

goat butter	50g
coriander seed	2g
fennel seed	1g
black cardamom	5g
cinnamon stick	3g
yellow mustard	4g
annatto seed	1.5g
star anise	2g
caraway seed	.5g
allspice berries	.25g
turmeric powder	1.25g
dry ginger, ground	.5g
black peppercorn	.75g
saffron	.05g
chipotle powder	1g
garlic, sliced thin	10g
shallot, sliced thin	115g
cashew milk	1.2L
kuzu	15g
cold water	28g
fermented tomato reduction	50g

Toast all the spices in the goat butter over medium-high heat until aromatic. Add the shallot and garlic, and cook until translucent. Whisk in the cashew milk, being sure to remove any fond that has formed on the bottom of the pan. Bring to a simmer, reduce the heat to medium-high, and allow to simmer for 20 minutes, stirring constantly with a rubber spatula to prevent scorching. Mix the kuzu with the cold water, then whisk into the sauce base and bring back to a simmer for one minute. Lastly, add the fermented tomato reduction. Allow the sauce to cool and infuse overnight in the refrigerator. The next day, pass through a fine-mesh strainer and reserve.

lamb dolma

dry-aged lamb, ground	454g
dolma spice (see below)	7g
golden raisins, roughly chopped	20g
kosher salt	9g
fresh mint, roughly chopped	4g

Mix all ingredients together until well combined. Separate into 15g portions and wrap in cured Swiss chard leaves. Steam at 80°C until reaching an internal temperature of 65°C. Let rest for 15 minutes.

cured swiss chard leaves

Swiss chard leaves, stems removed and reserved for chutney	200g
filtered water	1L
kosher salt	30g

Place the Swiss chard in a 4-quart Cambro or container. Bring the water and salt to a boil. Pour over the leaves and weigh down with a plate. Allow to cool at room temperature, then transfer to a refrigerator for 48 hours.

dolma spice

bishop's weed	2g
cumin seeds	7g
black peppercorn	9g
ground cinnamon	4g
marjoram	1g
chipotle powder	2g

Toast the bishop's weed, cumin, and black peppercorn until aromatic. Allow to cool, and grind to a fine powder. Mix all ingredients together and reserve in an airtight container until needed.

swiss chard chutney

cinnamon sticks	14g
star anise pods	2ea
green cardamom pods	5ea
coriander seeds	4g
arbol chilies	4ea
ginger, minced fine	45g
garlic, minced fine	25g
Swiss chard stems, diced small	3,000g
grapeseed oil	50g
sugar	1,500g
Omed cider vinegar	1.5L

Place the cinnamon, star anise, cardamom, coriander, and chilies in a cheesecloth sachet. In a pot over medium heat, sweat the ginger, garlic, and Swiss chard stems until they begin to soften. Add the rest of the ingredients and reduce until most of the moisture has evaporated and a jam consistency is achieved.

garam masala

black cardamom	47g
cinnamon sticks	20g
black peppercorns	32g
cloves	5g
cumin seed	60g
coriander	35g
star anise	4g

Toast all ingredients over medium-high heat until aromatic. Allow to cool, and grind as fine as possible.

lamb mop

sorghum	600g
garam masala	23g
lemon juice	200g

Simmer over medium-high heat for 20 minutes. Allow to cool and reserve until needed.

cashew yogurt

filtered water	1,440g
cashews	454g
probiotic culture	12caps
salt	t.t.

Pulse waters, cashews, and salt in blender and soak for 48 hours. Puree until smooth and pass through a fine-mesh strainer. Bring to 74°C while stirring constantly to prevent scorching. Allow to cool to 43°C and stir in culture. Ferment at 43.3°C for 12 hours, or at room temperature for 24 hours.

lamb ribs

rack of Denver cut ribs	1ea
filtered water	1L
kosher salt	10g

Brine the ribs in the water and salt for 10 hours. Remove from the brine, pat dry, and seal in a Cryovac bag on full pressure. Cook in a water bath at 71°C for 12 hours. Chill in an ice bath. Portion the ribs by cutting between each bone. French the top end of the rib by removing any meat and tissue with a paring knife. Wrap the exposed bone in aluminum foil and reserve.

onion marinade

barrel-aged fish sauce	100mL
sugar	30g
white vinegar	15mL

Mix to dissolve the sugar, and reserve.

additional ingredients & to finish

goat butter
green garlic fry bread (see page 28)
spring onion bulbs
preserved lemons
lemon wedge
lemon zest
Maldon sea salt
mint

For the onion salad Slice spring onions as thin as possible on a mandolin. Chiffonade mint leaves and add to the onions. Dress with desired amount of onion marinade. Allow to marinate for at least 5 minutes.

For the rib Season the ribs with the garam masala and slowly grill over hardwood embers. Glaze constantly with the lamb mop until caramelized and hot all the way through.

For the lamb T-bone Season with garam masala and kosher salt. Slowly roast over hardwood embers, glazing constantly with the lamb mop, to desired doneness. Let rest for 5 minutes before removing from the bone.

For the condiments Place a small spoonful of each of the Swiss chard chutney, cashew yogurt finished with lemon zest, and onion salad on the serving plate.

For the dolma Rewarm over the grill and garnish with a slice of preserved lemon.

For the green garlic fry bread Finish by brushing with good goat butter and Maldon sea salt.

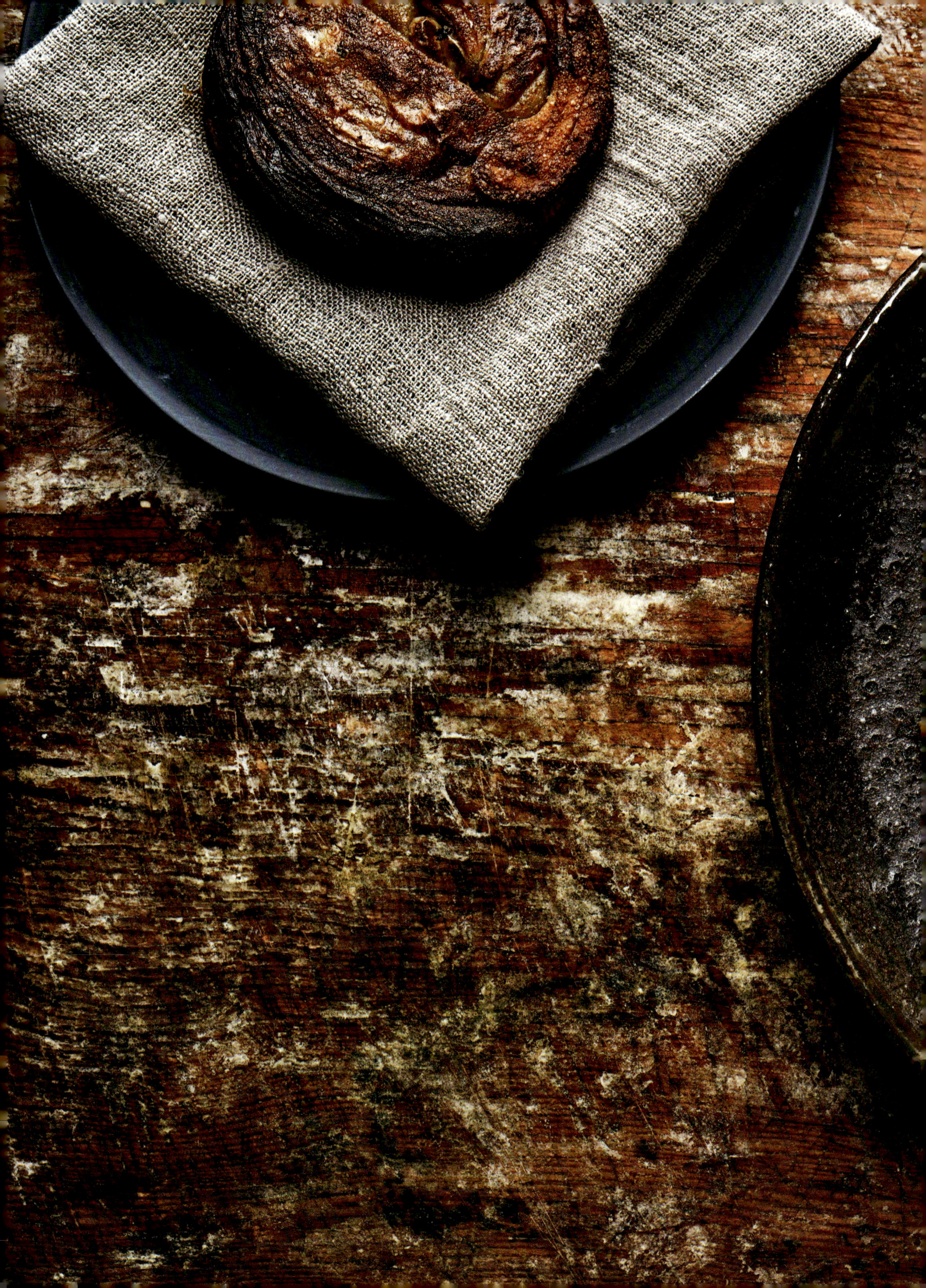

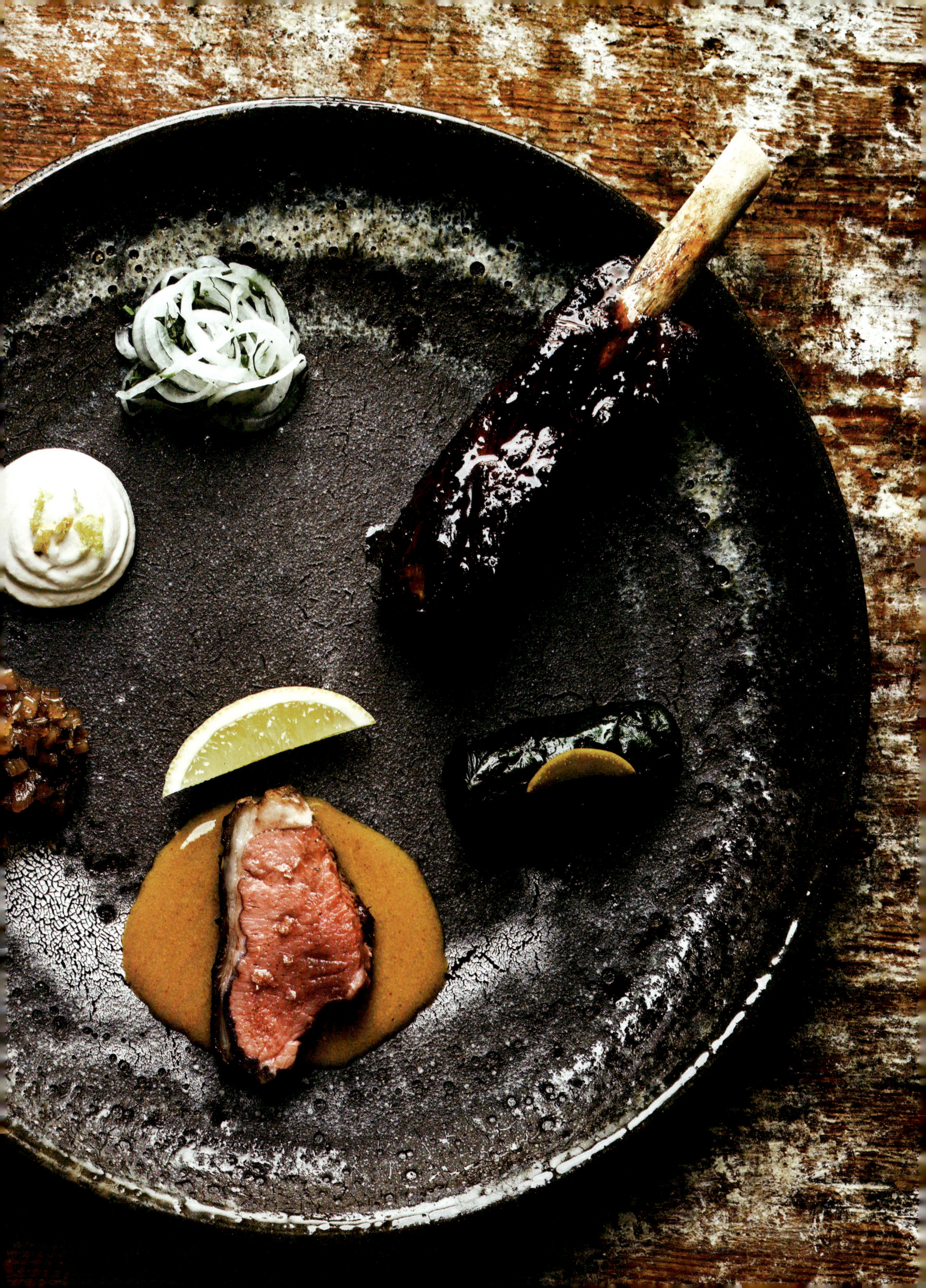

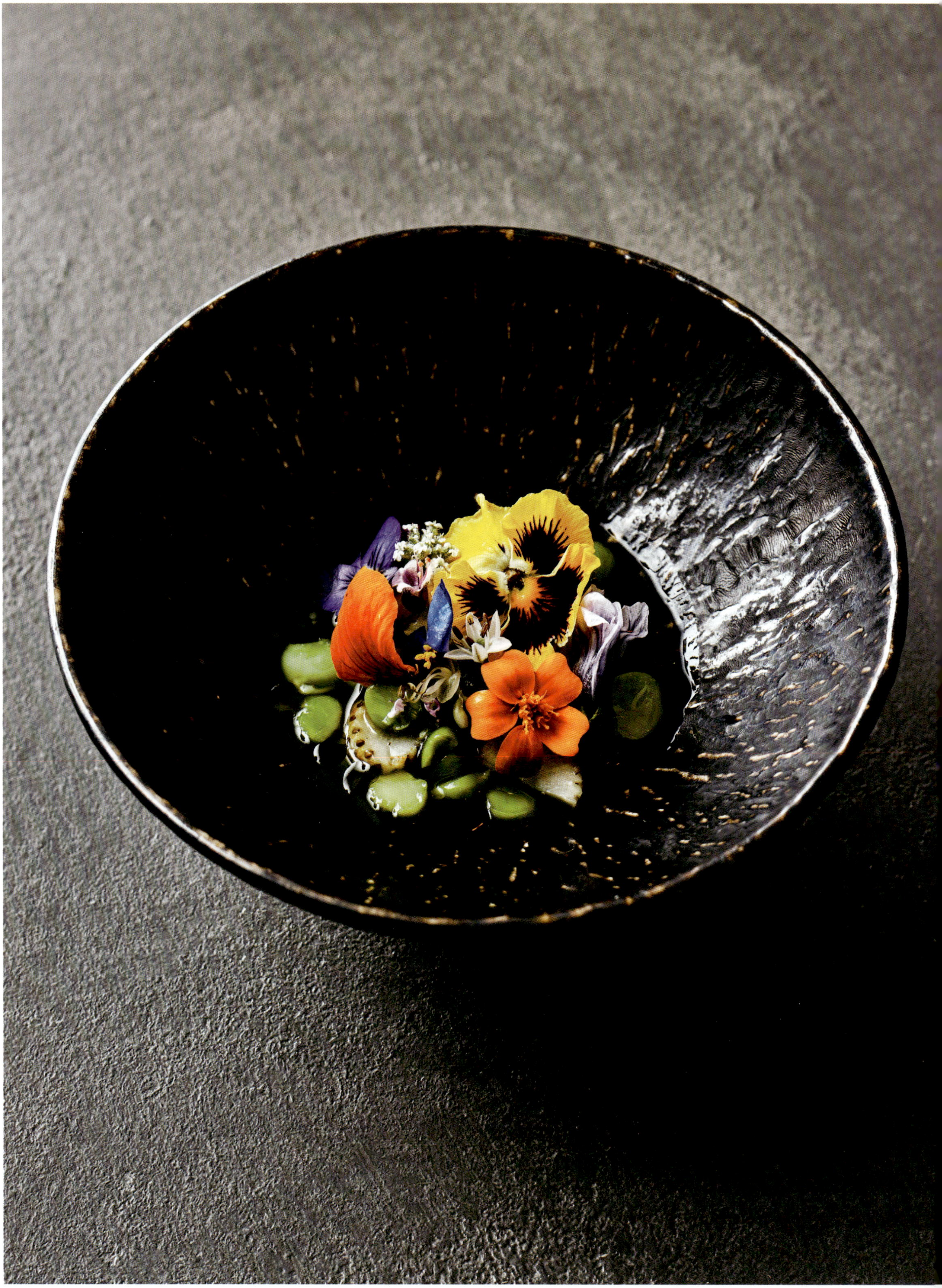

SALAD OF ENGLISH PEAS, GREEN STRAWBERRIES & GREEN CHARTREUSE

This was one of my favorite salads that we did, because it wasn't similar in any way to anything that people had ever had. Sweet peas were dressed with a vinaigrette made from green chartreuse, sugar snap pea juice, and pickled green strawberries folded in at the last second. We finished it with a very intense tarragon oil, lime zest, and mix of flowers that shared some similar characteristics to the nuances of the chartreuse.

---

green chartreuse vin

green chartreuse, alcohol burned off	225mL
sugar snap pea juice	375g
sugar	185g

Mix the sugar into the chartreuse once the alcohol has burned off. Cool and mix with the pea juice. Reserve chilled until needed.

tarragon oil

tarragon	100g
grapeseed oil	200g

Blend in a Vitamix on high speed until the mixture reaches 64°C. Strain through a coffee-filter-lined fine-mesh strainer. Cool and reserve.

pickled green strawberries

green strawberries, washed well and stems removed	1kg
filtered water	850mL
white vinegar	840mL
granulated sugar	600g
lemongrass stalks, bruised and cut into 3" pieces	1ea
ginger, 3" piece, peeled and sliced thin	1ea
mace	1g
allspice berries	3ea
bay leaves	4ea
cloves	3ea
cinnamon stick, 3" pieces	1ea
Thai long peppercorns	5ea

Mix ingredients together. Bring to a boil and pour over the green strawberries. Allow to cool at room temperature, and store in the refrigerator for at least 1 week.

additional ingredients & to finish

English peas, shelled and skin removed
herbs and flowers

Blanch the peas in a large pot of boiling water seasoned with 5% salt and 2% sugar. Cool on a tray by immediately transferring to blast chiller or freezer. Do not let them freeze. In a small mixing bowl, mix the green chartreuse vinegar with 25% its weight of the pickled strawberry brine. Slice a pickled green strawberry ⅛" thick, mix with a spoonful of the peas, and dress with the green chartreuse-pickle brine mixture. Place in a serving bowl, dress with a teaspoon of the tarragon oil, and garnish with the herbs and flowers.

YEAST DONUT, FOIE GRAS, STRAWBERRY & ELDERFLOWER

The glaze for this donut is one of my favorite springtime flavor pairings. I have used it in different ways over the years and look forward to using it still in the future. We cooked strawberries down in 50% sugar until completely softened. We then slowly dried them until they were chewy. The preserved strawberry juice we cooked down with St-Germain and thickened with 10x sugar. We glazed the donut in the strawberry syrup and diced the preserved strawberries (see below) and folded them into the pastry cream. We finished the donut by sprinkling pickled elderflowers over the top.

---

preserved strawberries

strawberries, washed and halved	450g	Cook over a double boiler until the strawberries are completely tender but still hold their shape. Drain and reserve the syrup for another use. Dry the strawberries at 110°F until most of the moisture has evaporated and they have the texture of a raisin. Cut into ¼" dice.
granulated sugar	225g	
St-Germain Elderflower Liqueur	50g	

strawberry glaze

reserved strawberry syrup	60mL	Mix until completely combined. Chill.
10x sugar	125g	
elderflower cordial	15mL	

additional ingredients & to finish

donut dough (see page 66)	Make a small hole in the side of the donut and fill with the pastry cream. Glaze the top of the donut and season with the sea salt. Finish with a few pickled elderflowers.
foie pastry cream (see page 66)	
pickled elderflower (see page 35)	
Maldon sea salt	

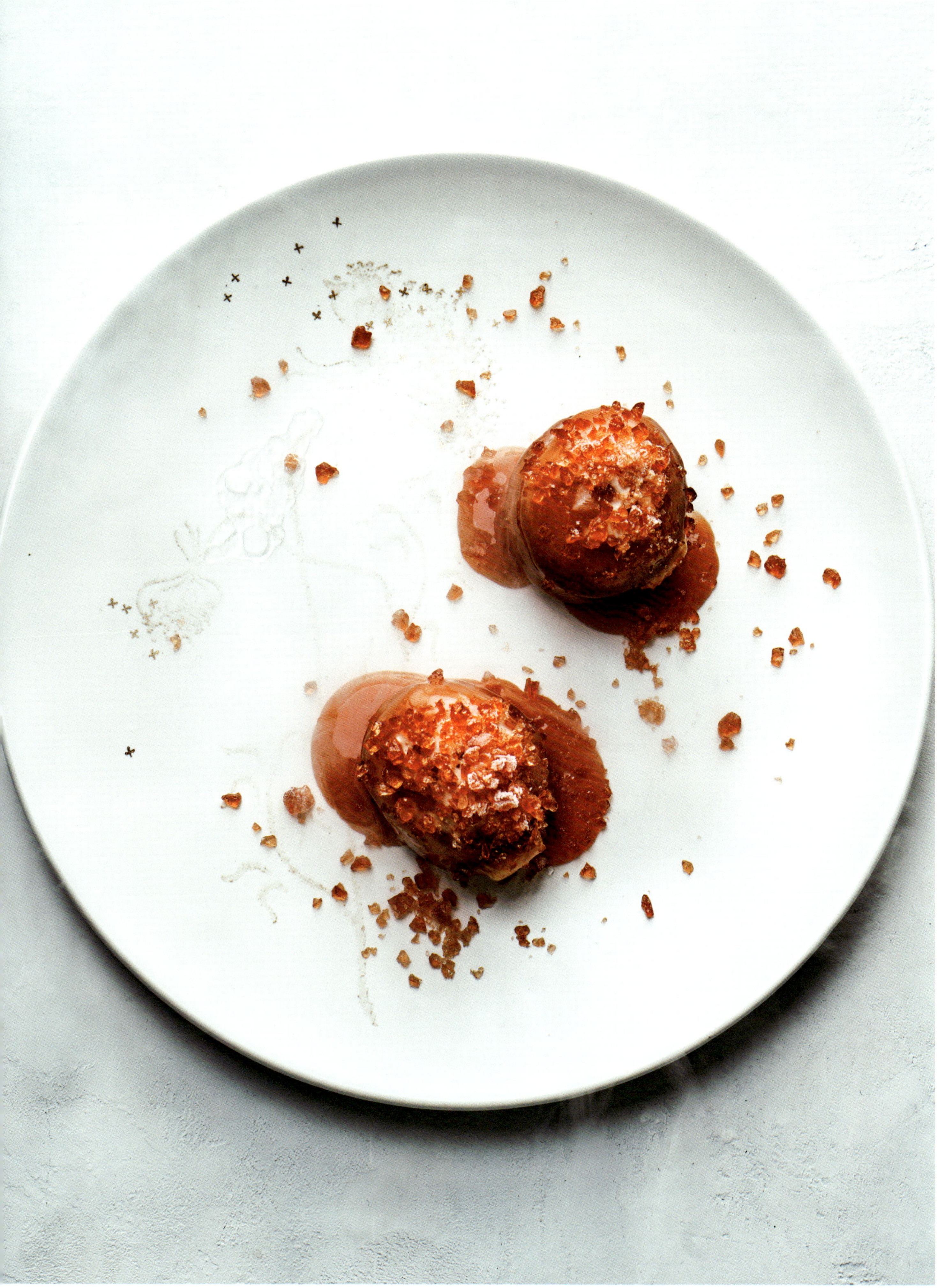

COOKING WITH CONFIDENCE
AFTER THE FIRST FOUR SEASONS

"Believe in yourself. Have faith in your abilities. Without a humble but reasonable confidence in your own powers you cannot be successful or happy." —Norman Vincent Peale

I have begun to realize over the past year that I like to cook with my instincts, to be reactive. To have the confidence to think with one or two ingredients in mind, show up to work, and say "I am putting this on the menu in a few hours." This forces me to trust and rely on my senses, flavor memories, and skills to create something without overthinking. Sometimes the dish comes from a smell, like the reginette with mussels and foie gras (page 219), and other times it comes from a memory, like the salad of green pepper with scuppernong (page 155). It's important to taste a wide variety of foods over your career and do it consistently, as the palate and mind can forget. I will always try everything once. Tasting different foods and paying attention to the nuances in each of them gives me the ability to store them like a flavor library I can keep returning to for inspiration. So, at any time, if a farmer drops off a new product, I can taste it and think back to what would go well with it, like a sixth sense.

I have realized that any time I write out an elaborate idea for a dish with recipes and have everything figured out, 99 percent of the time I am thoroughly disappointed and must start completely over. Once I taste an ingredient and approach it with an open mind, I usually know what I want to do with it. From years of tasting every single component over and over, the flavors have become second nature. One night toward the end of year one, we had an allergy pop up in the middle of service and had to come up with a new dish for them on the fly. I had just received some incredibly delicious Iberian pork collar from Encina Farms in Lake County, California. I looked on my station and had a vinegar made from velvet horn seaweed. It was sweet, acidic, and salty. I decided to make an "agro dulce" by reducing the vinegar with shallots and smoked onion oil. I reduced it until just before it began to caramelize. I then emulsified in a small amount of cabbage puree that I had and a little butter for richness and body. The caramelly sauce needed some more brightness, so I folded in fresh strawberries for some acidity and grilled hazelnuts for nuttiness and texture. The entire dish was finished with isot pepper to add just a touch of smoky heat. Without confidence, I would not be able to cook like this successfully.

If I had not faced the adversity in my life and my career, I wouldn't be who I am today. Living a healthy and sober lifestyle has helped to give my palate the ability to notice the nuances in the ingredients. Having to force myself to work through the pain after surgery and the times when I physically or mentally wanted to quit helps me to be excited about going in to work even when I've only had a few hours of sleep and don't think I can work fourteen hours. Continuing to try to be creative even when I didn't think anyone was enjoying my food has allowed me to believe in what I am giving to the guests each time. And having the restaurant that I have poured my heart into over the last year be named eleventh best in the country by *Opinionated About Dining* has proven to me that all the hard work by my staff and myself hasn't gone unnoticed.

Although I say I try not to pay attention to what the lists or critics have to say, it is a good way to measure where I am versus where I want to be. Am I continuing to get better and move up, or am I regressing? No matter what, it does not define who I am. I have recently begun to think about my future and my legacy. What will make me a great chef and a great person when I finally step away from cooking? People may look at someone and say "Look at all they have accomplished or didn't accomplish. Did they get a Michelin star? Win a James Beard award?" In reality, they're missing the whole story. It is so much more than awards. It is people's lives and watching them develop into good cooks and good people. We cannot accomplish any of this on our own without a staff that believes in our vision and our belief in their hard work to help share it with the guests. We cannot accomplish this without mentoring young cooks and investing in them the way those I've learned from invested in me. It is also a matter of what I have done for the world. Have I given back to those who are less fortunate than myself? Am I mindful about sustainability and how certain things will affect the environment? Have I been a good mentor and role model, and will I have made the world a better place? At The Catbird Seat, I have tried to focus on these points, although the space has its limitations. We try to use all of any ingredient before just throwing it in the trash, but we have to be mindful of how much space we have, which isn't a lot.

Using all of an ingredient could mean anything from curing and drying the bloodline of fish to fermenting and drying a vegetable skin to make into an oil. On a personal level, I try to take the time with my staff to be aware of what is going on in their lives and be aware of how they are feeling at work. Do they feel supported, are they frustrated or not, and is there anything they need to make their life easier? I believe that I've created an environment that allows the staff to feel confident in themselves as well. Above all, the main thing I can pass on to aspiring cooks is this:

Cook for yourself!

MY SECOND YEAR IN THE CATBIRD SEAT
2021 to 2022

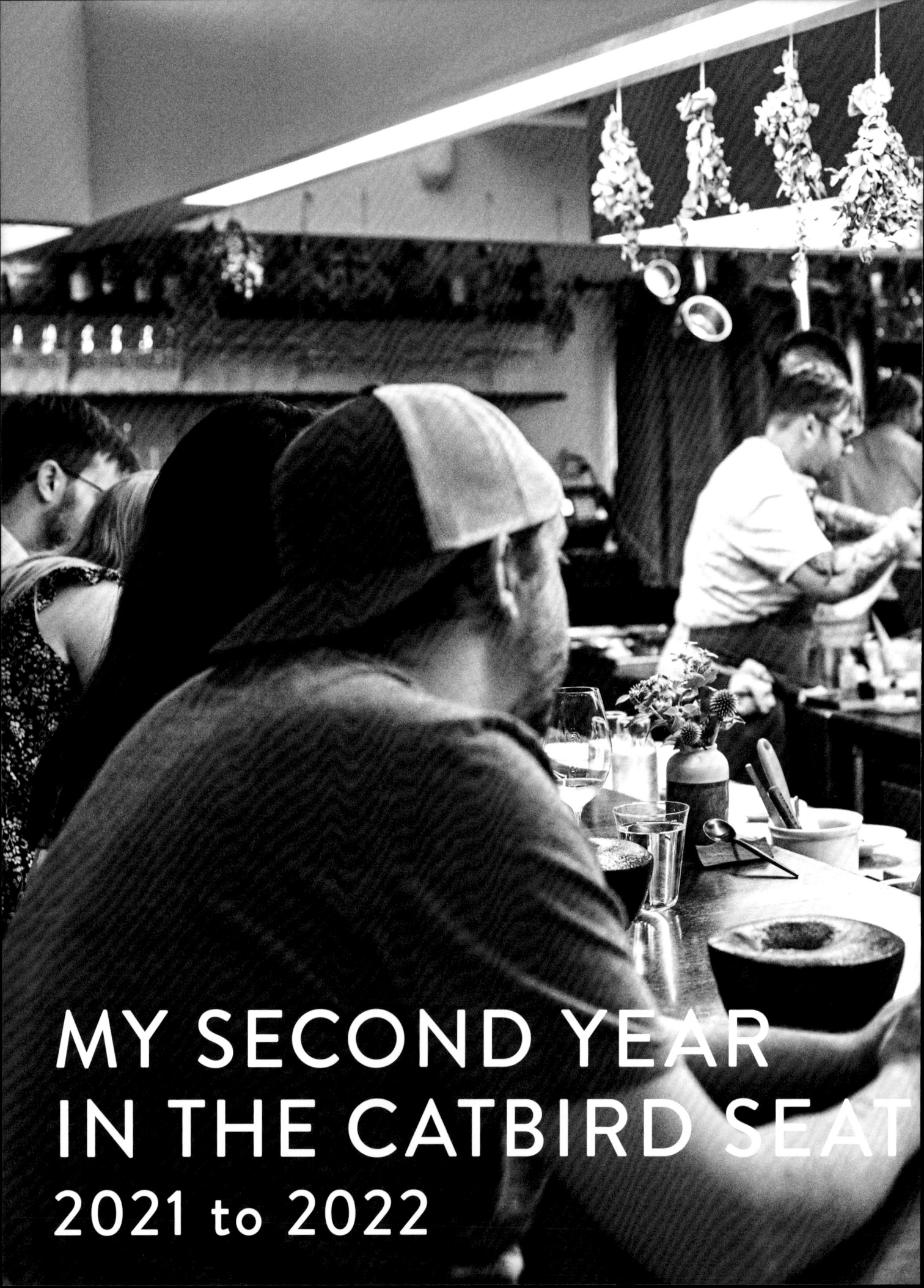

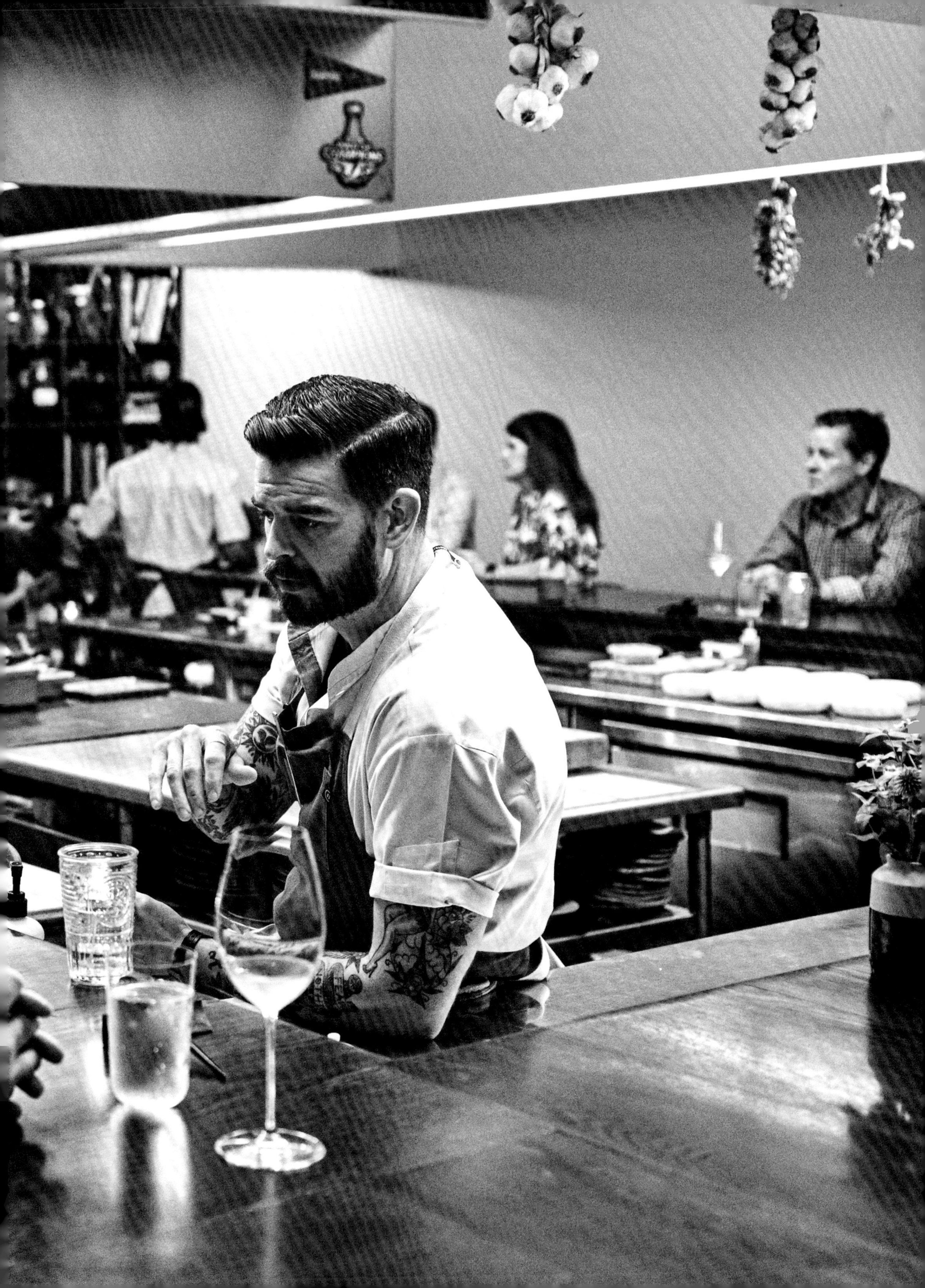

SUMMER 2021

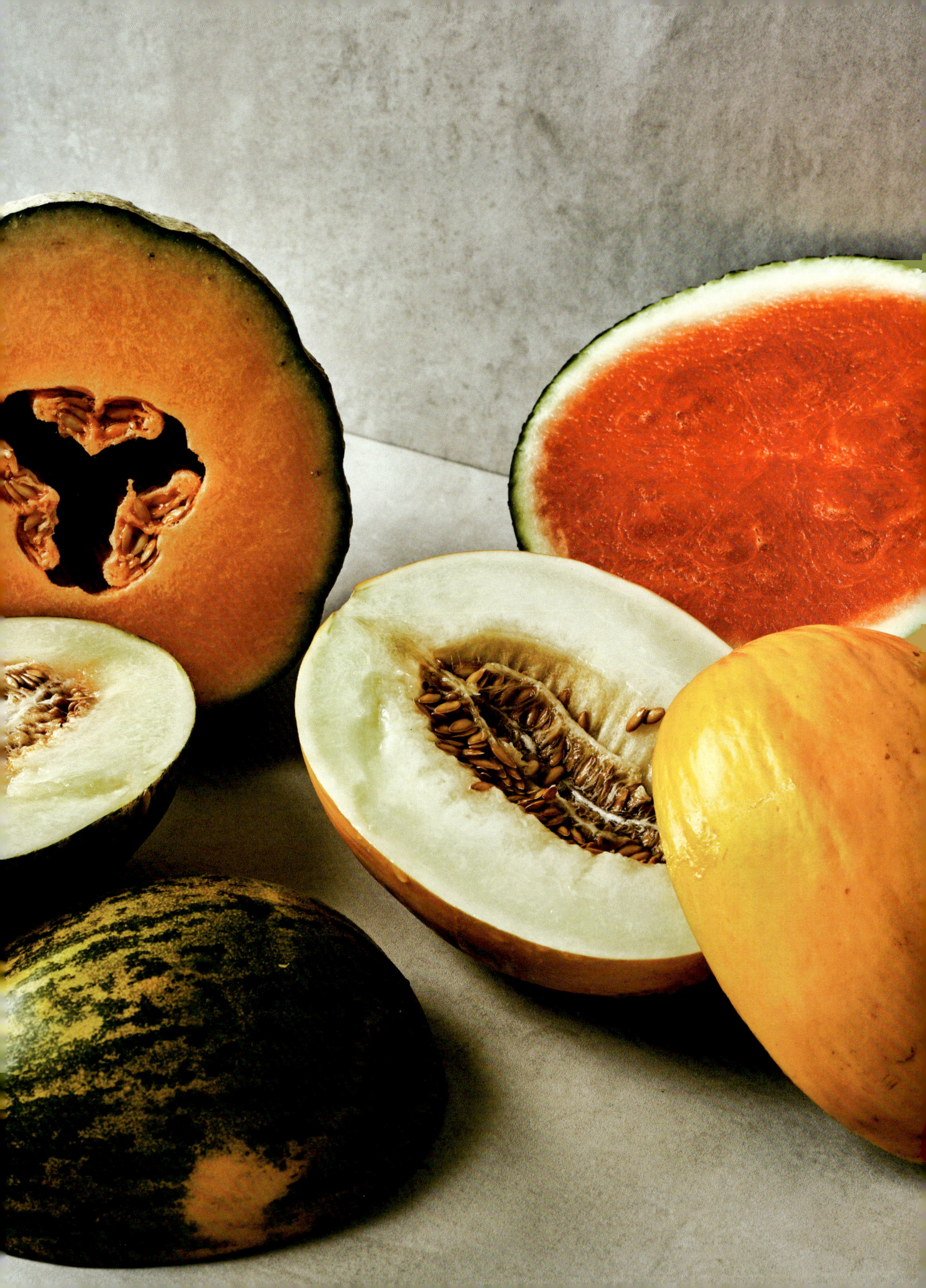

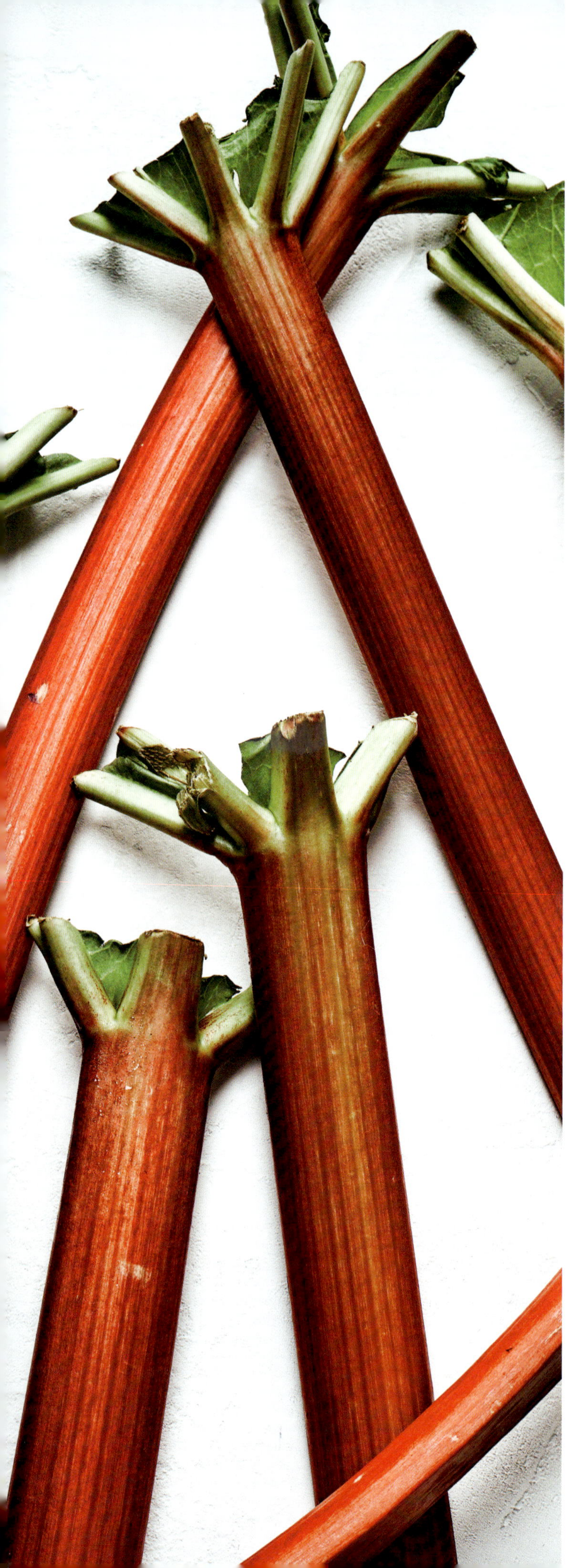
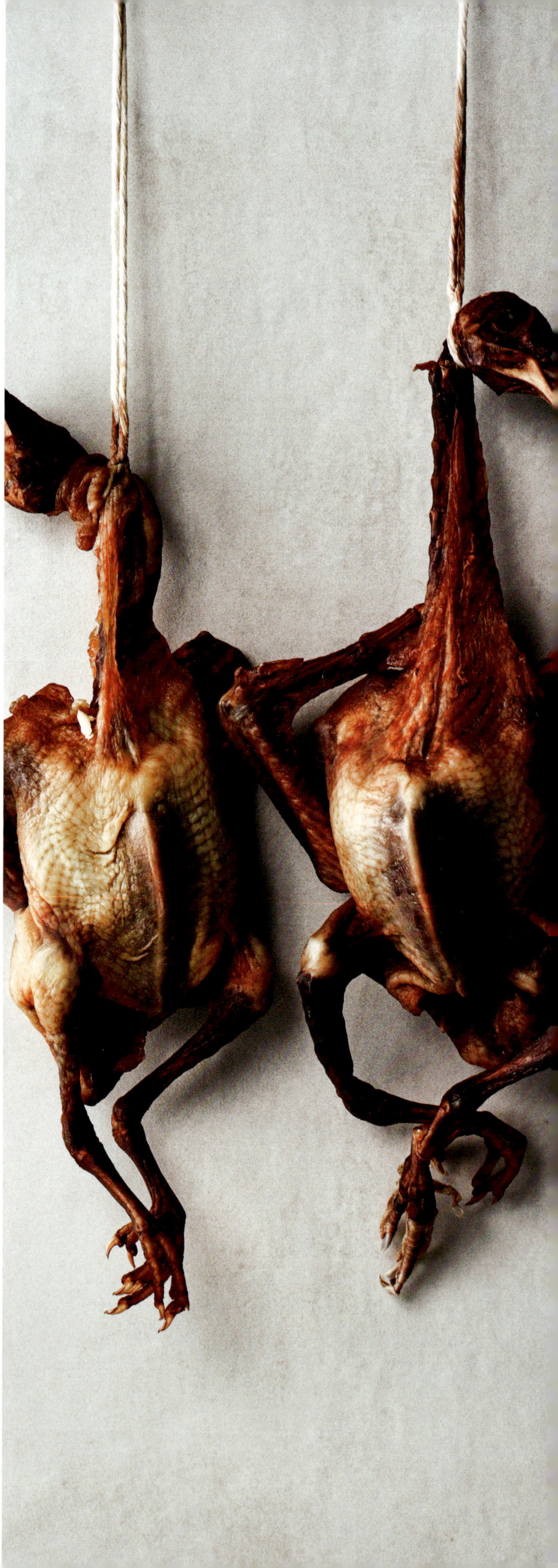

The date was July 13, 2021, a year into my tenure at Catbird. My buddy Logan sent me a succinct text: "Bro!" along with a screenshot of his phone screen. I was packing to head to Florida for my sister's wedding and opened it really quick, not really paying attention and thinking he'd just sent me a dumb screenshot of a list of restaurants he wanted to eat at. I then realized he'd sent a pic of the *Opinionated About Dining* publication's Top 100 North American restaurants list, and we were number 15. While rewards and lists are not something I focus on as validation, it was nice to be recognized *and* have an old friend reach out to me about it. Lists are not why I cook, but it felt good to know that we were on the right track to maintaining the restaurant's stature as one of the top places to dine in the country. Trevor Moran and Ryan Poli had both been ranked in the top 10 when they were the chefs here at Catbird. They are super-talented, amazing chefs and friends of mine, but the list was a small amount of encouragement that helped to remind me that I was at least upholding the restaurant's high standards.

Over the past year, I'd had a lot of guests come through the doors, eat my food, and hold conversations with me throughout the evening. This was a special place to be cooking, as we got to talk and engage with nearly every guest who came through the door. We don't always want feedback, especially when it's negative or ingenuous; but in this instance the frank, honest, real-time feedback is helpful. It shows that we've made the guest feel comfortable enough to open up to us about their experience. This made me realize over time that some of my stranger ideas seem to be the more popular among the guests. This is something that I will continue to pursue moving forward. As I sit here and write about summer again, I realize that I just get excited with every season change. I always look forward to cooking with the many cucurbits that are available in the summer (melons, cucumbers, and summer squash), and the wide varieties of peppers, tomatoes, and berries, a lot of which we'll preserve for use later in the year. And of course there's always corn and the multitudinous ways to use, preserve, and ferment it. This year we wanted to explore more of the ways these ingredients could be manipulated and used in more savory recipes like the grilled mussels and cantaloupe kimchi (page 152) and the salad of green pepper with scuppernong (page 155), or turn it on its head and use corn in a sweet ice cream to be served with Australian winter truffle (page 168). Our take on ambrosia salad—the church picnic classic—was amplified by a favorite flavor combination of mine: rhubarb and angelica root. But before diving into the recipes, I'd like to share one more journal entry from right in the middle of this summer season:

Day 395

I still get excited to go in to work every day. Every day is a new day and an empty canvas to create. This next year, I want to push even harder. We can never be complacent. Like William M. Chase said, "Never be satisfied with reaching for a mere star but for the greatest one." Another quote I saw recently, from an unknown source, has me inspired as well: "It feels good to be recognized but better to be respected."

Credit: Brian Baxter

SUMMER 2021 MENU

shigoku oyster, charred cucumber, succulents **148**

charred zucchini, salted buttermilk & marjoram **151**

grilled mussels & cantaloupe kimchi "jjigae" **152**

salad of green pepper, scuppernong & pistachio **155**

dry-aged ora king salmon, raspberry & angelica **156**

norwegian langoustine, fermented ramps, hickory king corn grits **159**

amadai with a curry of fermented golden beet **160**

devil's gulch ranch squab, romanesco & pechuga **162**

————————

ambrosia salad **167**

sweet corn ice cream, huitlacoche & australian winter truffle **168**

seaweed ice cream, fermented cucumber & sea urchin butterscotch pudding **171**

SHIGOKU OYSTER, CHARRED CUCUMBER, SUCCULENTS

For the first bite of the summer menu, I wanted the guests to know exactly what season they were in. We used Shigoku oysters and paired them with a clarified salsa verde made from charred cucumbers and fresh succulent herbs picked near the ocean. The mildly salty aspect of the beach herbs and brightness of the cucumber mignonette beautifully highlighted the brininess and sweet cucurbit flavor of the West Coast oysters.

---

charred cucumber salsa verde

whole cucumber	1,015g
olive oil as needed	
cucumber, diced	745g
garlic	15g
onion, medium dice	180g
cilantro	50g
white vinegar	415g
jalapeno, deseeded and chopped	50g
salt	5g
bourbon barrel smoked peppercorn	3g
gelatin, bloomed in ice water	1%

For the charred cucumber Toss the whole cucumber in enough olive oil to coat and season with salt and pepper. Char over the embers with 1 half-burnt-down log, allowing to smoke as it chars. Wrap in plastic and allow to rest for 30 minutes. Puree all ingredients except the gelatin until smooth. Separate 1 cup of the puree and reserve the rest. Wring out the bloomed gelatin, add to the one cup of puree, and melt over medium heat, stirring constantly. Once melted, add back to the reserved puree and puree until fully incorporated. Freeze in a thin layer. Once frozen, place in a cheesecloth-lined perforated hotel pan over a deeper hotel pan and allow to clarify overnight.

additional ingredients & to finish

oysters
succulent herbs such as: sea beans, ice plant, beach arugula, oyster leaf
Mexican tarragon leaves, picked
coriander capers
(see base recipes on page 270)

Shuck the oysters and remove from the shell. Place in a bowl, dress with the salsa verde, and top with one coriander caper and one of each herb.

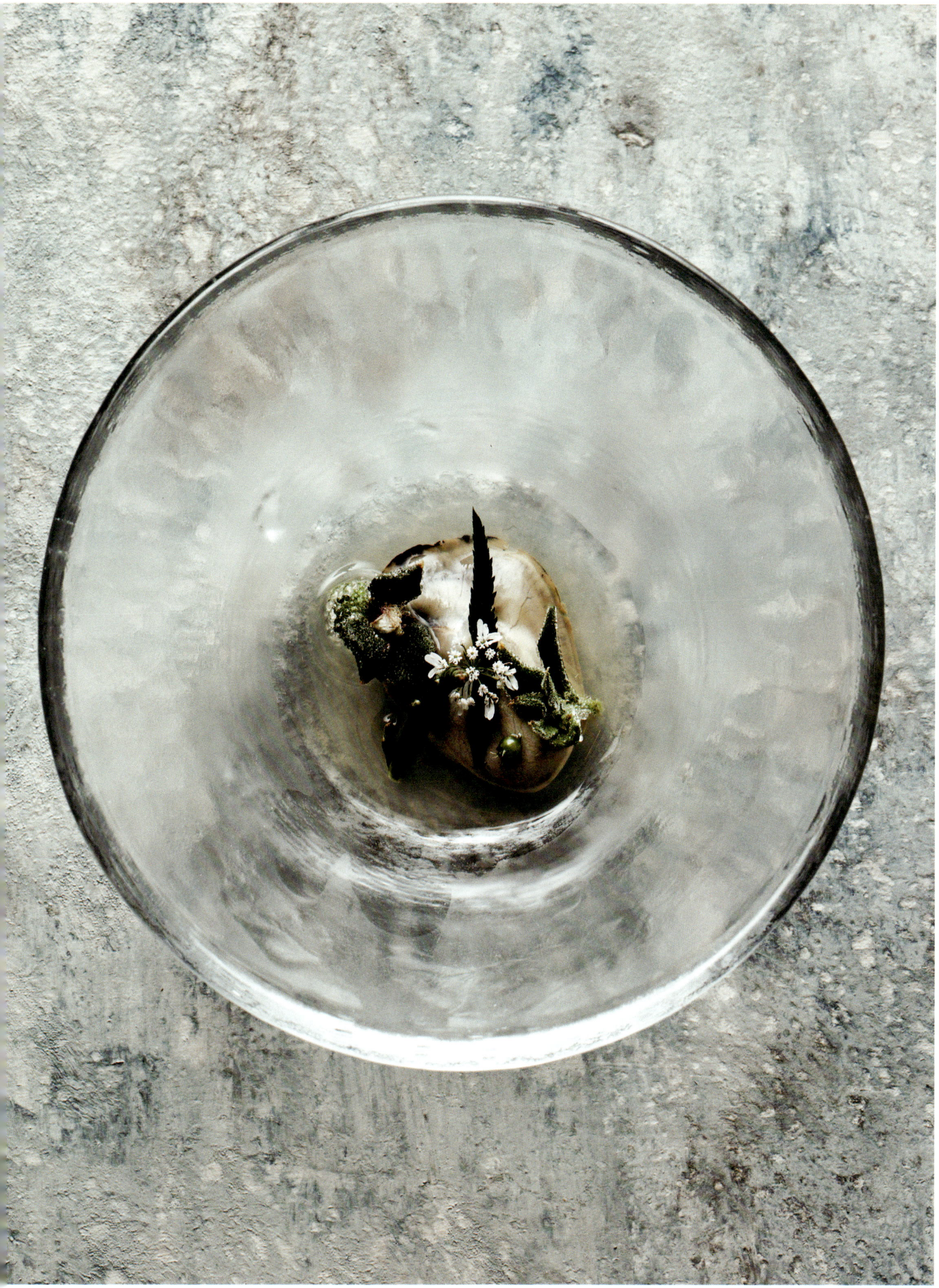

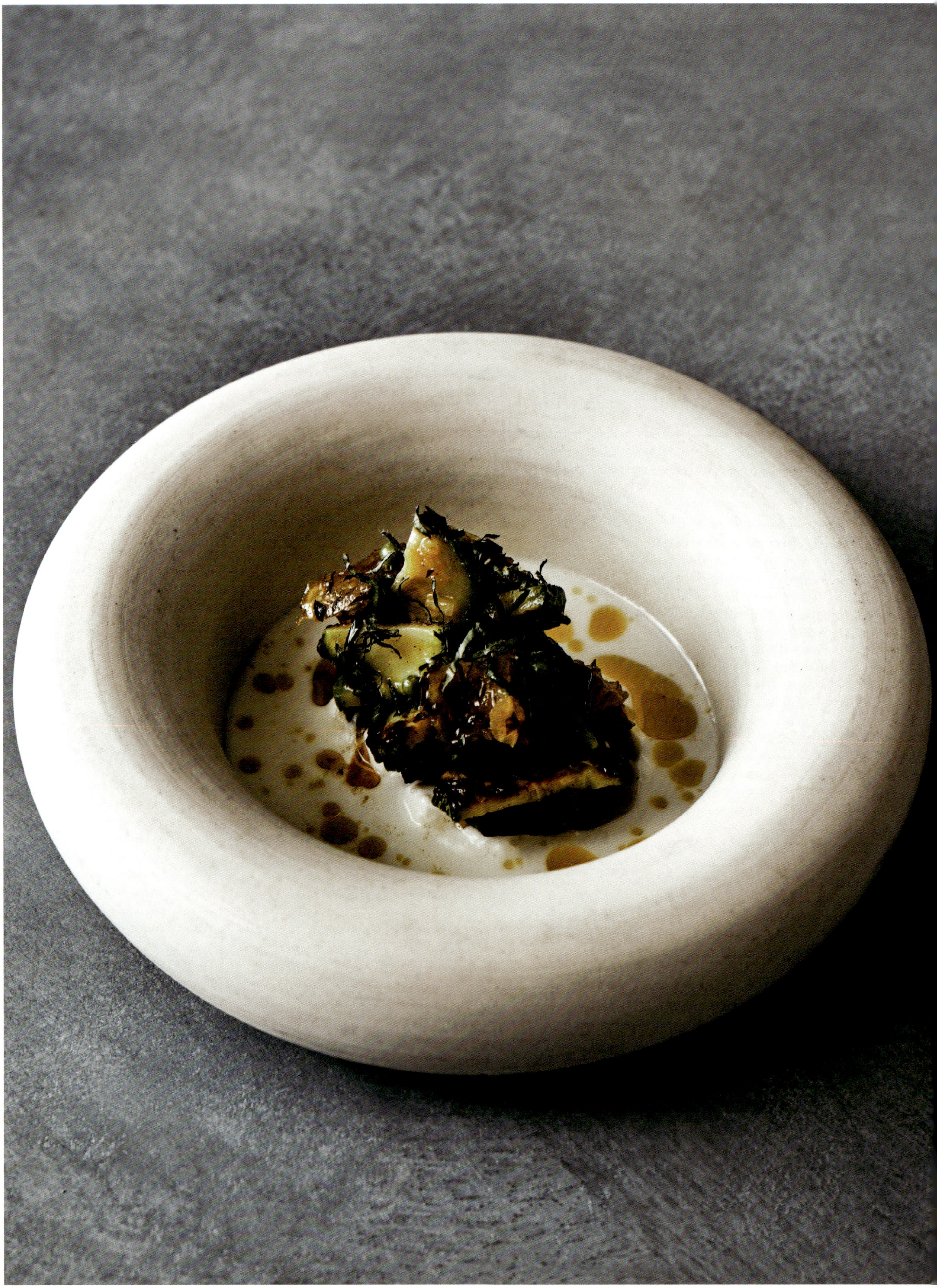

CHARRED ZUCCHINI, SALTED BUTTERMILK & MARJORAM

I love the pairing of summer squash with fresh cheese or buttermilk. For this one, we made a dressing from salted buttermilk and burrata cheese. Zucchini that retains some texture is interesting, so for this next dish we grilled zucchini very hard and fast until it was just beginning to char. We then dressed that in a chimichurri, some fresh marjoram from our garden, lacto-fermented green tomato, fresh tomato, and fresh coriander berries from our garden. Lastly, we finished it with a lovely olive oil from France with the taste of preserved black olives and an amazing peppery finish.

---

chimichurri

garlic, minced fine	30g	Mix all ingredients but the herbs together. Before serving, fold in the herbs.
shallot, minced	40g	
parsley leaves, minced fine	25g	
flowering marjoram, minced fine	5g	
white balsamic vinegar	90mL	
olive oil	110mL	
lemons, juiced and zested	2ea	
salt	t.t.	
black pepper	t.t.	
Aleppo pepper	t.t.	

salted buttermilk

buttermilk	1L	Allow to steep at room temperature for 7 days. Pass through a fine-mesh strainer and reserve.
kosher salt	20g	
garlic cloves, minced	12g	

additional ingredients & to finish

lacto-fermented green tomato, small dice
fresh heirloom tomatoes, peeled and small diced
fresh coriander berries
burrata, fine dice
CastelineS Noir D'Olive
zucchini, washed well

Slice the zucchini into ¼"-thick half-moons, toss in a small amount of neutral oil, and grill quickly on one side until they begin caramelizing but are still firm. Mix the burrata with some of the salted buttermilk to resemble the texture of a blue cheese dressing. Mix the chimichurri with equal parts of the fermented green tomato and fresh tomato, and fold in the grilled zucchini. Spoon some of the buttermilk dressing into the bottom of a bowl, and top with the zucchini mixture and some fresh coriander berries. Finish with Noir D'Olive, a French olive oil, or another peppery, aromatic olive oil.

GRILLED MUSSELS & CANTALOUPE KIMCHI "JJIGAE"

This dish came about from my love of Korean seafood dishes. One of my favorites here in town is at a restaurant called Hai Won Dai. They serve spicy braised octopus stir-fried with vegetables, or Ojinguh Bokum. We had just received some beautiful Korean melons from one of our local farmers. I wanted to do a spicy mussel soup base, thicken it to just be able to glaze grilled mussels, and finish it all with the melons, cut to order and dressed in a kimchi made from leftover cantaloupe pulp. We finished it with some thin slices of Korean chili for some fresh spice and pepper flavor.

---

cantaloupe kimchi

cantaloupe pulp (leftover from juicing)	900g
garlic, minced	30g
ginger, minced	22g
Aleppo chile flake	12g
Fresno chile, roughly chopped	60g
green onion, minced	45g
fish sauce	20g
honey	15g
salt	22g

Puree all ingredients and seal in a Cryovac bag on full pressure. Allow to ferment in a warm place for a minimum of 14 days.

steamed mussels

mussels	10lbs
sweet vermouth	1 (750ml) bottle
Korean soup stock	2 pouches
ginger	40g
shallot	150g
garlic, halved	1 head

Wash the mussels in cold water until completely purged. Place all ingredients in a wide rondeau, cover with a lid, and bring to a boil over medium-high heat. Once the mussels have opened, remove them, and continue to reduce the mussel stock to 1,000mL. Pass through a fine-mesh strainer; cool and reserve. Remove the mussels from the shells and remove the beards from the mussels. Cool immediately.

mussels soup base

Korean chilies	40g
shallot	25g
grapeseed oil	40g
garlic	8g
gochujang	25g
Aleppo	12g
fermented green plum honey	50mL
mussel stock (reserved from cooking)	1L
tsuyu soup base	32mL
xanthan gum	.15%

Roast chilies, shallot, and garlic in grapeseed oil over medium-high heat. Add gochujang and Aleppo and cook until aromatic, 4 to 5 minutes. Next, add the honey and bring to a boil, but do not let it burn. Add mussel stock and soup base, scraping any fond from the bottom of the pan. Reduce to 660g. Place in a Vitamix with the xanthan gum and puree on high speed. Pass through a chinois and reserve.

mussel paste

mussels, cured and smoked (not dried)	175g
mussel garum lees	12g
doenjang	125g

Puree until as smooth as possible. Reserve in a piping bag.

additional ingredients & to finish

Korean melon, peeled and sliced into ¼"-thick slices (same length as mussels)
Korean chilies, julienned into 1" pieces
hanguk seasoning

Dress three mussels in a little neutral oil, and grill until they begin to char. Place a small amount of mussel paste on the bottom of a plate. Place the mussels side by side on top of the fudge and glaze in the soup. Toss the sliced melon with the cantaloupe kimchi, and shingle over the mussels. Finish with a few pieces of the julienned chile and some of the hanguk seasoning.

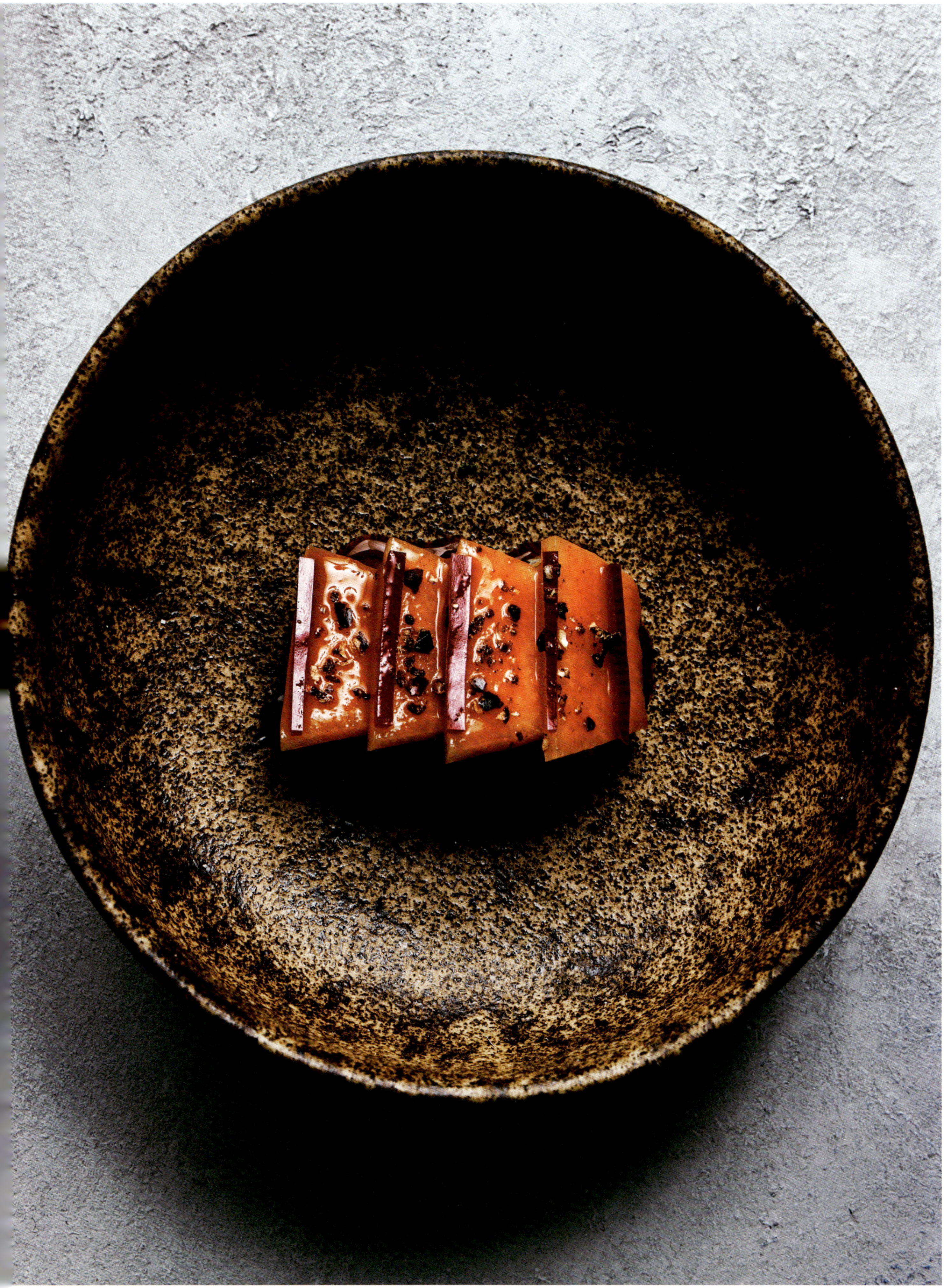

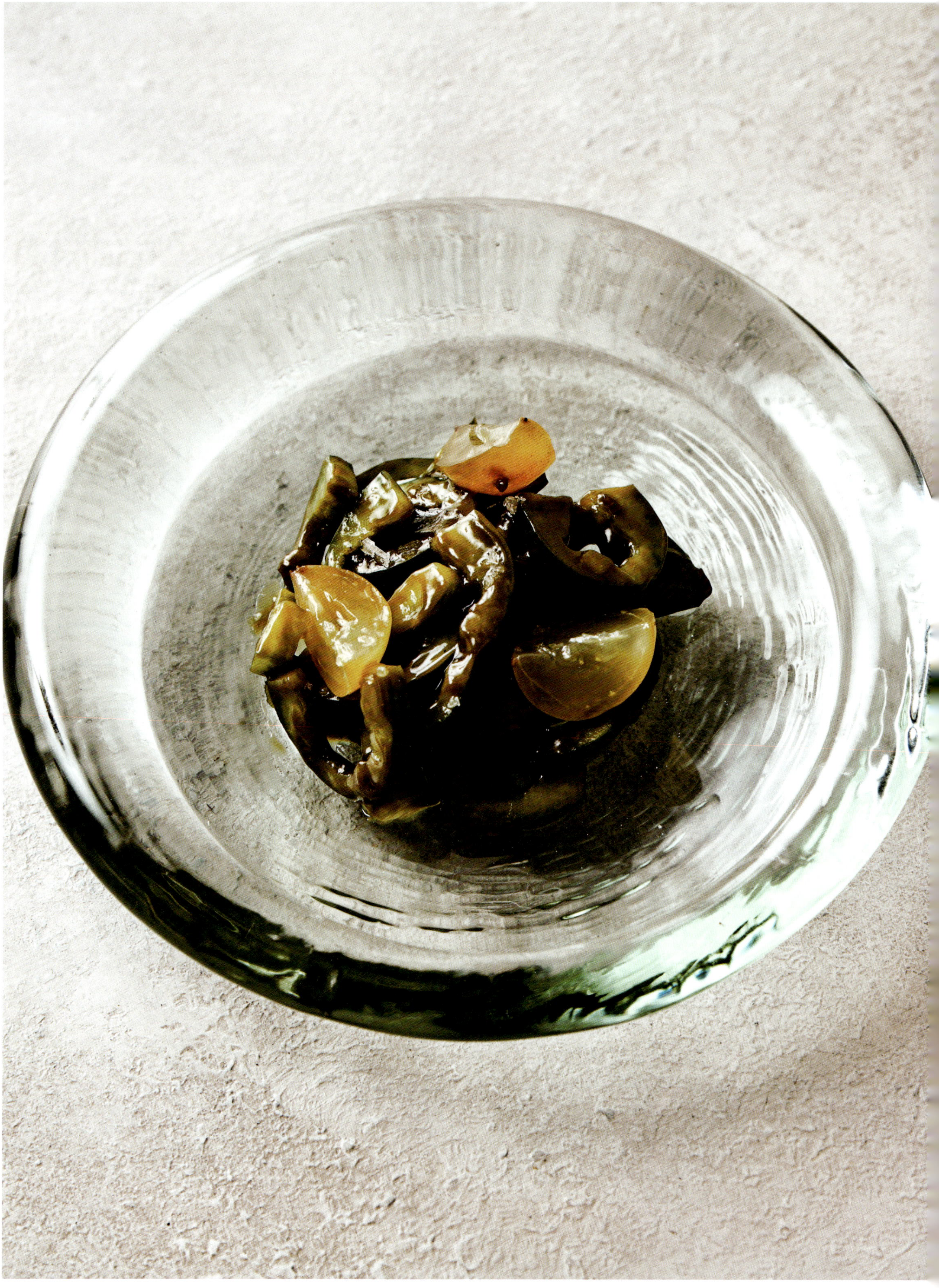

SALAD OF GREEN PEPPER, SCUPPERNONG & PISTACHIO

This dish is very special to me. I wasn't sure how the guests were going to react to it, but I decided to go for it anyway. When I was young, we moved in with my grandmother. In the summer, she would go out to her garden, pick fresh green bell peppers, slice them, and make a peanut-butter-and-pepper sandwich. The first time I saw her do it, I asked her "What the heck are you doing?" She replied "Haven't you ever had a green-pepper-and-peanut-butter sandwich before?" She knew very well that I never had, but I tried it anyway. To my surprise, it actually wasn't that bad. I appreciate it more now than I did back then. For this dish, we would make a pistachio vinaigrette in a mortar and pestle a la minute. We would cut the green pepper to order, dress the slices directly in the bowl of the mortar, and serve it with cured foie gras and scuppernong grapes that were cut right before serving. There is something about the skin of a freshly cut scuppernong that has a similar grassy or "green" flavor to the freshly cut peppers.

---

cured foie gras

rouge foie gras, sliced 1" thick and frozen	1kg
country ham cure	t.t.

Season liberally with the country ham cure. Place into a vacuum bag and place back in the freezer. Once frozen, seal at full pressure. Cook in a water bath at 60°C for 30 minutes. Chill and allow to mature in the refrigerator for 3 days. Dice into 1½" × 1½" squares and keep cold.

pistachio dressing

shallot, minced fine	4g
Maldon sea salt	pinch
pistachio butter	34g
pistachio oil	14g

In a mortar and pestle, add the shallots and salt. Mash until a smooth paste begins to form. Add the pistachio butter and continue to mix well. Slowly emulsify in the pistachio oil. Adjust the seasoning as needed with more of the salt, pistachio butter, or pistachio oil.

additional ingredients & to finish

scuppernong, seeded and quartered
green bell pepper or other sweet green pepper, deseeded
Maldon sea salt

Place a piece of the foie gras in the center of a plate and season with a pinch of sea salt. Slice the peppers into ¼"-thick slices about 1" to 1½" in diameter. Toss the peppers and grapes with the dressing, and spoon over the foie gras.

DRY-AGED ORA KING SALMON, RASPBERRY & ANGELICA

In our attempt to buy as much as possible and eliminate as much waste as possible, we found (as you can probably tell by now) that fermentation and the depth of flavor it adds has become a basis in most of our dishes. The next bite here was a nice acidic contrast to the rich pepper-and-foie-gras dish. We dressed dry-aged ora king salmon in a vinaigrette made from fermented raspberry juice, raspberry vinegar-soaked raspberry pearls, and an oil made from loquat pits, which lends a bitter almond flavor to the dish. Lastly, we finished it with an angelica-infused almond milk mousse and freeze-dried raspberries.

---

almond angelica puree

shallot	30g
angelica root	3g
butter	25g
mirin	20g
sake	30g
white shoyu	65g
almond milk	420g
salt	t.t.
scalded cream, cooled	100g
agar-agar	1%

Sweat the shallot and angelica in the butter until the shallots begin to soften. Add the mirin and sake and cook until all the alcohol has burned off. Next, add the white shoyu and almond milk and bring to a simmer for 10 minutes. Puree until smooth and pass through a fine-mesh strainer into a sauce pot. Using a bamix or stick blender, shear in the agar-agar, followed by the scalded cream. Bring to a simmer for 2 minutes. Season to taste with salt. Pass through a chinois into a shallow tray and allow to completely cool. Once cooled, cut the gel into cubes, and puree in a Vitamix on high speed until completely smooth. Pass through a fine-mesh strainer into an ISI canister and charge with two no. 2 charges. Allow to cool, shaking every 15 minutes or so.

loquat oil

loquat pits	40g
grapeseed oil	200mL

Puree on high in a Vitamix to a temperature of 65°C. Allow to strain through a coffee-filter-lined fine-mesh strainer. Cool and reserve.

additional ingredients & to finish

aged ora king salmon belly, brunoised and kept chilled
raspberry pearls
Jean-Marc Montegottero Huilerie Beaujolaise Vinaigre de Framboise
freeze-dried raspberries
Pacific sea salt

Marinate the raspberry pearls in the raspberry vinegar for a minimum of 2 hours. Place two ounces of the diced salmon on a plate and dress with the loquat oil, Pacific sea salt, and a spoonful of the marinated raspberry pearls. Cover with the angelica mousse and finish by crushing a few freeze-dried raspberry pieces over the mousse.

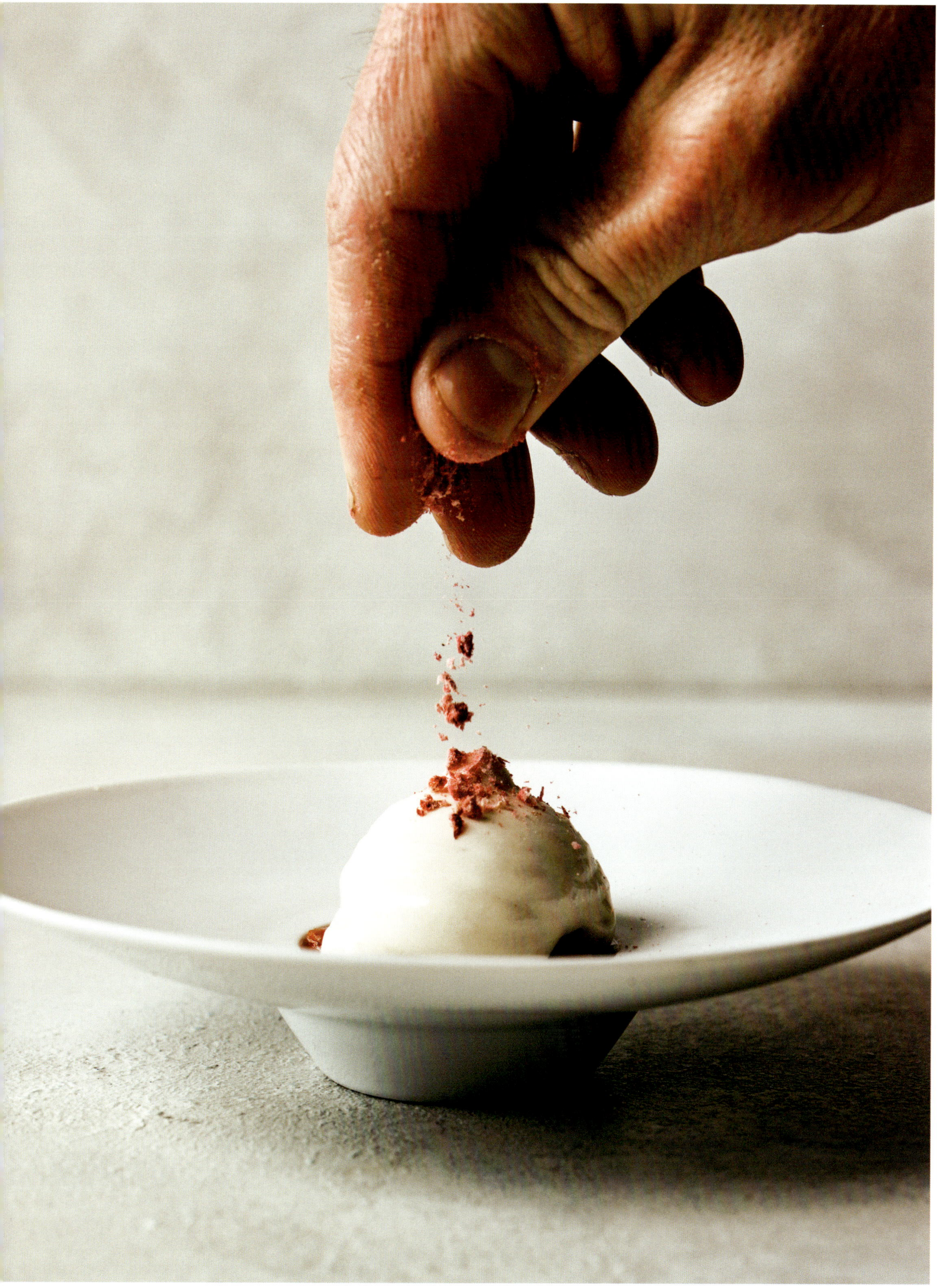

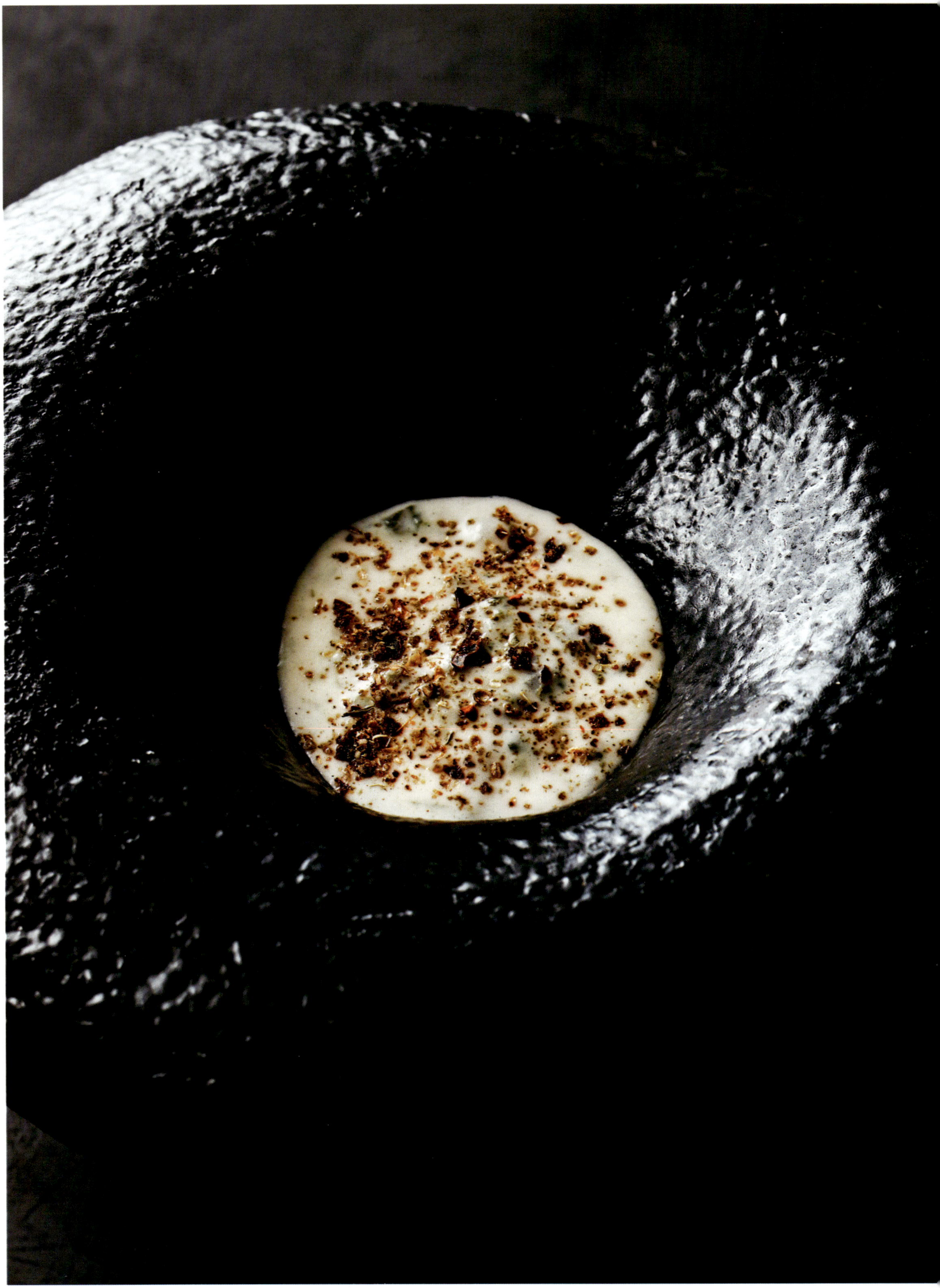

NORWEGIAN LANGOUSTINE, FERMENTED RAMPS, HICKORY KING CORN GRITS

This is essentially shrimp and grits. At Husk, we had an ever-changing shrimp and grits on the menu, and I kind of missed getting to come up with different variations of them. This version used live langoustine from Norway that we cooked down in a butter made from the shells, served with Hickory King corn grits seasoned with a popcorn shio koji and warm butter sauce made from ramps fermented like white kimchi.

---

half-sour ramps

white vinegar	750mL
Lindera Farms ramp vinegar	750mL
filtered water	750mL
sugar	240g
salt	120g
turmeric, ground	2.5g
celery seed	6.5g
mustard seed	14g
chili flake	7g
coriander seeds	7g
garlic, sliced thin	20g
fresh dill, stems and leaves	180g
lacto-fermented ramps	1kg

Bring all the ingredients except the ramps to a boil. Allow to cool to room temperature, adjust the pH to 4.6 by adding more white vinegar as needed. Add the ramps and cool completely. Once cooled, seal on full pressure in a Cryovac bag and allow to age for one month.

langoustine consommé

langoustine heads	500g
miso consommé	250g
filtered water	250g
egg whites	2ea

Blend the heads with the miso consommé and water. Whisk in the egg whites, and seal in a Cryovac bag on full pressure. Steam in a Rational at 87°C for 30 minutes. Allow to strain through a coffee-filter-lined mesh strainer. Cool and reserve.

half-sour ramp butter

shallot, sliced thin	35g
garlic, sliced thin	5g
sweet vermouth	185mL
half-sour ramp brine	75mL
langoustine consommé	185mL
xanthan gum	.25g
butter, cubed	205g

Reduce the shallot, garlic, vermouth, ramp brine, and consommé to 205g. Place in a Vitamix, add the xanthan gum, and puree on high speed until completely smooth. Slowly emulsify in the butter. Pass through a chinois and reserve in a warm place.

popcorn shio

popped popcorn	205g
rice koji	205g
filtered water	550mL
kosher salt	96g

Blend all ingredients together and seal in a Cryovac bag on full pressure. Allow to ferment in a warm place for 7 to 10 days. Cool and reserve until needed.

langoustine butter

langoustine shells chopped into 2" pieces	12ea
butter	2lb
garlic	25g
bay leaf	1ea

Bring all the ingredients to a boil and cook until the butter has clarified.

additional ingredients & to finish

cooked grits	
langoustine tail, small dice	
half-soured ramps, chopped fine	
lemon juice	
hanguk seasoning	

Season the grits with the popcorn shio and salt, and mount with butter until creamy. Gently warm the langoustine tails in the langoustine butter. Place a spoonful of grits in a bowl and top with the langoustine, being sure to strain off the butter. Season with fresh lemon juice. Fold a spoonful of the chopped ramps into the ramp butter and completely cover the shrimp. Season to taste with the hanguk.

AMADAI WITH A CURRY OF FERMENTED GOLDEN BEET

One of my favorite fishes is tilefish. For this particular dish, we used amadai, or Japanese tilefish. Amadai are great because you can actually eat the scales if cooked properly. In this preparation, the fish is cleaned, lightly seasoned before cooking, and then slowly roasted by pouring hot oil over the scales. This not only crisps up the scales but also slowly cooks the fish. We served it with a sauce made from a reduction of fermented golden beet juice, house-made vadouvan spice, and a pistachio dukkah. We also dressed it in some fermented golden beet juice and lime zest added at the last second.

---

golden beet vadouvan

vadouvan spice	30g
coconut fat	60mL
coconut milk	500mL
golden beet juice	500mL
makrut lime leaf	1ea
butter, cubed	100g
soy lecithin	2.5g

Toast the vadouvan in the coconut fat over medium heat. Add the coconut milk, beet juice, and lime leaf. Bring to a simmer and allow to cook for 15 minutes. Pass through a fine-mesh strainer, mount in the butter, and add the soy lecithin. Reserve warm until needed.

dukkah

Sicilian pistachio	125g
sesame seeds	70g
shredded coconut	12g
fennel seed	9g
cumin seed	3g
coriander seed	3g
espelette pepper	1g
black peppercorns	.5g

Toast all the ingredients at 325°F for 5 minutes. Remove from the oven and stir well and return for another 5 minutes. After 10 minutes, allow to cool completely and roughly chop in a robot coupe. Reserve in an airtight container.

lacto-fermented golden beet juice

golden beet juice	1L
kosher salt	20g

Place in a Cryovac bag and seal on full pressure. Allow to ferment a minimum of 14 days. Pass through a coffee-filter-lined fine-mesh strainer, cool, and reserve.

additional ingredients & to finish

lemon juice	
lime zest	
amadai, scales left on, cut into 56g portions	
500mL neutral oil	

Heat the oil to 180°C. Place the amadai on a roasting rack-lined half hotel pan. Slowly ladle the oil over the fish, roasting the scales and cooking the fish to medium-well. Take care not to burn the scales or overcook the fish. Place the fish in a serving bowl and season with the fermented beet juice, a spoonful of dukkah, and lime zest. Season the beet curry with fresh lemon juice to taste, rewarm, and aerate with a bamix or immersion blender. Spoon a couple of ounces around the fish and serve immediately.

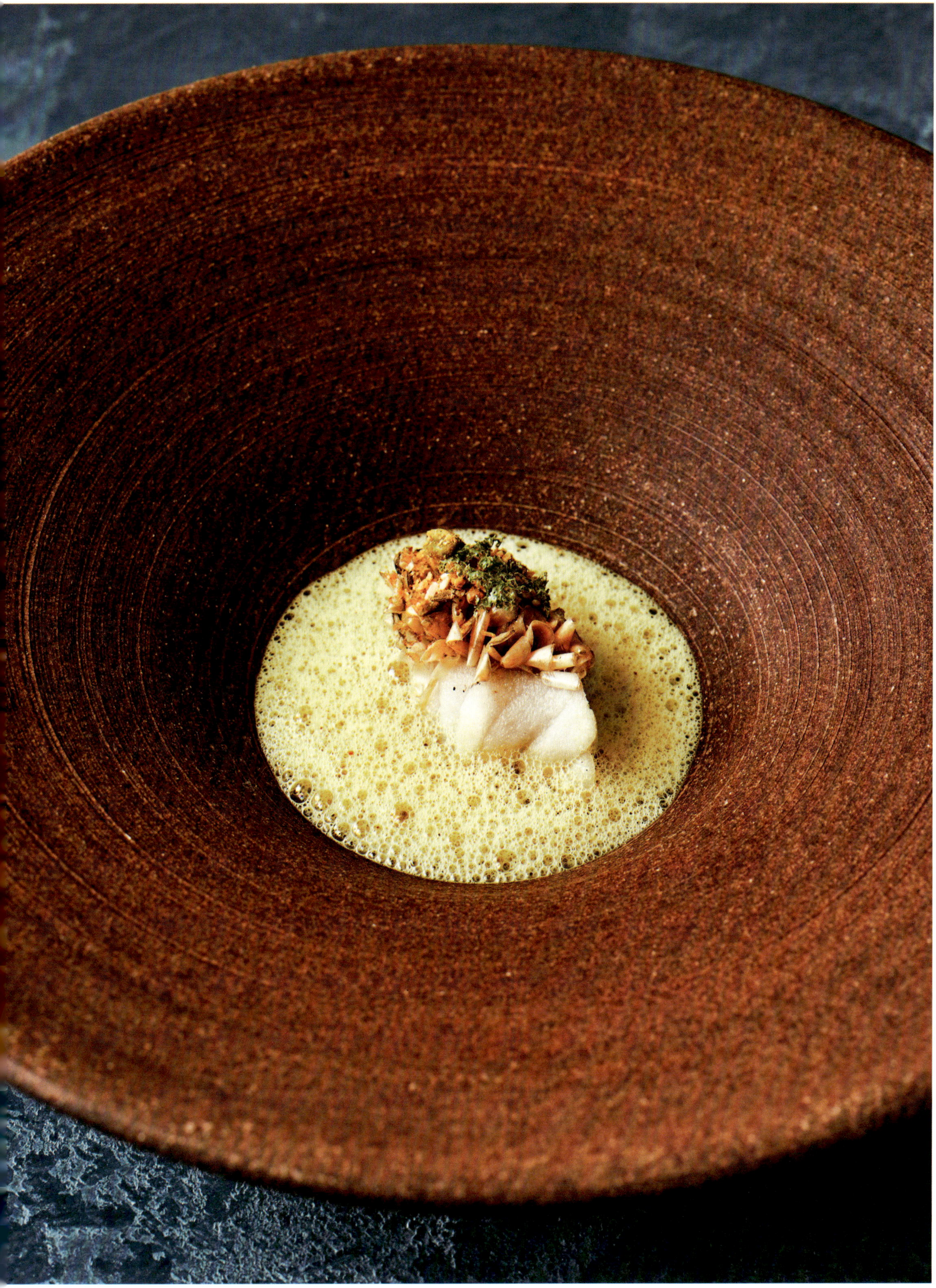

DEVIL'S GULCH RANCH SQUAB, ROMANESCO & PECHUGA

The idea for this dish came from talking with our opening beverage director Cole Just. We were discussing how cool it would be to do a Southern-style pechuga mezcal made by hanging a country ham over the still during the distillation. Pechuga mezcal is a type of mezcal made by hanging a chicken breast above the still during the final distillation. Other variations use rabbit, turkey, and jamon, among other things. For this dish, I decided to do dry-aged squab from Devil's Gulch Ranch that were cod-smoked and roasted quickly by basting, ladling hot oil over the squab. We finished it by slowly roasting it over hardwood charcoal and constantly glazing with a honey infused with dried chilies and pechuga. The sauce was made from roasting shallots in foie gras fat, deglazing with pechuga and mango vinegar, and adding a stock made from the smoked squab carcasses charred on the grill after carving. We served it alongside Romanesco roasted in foie gras fat and dressed in a Marcona almond salsa macha, a tamale made from fresh masa, and a chorizo made from the squab legs. We topped the chorizo with a grilled avocado mayo.

---

squab chorizo

squab legs, diced into 1" pieces	485g
pechuga	10g
Lindera Farms ramp vinegar	10g
salt	7g
chipotle Morita powder	6g
onion powder	1.7g
smoked paprika	2g
guajillo powder	1.25g
white pepper, toasted and ground	.3g
cumin, toasted and ground	.3g
Mexican oregano	.3g

Dress the squab legs in the pechuga and vinegar and allow to marinate for 30 minutes. Place the legs in the freezer for 5 minutes. Grind through a medium die. Toss with the remaining ingredients and grind through the fine die. Reserve until needed.

tamale dough

room temperature duck fat	300g
fresh masa	1,000g
reduced squab stock	80g
salt	10g
baking powder	10g

Whip duck fat with whip attachment until light and airy. Add the remaining ingredients and whip with paddle attachment until well combined.

tamales

squab chorizo	
tamale dough	
corn husks	

Fill corn husks with 50g tamale dough stuffed with 20g squab chorizo. Steam at 212°F for 18 minutes.

salsa macha

Aleppo chile, smoked and dried	6g
Guajillo chile, dried	10g
Morita chile, dried	4g
Pasilla chile, dried	10g
Marcona almond	260g
sesame seeds	30g
garlic, minced	35g
olive oil	390g
thyme leaves	2g
Mexican oregano	3g
Omed cider vinegar	10g
Maldon sea salt	t.t.

Toast the chilies, allow them to cool, remove the seeds, and small-dice them. Set aside. Slowly cook the almonds, sesame seeds, and garlic in the olive oil over medium heat until the garlic and nuts begin to caramelize, 7 to 8 minutes. Stir in the chopped chilies and transfer to a robot coupe. Add the vinegar, thyme leaves, and oregano. Puree in the robot coupe until everything is coarsely chopped. Season to taste with sea salt, cool, and reserve.

grilled avocado mayo

grilled avocado	425g
Kewpie mayo	260g
sorrel	120g
vitamin C powder	3g
jalapeno	10g
salt	t.t.

Combine all ingredients. Puree in a Vitamix on high speed until completely smooth. Pass through a fine-mesh strainer and reserve in a piping bag.

squab jus

shallot	60g
foie fat	30g
sugar	50g
Jean-Marc's Huilerie Beaujolaise mango vinegar	40g
pechuga	90g
squab stock	675mL

Sweat the shallot in the foie fat over medium heat until it begins to caramelize. Add the sugar, vinegar, and pechuga. Reduce until it just begins to caramelize as if making a gastrique. Add the squab stock and bring back to a simmer. Reduce the heat and cook at a lazy simmer until the sauce is napé and thick enough to coat the back of a spoon.

honey pechuga glaze

garlic, minced fine	10g
pechuga	60g
clover honey	205g
Morita, dried	8g
chipotle, dried	4g

Bring all the ingredients to a boil in a small sauce pot. Remove from the heat, transfer to a small container, and reserve in a warm place until needed.

squab spice

coriander	35g
white pepper	12g
fennel seed	6g
bee pollen	17g
chipotle powder	2g
fennel pollen	5g
Spanish orange peel, dried	20g
Maldon sea salt	10g

Toast the coriander, white pepper, and fennel seed. Allow to cool. Mix with the remaining ingredients and grind in a spice grinder. Reserve in an airtight container.

additional ingredients & to finish

- aged squab breasts
- Romanesco, cut into bite-size pieces
- rendered duck fat
- lime juice
- lime zest
- espelette

For the Romanesco Place a Silpat-lined sheet pan in the oven and preheat to 425°F. Toss the Romanesco in rendered duck fat and season with salt. Dump onto the hot pan in the oven and roast until caramelized and tender. Season with lime juice, toss with the salsa macha, and place in a bowl. Finish with lime zest.

For the tamale Unwrap the tamale, top with the avocado mayo, and season with espelette.

For the breast Keep the aged breasts on the cage. Season liberally with salt. Slowly roast the breast over hardwood charcoal, glazing constantly with the honey. Allow the breast to rest, carve off of the cage, and return to the grill to crisp the skin. Brush one last time with honey glaze, season with the squab spice, and place on a serving plate. Dress with an ounce or two of the squab jus.

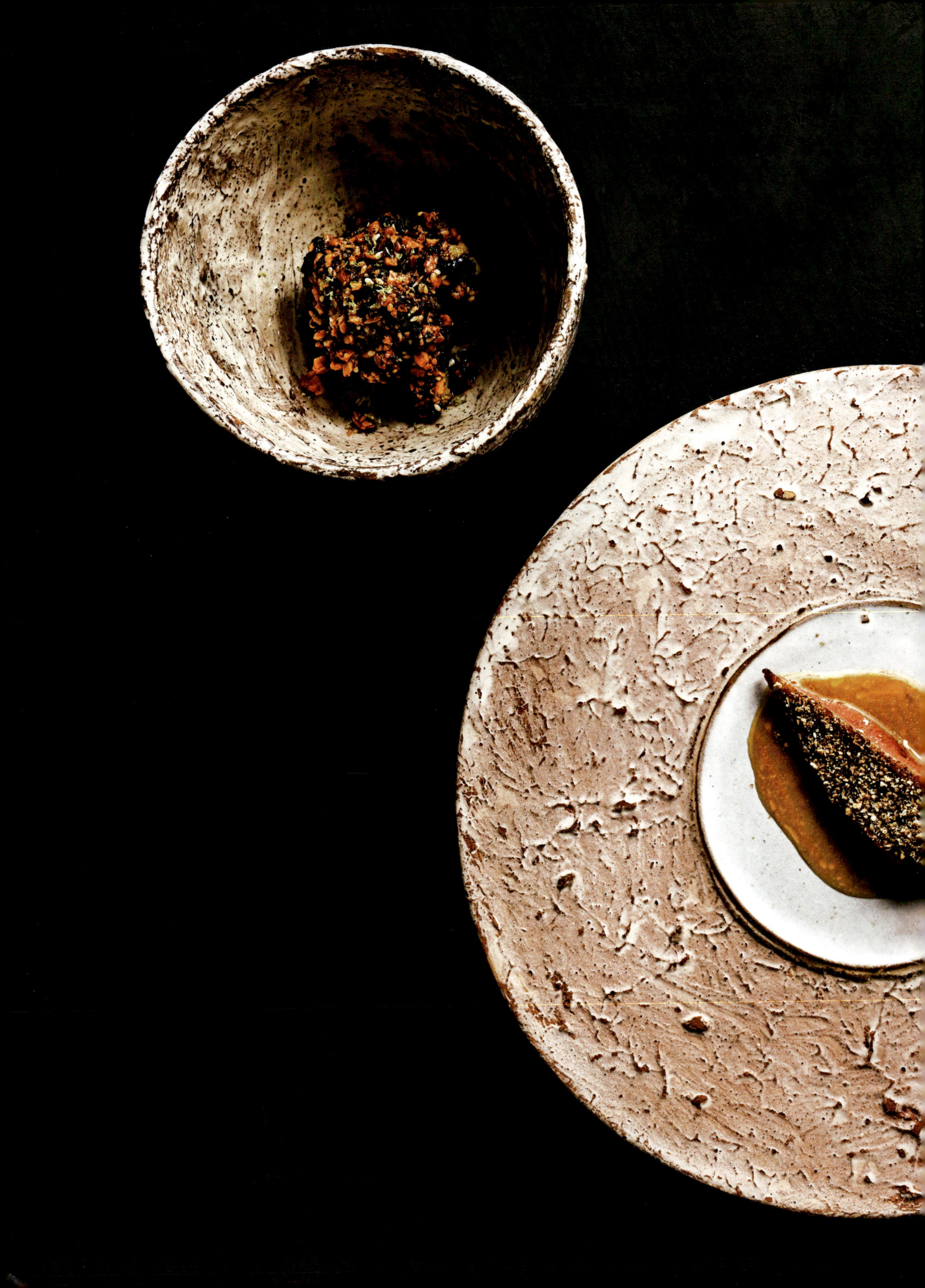

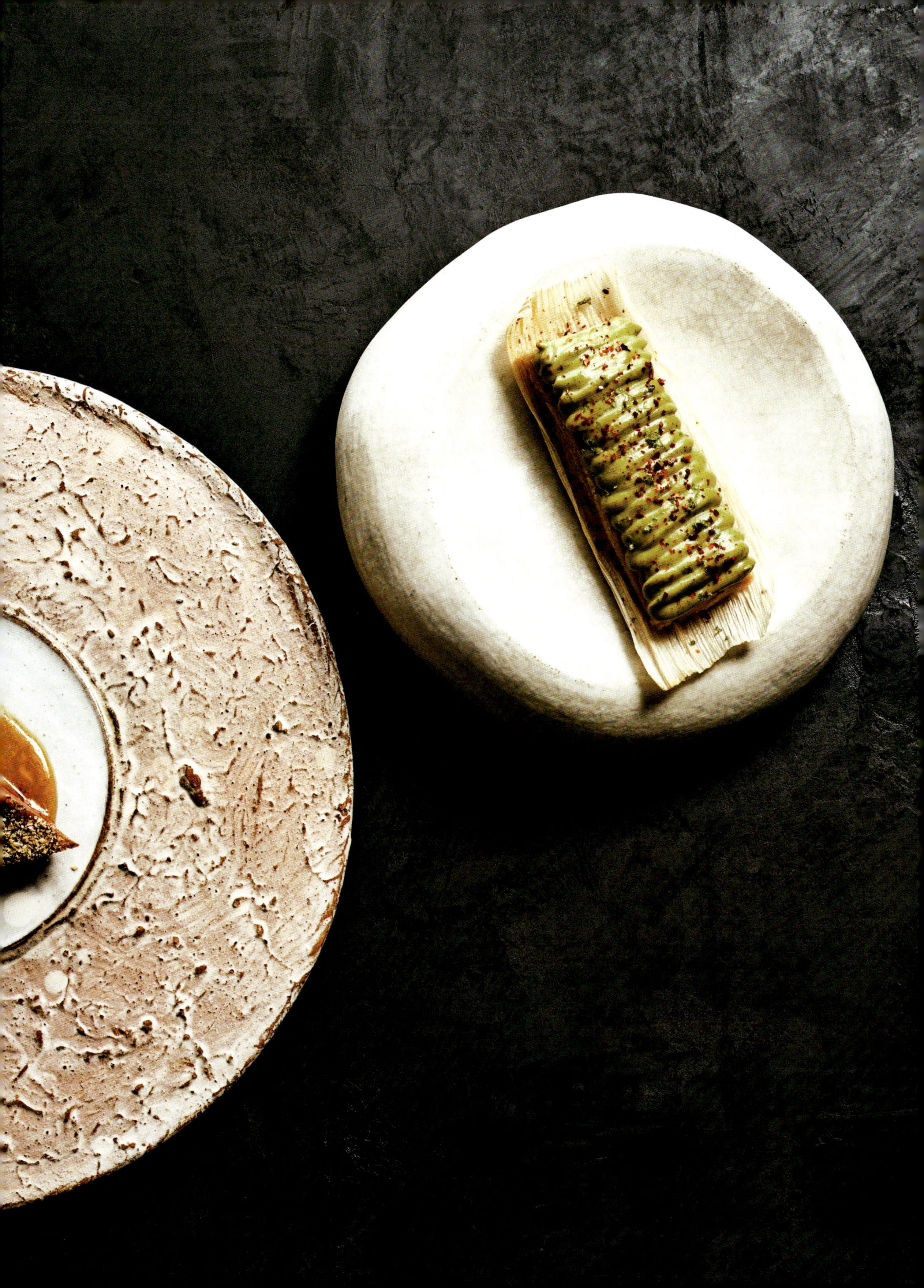

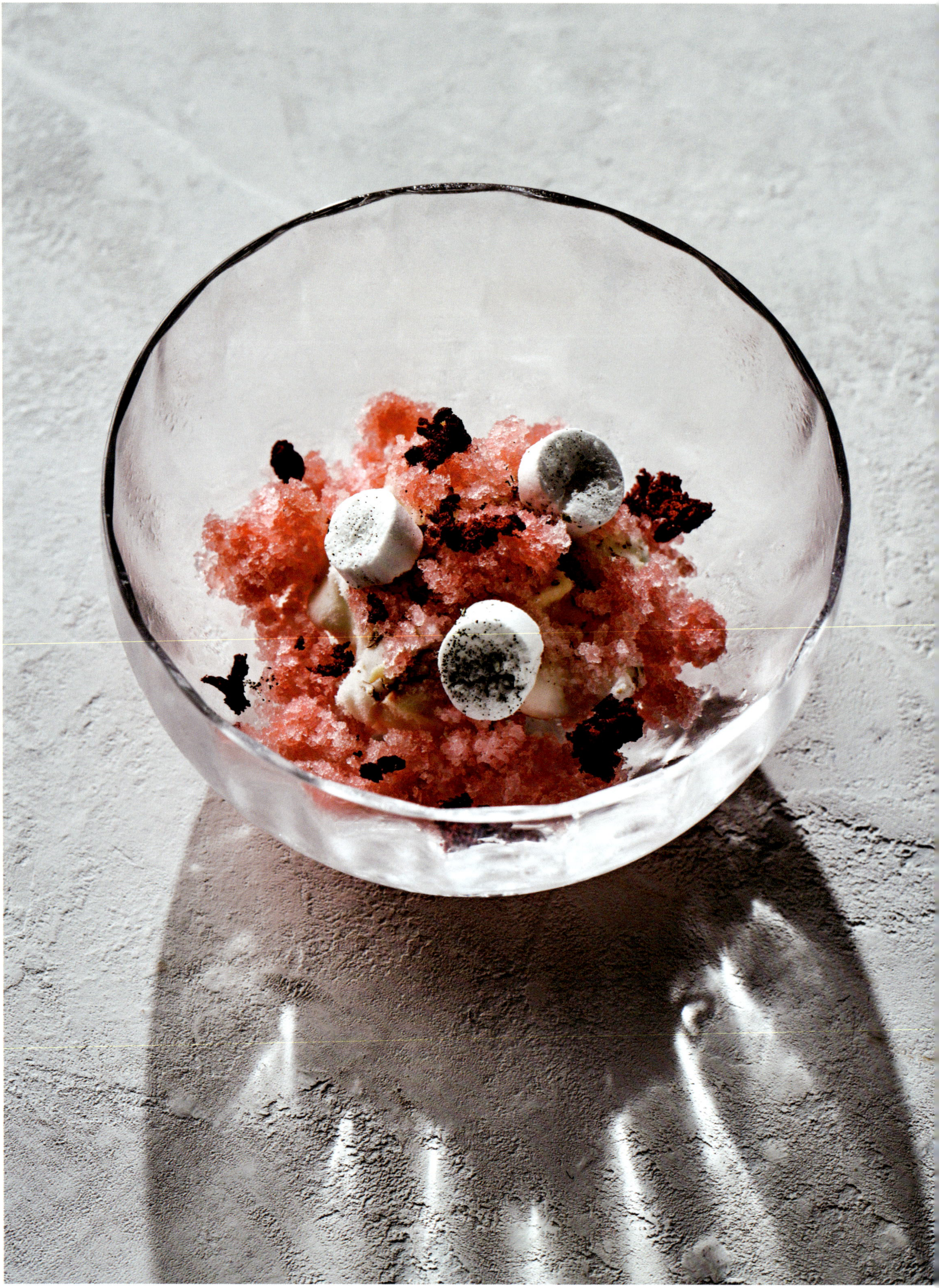

AMBROSIA SALAD

Usually, when you see ambrosia salad at a church potluck or family gathering, you rarely see it actually get eaten—though somehow, someone always makes it and adds it to the spread. I personally like ambrosia salad, which was sometimes the only way I could get something sweet off the dessert table as a kid. Our version consisted of rhubarb, preserved kumquat, grapes, sherbet made from coconut crème fraiche, pecan miso, freeze-dried cherries, and angelica root marshmallows.

---

coconut crème fraiche

sugar, split 15g/10g	25g	Mix 10g of sugar with the stabilizer and set aside. Bring the coconut milk and coconut water to a simmer over medium heat. Mix the 15g of sugar with the dextrose, and whisk into the coconut mixture, along with the trimoline. Bring it to 110°F and whisk in the stabilizer/sugar mixture, followed by the crème fraiche. Bring the mixture to 185°F, whisking constantly to prevent scorching. Pass through a fine-mesh strainer into a Paco canister and freeze immediately. Spin before serving.
Uno ice cream stabilizer	1g	
coconut milk	125g	
coconut water	150mL	
dextrose	70g	
trimoline	35g	
crème fraiche	100g	

rhubarb granita

rhubarb juice	400g	Combine ingredients. Freeze in a shallow pan until needed. Scrape with a fork before serving.
strawberry juice	500g	
drops of angelica root extract	10ea	

roasted pecan dressing

pecans, roasted at 350°F for 10 minutes, chopped fine	180g	Combine all ingredients. Puree in a Vitamix on high speed until as smooth as possible. Cool and reserve.
white miso	85g	
white shoyu	25g	
birch syrup	35g	
shallot, minced	10g	
grapeseed oil	140g	
ginger	5g	

celery leaf powder

celery leaf, picked, washed, and dried well	200g	Dry at 115°F for 2 hours or until completely dried. Grind to a fine powder and pass through a tea strainer.

angelica root meringue

egg whites, at room temperature	200g	Whip the whites in a stand mixer until soft peaks form. Add the cream of tartar and slowly add the sugar and whip to stiff peaks. Stir in the angelica root extract and transfer the mixture to piping bags. Pipe desired shape onto Silpat-lined sheet trays. Bake at 200°F for 2 to 2½ hours. Dust with the celery leaf powder and hold in a dehydrator set at 100°F until needed.
cream of tartar	1tsp	
granulated sugar	200g	
drops of angelica root extract	6ea	
celery leaf powder as needed		

additional ingredients & to finish

peeled concord grapes, sliced into ¼" coins	Place a teaspoon of the roasted pecan dressing in the bottom of a chilled bowl. Place a small spoonful of the sherbet in the bowl and mix in the grapes, kumquat, and roasted pecans. Place the mixture in the center of a bowl and top with a few shavings of the rhubarb granita, a few pieces of the angelica meringue, and some crushed freeze-dried cherry. Serve immediately.
preserved kumquat, quartered	
roasted pecans, chopped	
freeze-dried cherries	

SWEET CORN ICE CREAM, HUITLACOCHE & AUSTRALIAN WINTER TRUFFLE

I had never used huitlacoche for anything. I didn't even know what it tasted like, but I ordered a bunch anyway. Huitlacoche—or corn smut—is also called Mexican truffle. It is a fungus that grows off the kernels before the corn is fully developed and produces a puffy gray and sometimes black kernel with a very aromatic mushroom-like flavor. I decided it would be interesting to cook into a butterscotch. We served the butterscotch warm over a sweet-corn ice cream that was seasoned liberally with crunchy flakes of Maldon sea salt and fresh Australian winter truffles. The dish was very simple, but it was made quite flavorful by the depth of the huitlacoche and truffles.

---

huitlacoche butterscotch

cream	225g
huitlacoche	225g
sugar	400g
glucose	120g
mirin	100g
Nixta Licor de Elote (corn liqueur), divided 100g/30g	130g
salt	2g
butter	85g

Mix the cream and huitlacoche in a sauce pot and bring to a boil. Puree the mixture in a Vitamix on high speed until smooth. Pass through a fine-mesh strainer and reserve. Mix the sugar, glucose, mirin, and 100g of the Nixta Licor de Elote in a sauce pot and bring to 320°F. Whisk in the huitlacoche cream, being mindful that it will bubble as you add it in. Bring this mixture to 245°F. Remove from the heat and whisk in the salt, remaining 30g of Nixta Licor de Elote, and butter until completely emulsified. Cool and place in piping bags until needed.

corn ice cream

milk	480mL
heavy cream	480mL
granulated sugar, divided 165g/30g	195g
corn kernels, cobs reserved	700g
vanilla extract	7g
egg yolks	9ea
salt	t.t.

Bring the milk, cream, 165g sugar, corn, and corn cobs to a boil. Remove from the heat and cover for 30 minutes. Remove the corn cobs, puree with a bamix or immersion blender, and pass through a fine-mesh strainer into a clean sauce pot. Whisk the remaining sugar with the egg yolks until pale and airy, and slowly temper in the warm corn milk. Place back in the pot and cook over medium heat, stirring constantly with a rubber spatula to prevent scorching. Cook the mixture to 175°F. Season with salt, then pass through a fine-mesh strainer into Paco canisters and freeze immediately. Spin before serving.

additional ingredients & to finish

Australian winter truffle
Maldon sea salt

Warm the huitlacoche butterscotch. Spoon a small amount of ice cream into a bowl, and glaze with the huitlacoche butterscotch. Season with the sea salt and microplane desired amount of fresh truffle to top.

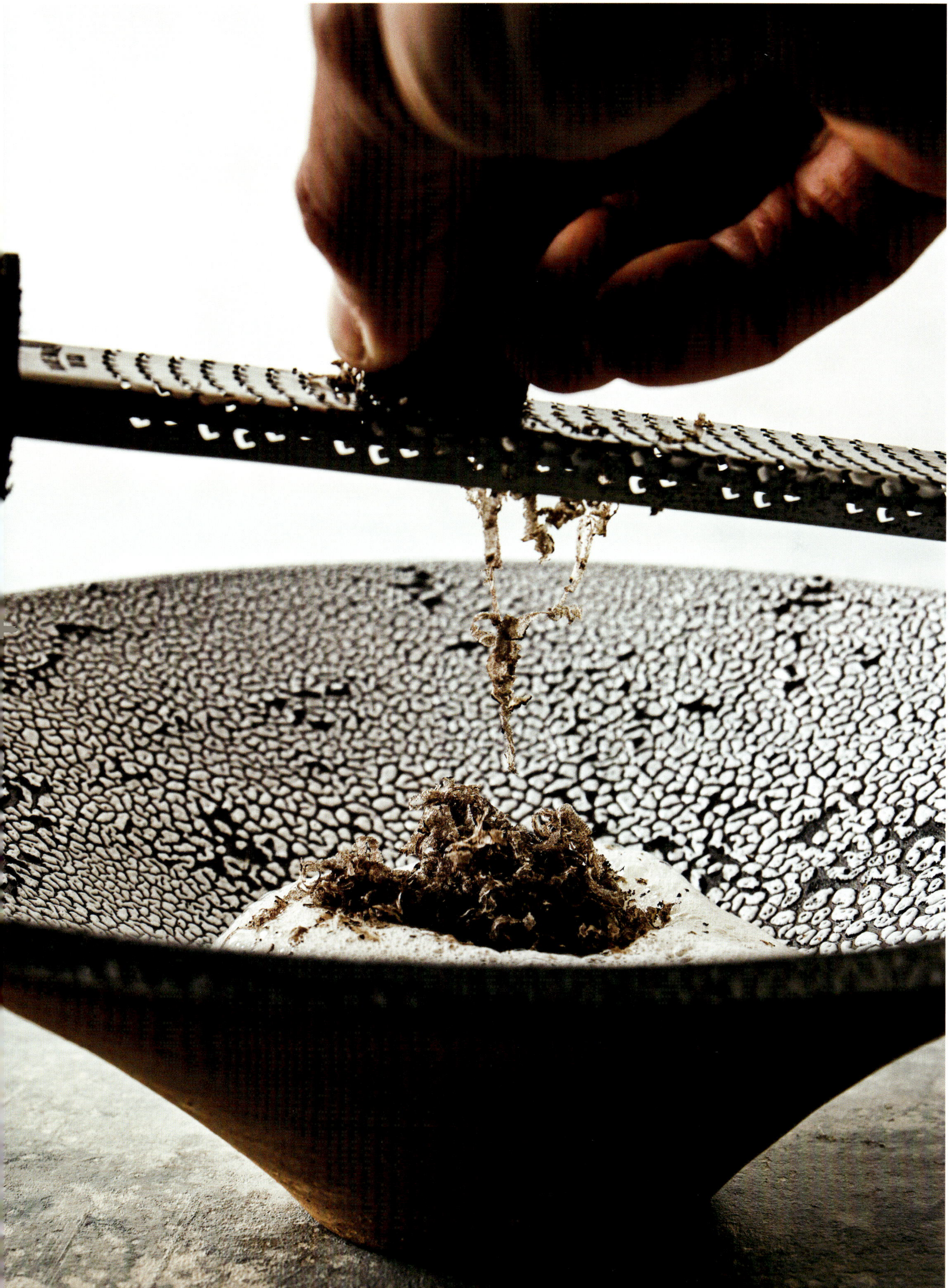

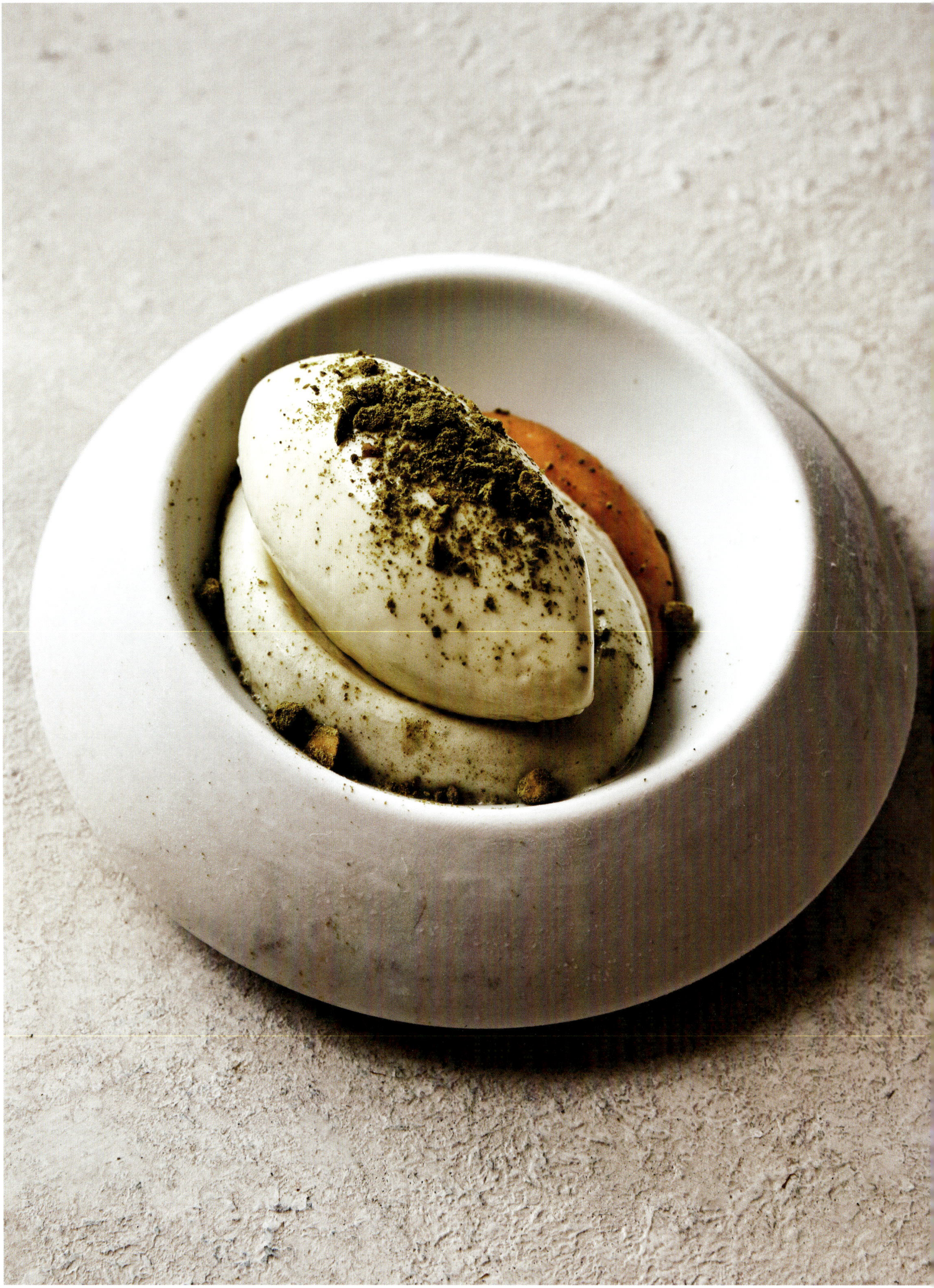

SEAWEED ICE CREAM, FERMENTED CUCUMBER & SEA URCHIN BUTTERSCOTCH PUDDING

One day, my sous chef, Connor Carlson, said he had something weird for me to taste, so I said "Okay." He gave me two quenelles side by side and said to make sure I got both in each bite. I wasn't quite sure what I had just eaten. It was a seaweed ice cream and fermented cucumber curd. It was almost like a sweet dill pickle. I didn't know what to think, but I couldn't stop eating it. I told him it needed something, but I wasn't sure what. In the middle of service, it came to me. I called him over and said "We need to make a butterscotch pudding with sea urchin." The dulse, or seaweed-like flavor, of the sea urchin, plus the natural sweetness it has, tied everything together, while the pudding added some richness. It freaked most people out; but once they got past sea urchin in a dessert, they cleaned the bowl . . . most of the time.

---

seaweed ice cream

milk	500mL
heavy cream	100g
grilled kombu	10g
seaweed powder	30g
sugar	100g
nonfat dry milk solids	50g
guar gum	1g
ice cream stabilizer	1g

Bring the milk, cream, and grilled kombu to a boil. Cover with a tight-fitting lid and steep for 30 minutes. Strain into a clean sauce pot and bring to a simmer over medium-high heat. Mix the remaining dry ingredients and slowly whisk into the milk/cream. Continue to whisk until the mixture returns to a simmer. Simmer for 3 minutes. Strain through a fine-mesh strainer. Freeze in a Paco container until needed. Spin 1 hour before using.

sea urchin butterscotch pudding

kosher salt	4g
cornstarch	20g
egg yolks	80g
milk	200g
sea urchin butterscotch	240g

Mix the salt and cornstarch together. In a medium-size sauce pot, bring the milk to a simmer. Whisk the cornstarch into egg yolks and temper in the milk. Add back to the pot and stir vigorously with a whisk until the mixture comes to a boil for one minute. Emulsify in the sea urchin butterscotch until completely combined. Season with more salt as needed. Pass through a fine-mesh strainer. Place in a shallow container covered directly with plastic wrap to prevent a skin from forming. Cool immediately. Before using, whip with a whisk until airy, transfer to a piping bag, and reserve.

fermented cucumber curd

granulated sugar	498g
egg yolks	15ea
granulated sugar	100g
water	138g
Uno ice cream stabilizer	1.3g
lacto-fermented cucumber juice	425g
butter, cubed and chilled	175g
mascarpone	300g

Beat 498g sugar and the egg yolks until creamy. Bring the 100g sugar, water, and stabilizer to a simmer. Whisk in the lacto-fermented cucumber juice and temper into the egg-yolk mixture. Cook until the mixture is napé or coats the back of a rubber spatula. Using a bamix or immersion blender, emulsify in the butter, followed by the mascarpone. Pass through a fine-mesh strainer into a Paco canister and chill immediately. Spin before using and place in a piping bag.

toasted pistachio

Sicilian pistachios, toasted and cooled	200g
seaweed powder	10g

Pulse together in a robot coupe until a coarse crumb is achieved.

additional ingredients & to finish

Pacific sea salt	

Pipe a small amount of the pudding into the bottom of a bowl. Place a quenelle of cucumber curd on top and flatten with the back of the spoon. Next, add a quenelle of the seaweed ice cream. Season with a pinch of Pacific sea salt and top with the pistachio crumble.

FALL 2021

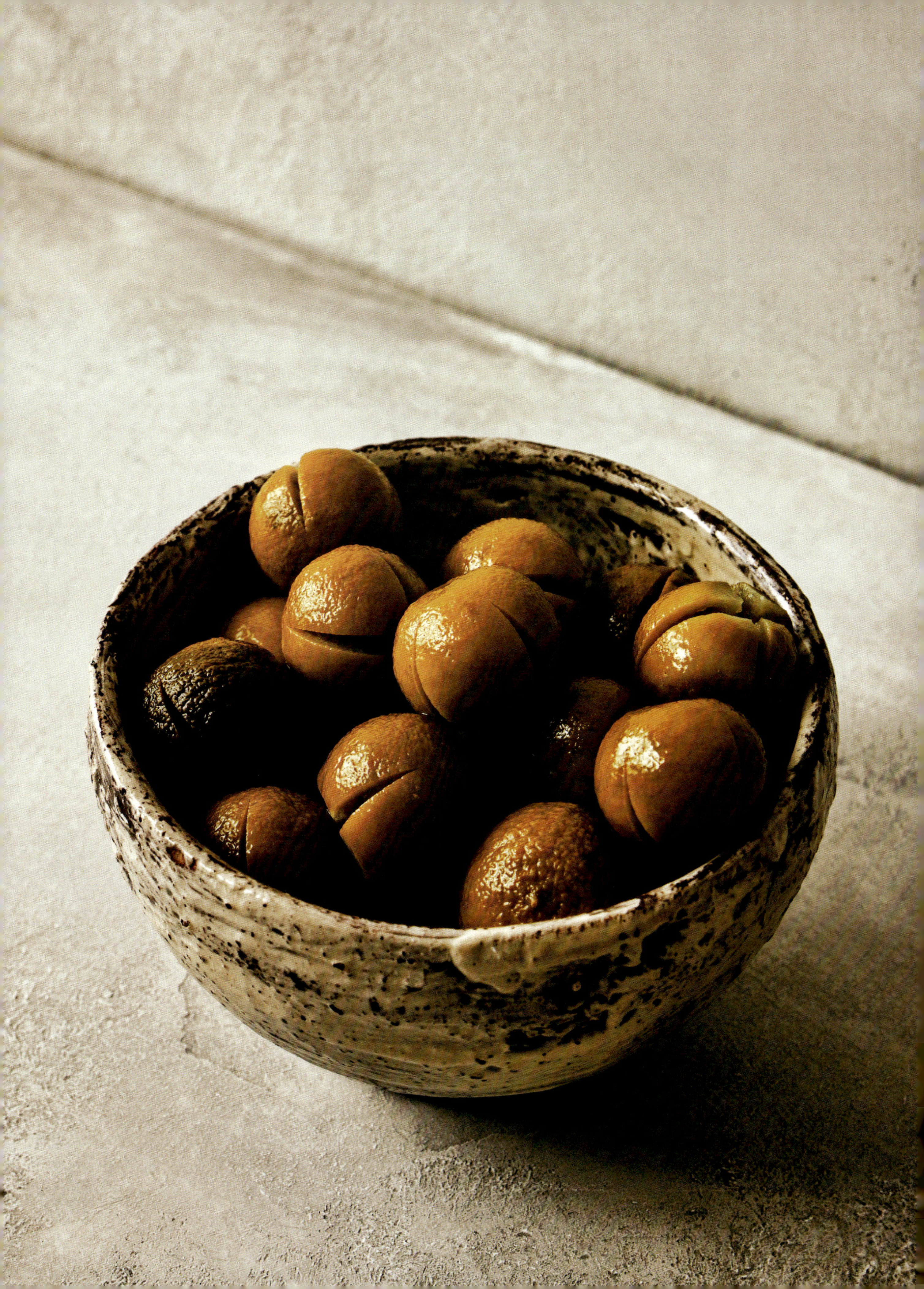

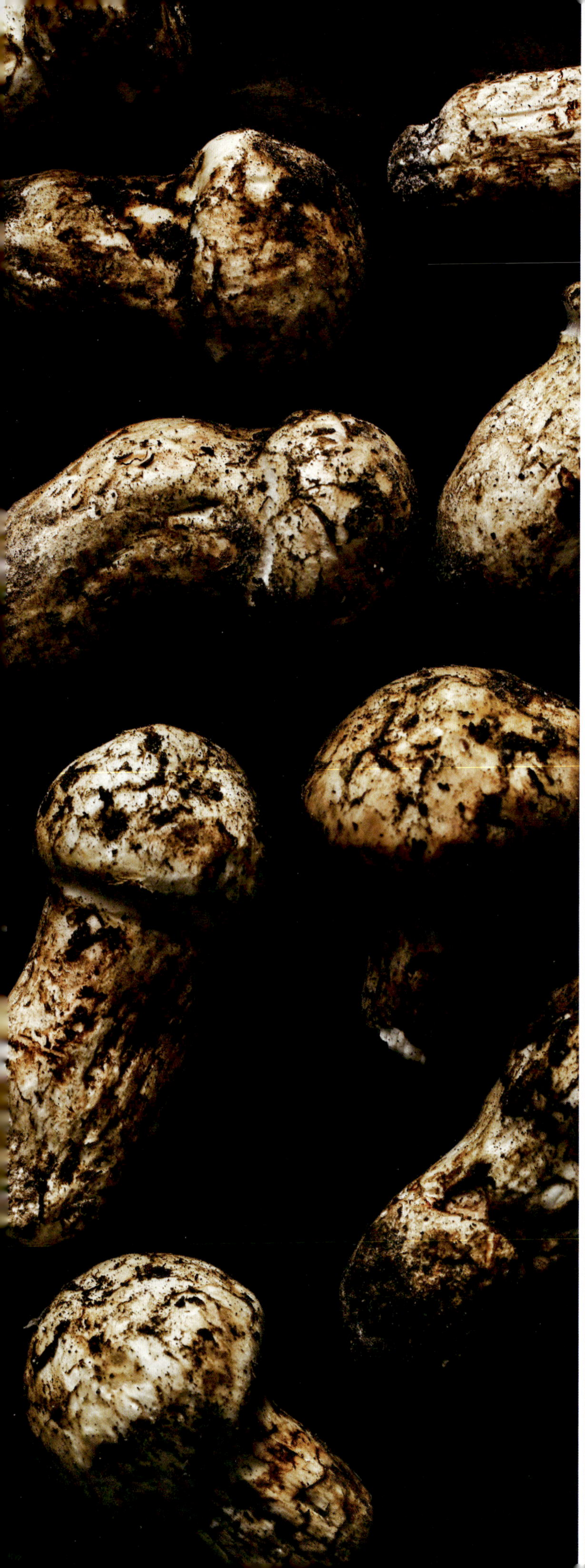
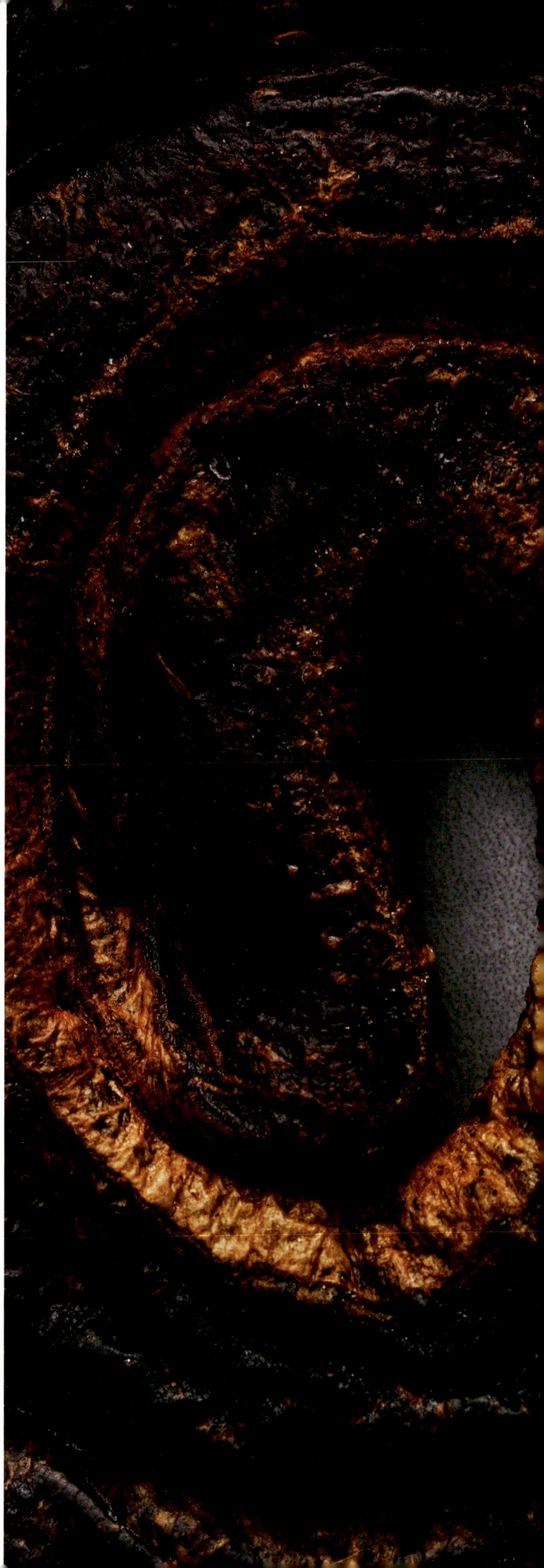

After making it through a hot and relatively dry summer season in Nashville, I wanted to focus on earthier flavors for this particular fall menu. I love the rustic qualities of a good oyster pie, so for our first bite I contrasted that with the richness of porter beer, making a cream sauce with it. As carrot season hit its peak, we decided to treat them like barbecue (page 185), roasting them in brown butter and finishing them on charcoal for a smoky intense character. Fermented sea buckthorns—a wild edible native to China but growing all over the Eastern Seaboard of North America as well—gave an herbaceous, oceanic quality to the dish backed up by blue mussels smoked with hay. It was one of my favorite dishes from this—or any—season.

To bring an earthy quality to squab liver mousse (page 182), I cooked down a few different types of alcohol: Calvados (French apple brandy), Madeira, and port all brought a new level of spice and caramel-like depth that I doubled down on by freeze-drying sheets of PX sherry and serving it alongside. My love for maitake mushrooms was once again on display as I treated them like steak in a dish with uni butterscotch and furikake. Slow-roasting the mushroom on coals intensified the meaty flavor, and we got plenty of great feedback on the dish from vegetarians and meat-eaters alike. Then we flipped it all on its head for the last course by serving matsutake mushrooms in a dessert. We made mushroom ice cream and served it with the bright citrus quality of Virginia Pine, a pine variety native to the Southeast and a nod to the fact that matsutake mushrooms are often found in pine-laden forests.

Some of the preservation techniques we leaned on for this season included black garlic, preserved Virginia Pine pine cones, cured tuna heart, and the aforementioned fermented sea buckthorn, which brought out a light note of anise in the flavor.

Credit: Brian Baxter

FALL 2021 MENU

oyster pie with porter beer cream **178**

tartare of toro sawara & otoro with japanese citrus & shiro dashi custard **181**

squab liver mousse, onion jam, crispy px sherry **182**

barbecued carrot, blue mussels & fermented sea buckthorn **185**

grilled maitake mushroom, uni butterscotch, furikake **186**

barely cooked scallops with brown butter roasted hazelnut **189**

charred broccoli, anchovy & cured tuna heart **190**

kani miso chawanmushi, burnt vanilla, matsutake & virginia pine **193**

dry-aged devil's gulch ranch squab with sunchokes, black garlic & malted milk **194**

———————

fig & coconut **199**

matsutake mushroom ice cream, preserved virginia pine cones, pine nut milk **200**

OYSTER PIE WITH PORTER BEER CREAM

This was a fun little bite and a nice start to our fall menu. A play on an oyster pie, we gently warmed oysters in a tart shell made with roasted kombu powder. We topped the pie with a cream we whipped to order and seasoned with the liquid from oyster shiokara and porter beer from Anchor Brewing. We finished by dusting it with a powder made from cured, smoked, and dried oysters.

---

kombu oil

kombu, roasted over hardwood coals	25g
grapeseed oil	250g

Combine and puree in a Vitamix until completely smooth. Allow to pass through a cheesecloth-lined fine-mesh strainer. Reserve the paste for another use.

tart dough

AP flour	450g
kosher salt	7g
kombu, roasted over hardwood coals, ground fine and sifted	10g
roasted kombu oil	225g
ice water	120g

In a robot coupe, mix the dry ingredients. Pulse in the kombu oil. Do not overmix. The dough should be a sandy texture. Lastly, pulse in the ice water, remove from the robot coupe, and quickly knead into a smooth dough. Do not let the dough get too warm and do not overmix it. Wrap in plastic and cool overnight.

To bake Roll dough to ⅛" thickness, punch circles large enough to fill 2" tart molds. Gently flatten the dough into the molds, add a second mold to the top, and trim away any excess dough. Place on a pass tray and top with a second tray. Bake at 325°F on fan 3 for 9 minutes. Remove the top passing tray, rotate the bottom tray 180°, and place back in the oven uncovered. Bake for an additional 9 minutes. Remove from the oven, allow to cool, and carefully transfer the tart shells to an airtight container.

oyster shiokara

oysters, washed well, shucked from their shells and free of any debris	500g
kosher salt	15g
mirin	30g
sake	30g
kombu, rinsed	10g
rice koji	18g
filtered water	250mL
bloomed gelatin	1%

Toss all ingredients except water and gelatin together well and seal in an appropriately sized Cryovac bag. Ferment under refrigeration for 2 weeks. Puree until smooth. Take 250mL filtered water and 1% bloomed gelatin of the total weight of the water and puree. To calculate the proper weight of gelatin, add the puree and 250mL of water and multiply by .01. Warm the water to melt the puree and blend with the oyster puree. Freeze in a shallow pan. Transfer to a cheesecloth-lined fine-mesh strainer and allow to defrost overnight. Reserve the clarified liquid.

oyster glaze

oyster liqueur, reserved from shucking	200mL
mirin	20mL
5-year aged kombu, rinsed	5g

Combine. Reduce over medium heat until a glaze is formed. Strain and cool.

additional ingredients & to finish

heavy cream
Anchor beer
kosher salt
lemon juice
smoked and dried oyster powder (see page 272)

Brush the oyster with the oyster glaze and grill on a fine-mesh grill screen, quickly, over hardwood. Transfer to the tart shell. Gently whip the cream until just before soft peaks begin to form. Season with a few drops of the beer, lemon juice, shiokara, and salt. Continue to whisk gently, adjusting the seasoning by adding more as needed. The pH of the cream will change, so be sure not to overwhip it. Top the oyster with the cream, and finish with a dusting of the smoked oyster powder. Serve immediately.

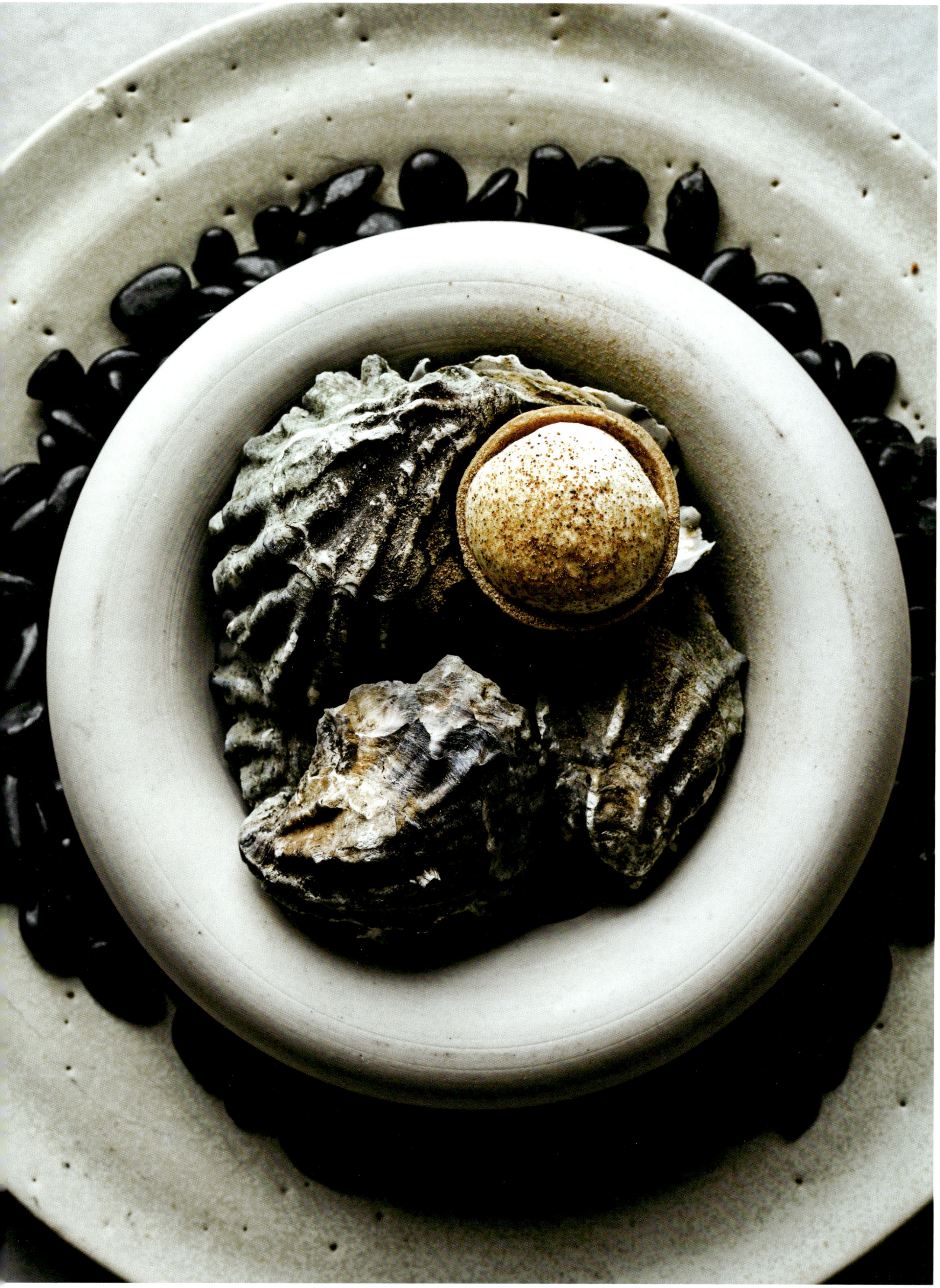

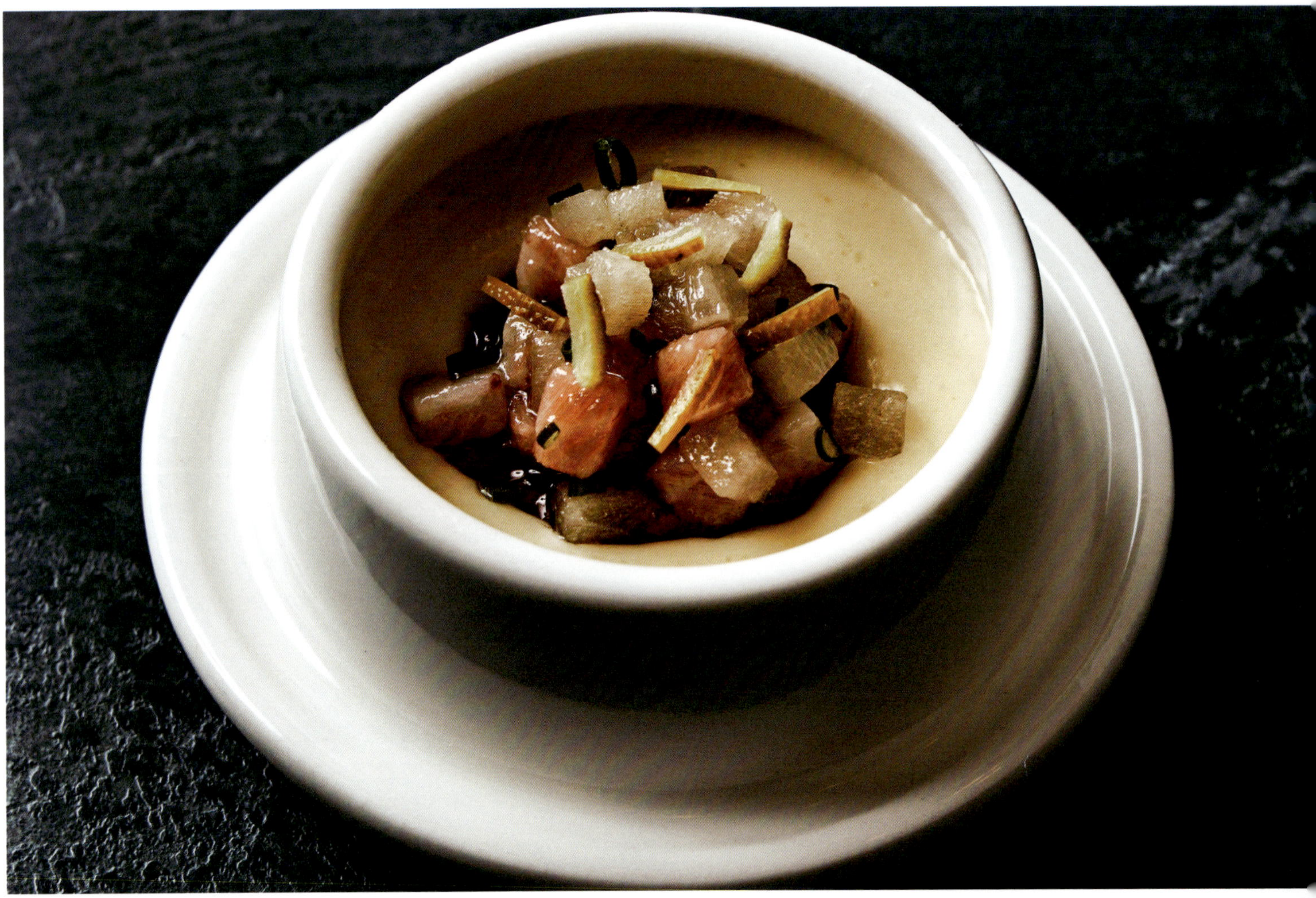

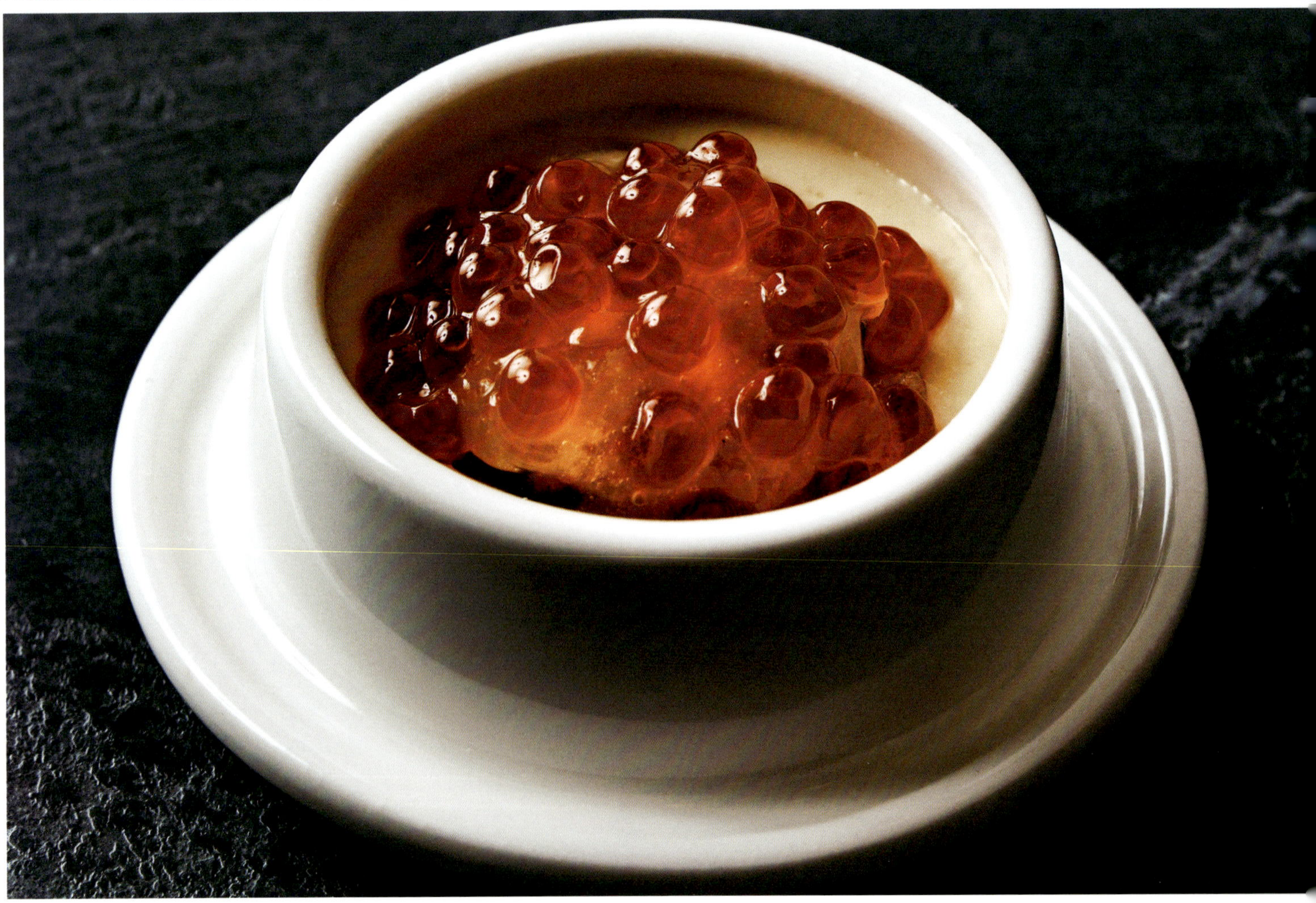

TARTARE OF TORO SAWARA & OTORO WITH JAPANESE CITRUS & SHIRO DASHI CUSTARD

This was on the menu longer than any other dish besides the donut, and it was always one of the favorites. We dressed aged toro sawara (fatty Spanish mackerel) and aged otoro (fatty tuna belly) with lovage oil and an oil made from cured, smoked, and dried fish bones. It is topped with a gelee made from yuzu and sake alongside masa ikura (sake and shoyu-cured salmon roe). We served it over a cream infused with 5-year aged kombu and shiro dashi.

---

shiro dashi custard

heavy cream	150mL
shiro dashi	45g
5-year aged kombu	3g
iota carrageenan	.45%

Bring the cream, shiro dashi, and kombu to a simmer. Allow to steep for 15 minutes. Strain and weigh. Return to a clean pot and shear in the proper weight of the iota carrageenan using a bamix or immersion blender. Whisking constantly, bring to a boil for 1 minute. Immediately transfer to 2-ounce ramekins using a warmed spoon or sauce gun—approximately 15g per portion. Allow to cool to room temperature.

yuzu gelee

yuzu juice	125mL
mirin	15mL
sake	20mL
gelatin sheets, bloomed	4.8g

Bring the yuzu, mirin, and sake to a boil and stir in the bloomed gelatin until completely melted. Pour in a shallow tray and cool in a refrigerator until completely set. It is a soft gel; so, once set, gently break up to desired texture using a fork. Reserve chilled until needed.

bone oil

cured, smoked, and dried fish bones	100g
grapeseed oil	200g

Seal the ingredients in a Cryovac bag on full pressure. Place in a pot of boiling water for a minimum of 4 hours. Cool and allow to steep in the bag overnight. Pass through a coffee-filter-lined fine-mesh strainer and reserve.

lovage oil

lovage leaves, picked and washed	105g
grapeseed oil	275g

Place in a Vitamix and blend on high speed until it reaches 64°C. Pass through a coffee-filter-lined fine-mesh strainer. Cool and reserve.

preserved sudachi

sudachi rind	200g
kosher salt	10g

Combine and Cryovac at full pressure and allow to ferment for 6 months. Remove the pith from the rind and cut into ½"-long julienne.

additional ingredients & to finish

toro sawara, small dice
otoro, small dice
Pacific sea salt
masu ikura

Mix the toro sawara and otoro together in a small bowl and dress with the bone oil and a small amount of sea salt. Do not over-season, as the custard is salty. Place an ounce of the fish mixture onto the custard. Dress with a teaspoon of the lovage oil, a teaspoon of the yuzu gelee, 3 strips of sudachi, and, lastly, the ikura.

SQUAB LIVER MOUSSE, ONION JAM, CRISPY PX SHERRY

I wanted to take flavors traditionally served with a torchon or other charcuterie preparation and cram them all into one perfect little bite. To accomplish this, I tried to pack as much flavor into the bite as possible, while also keeping it as simple as I could. We created a crispy tart made with rendered foie gras fat, filled with a caramelized onion jam, mousse made from quail livers, and foie gras, and topped with crispy, freeze-dried Pedro Ximenez sherry. The acidity in the onion jam helps cut the richness of the bird livers, and the sweetness and crunch of the freeze-dried Pedro Ximenez sherry helps round out the flavors.

---

squab liver mousse

port	150mL
Calvados	150mL
Madeira	150mL
shallots, sliced thin	120g
garlic, sliced thin	15g
thyme sprigs	4ea
fresh bay leaf	1ea
black peppercorn	5g
quail liver	200g
foie gras	250g
salt	t.t.
butter, melted	400mL
pink salt or cure 1	1.2g
whole eggs	4ea

Cook the port, Calvados, Madeira, shallots, garlic, thyme, bay leaf, and peppercorns in a sauce pot over medium heat. Allow to slowly reduce until au sec. Transfer to a Vitamix, add squab liver and foie gras, and puree on high speed. Once smooth, add the pink salt and the eggs one at a time, being sure each is completely incorporated before adding the next. Slowly emulsify in the butter. Continue to blend until the mixture reaches 70°C. Season to taste with salt. Pass through a fine-mesh strainer into an ISI canister. Charge with one charge and submerge in an ice bath. Be sure to shake every 15 minutes or so until fully cooled. Reserve in the refrigerator until needed. Before using, allow to come to room temperature.

tart dough

AP flour	450g
kosher salt	7g
rendered foie gras fat, chilled	100g
olive oil	125g
ice water	120g

In a robot coupe, mix the dry ingredients. Pulse in the foie gras fat followed by the olive oil. Do not overmix. The dough should be a sandy texture. Lastly, pulse in the ice water, remove from the robot coupe, and quickly knead into a smooth dough. Do not let the dough get too warm. Wrap in plastic and cool overnight.

To bake Roll dough to ⅛" thickness and punch circles large enough to fill 2" tart molds. Gently flatten the dough into the molds, add a second mold to the top, and trim away any excess dough. Place on a pass tray and top with a second tray. Bake at 325°F on fan 3 for 9 minutes. Remove the top passing tray, rotate the bottom tray 180°, and place back in the oven uncovered. Bake for an additional 9 minutes. Remove from the oven, allow to cool, and carefully transfer the tart shells to an airtight container.

onion jam

sugar	100g
apple pectin	1g
onion, brunoised	200g
Pedro Ximenez vinegar	200g

Mix the sugar with the apple pectin. Bring the onion and vinegar to a boil. Whisk in the sugar mix. Reduce the heat to allow the mixture to slowly simmer until a jam consistency is achieved. Season to taste with salt, and cool.

additional ingredients & to finish

freeze-dried PX sherry	
Maldon sea salt	

Place a teaspoon of the onion jam in the center of a tart mold. Pipe in a small dollop of mousse. Finish with a pinch of Maldon and a few pieces of the freeze-dried sherry.

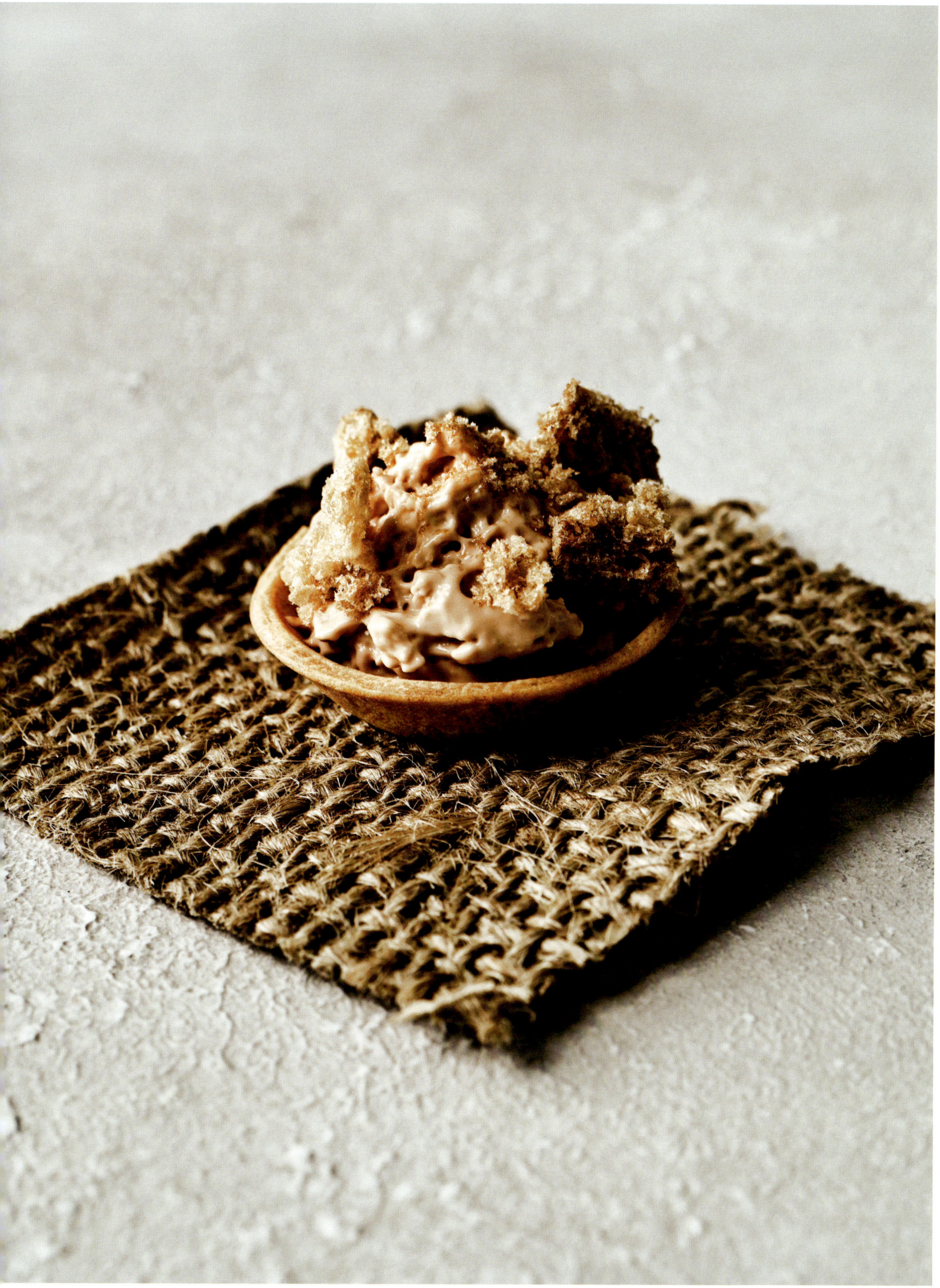

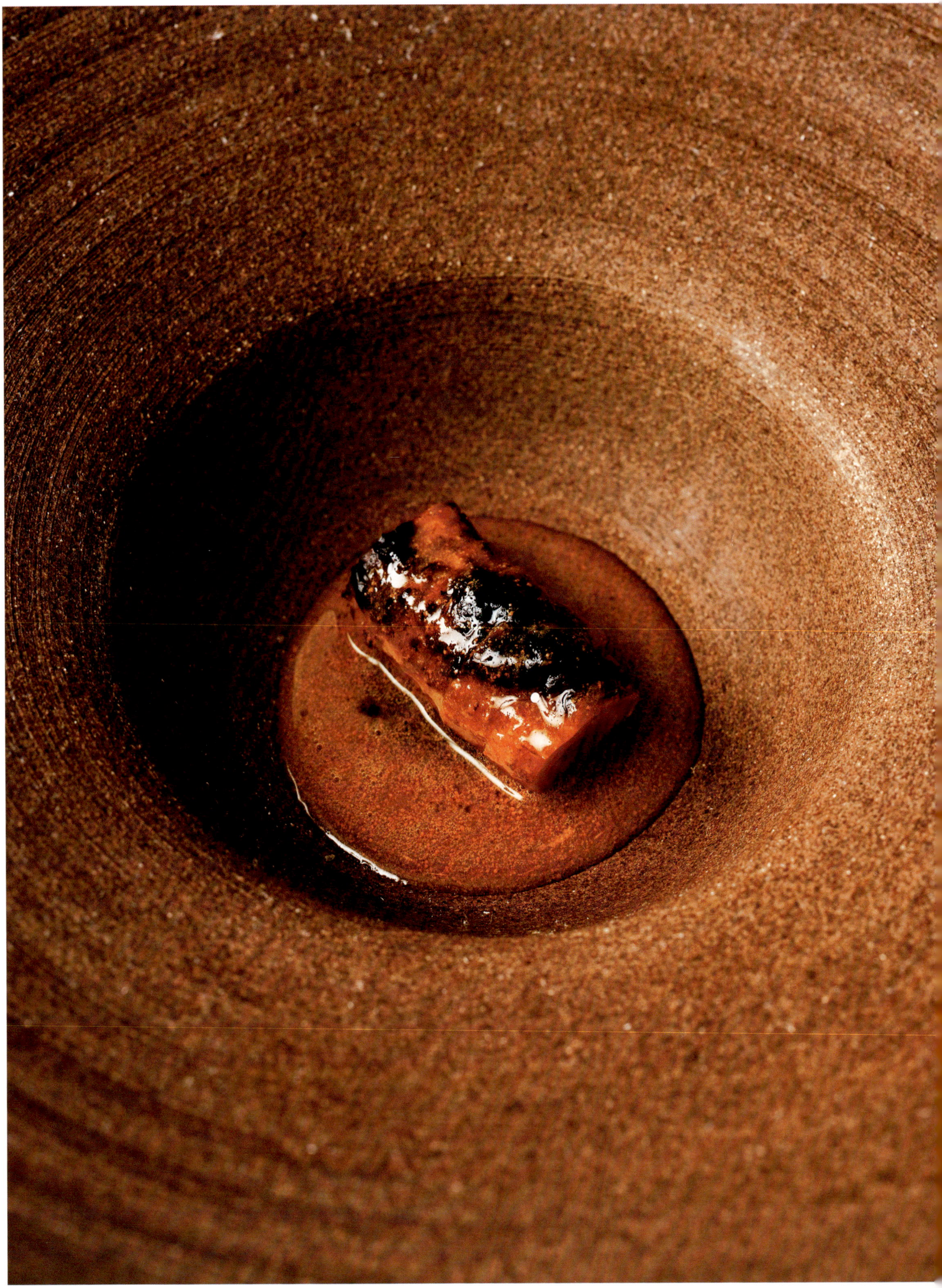

BARBECUED CARROT, BLUE MUSSELS & FERMENTED SEA BUCKTHORN

The intention of this dish was to highlight carrots, though it actually evolved from a dish originally made with smoked mussels. The carrots are roasted in brown butter and then finished over charcoal. They sit on top of an emulsion made from mussel garum and smoked hay oil, and then they are dressed in a sauce made from the cuisson of the mussels, carrot juice, and fermented sea buckthorn juice. This is another one of my favorite dishes that I put on the menu in my time here.

---

mussel & carrot bbq

blue mussels	10lbs
shallots, sliced thin	245g
garlic, sliced thin	10g
absinthe	200mL
vermouth	400mL
hay	1qt
carrot juice	450mL
xanthan gum	.5g
black licorice	3g
salt	t.t.

Place mussels, shallots, garlic, and both spirits in a large enough pot to allow room for the hay to be added later. Cook covered with a lid until the mussels begin to open and the alcohol has burned off. Add the hay to the pot and light on fire with a torch. Once burning, cover with a lid and allow to smolder until it has stopped smoking. Remove all the mussels and most of the hay (it is okay if some burned bits remain). Add the carrot juice and slowly reduce until it has a concentrated flavor. Puree in a blender with the xanthan gum and licorice. Season to taste with salt and pass through a fine-mesh strainer. Cool and reserve.

mussel fudge

egg yolk	1ea
mussel garum solids, dried and ground into a fine powder	25g
Minus 8 Vidal Vinegar	35g
filtered water	10g
grapeseed oil	70g
hay-smoked oil	50g

Mix egg yolk, mussel powder, vinegar, and water in a robot coupe and process until frothy. Slowly emulsify in grapeseed oil, followed by hay oil. Pass and reserve in a piping bag.

mussel butter

mussel reduction (see mussel stock, page 275)	75g
saffron	.15g
butter, cubed	250g
salt	t.t.

Warm the mussel reduction and saffron over low heat. Slowly emulsify in the butter, season to taste with salt, and reserve in a warm place until needed.

roasted carrots

carrots, scrubbed well	5–6ea
butter, cubed	100g
kosher salt	t.t.

Place the carrots in foil, lay the cubes of butter over the carrots, and season with salt. Close the foil and place in the middle rack of an oven. Roast at 425°F for 18 minutes. Remove from the oven and allow to cool.

additional ingredients & to finish

fermented sea buckthorn juice (see page 269)

Slowly roast the carrots over hardwood until beginning to caramelize and hot through. Cut the carrots into 2"-long portions. Toss them in the mussel butter. Meanwhile, rewarm the carrot BBQ sauce and season to taste with the fermented sea buckthorn juice. Place a small amount of the mussel fudge in the bottom of a plate, top with one of the carrots, and glaze with a spoonful of the carrot BBQ sauce. Serve immediately.

GRILLED MAITAKE MUSHROOM, UNI BUTTERSCOTCH, FURIKAKE

I love maitake mushrooms. They are a great vegetarian substitute due to their rich, meaty flavor and succulent texture. This was a very simple presentation, and once again I tried to pack as much flavor into this dish as I could. We marinated the mushrooms in a dressing of mushroom soy sauce and sesame, then slowly roasted them over the coals until they began to char like a nice piece of steak. We glazed them in a sweet and salty, umami-packed butterscotch made from sea urchin, and finished the dish with katsuo mirin furikake and a bottarga made from sea urchin. For a vegetarian version, substitute a miso butterscotch and nori fume furikake.

---

uni butterscotch

heavy cream	225g
uni garum (see base recipes on page 272)	3g
sugar	400g
glucose	120g
sake	100mL
mirin	100mL
sea urchin	225g
Laphroaig 10-year scotch	30mL
salt	2g
butter, cold and cubed	85g

Mix the cream and sea urchin in a sauce pot and bring to a boil. Puree the mixture in a Vitamix on high speed until smooth. Pass through a fine-mesh strainer and reserve. Mix the sugar, glucose, mirin, and sake in a sauce pot and bring to 320°F. Whisk in the sea urchin cream, being mindful that it will bubble as you add it in. Bring this mixture to 245°F. Remove from the heat and whisk in the salt, Laphroaig, uni garum, and butter until completely emulsified. Cool and place in piping bags until needed.

maitake marinade

matsutake shoyu	245mL
garlic, microplaned	2g
mirin	120mL
sesame oil	120mL
tamari	100mL
sesame seeds, toasted (divided into 75g/30g)	105g

Puree all ingredients except the 30g sesame seeds until as smooth as possible. Fold in the remaining 30g sesame seeds.

additional ingredients & to finish

uni bottarga
maitake mushroom, cut into quarters, stems left intact
uni garum
Seto Fumi furikake

Marinate the maitake mushrooms by completely submerging them in the marinade and allowing the excess to drain off. Marinate for 30 minutes. Slowly roast over the coals until well caramelized and cooked through. Spray with the uni garum, glaze completely with the butterscotch, season with the furikake, and grate some of the bottarga over the top.

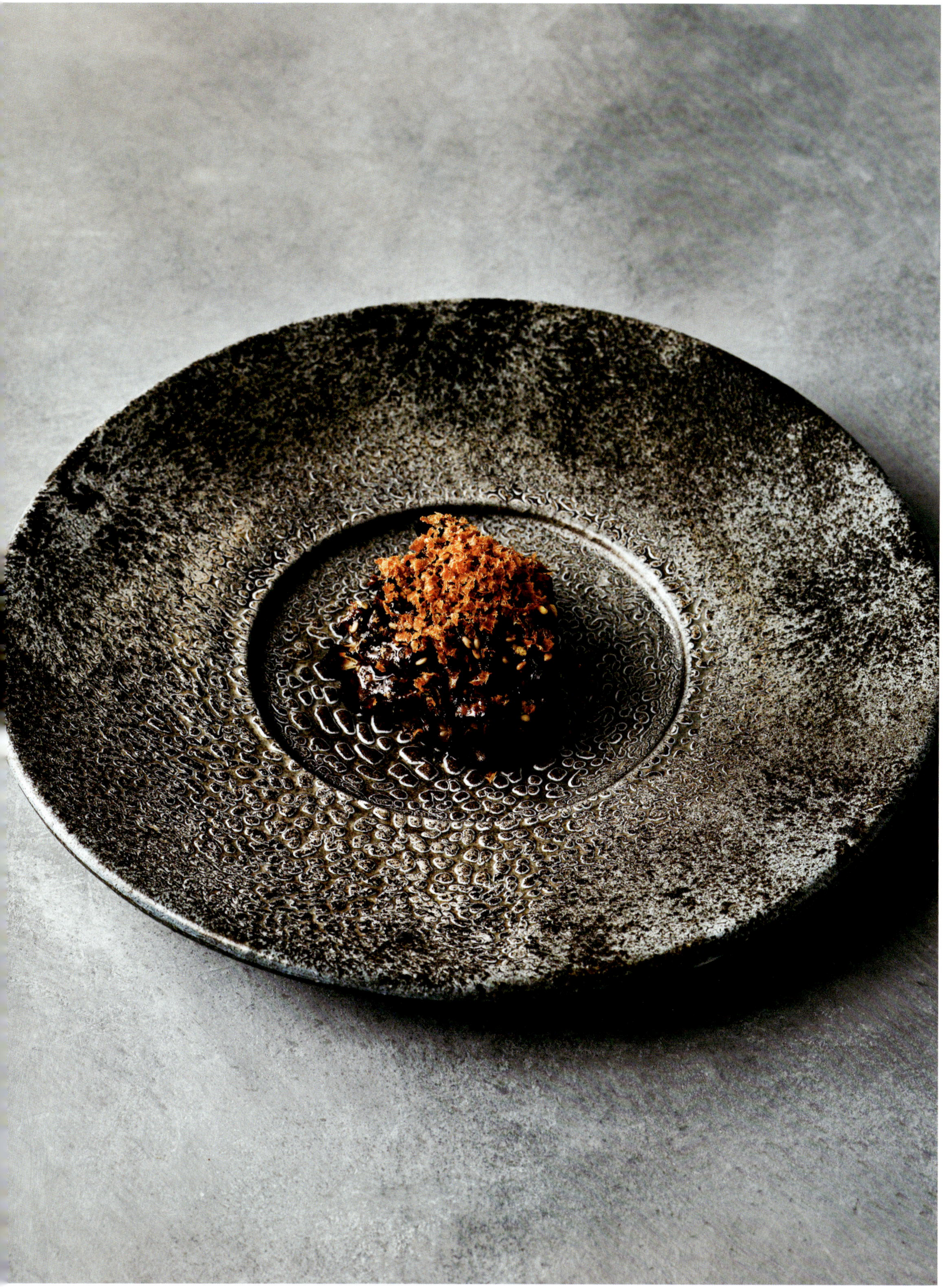

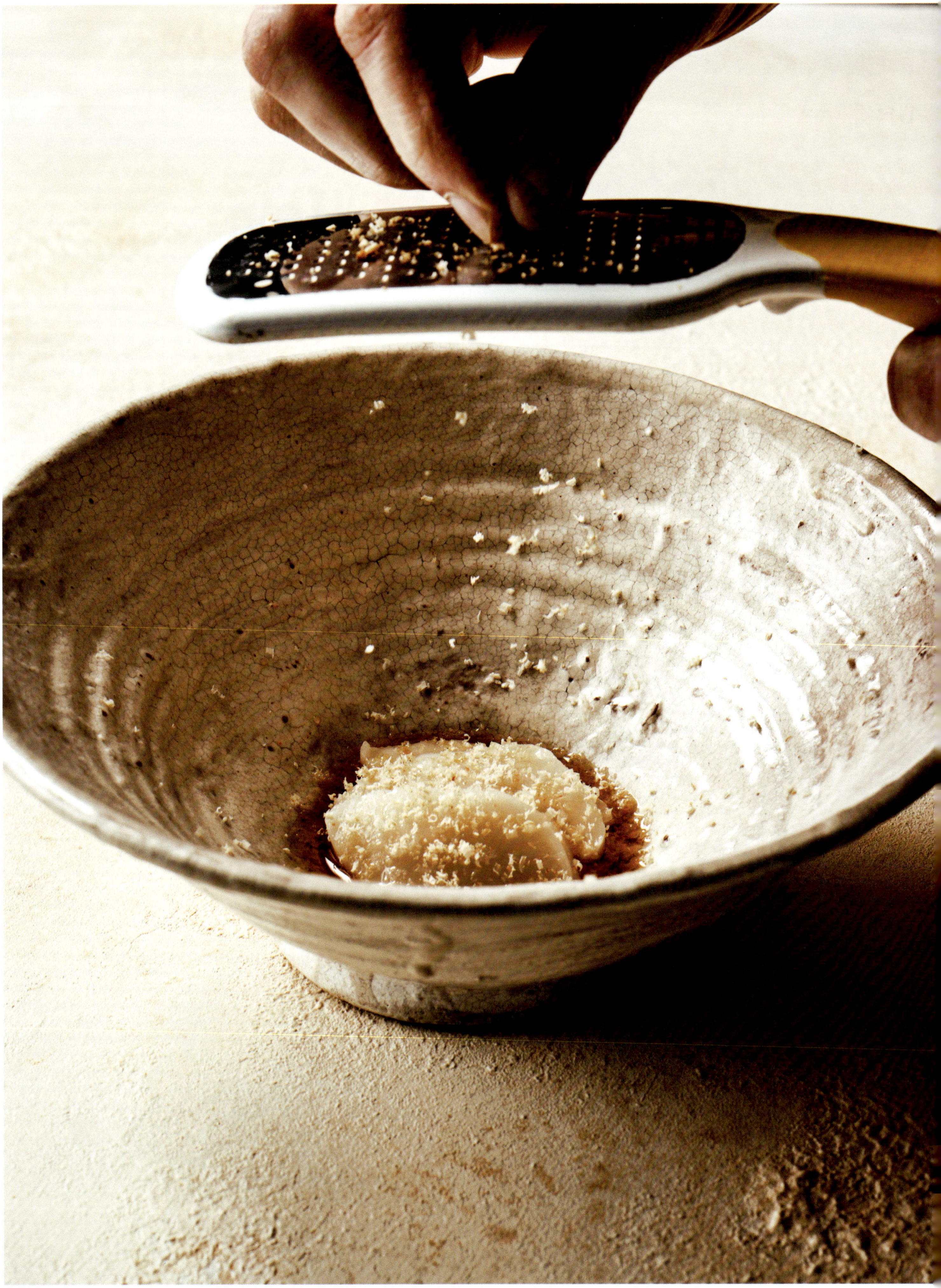

BARELY COOKED SCALLOPS WITH BROWN BUTTER ROASTED HAZELNUT

Over time, I've come to believe that scallops are the most versatile shellfish due to their natural sweetness and rich quality. You can eat them raw, grilled, poached in a broth, roasted or sauteed in a pan, broiled, or fried. For this dish, I wanted the texture of a raw scallop with the rich creaminess that the raw scallop has, but I wanted to serve it warm. We would cure and quickly but gently confit the scallops in olive oil, slice them thin, and dress them in hot brown butter that we had previously roasted hazelnuts in. They were dressed in a sweet and sour quince vinegar with crunchy flakes of Pacific sea salt, and we shaved the warm hazelnuts over the top at the last second.

---

confited scallops

olive oil	1L
kosher salt	50g
sugar	50g
scallops	12ea

Warm the olive oil to 45°C. While the oil is heating up, mix the salt and sugar and season the scallops liberally. Place in a shallow tray that will allow them to be submerged once the oil is added. Once the oil reaches 45°C, pour over the scallops and place in a Rational set to 45°C and full humidity. Cook for 20 minutes. Remove from the oven and allow to cool completely in the refrigerator.

brown butter roasted hazelnuts

butter	400g
hazelnuts	100g

Melt the butter in a small sauce pot over medium heat. Once melted, add the hazelnuts, and slowly roast in the butter until deep golden brown. Strain and dry on a tray lined with paper towels. Reserve the butter in a small pot until needed.

hazelnut puree

hazelnuts	222g
butter	225g
filtered water	450mL
white miso	70g
sugar	6g
shiro dashi	48g
mirin	16g
sake	16g
hazelnut oil	50g

Slowly toast the hazelnuts in the butter until golden brown. Strain off the butter, and reserve in a warm place. Add the water and toasted hazelnuts to a pressure cooker on high for 60 minutes. Strain off the water and reserve. Add all the remaining ingredients except the hazelnut oil with the hazelnuts, and puree until smooth. Add some water if needed to adjust the consistency of the puree. Finish the puree by adding 50g of the hazelnut oil.

additional ingredients & to finish

quince vinegar
hazelnut oil
Pacific sea salt

Remove the scallops from the olive oil and dry well. Gently warm in 140°F oven for 5 minutes. Place a small amount of hazelnut puree on a plate. Slice the scallop into thin disks and shingle over the hazelnut puree. Reheat the brown butter until just before its smoke point. Spoon immediately over the scallops. Dress with a teaspoon of the quince vinegar, a few drops of hazelnut oil, and a pinch of sea salt. Microplane one of the roasted hazelnuts over the top and serve immediately.

CHARRED BROCCOLI, ANCHOVY & CURED TUNA HEART

For this dish, I took the idea of broccoli smothered in a cheese sauce and combined it with my love for the broccoli salad at my good friend Pat Martin's restaurant, Martin's Bar-B-Que Joint. Tender heads of broccoli are marinated and charred directly on the burning coals. They're served warm, dressed in a healthy amount of lemon juice and probably an unhealthy amount of a hollandaise made from a spice of roasted anchovies, capers, and garlic. We finished with shavings of a nice salty, cured, and dried tuna heart.

---

broccoli marinade

olive oil	250g	Combine ingredients, mix well, and reserve.
lemon zest	5g	
shallot, minced	75g	
garlic, minced fine	20g	
Aleppo chile flake	5g	

anchovy hollandaise

egg yolks, cooked at 65°C for 45 minutes	6ea	Add the cooked yolks, anchovy powder, and lemon juice to a blender. Puree until smooth, and slowly emulsify in the melted butter. Finish by mixing in the vinegars and seasoning to taste with salt. Transfer to a piping bag and reserve in a warm place.
anchovy powder (see base recipes on page 273)	8g	
lemon juice	20g	
melted butter	225g	
bitter lemon vinegar	14g	
25% vinegar	1g	
kosher salt	t.t.	

additional ingredients & to finish

broccoli, cut into 2" pieces and marinated for 1 hour	Drain the broccoli from the marinade, season with kosher salt, and char directly on the embers until beginning to cook while still retaining some snap. Place the charred broccoli in a bowl and dress heavily with fresh lemon juice. Pipe the hollandaise over the broccoli. Finish by shaving lemon zest and desired amount of tuna heart over the hollandaise.
lemon juice	
lemon zest	
cured tuna heart	

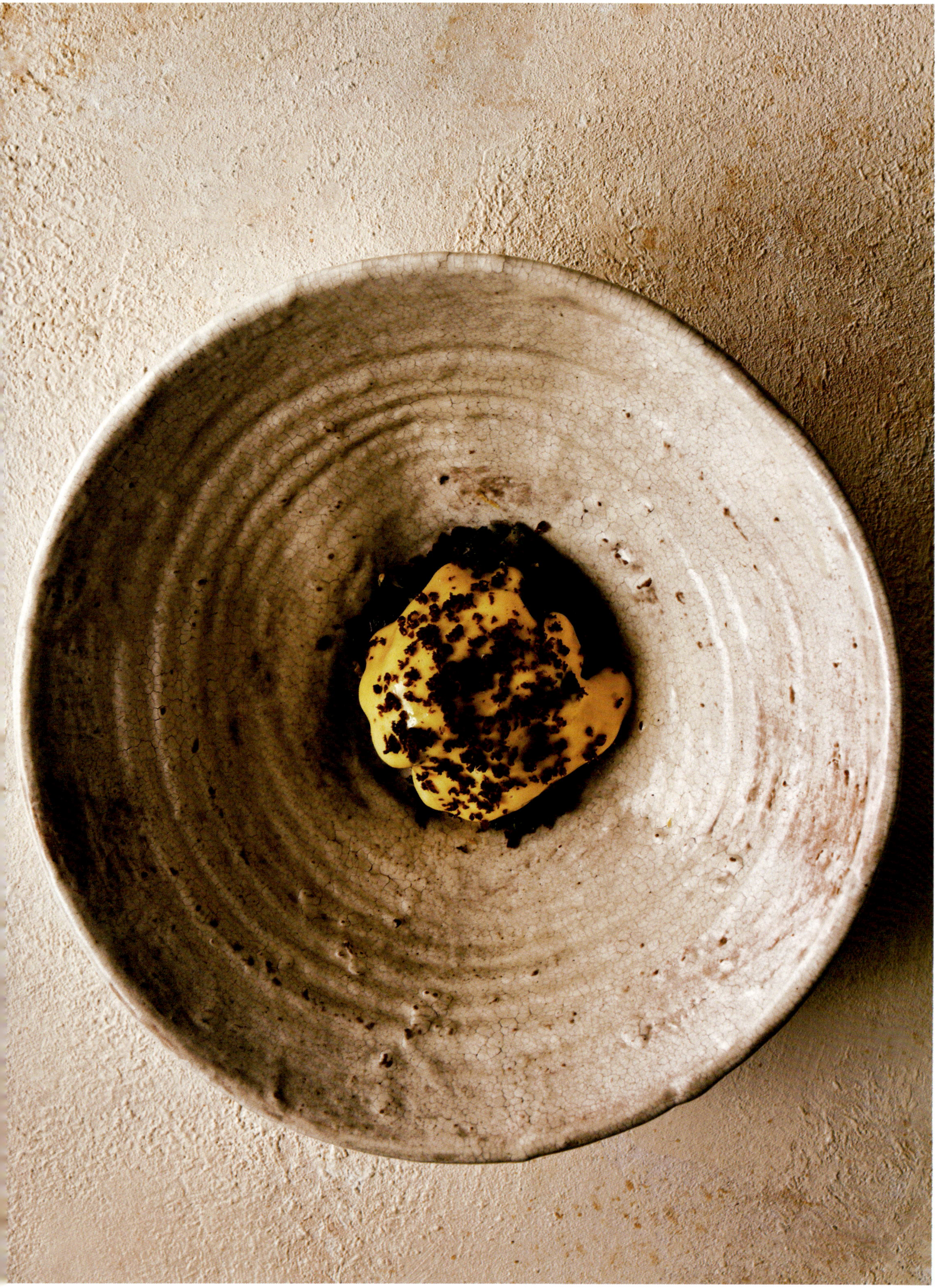

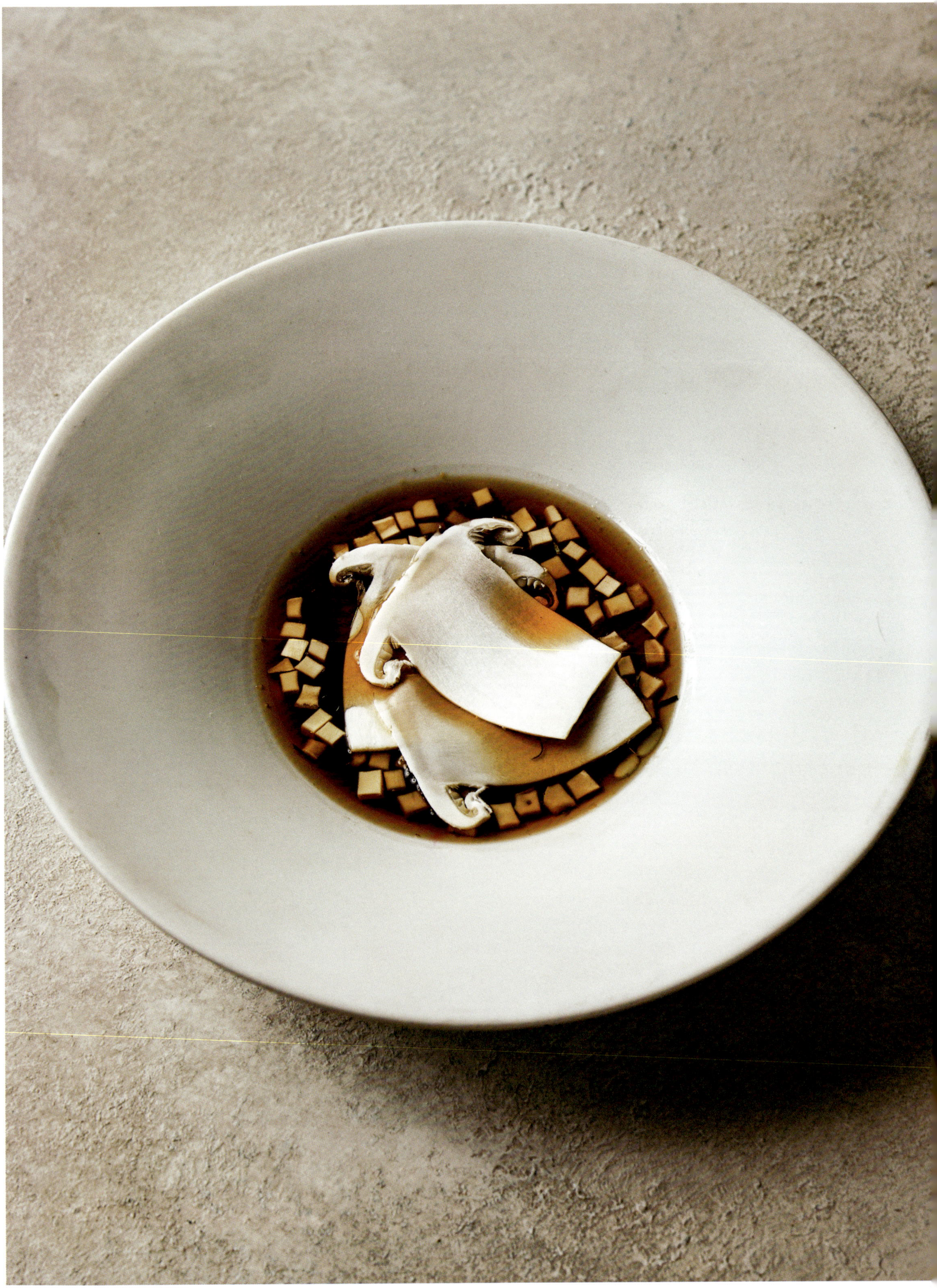

KANI MISO CHAWANMUSHI, BURNT VANILLA, MATSUTAKE & VIRGINIA PINE

For this version of our chawanmushi, I wanted to utilize the entirety of the kegani. Kegani is a "hairy" crab, also known as a horsehair crab, and hails from the coast of Hokkaido, Japan. It is very sweet, so the idea with this dish was to build off the sweetness. We made the custard base from a dashi fortified with the shells and seasoned with kani miso. Kani miso utilizes the innards and mustards of the crab that have been cooked down until thick and creamy. It is very rich and full of flavor. We then dressed it with an oil made from burnt pompona vanilla, an extremely complex varietal coming from Peru via our friend Knox of Larder Foods out of Birmingham, Alabama. We then warmed the picked crab meat in a seasoned dashi along with matsutake mushrooms that had been grilled and smoked over Virginia Pine needles. Lastly, we added a few drops of fresh yuzu juice, zest, and an oil made from burnt pine needles.

---

kani miso dashi

ingredient	amount	method
filtered water	1,100mL	Place all ingredients in a Cryovac bag sealed on full pressure. Cook at 60°C for 45 minutes. Remove from the water bath and allow to steep an additional hour. Strain through a fine-mesh strainer and reserve.
kani miso (see below)	100g	
kombu	20g	

kani miso

ingredient	amount	method
Kegani innards	5–6ea	Slowly reduce over medium heat, stirring constantly with a rubber spatula until a thick paste is formed.

kani miso chawanmushi base

ingredient	amount	method
kani miso dashi	1L	Mix ingredients together well and pass through a fine-mesh strainer. Reserve until needed.
whole egg	360g	
white shoyu	60g	
mirin	45g	
sake	20g	

matsutake & pine dashi

ingredient	amount	method
filtered water	1L	Place all ingredients in a Cryovac bag and seal on full pressure. Cook at 60°C for 45 minutes. Remove from the water bath and allow to steep an additional hour. Strain through a fine-mesh strainer and reserve.
kombu	20g	
Virginia Pine needles, smashed with the back of a knife	20g	
dried matsutake mushrooms	50g	

seasoned matsutake dashi

ingredient	amount	method
kuzu	15g	Mix the kuzu and water to form a slurry. Bring the dashi, mirin, and sake to a boil over medium-high heat. Whisk in the slurry and boil for one minute. Pass through a fine-mesh strainer and reserve.
cold filtered water	30mL	
matsutake and pine dashi	660g	
mirin	250g	
sake	250g	

grilled vanilla oil

ingredient	amount	method
pompona vanilla, charred over hardwood	65g	Combine ingredients and puree in a Vitamix on high speed until the temperature reaches 65°C, retaining some of the bean in the oil. Pass through a fine-mesh strainer and reserve.
grapeseed oil	200g	

burnt pine oil

ingredient	amount	method
dried pine needles	50g	Place the pine needles in a deep third pan, light them on fire, cover with the oil, and wrap tightly for 15 minutes. Transfer to a Vitamix and blend on high speed until the temperature reaches 65°C. Pass through a coffee-filter-lined fine-mesh strainer and reserve.
fresh pine needles	25g	
grapeseed oil	200g	

additional ingredients & to finish

- yuzu juice
- yuzu zest
- matsutakes, washed and cleaned, shaved into 1.5mm thickness
- cleaned kegani meat

Divide 15g of the kani miso chawanmushi base into separate bowls. Cover with plastic wrap. Steam at 82°C for 8 minutes or until just set through, while allowing the custard to have a slight jiggle to it. Warm the seasoned matsutake dashi over medium heat and season with yuzu juice to taste. Add an ounce of the crab and continue to warm. Spoon an ounce of the seasoned dashi with the kegani over the top of the custard. Finish with the yuzu zest, pine oil, vanilla oil, and shaved matsutakes.

DRY-AGED DEVIL'S GULCH RANCH SQUAB WITH SUNCHOKES, BLACK GARLIC & MALTED MILK

In this dish, I wanted to take the idea of Peking duck—but, instead of a hoisin sauce, I wanted to try to mimic those flavors with malt. I slowly roasted dry-aged squab on the bone by basting with hot oil until the skin was crispy. The breasts were sliced and served with sunchokes that had been confited and then roasted in brown butter in a hot cast-iron pan until well caramelized. We deglazed the pan with a sauce made from black garlic and a black garlic molasses, and finished the dish with puffed wild rice and a cream infused with black malted barley. Alongside the roasted breasts, we served the slowly grilled legs that had been lacquered with the same black garlic glaze.

---

confited sunchoke

sunchokes, washed and scrubbed well, cut into ¼" dice	450g	Place all the ingredients in a pan that allows the sunchokes to be completely submerged. Cover in plastic wrap, then foil, and cook in a Rational at humidity and 85°C until tender, 18 to 20 minutes. Allow to cool at room temperature. Drain the sunchokes and reserve until needed.
melted butter	800g	
kombu	20g	

sunflower seed puree

sunflower seeds	460g	Slowly toast the sunflower seeds in the butter until golden brown. Strain off the butter. Add enough water to cover the toasted seeds and place in a pressure cooker on high for 45 minutes. Strain off the water and reserve. Add all the remaining ingredients with the sunflower seeds and puree until smooth. Add some of the water if needed to adjust the consistency of the puree.
butter	500g	
water as needed		
black sesame miso	75g	
black garlic	75g	
black garlic shoyu	45g	

malt cream

shallots, sliced thin	30g	Sweat the shallots and garlic in butter until translucent. Add the malted wheat, and toast until aromatic, 3 to 4 minutes. Add the beer and reduce by half or until all the alcohol has burned off. Add the cream and yeast to the reduction and continue to reduce by ⅓ of its original volume. Pass through a fine-mesh strainer and season to taste with salt.
garlic, minced fine	1g	
butter	30g	
dark malted wheat	35g	
Anchor Brewing porter beer	125g	
heavy cream	315g	
yeast reduction	30g	
kosher salt	t.t.	

black garlic hoisin

onion jus	500g	Combine all ingredients and puree until completely smooth. Pass through a fine-mesh strainer and reserve.
black garlic molasses	20g	
black garlic shoyu	84g	
brown rice vin	45g	
fermented black beans	25g	
black garlic	80g	
sesame oil	7g	
five spice	3g	
szechuan peppercorn	1g	

additional ingredients & to finish

puffed wild rice
squab

For the squab Remove the legs from the birds and reserve. Season the breast/cage liberally with salt and let sit for 30 minutes at room temperature. Meanwhile bring 400mL neutral oil to 350°F in a wide sauteuse. Using a ladle, slowly baste the bird until the skin is golden brown and crispy. Let rest for one minute, then remove the breasts from the cage. Brush the skin with the hoisin and grill until it begins to caramelize. Flip it over and grill the bottom of the breast for 15 seconds. Let rest another minute and slice into thin pieces and plate. Place a tablespoon of the sunflower seed puree to the right of the breast. Meanwhile, season the legs with salt, and slowly roast over lower-temperature embers, glazing constantly with the black garlic hoisin. Once cooked through, move the legs over hotter embers to crisp the skin. Season with puffed rice and serve immediately.

For the sunchoke Season the sunchokes with salt and set aside for 5 minutes. Melt 200g butter over medium-high heat in a cast iron. Once it begins to bubble, add the sunchokes and continue to roast in the butter as it browns until golden brown and crispy. Strain off the butter, return to the heat, and deglaze with a couple ounces of the black garlic hoisin. Continue to cook until a sticky glaze is formed. Place next to the portioned breast, and top with puffed rice.

Rewarm the malt cream and aerate with a bamix or immersion blender until frothy. Season to taste with salt and spoon an ounce or two over the sunchokes. Serve immediately.

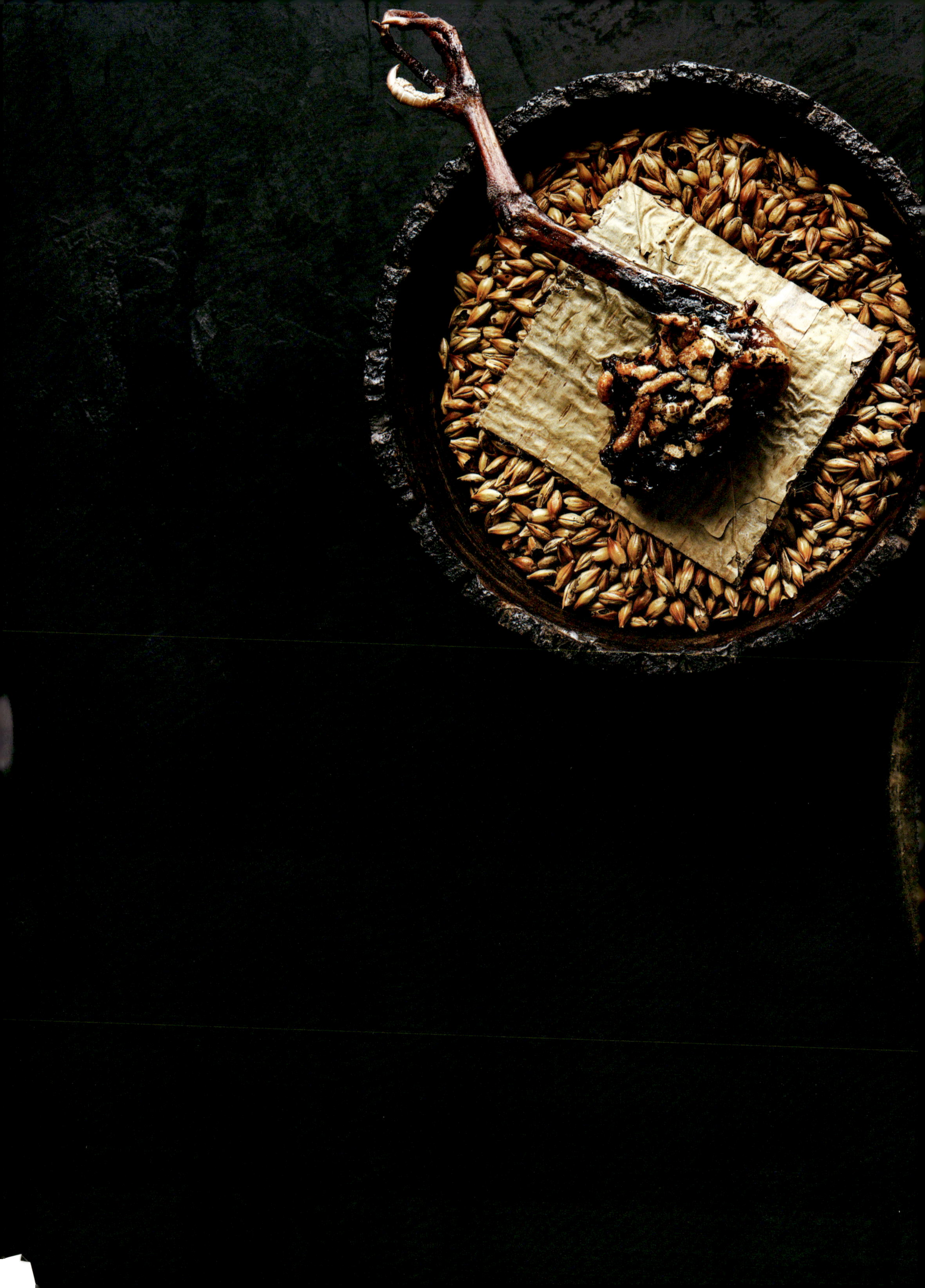

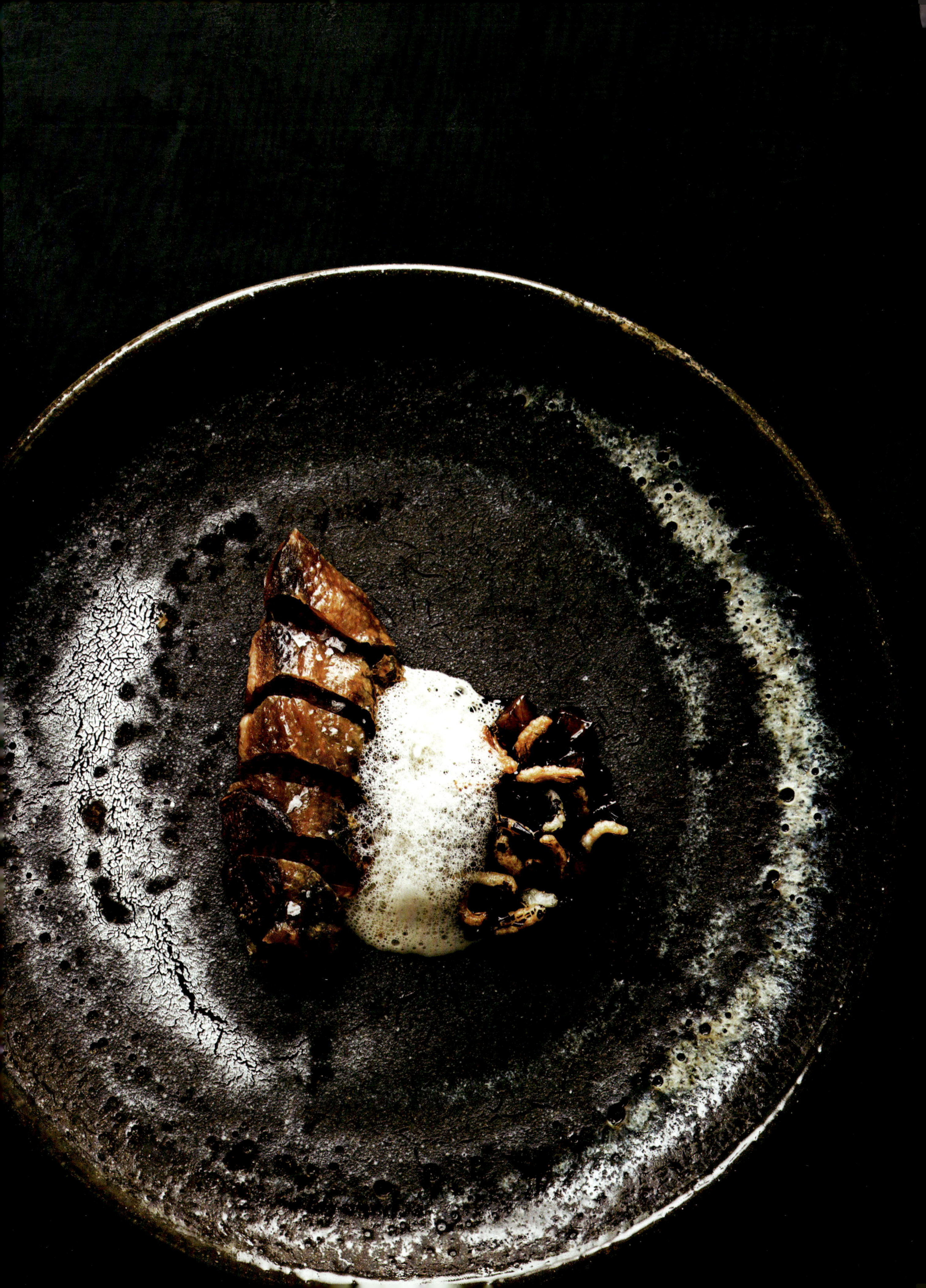

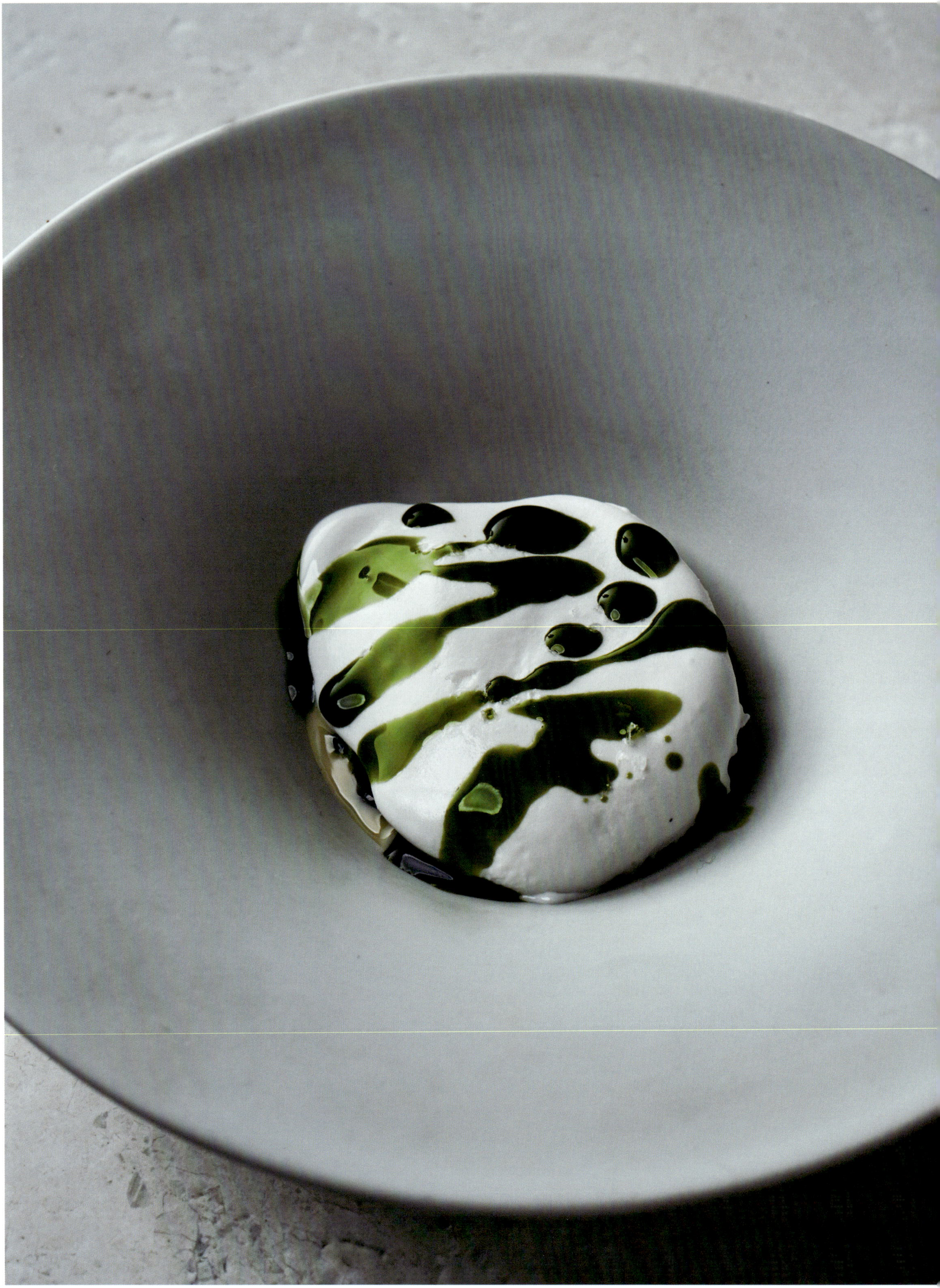

FIG & COCONUT

Fresh figs from Bloomsbury Farm in Smyrna, Tennessee, were the star of this dish. We charred the fresh figs over burning guava branches and dressed them in a fig syrup. I wanted to utilize the tender fig leaves as well, so we made a vibrant green oil with them. To play off their toasted coconut flavor, I decided to serve them with a frozen coconut meringue. My sous chef Ian decided to infuse the anglaise with some fresh eucalyptus leaves and star anise. This was our take on the classic floating island.

fig leaf oil

tender fig leaves	200g	Add fig leaves and grapeseed oil to a Vitamix and puree on high speed until the oil reaches 64°C. Allow to strain through a coffee-filter-lined fine-mesh strainer. Chill and reserve.
grapeseed oil	300g	

fig syrup

fig puree	1,000g	Cook all the ingredients together in a heavy-gauged sauce pot over medium heat until the mixture reaches 220°F. Stir often with a whisk or rubber spatula to prevent scorching.
granulated sugar	250g	
port wine	250mL	
citric acid	12g	

coconut meringue

coconut milk	2,300g	Strain the coconut milk in a cheesecloth-lined fine-mesh strainer overnight or until it resembles yogurt. Bring the 270g granulated sugar and the 270g coconut water to a boil, add the bloomed gelatin, and stir until dissolved. Allow to cool to room temperature. Next, add the vinegar and coconut milk.
kosher salt	2g	
coconut vinegar	125g	
granulated sugar	270g	
coconut water	270g	
gelatin, bloomed in ice water	23g	
granulated sugar	1,260g	
salt	4.7g	
egg whites, at room temperature	630g	

Meanwhile, make a Swiss meringue by cooking the remaining sugar, salt, and egg whites in the bowl of a stand mixer placed over a double boiler until it reaches 79°C. Be sure to continually stir the mixture with a whisk until it reaches the proper temperature. Transfer to a stand mixer and whip with the whisk attachment until stiff peaks form and it is completely cool.

Fold the meringue into the coconut mixture in thirds until no streaks remain. Place into Paco canisters and freeze immediately in a blast chiller or with nitrogen. Reserve, covered, in the freezer until needed.

eucalyptus anglaise

granulated sugar	125g	Mix 50g of the sugar with the egg yolks and whip until pale and airy. Bring the rest of the ingredients to a boil over medium heat. Slowly temper into the egg mixture. Add back to the pot and cook, stirring constantly with a ladle, until the anglaise reaches 180°F or coats the back of a spoon. Pass through a chinois and cool immediately.
egg yolks	6ea	
milk	500mL	
burnt vanilla paste	1.75g	
star anise	1g	
fresh eucalyptus	3g	

additional ingredients & to finish

fresh figs, halved, cut side dusted with granulated sugar	Spin the meringue in a Pacojet and reserve in the freezer until needed. Spoon an ounce or so of anglaise into the bottom of a bowl. Char the figs, cut side down, over hardwood embers and burning guava branches. Dice into ¼" pieces and dress in the fig syrup. Place a spoonful in the center of the bowl and season with Maldon sea salt. Top with a scoop of the meringue and finish with a few drops of fig leaf oil.
Maldon sea salt	

FALL 2021

MATSUTAKE MUSHROOM ICE CREAM, PRESERVED VIRGINIA PINE CONES, PINE NUT MILK

This is one of my favorite desserts. Most people have never had mushrooms in a dessert and probably wouldn't expect this one to be as light as it was. We cooked down matsutake mushrooms into an ice cream, then dressed it in candied young pine cones, pine cone syrup, and yuzu zest. A little Maldon salt helps bring the mushroom flavor forward, and the last-second addition of some crunchy, nitro-frozen pine nut milk meringue brings just enough sweetness and fattiness to balance the bitterness from the matsutake. Side note: the candied pine cone syrup tastes like Sprite if you add soda water to it!

---

matsutake mushroom ice cream

nonfat dried milk solids	50g
guar gum	1g
sugar	100g
salt	5g
Uno ice cream stabilizer	1g
matsutake, chopped fine	250g
milk	500g
heavy cream	100g

Mix the dry ingredients and reserve. Bring the matsutake, milk, and heavy cream to a simmer. Cover and steep for 30 minutes. Pass through a fine-mesh strainer into a clean saucepan. Whisk in the dry mix and bring to a boil for one minute, whisking constantly to prevent scorching. Pass through a fine-mesh strainer into a Paco canister and freeze. Spin before using.

pine nut meringue

iota carrageenan	1.5g
sugar	75g
nonfat dry milk solids	25g
kosher salt	.5g
pine nut milk	250g

Mix the dry ingredients together. Warm the pine nut milk over medium heat, whisk in the dry mix, and bring to a boil for one minute. Pass through a fine-mesh strainer into an ISI canister. Charge with one no. 2 charger. Cool in an ice bath, shaking every 15 minutes or so until completely cool.

preserved virginia pine cones

tender pine cones	200g
filtered water	500g
sugar	500g
citric acid	5g

Cook the ingredients over medium heat in a sauce pot covered with a cartouche. Once the syrup begins to thicken and the pine cones are tender, remove from the heat and allow to cool. Store until needed.

additional ingredients & to finish

fresh yuzu zest
Maldon sea salt

Separate the pine cones into small pieces. Place a quenelle of the matsutake ice cream in a bowl. Spoon over a few pieces of the pine cone and its syrup. Season with a pinch of Maldon sea salt and some fresh yuzu zest. Pipe some of the pine nut meringue into liquid nitrogen. Bust the mousse into small pieces, spoon over the ice cream, and serve immediately.

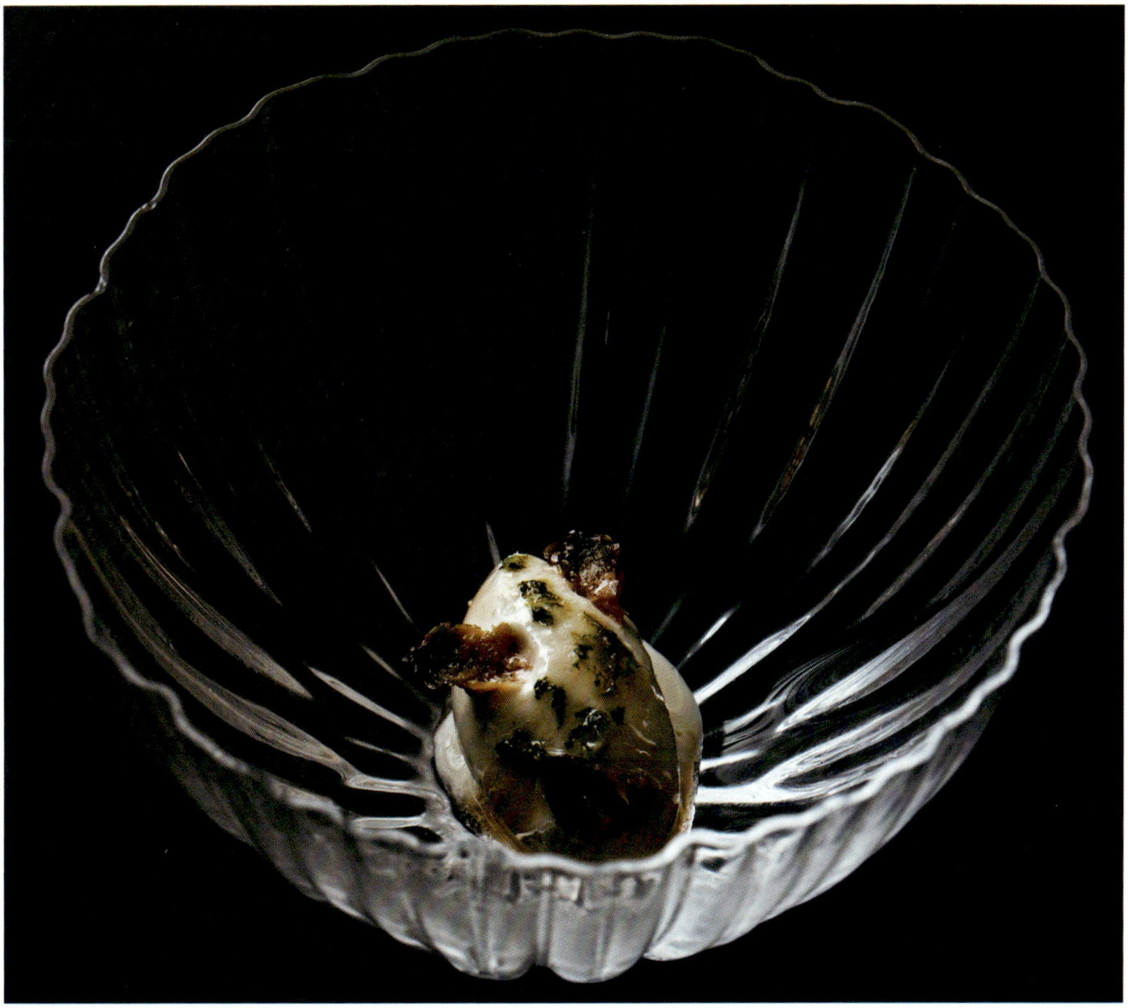

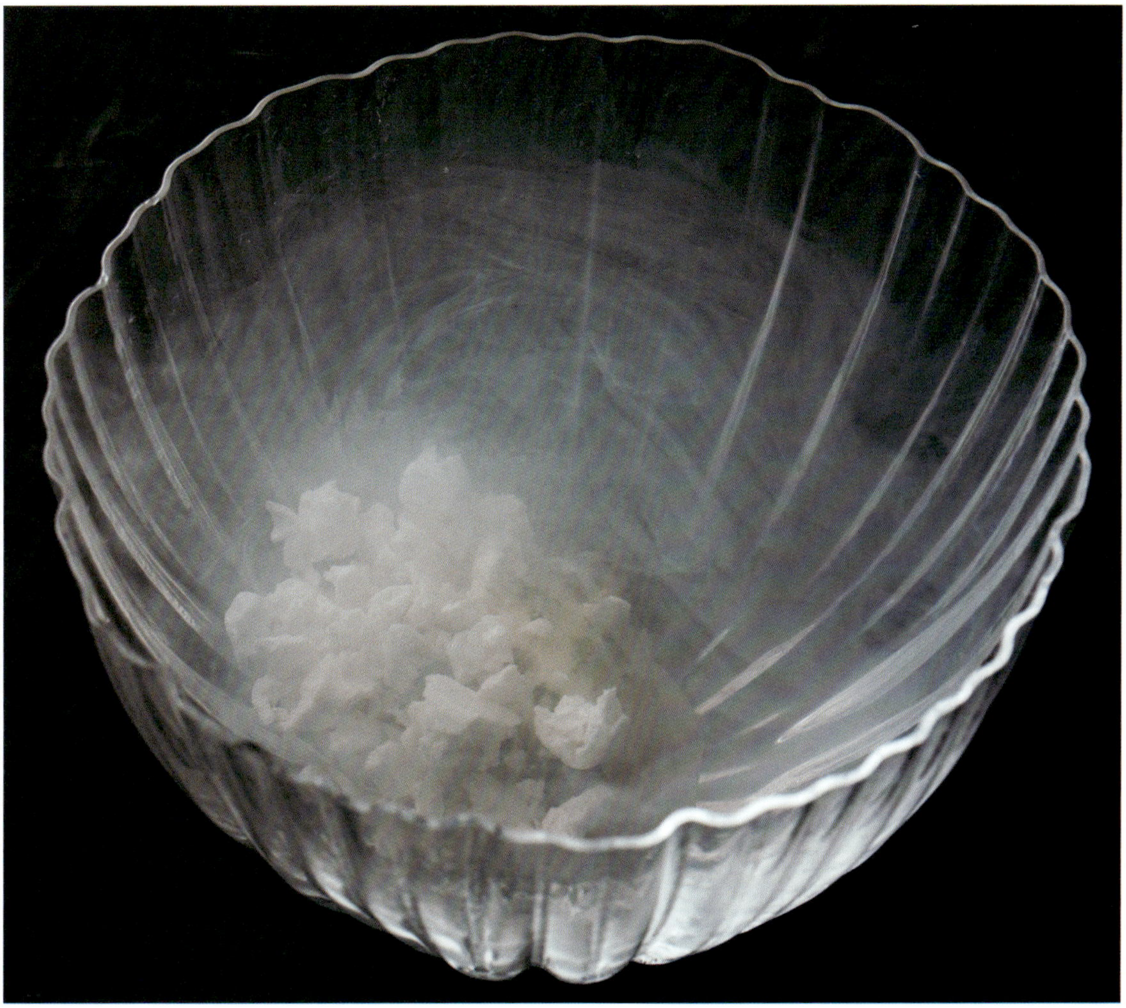

WINTER 2021–2022

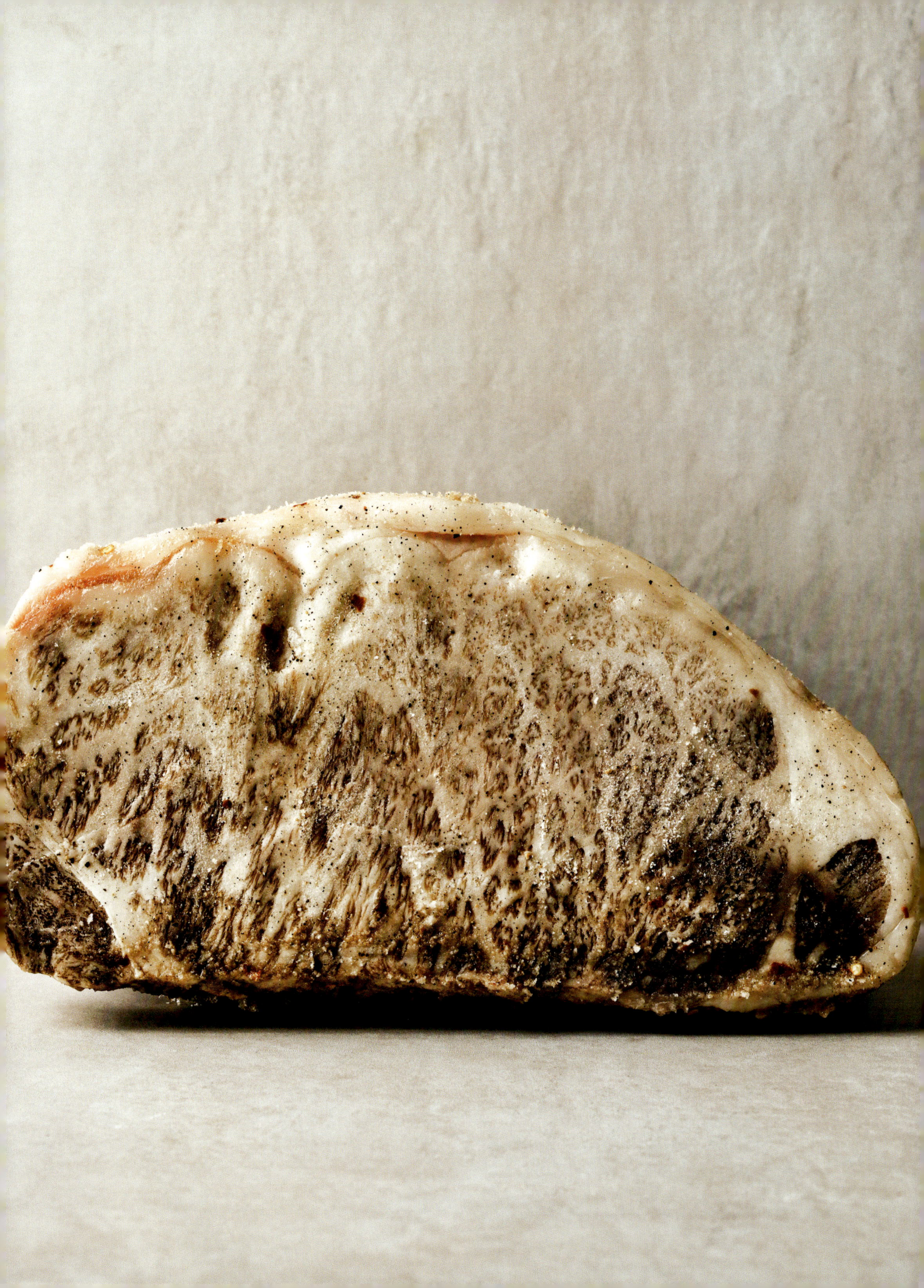

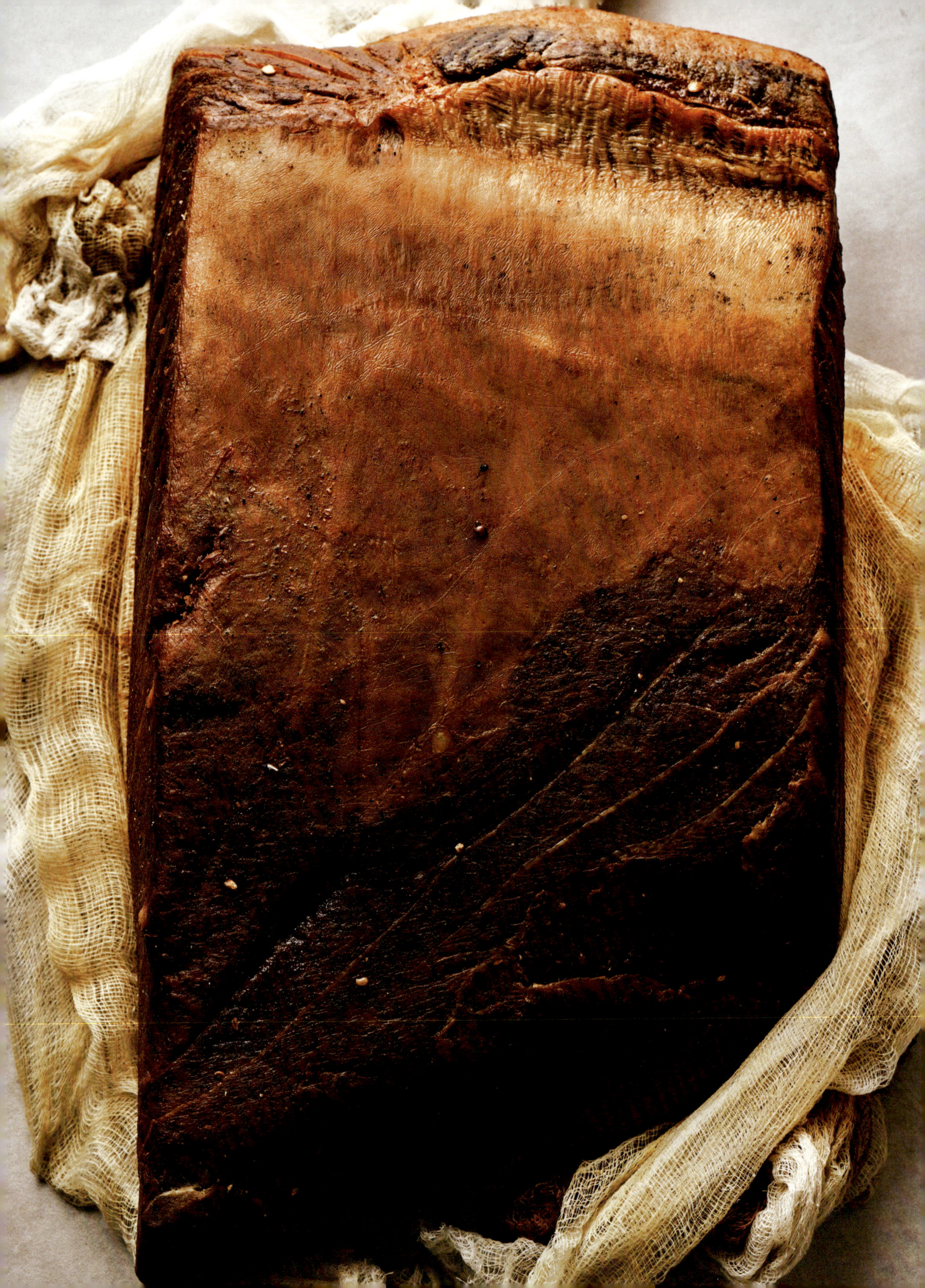

This menu saw us once again turning to the ocean for inspiration as we embarked on our second winter season. We combined the freshness of sea scallops with the umami blast of aged pork belly and fermented heirloom pumpkin (page 216). The delicate flavor of steamed grouper came alive with the addition of preserved tomato and foraged wild fennel. This was a season where I experimented with different ways to add acid and heat to some of the dishes. To add a surprising depth to an Asian pear dish (page 225) inspired by the Korean salad musaengchae, I made a kimchi-like dressing with radish and chile flake and topped it with a pear "snow," bringing a cooling contrast to the spicy flavors. For a pasta dish with grilled mussels (page 219), I used preserved black currants from a previous season, making for a surprising combination that added depth of flavor and acid in a beautiful way.

Two names that have come up a lot in my career also played a vital role in this season's menu: Alan Benton and Nat Bradford. Alan Benton has been smoking and curing hams in his own unique way (no other ham comes close to his smoky complexity) in the foothills of Tennessee's Smoky Mountains for over fifty years. Last I heard, he was curing and aging over 18,000 hams and 50,000 bacon bellies every year. What I have always appreciated about Mr. Benton is his steadfast, simple approach to curing that never changes, because it doesn't need to. He uses salt, brown sugar, black and red pepper, hickory wood, and time. That's it. One of the first things you smell when adding Benton's bacon into the pan or slicing through some of the cured country hams is a big fire burning that sweet hickory wood in the middle of the woods. While I appreciated being able to get incredibly fresh seafood from all over the world for The Catbird Seat, I love that we can use unique local products to help tell the story of this region as well.

Nat Bradford is a fifth-generation farmer, landscape architect, and seed saver. His namesake—the famous Bradford Watermelon—was developed around 1840 when the Lawson watermelon of South Carolina was crossed with the Mountain Sweet variety. By 1860, the Bradford Watermelon was so prized in the Southeast that fields had to be guarded by dogs and men with guns; it is now recognized as one of the three oldest surviving watermelon varieties in North America. Nat Bradford is also known for helping keep alive a rare variety of pumpkin indigenous to South Carolina and grown in that region for hundreds of years by Native Americans, the Dutch Fork pumpkin. They've been described as a giant native variety of butternut squash and have incredible flavors of orange and vanilla, and they go well with everything from salmon to pork. I was fortunate to get my hands on some of these incredibly rare pumpkins and fermented the juice to use in a Vin Jaune sauce for the scallop, pork, pumpkin, and black truffle dish (page 216). Being able to touch on both Alan Benton and Nat Bradford's histories in one dish was one of the more memorable moments from this winter menu.

Credit: Brian Baxter

WINTER 2021–2022 MENU

redneck sushi with aged otoro & wagyu "ham" **208**

blue crystal prawn tartare, fermented kiwi, belgian osetra caviar **211**

steamed kue grouper, preserved tomato & wild fennel **212**

spiny lobster, preserved périgord truffle, hickory king corn grits **215**

scallops wrapped in 45-day aged pork belly, fermented pumpkin & smooth black truffle **216**

reginette pasta with grilled mussels dressed in foie gras & preserved black currants **219**

pork ribs, winter squash & peanut **220**

dry-aged bear creek farm ribloin, savoy cabbage, black walnut & périgord truffle **222**

_____

asian pear & kimchi **225**

razor clam, fermented raspberry, rose & horseradish ice cream **226**

burnt banana, black walnut, cultured butter & caviar **229**

yeast donut, foie gras, candy cap mushrooms **230**

REDNECK SUSHI WITH AGED OTORO & WAGYU "HAM"

In another version of our redneck sushi, this time we highlighted the combo of fatty A5 wagyu from Kumamoto, Japan, with aged otoro from the same prefecture. We served it with freshly grated Mazuma wasabi and brushed in a smoked onion shiro dashi, adding depth of flavor to the meatiness of the wagyu.

---

smoked onion nikiri

smoked onion shiro dashi (see page 271)	225g
mirin	225g
dashi	40g
Madeira	25g

Mix all ingredients together in a pot. Bring to a simmer and allow to slowly reduce about 15 to 20 minutes until all the alcohol has burned off and the sauce has a nice napé consistency.

sushi grits

cooked grits	850g
mirin	15g
brown rice vinegar	20g
salt	2g
glutinous rice flour	30g

Mix until well combined. Allow to cool. Quenelle and reserve in the freezer.

additional ingredients & to finish

otoro, sliced thin
wagyu ham, sliced thin
(see base recipes on page 273)
wasabi

Fry the grits until golden brown and warm all the way through. Top with a small amount of fresh wasabi and lay down the tuna, then the wagyu ham. Brush with the nikiri and serve immediately.

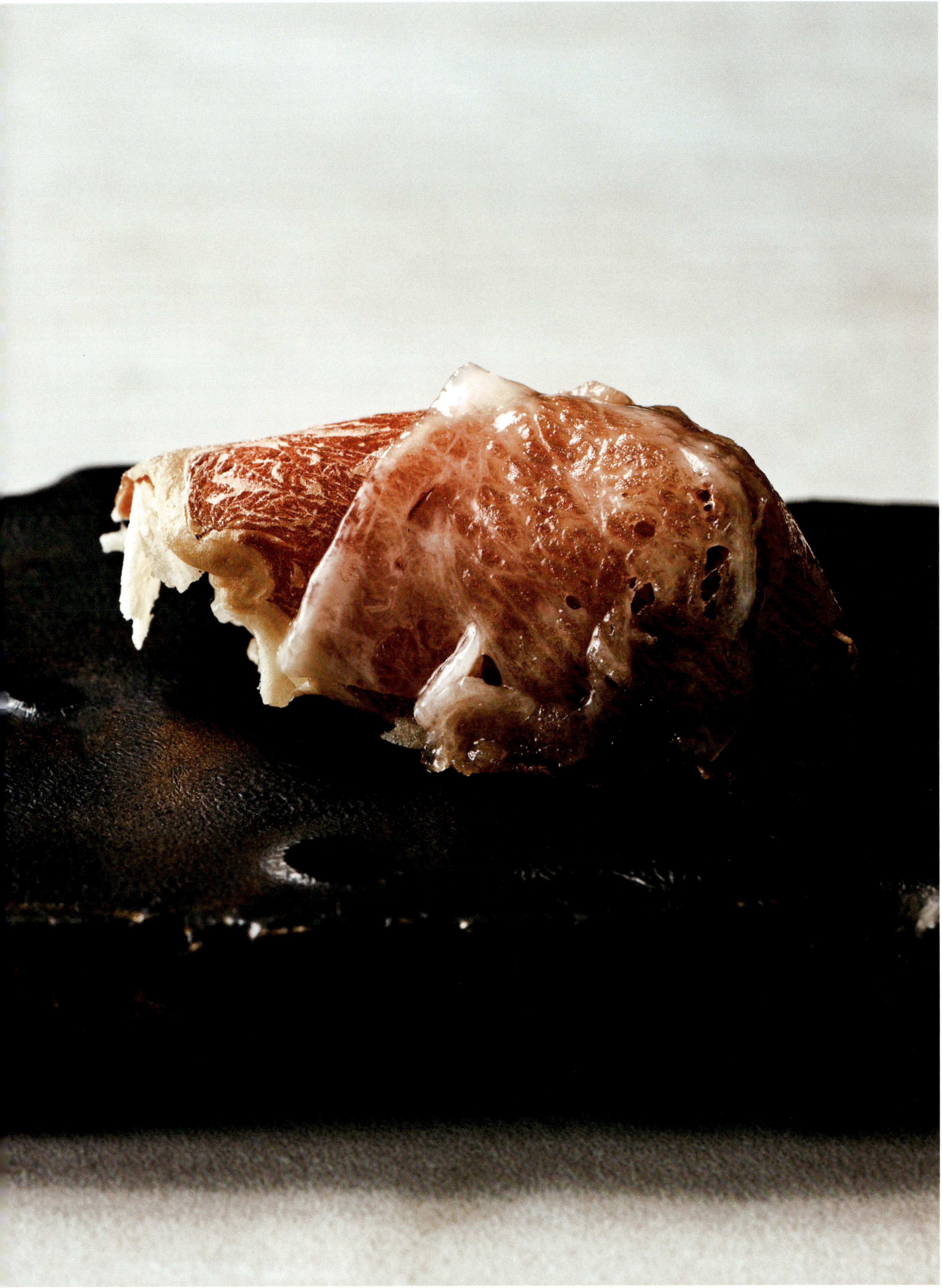

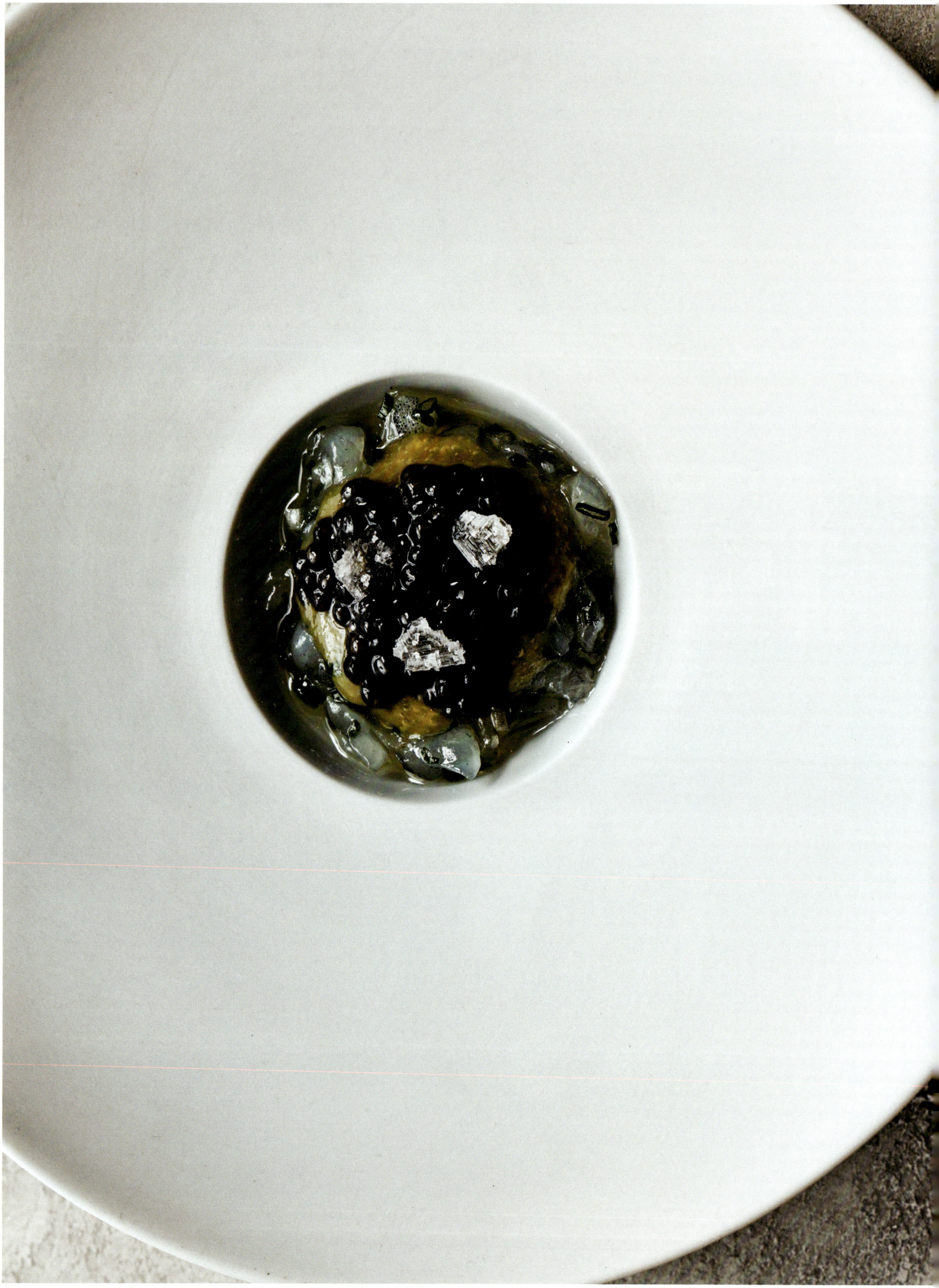

BLUE CRYSTAL PRAWN TARTARE, FERMENTED KIWI, BELGIAN OSETRA CAVIAR

Blue crystal prawns are delicious raw. They're sweet with just a touch of brininess and a rich, velvety mouthfeel. I wanted to try to highlight these characteristics by adding touches of sweetness, acidity, and salt. We dressed diced shrimp in an oil made from the shells with minced chives and finished with reduced, fermented kiwi juice and crunchy Pacific sea salt.

---

fermented kiwi

kiwi juice	1kg
kosher salt	20g

Mix the kiwi juice and salt together and place in a vacuum-seal bag. Seal and place in a warm place for 5 to 6 days. Burp the bag as needed as it fills with gas, and reseal in a clean vacuum bag. Allow to ferment another week. Once it has reached the desired sourness, strain through a fine-mesh strainer lined with cheesecloth and process in the centrifuge at 4500RPM for 15 minutes. Reduce slowly over medium-low heat until a nice glaze is achieved.

prawn shell oil

prawn shells	100g
grapeseed oil	250g

Bring the mixture up to 250°F in a sauce pot. Allow the shells to slowly fry until toasted and aromatic. Puree in a Vitamix on high speed until smooth. Pass through a coffee-filter-lined mesh strainer, cool, and reserve.

celeriac puree

celery root, peeled and sliced thin	400g
butter	100g
heavy cream	700mL
xanthan gum	Pinch
kewpie mayonnaise	50g
salt	t.t.

Melt the butter over medium high heat. Add the celery root and begin to sweat, stirring constantly until it begins to soften. Cover with the cream and bring to a boil. Reduce the heat to a simmer and cook until the celery root is completely tender. Strain off all of the liquid and reserve. Place the celery root in a vitamix and puree on high until completely smooth. Add small amounts of the reserve liquid as needed to help the puree spin. Once smooth, add a pinch of xanthan gum and emulsify in the mayonnaise. Season to taste with salt. Pass through a fine mesh strainer and cool until needed.

additional ingredients & to finish

blue crystal prawns, peeled and deveined, brunoised
chives, minced fine
Pacific sea salt
Osetra caviar or other salty caviar

Dress the prawns in enough shell oil to just glaze them. Season to taste with the Pacific sea salt and a pinch of chives. Place a small amount of the celery root puree in the bottom of a bowl. Top with the dressed prawns. Completely glaze in the kiwi reduction, and top with the caviar. Season the caviar with a few flakes of sea salt.

STEAMED KUE GROUPER, PRESERVED TOMATO & WILD FENNEL

I love making cioppino when the weather begins to cool down. This dish is loosely inspired by those flavors and contains a clarified preserved tomato broth fortified with bacon, wild fennel, and reduced razor clam stock. The main protein here is Kue grouper, a long-tooth grouper from Japan. I chose the Kue grouper due to its high fat content and mild flavor. We finished the dish with pickled wild fennel to add some brightness and help cut through the richness of the grouper. You could serve this with a nice grilled piece of sourdough rubbed with olive oil and garlic to help soak up any remaining broth.

---

preserved tomato broth

Benton's bacon, small dice	125g
wild fennel, sliced thin	55g
garlic	5g
smoked pea or bean shells	5g
sweet vermouth	350g
absinthe or pernod	70g
clam juice	500g
preserved tomato juice or tomato cocktail	400g

Render the bacon over medium heat. Add the fennel and garlic and sweat until soft, taking care not to get any color on them. Add the pea shells, vermouth, and absinthe. Reduce until all the alcohol has evaporated. Add the clam and tomato juices, bring to a simmer, and allow to simmer for an additional 25 minutes. Pass through a fine-mesh strainer and reserve.

pickled wild fennel

Jean-Marc's Huilerie Beaujolaise calamansi vinegar	200g
filtered water	50g
absinthe	50g
sugar	50g
wild fennel, sliced thin	200g

Bring all the ingredients except the fennel to a boil. Pour mixture over the fennel and allow to cool at room temperature. Store in the refrigerator for a minimum of one week.

additional ingredients & to finish

grouper, skinned and brined in 3% salt brine for 20 minutes
fennel pollen

Steam the grouper until just cooked. Transfer to a bowl and dress with a few ounces of the hot tomato broth. Top with a teaspoon of pickled fennel and a pinch of fennel pollen.

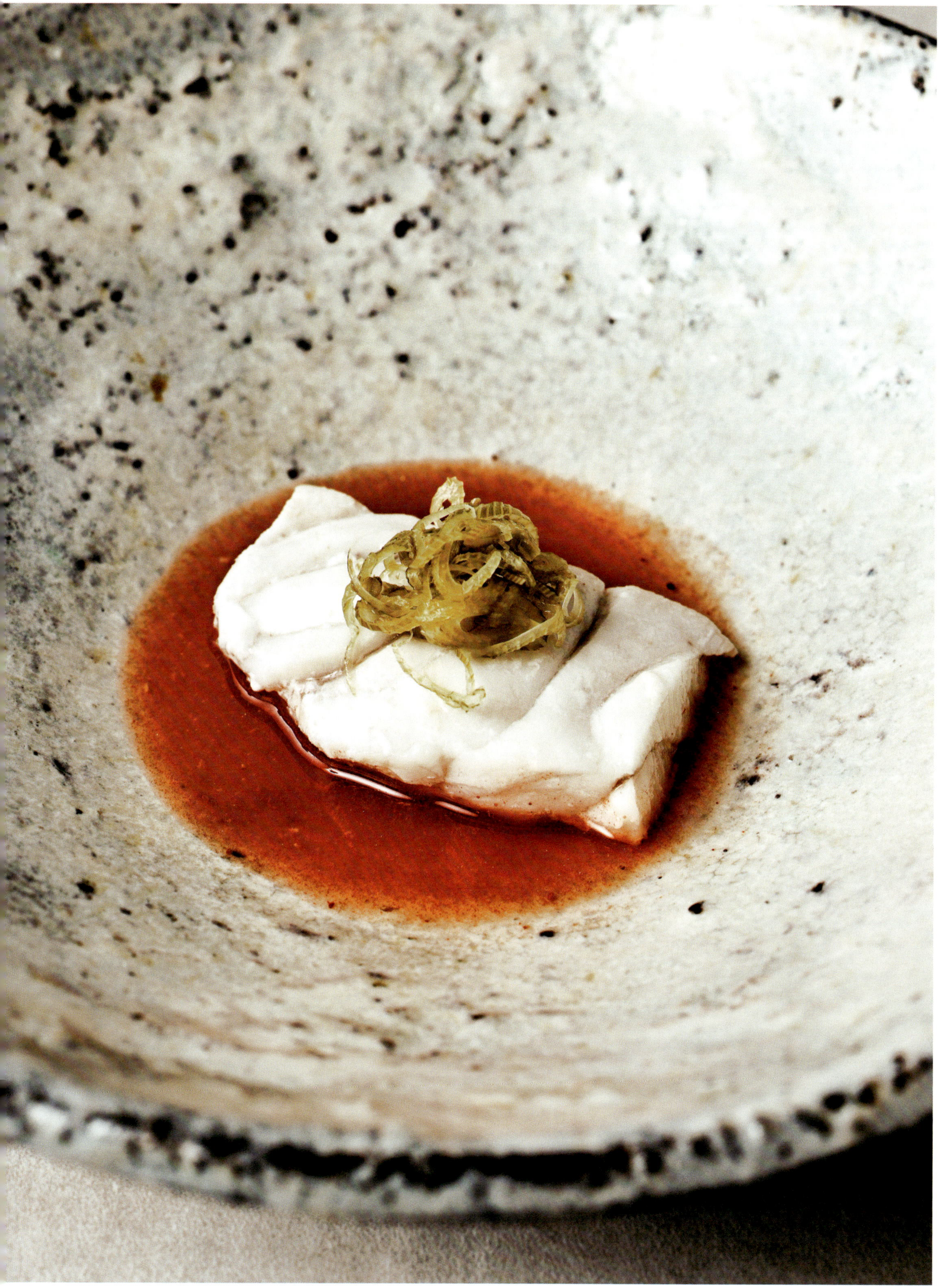

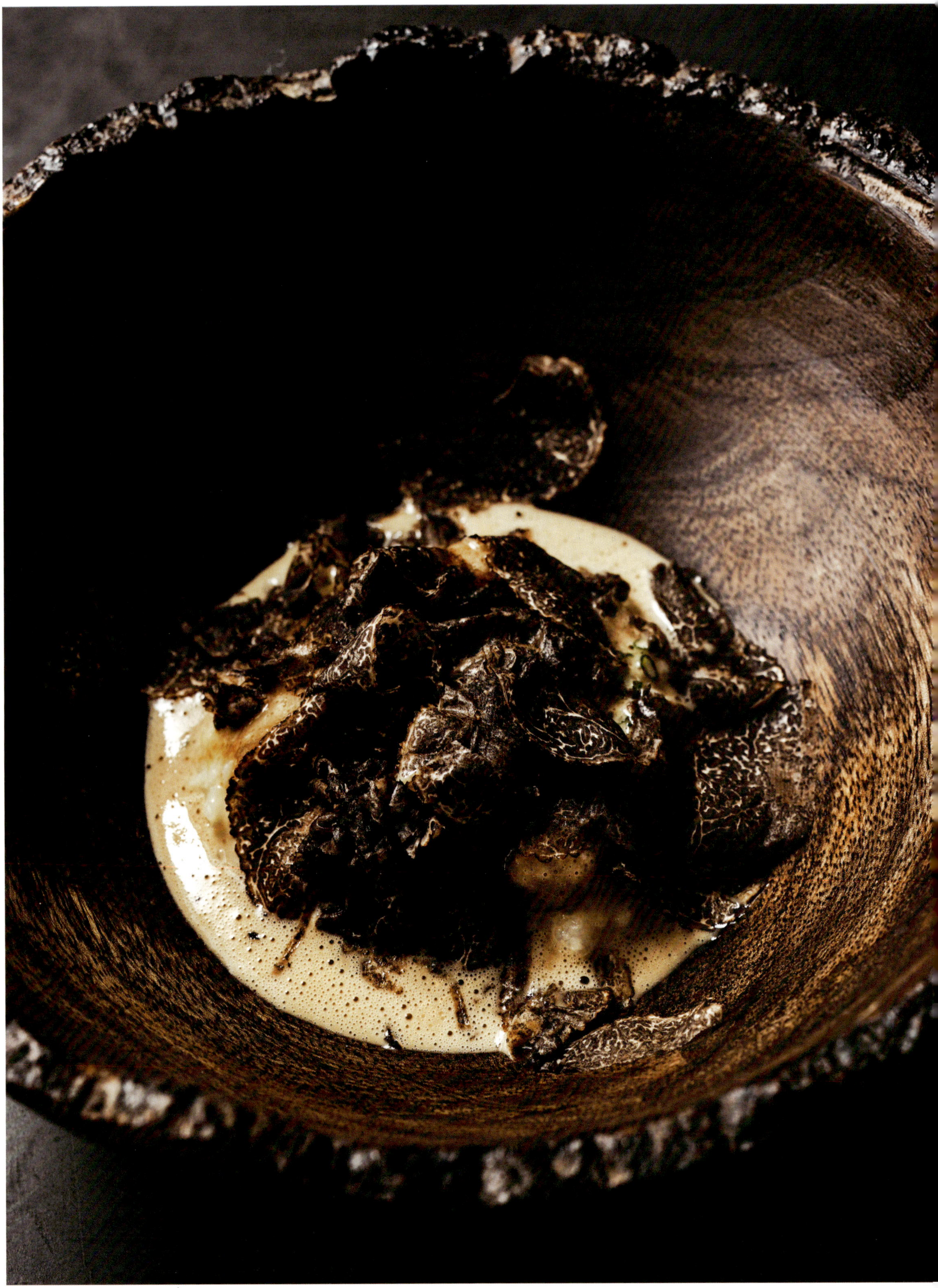

SPINY LOBSTER, PRESERVED PÉRIGORD TRUFFLE, HICKORY KING CORN GRITS

Spiny lobster is one of those products that can be served with light flavors but can also pair well with meatier flavors. I wanted to play off the nuttiness of the grits in this dish, so we made a butter from lobster heads rubbed in miso and roasted, cooked down with sherry, and finished with smoked shoyu. The smokiness gave the sauce the meaty depth I was looking for and added even more umami. The whole dish was finished with a healthy amount of Périgord truffle.

---

lobster glace

spiny lobster heads, split	8ea
miso as needed	
garlic head, halved	1ea
grapeseed oil as needed	
cream sherry	750mL
oloroso sherry	750mL
bay leaves	3ea
filtered water	5.5L

Rub heads with miso. Dress the heads and halved garlic with a small amount of grapeseed oil. Roast at 405°F for 10 minutes. Transfer to a wide rondeau and cover in the sherries. Reduce over medium heat until all the alcohol has burned off. Cover with the water, add the bay leaves, and slowly simmer for 2 hours. Pass through a fine-mesh strainer, being sure to push all the juices through with a ladle.

lobster sherry butter

shallot	125g
garlic	10g
smoked shoyu	175g
lobster glace	425g
butter, cubed and chilled	454g

Reduce everything but the butter down to 305g. Transfer to a blender and blend on high speed until smooth, and emulsify in the cubed butter. Pass through a fine-mesh strainer and reserve in a warm place.

additional ingredients & to finish

cooked grits
popcorn shio
lobster tails, brined in 10% salt brine for 10 minutes, cut into 1" pieces
black truffle

Season the grits with the popcorn shio and salt, and mount with butter until creamy. Gently cook the lobster to medium or medium-well in the sherry butter. Place a spoonful of the grits in a bowl, and dress with the lobster and a few spoonfuls of sherry butter. Finish with desired amount of freshly shaved winter truffles.

SCALLOPS WRAPPED IN 45-DAY AGED PORK BELLY, FERMENTED PUMPKIN & SMOOTH BLACK TRUFFLE

I created this dish around a beautiful piece of pork belly that we received from our friend Tank of Holy City Hogs. It had been smoked and aged for 45 days by Alan Benton of Benton's Bacon. I decided to do a little throwback to something I'd had for the first time with my grandma Carol: scallops wrapped in bacon. For this dish, we wrapped confited scallops in the aged belly and slowly warmed them, allowing the belly to melt into the scallop. We served it with a sauce made from Vin Jaune and fermented Dutch Fork pumpkin from Nat Bradford and dressed the scallop in a black truffle "barbecue" sauce and some fresh winter truffle.

---

truffle bbq

kuzu	15g
cold filtered water	30mL
truffle paste	265g
truffle juice	400mL
mushroom tamari	220mL
vegetable bouillon paste	40g
light brown sugar	68g

Mix the kuzu and water to form a slurry. Bring the remaining ingredients to a simmer over medium-high heat. Whisk in the slurry and continue to whisk until the sauce reaches a boil for one minute. Cool and reserve.

pumpkin-vin jaune sauce

shallot, sliced thin	130g
garlic, sliced thin	10g
grilled pompona vanilla	4g
Vin Jaune	270mL
fermented Dutch Fork pumpkin juice (process like fermented pear juice, page 269)	560mL
cream	840mL

Place the shallot, garlic, vanilla, and Vin Jaune in a heavy-gauged sauce pot and bring to a simmer over medium heat. Cook until all the alcohol has burned off the wine. Add the pumpkin juice and cream, return to a simmer, and cook until the sauce has reduced by ¼ of its original volume. Pass through a fine-mesh strainer and reserve.

confited scallops (see page 189)

Remove the scallops from the oil, pat dry, and wrap in bacon that has been sliced as thinly as possible.

additional ingredients & to finish

smooth black truffles

Place the scallops in an oven set at 140°F for 45 minutes. Transfer to a bowl and dress with a teaspoon of the black truffle BBQ. Rewarm the pumpkin Vin Jaune sauce, season to taste with salt, and aerate with a bamix or immersion blender. Spoon the sauce around the scallop and finish with shaved black truffle to cover.

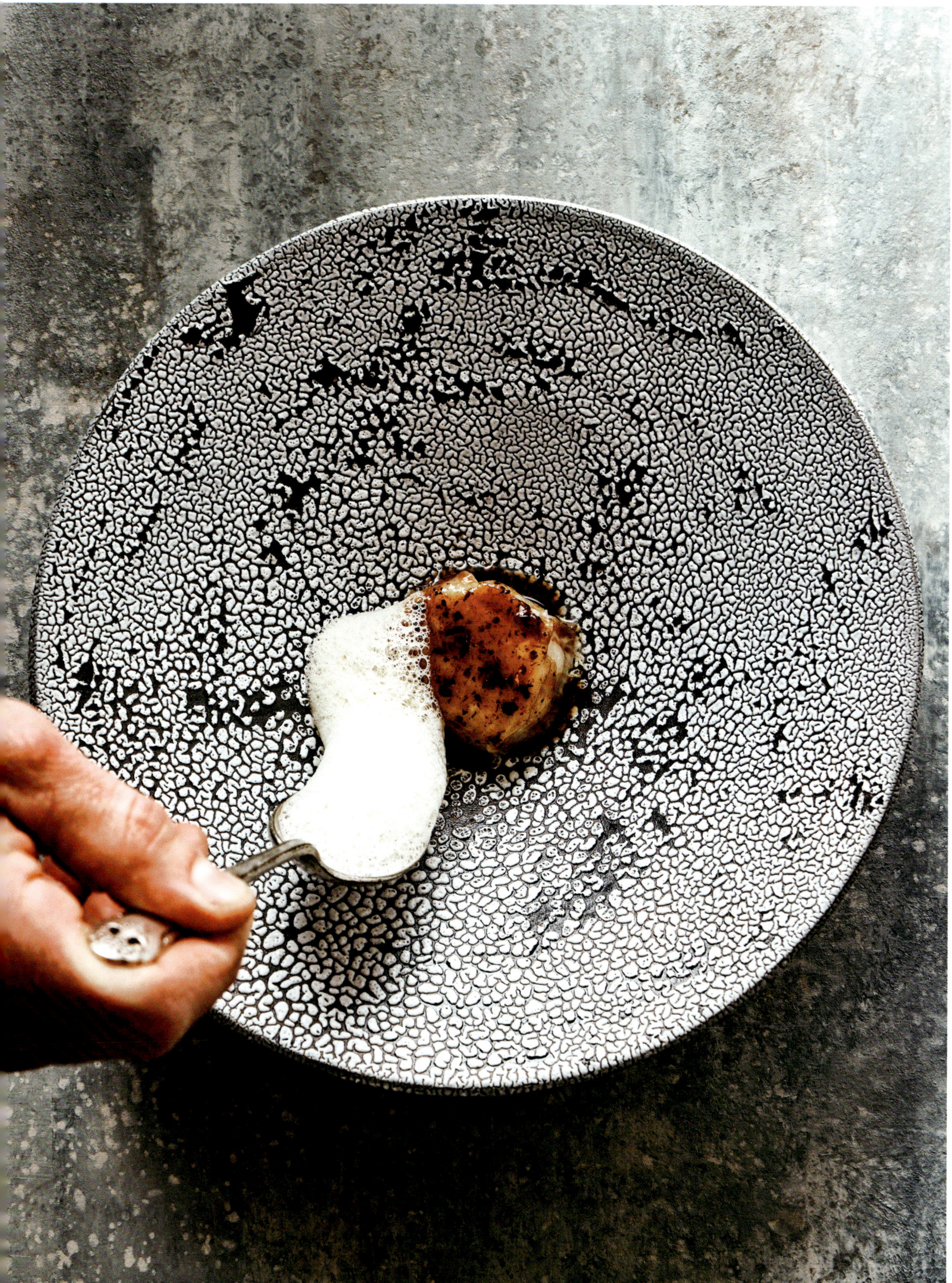

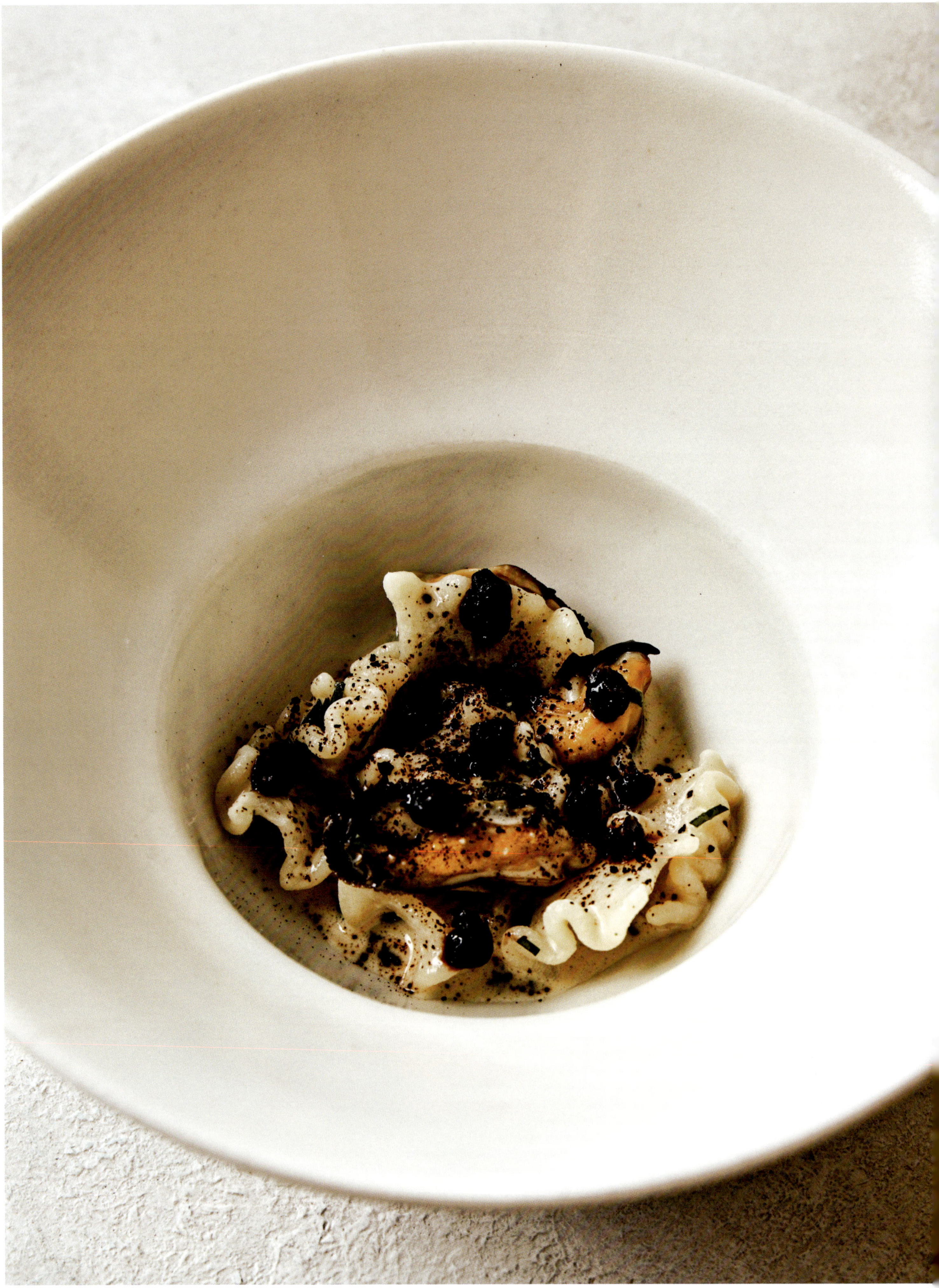

REGINETTE PASTA WITH GRILLED MUSSELS DRESSED IN FOIE GRAS & PRESERVED BLACK CURRANTS

The idea for this dish came to me one day when cooking mussels. There was something about the aroma that smelled like a piece of poached foie gras. So I thought if I made a rich enough sauce from foie gras and cream sherry, it would play well with the meatiness you can get from grilled mussels. I just had to figure out a way to add brightness to the dish to help cut through all the richness. I started thinking about different ways acid can be added to dishes where foie is the main focus. I eventually settled on black currants that had been dried in the summer and allowed to marinate in blueberry vinegar. We tossed the mussels and black currants with some reginette pasta cut to the same length as the mussels and finished with tarragon. The texture of the al dente pasta played well with the almost chewiness of the mussels.

steamed mussels

mussels	10lbs	Wash the mussels in cold water until completely purged. Place all ingredients in a wide rondeau, cover with a lid, and bring to a boil over medium-high heat. Once the mussels have opened, remove them, and continue to reduce the stock to 1,000mL. Remove the mussels from the shells and remove the beards from the mussels. Cool immediately.
sweet vermouth	1 (750ml) bottle	
Korean Soup stock	2 pouches	
ginger	40g	
shallot	150g	
garlic, halved	1 head	

foie parfait

shallot, sliced thin	100g	Reduce the shallot, garlic, aromatics, and alcohols until au sec. Add to a Vitamix with the foie gras and pink salt. Puree on high until smooth. Add the eggs one by one, being sure to fully incorporate after each addition. Slowly emulsify in the melted butter. Pass through a fine-mesh strainer and chill immediately.
garlic, sliced thin	25g	
bay leaf	1ea	
thyme sprigs	2ea	
Madeira	125mL	
cream sherry	125mL	
calvados	125mL	
foie gras	225g	
TCM pink salt	.5g	
eggs	2ea	
butter, melted	225g	

black currants

dried black currants	150g	Marinate the currants in the vinegar for a minimum of one month.
Jean-Marc Huilerie Beaujolais condiment aigre-doux de myrtille	200mL	

additional ingredients & to finish

reginette or other bite-size pasta	Sweat a small amount of the shallot in foie fat. Add 4 oz of sherry and reduce to au sec. Add 8 oz of mussel stock and reduce by half. Cook the pasta in heavily salted water to desired doneness. Meanwhile, grill the mussels over hardwood embers. Mount a few tablespoons of the foie parfait into the mussel stock, whisking constantly. Bring to a simmer and season to taste with kosher salt. Drain the pasta and place in a bowl with the grilled mussels, currants, and tarragon. Toss in enough of the foie sauce to glaze. Serve immediately.
tarragon, minced fine	
oloroso sherry	
shallot, minced fine	
foie fat	
reserved mussel stock	

PORK RIBS, WINTER SQUASH & PEANUT

One of my favorite places to eat in Nashville is King Market, a Lao-Thai grocery that also has a cafe inside. The first time I was there was with my old roommate, Chef Morgan McGlone. We ordered so much food that we received looks from the workers behind the counter. Some dishes were so spicy to me, but I couldn't stop eating them. We used to go there and try new dishes every few weeks. I wanted to do a dish inspired by one of my favorite Laotian salads, Tum Mak Hoong (papaya salad), and one of my absolute favorite things to eat in Nashville, Som Moo, a deep-fried, fermented sausage. We took Bear Creek Farm pork ribs, grilled them while slowly lacquering them with a black-garlic-and-onion hoisin sauce, and topped them with a spicy peanut crumble. Alongside, we served a raw butternut squash salad dressed with fish sauce, plenty of lime juice, and aromatic herbs.

---

pork brine

water	.5L	Mix together until completely dissolved.
salt	50g	
maple sugar	50g	
white pepper	5g	
makrut lime leaf	1ea	

pork ribs

St. Louis rib rack	1ea	Combine and Cryovac for 12 hours. Drain and place in a clean Cryovac bag and seal on full pressure. Cook at 71°C for 12 hours. Shock immediately in an ice bath to cool. Separate each rib by cutting between each bone. French the top 1½" of each bone and wrap the exposed bone in foil. Reserve until needed.
pork brine	.5L	

peanut crumble

garlic, minced fine	12g	Blanch the garlic in water three times by bringing it to a boil. Be sure to change the water each time. Fry at 300°F until golden brown, stirring constantly to prevent sticking. Drain and reserve. Fry the shallots at 300°F until golden brown, stirring constantly to prevent sticking. Drain and reserve. Place all ingredients in a robot coupe and grind to a fine crumb.
shallot, sliced paper-thin on a mandolin	20g	
peanuts, roasted at 325°F until golden brown	35g	
fermented chile powder (substitute dried, then ground sambal powder)	4g	

caramelized onion hoisin

onion jus	300g	Combine all ingredients. Puree in a Vitamix on high speed until smooth. Pass through a chinois and reserve.
black garlic molasses	20g	
black garlic shoyu	84g	
brown rice vin	45g	
fermented black beans	25g	
black garlic	20g	
sesame oil	7g	
prunes	60g	
five-spice powder	3g	
szechuan peppercorn	1g	

fish sauce vinaigrette

palm sugar	80g	Bring palm sugar, fish sauce, lemongrass, and chilies to a boil. Remove from heat and whisk to melt the sugar. Once cool, season with lime juice. Allow to sit overnight and strain the following day.
fish sauce	200g	
lemongrass, chopped	20g	
Thai bird chilies, halved	2g	
lime juice	40g	

additional ingredients & to finish

butternut squash, julienned on a mandolin	*For the ribs* Slowly grill the ribs, glazing every few minutes in the hoisin until caramelized and heated all the way through. Crust with the peanut crumble and finish with lime zest.
lime juice	
lime zest	*For the squash* Dress the julienned squash in fish sauce vinaigrette and lime juice to taste. Serve alongside the pork rib and finish with the fresh herbs.
Thai basil	
cilantro	
mint	
chive	

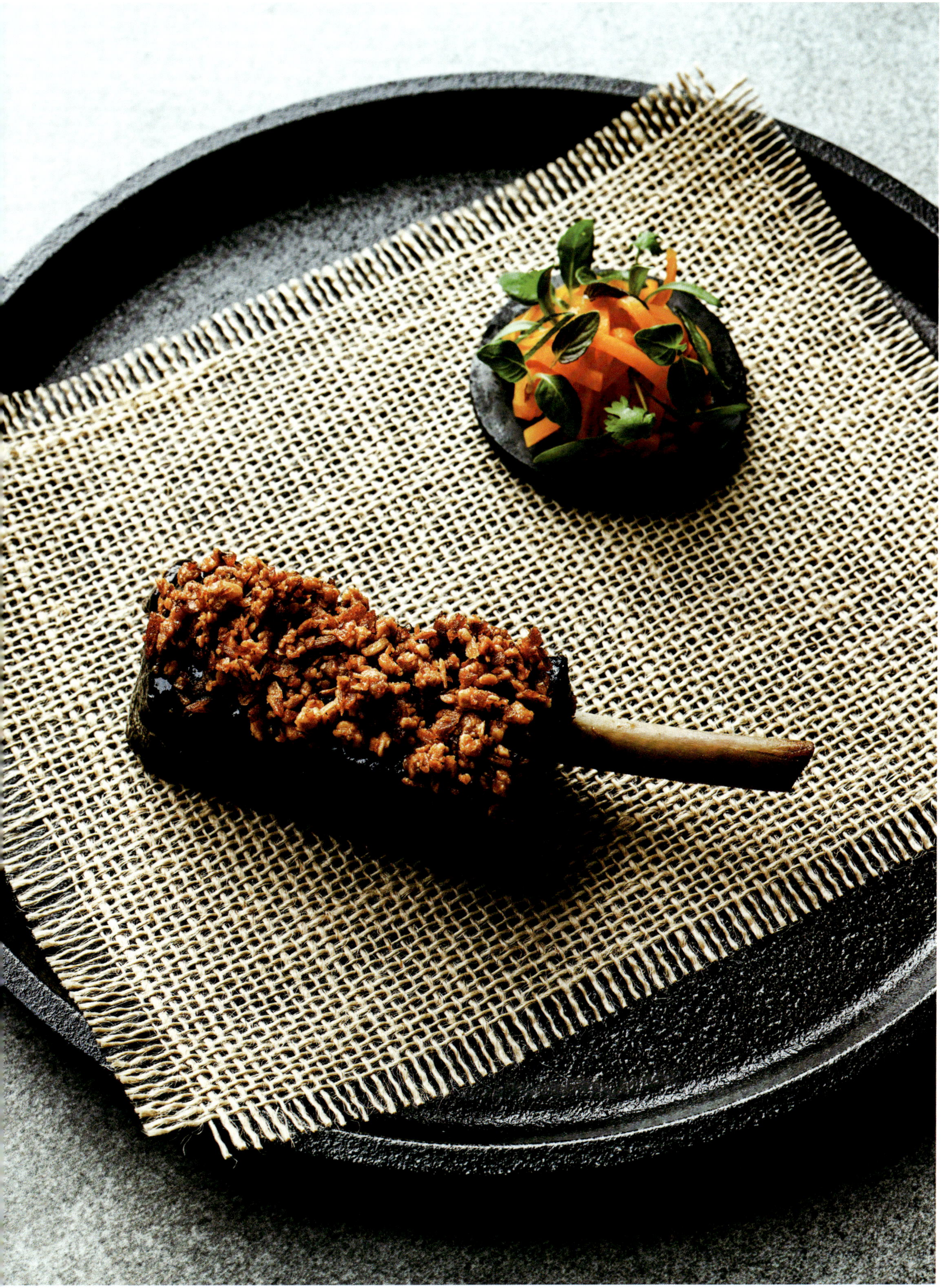

DRY-AGED BEAR CREEK FARM RIBLOIN, SAVOY CABBAGE, BLACK WALNUT & PÉRIGORD TRUFFLE

I love Bear Creek Farm beef. In my experience, it is some of the best beef in the country. For this dish, we aged a ribloin a little longer than we normally do, and, when grilling it, the aroma was an intense smell of roasted black walnuts. I told my sous chef, Connor Carlson, that we had to do a dish with beef and black walnuts. We ended up making a terrine with savoy cabbage leaves layered with a puree made from savoy cabbage, a black truffle puree, a haché of preserved Périgord truffles, and roasted black walnuts. We finished it with an intense sauce perigueux and shaved winter truffles. To help cut through the richness of the main course, we followed it with cabbage that had been fried in rendered bone marrow, creamed out with a cabbage puree, and hidden under Kumamoto A5 wagyu striploin that had been cured like country ham and aged for six months. We finished with a butter sauce made from all the unused parts of broccoli from the previous fall that had been charred, smoked, and then fermented. I think most people would've been happy with just a plate of the creamed cabbage.

---

sauce perigueux

beef tallow	100g	Melt the beef tallow. Once hot, add shallot and mushrooms. Cook until a deep golden brown is achieved. Add the Madeira and truffle juice and cook on medium heat until reduced by ¾ of its original volume. Add the demi-glace and reduce to 1L. Strain through a fine-mesh strainer and reserve.
shallot, sliced thin	300g	
mushroom stems, sliced	120g	
dried mushroom, such as maitake or morel	60g	
Madeira	750mL	
truffle juice	500mL	
demi-glace	3,500g	

seasoned perigueux

perigueux	100g	Combine, bring to a simmer, and reserve.
preserved truffle, haché	8g	
black truffle balsamic	2g	

cabbage puree

cabbage hearts, cores removed (outer leaves saved for cabbage terrine)	345g	Sweat the cabbage in the butter over medium heat until it begins to soften. Cover with the cream, preserved truffle juice, and a cartouche. Cook until completely soft. Strain off all remaining liquid, reserve, and place cabbage in a Vitamix. Blend on high, adding the reserved liquid only as needed. Once smooth, season to taste with salt and pass through a fine-mesh strainer. Cool and reserve in a piping bag until ready to use.
butter	50g	
heavy cream	600mL	
preserved truffle juice	50g	
salt	t.t.	

preserved winter truffle puree

porcini mushroom garum	250g	Bring all the ingredients except the gellan gum to a boil. Transfer to a Vitamix and blend on high speed until smooth. Shear in the gellan gum, pass through a fine-mesh strainer into a clean pot, and bring to a boil for 1 minute, stirring constantly. Cool in a shallow pan overnight. The next day, return to a blender and puree until completely smooth. Pass through a fine-mesh strainer into a piping bag and reserve.
heavy cream	175g	
vegetable bouillon paste	10g	
white pepper	1g	
clove	1ea	
preserved truffle	65g	
black walnut miso	50g	
low acyl gellan gum	2g	

to assemble the terrine

outer cabbage leaves, blanched and cooled	Cut the leaves to 3" × 1" strips. In a 3" × 1" rectangle mold, lay a leaf in the bottom. Add a thin layer of cabbage puree and pinch of black walnuts. Add another cabbage leaf. Pipe a thin layer of truffle puree and a pinch of truffle haché. Add another leaf and repeat the process to the top of the mold. Wrap in a foil and bake at 245°F for 25 minutes. Remove from the oven, remove the foil, and lay another 3" × 1" mold over the top. Add a few quarter sheet pans or other level item to gently weigh down the terrines. Allow them to set for one hour. Before serving, brush with rendered beef fat, season with sea salt, and warm in an oven.
black walnuts, toasted and chopped	
truffle puree	
preserved winter truffle, haché	

fried cabbage

beef tallow	50g
cabbage hearts, small dice	400g
salt	t.t.
cabbage puree as needed	

Melt the beef tallow over high heat and add the diced cabbage. Fry until golden brown, season with salt, and dress with enough cabbage puree to make the texture of creamed cabbage (this will vary depending on how much water may be released from the cabbage).

brassica butter

shallot, sliced thin	60g
2% charred brassica stems (see base recipes on page 267)	90g
miso consommé	190g
butter, cubed and chilled	190g
xanthan gum	.25g

Place all the ingredients except the butter and xanthan gum in a small sauce pot with a tight-fitting lid. Cook over medium heat until the shallots are tender. Place in a Vitamix and puree on high speed until as smooth as possible. Add the xanthan gum and slowly emulsify in the chilled butter. Pass through a fine-mesh strainer and reserve in a warm place.

additional ingredients & to finish

wagyu ham (see base recipes on page 273)
ribloin, grilled and rested
winter truffle
Maldon sea salt

Place a slice of the grilled beef on the left side of a plate. To the right, place a cabbage terrine. Spoon an ounce of perigueux sauce over the steak and finish with shaved truffle.

In a separate dish, spoon some of the creamed cabbage, cover with a slice of the wagyu ham, and pour the hot brassica butter over the top.

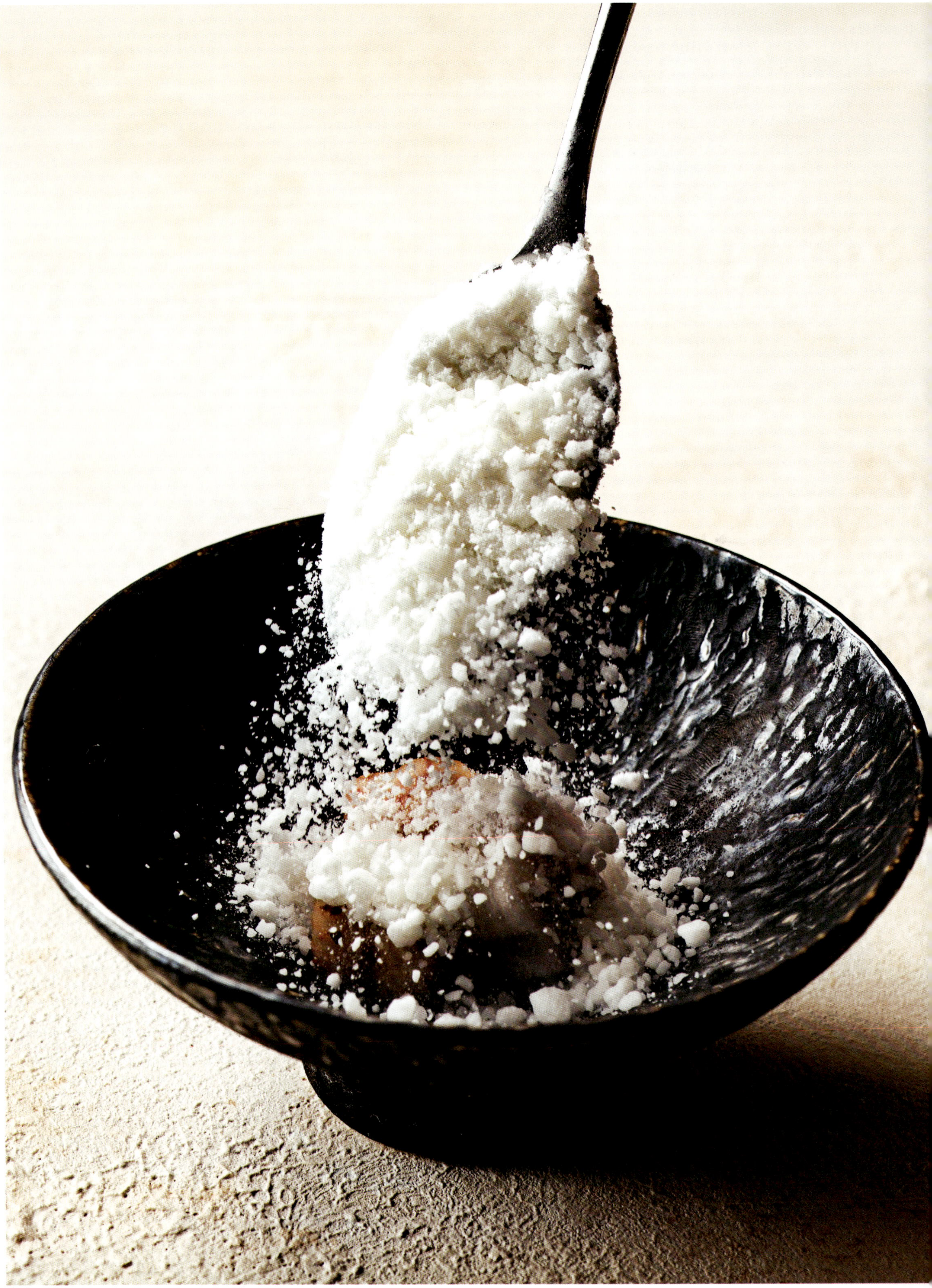

ASIAN PEAR & KIMCHI

This dish was inspired by the Korean salad musaengchae. Crunchy Korean radish, or mu, is dressed in a spicy sweet-and-sour dressing. For this version, we used purple daikons from Bells Bend Farms dressed with a vinaigrette made from fermented pear juice and finished with an ice-cold, refreshing pear snow. This was the spiciest transition to desserts that we ever did, but texturally it was by far my favorite.

radish dressing

fermented pear juice (see page 269)	70g
fish sauce	25g
aged pear vinegar	30g
sugar	17g
Korean chili flake	14g

Combine ingredients and mix well until sugar is fully dissolved. Chill and reserve.

asian pear snow

Asian pear juice	900g
ascorbic acid	5g
dextrose	30g
cornstarch	10g
gelatin, bloomed	5g

Mix pear juice, ascorbic acid, dextrose, and cornstarch and bring to a boil. Stir in bloomed gelatin. Allow to freeze in a shallow hotel pan. Once frozen, break up into small chunks and toss with liquid nitrogen. Process in a robot coupe or Thermomix until a fine snow is formed. Reserve in the freezer until needed.

additional ingredients & to finish

Shinko pear, diced into ½" cubes
purple daikon, cut into ½" × ½" × ¼" slices
Maldon sea salt

Dress the radish and the pear in the dressing and marinate for 5 minutes. Spoon into the center of a plate, season with sea salt, and top with the pear snow.

RAZOR CLAM, FERMENTED RASPBERRY, ROSE & HORSERADISH ICE CREAM

This was originally meant to be a savory dish. I had done similar flavors with live sea urchin from Maine, which has an amazing floral, roselike quality. However, the addition of the horseradish ice cream made this the first course into the sweeter end of the menu. We served East Coast razor clams raw and dressed with a vinaigrette made with fermented raspberry juice, raspberry vinegar, and rose water. It is finished with a few drops of loquat pit oil, preserved horseradish juice, a very crunchy Pacific sea salt, and horseradish ice cream that had been frozen and shaved on a microplane into liquid nitrogen.

---

fermented raspberry vinaigrette

fermented raspberry juice (see page 270)	45g	Mix until well combined and keep chilled.
Jean-Marc's Huilerie Beaujolaise vinegar de Framboise	1g	
rose water	.5g	

salted buttermilk

good buttermilk	1L	Mix well and allow to sit covered at room temperature for 3 days.
kosher salt	10g	
preserved horseradish	30g	

horseradish ice cream

eggs	15ea	Whip the eggs and sugar until nice and airy. Meanwhile, bring the base syrup and buttermilk to a simmer over medium heat, whisking constantly. Temper into the egg mixture. Return to the heat and bring to 170°F, whisking constantly so the mixture doesn't begin to scorch or curdle. Once it has reached 170°F, remove from the heat, whisk in the 40g preserved horseradish and the cold butter. Add enough titanium dioxide until the ice cream is an opaque white color. Pass through a fine-mesh strainer into a Paco canister and freeze. On the day of, process the Paco canister one full cycle, place into a ninth pan or small 2" × 2" mold, and refreeze. Reserve until needed.
granulated sugar	500g	
base syrup (see below)	250g	
salted buttermilk	725g	
preserved horseradish	40g	
butter, cold, cut into small cubes	175g	
titanium dioxide	t.t.	

base syrup

Uno ice cream stabilizer	6g	Mix the ice cream stabilizer and sugar together. Warm the water over medium heat to 150°F. Blend the sugar mixture into the water with an immersion blender, return to the heat, and bring to a boil, whisking constantly. Pass through a fine-mesh strainer, cool, and reserve.
sugar	440g	
filtered water	600g	

additional ingredients & to finish

razor clams, removed from their shells, cleaned, frozen, and sliced on a slight bias to a ¼" thickness (shells and trim reserved for stock)	Shave the horseradish ice cream on a microplane into liquid nitrogen, and reserve. Place one of the diced razor clams into one of the shells or into a small bowl on ice. Dress with desired amount of raspberry vinaigrette, 4 to 5 drops of loquat oil, desired amount of horseradish juice, and a pinch of Pacific sea salt. Before serving, top with the horseradish ice cream and some of the freeze-dried raspberry.
horseradish juice, strained from preserved horseradish	
loquat oil (see page 156)	
Pacific sea salt	
freeze-dried raspberries, pulverized	

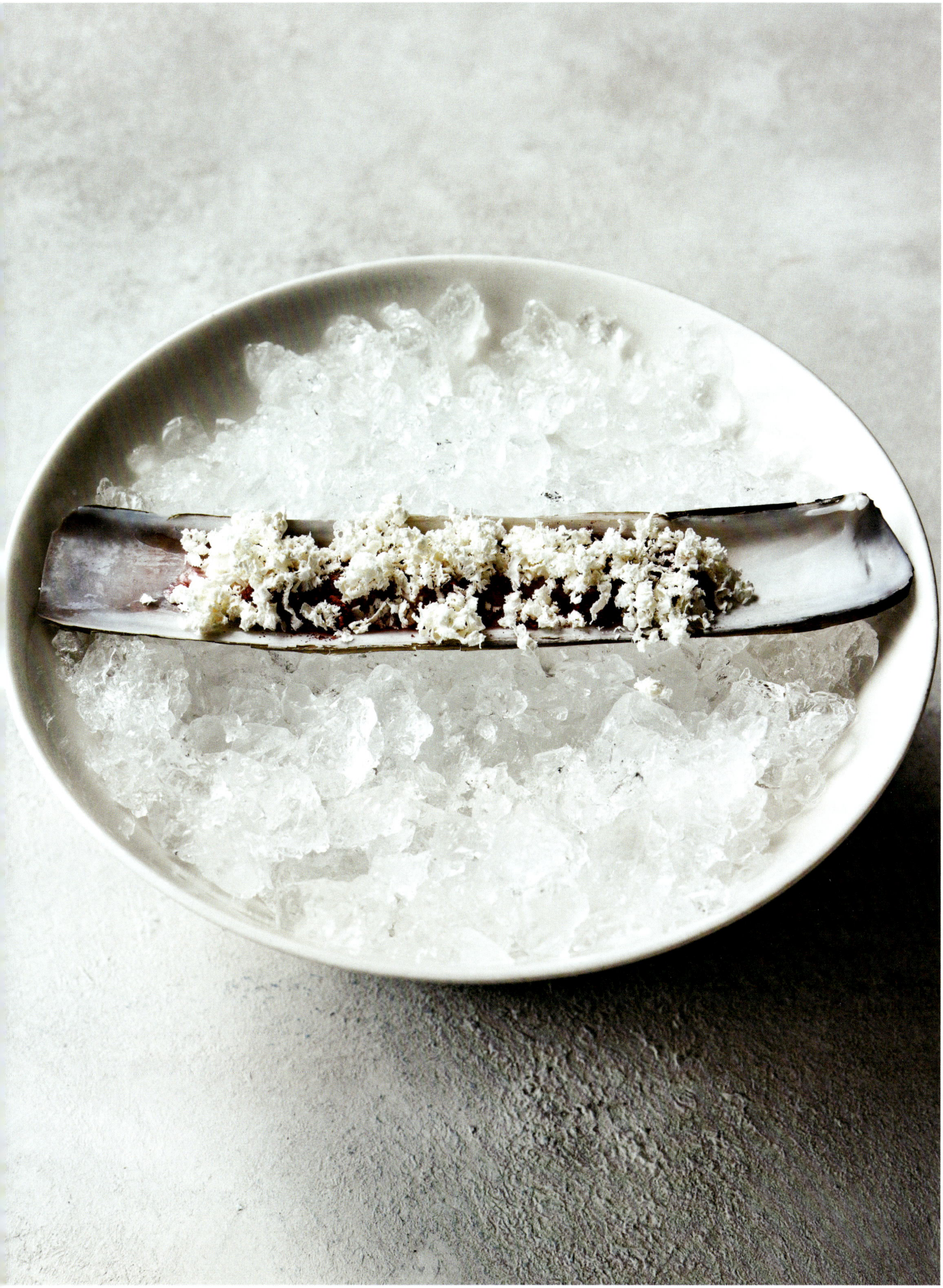

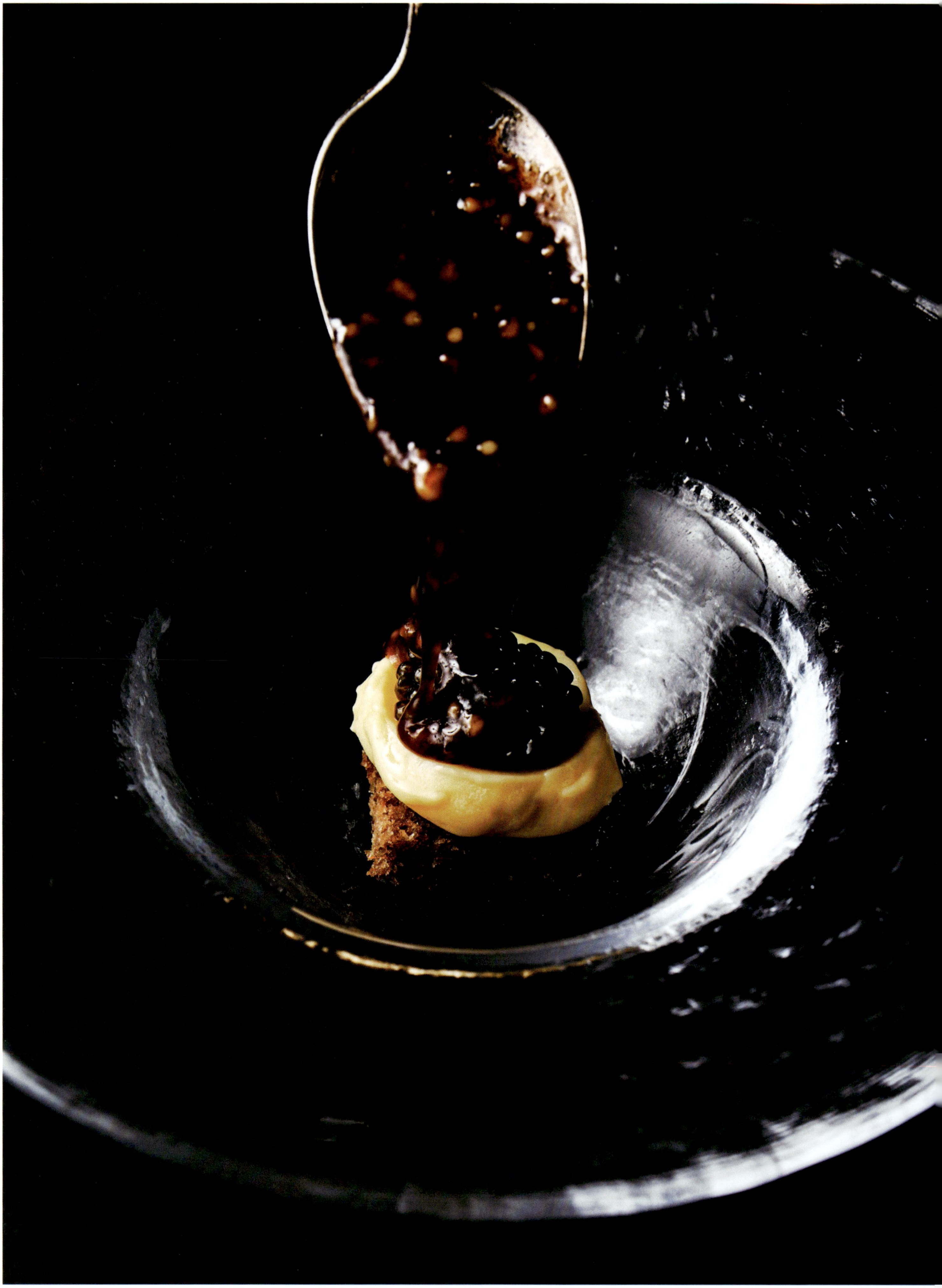

BURNT BANANA, BLACK WALNUT, CULTURED BUTTER & CAVIAR

My grandmother often made banana bread at the house. I always loved when she did, and I was always in the kitchen fast so I could get a fresh, warm slice. She would put what I like to call a healthy amount of margarine on it before giving it to me. This dish evolved over the past couple of years, but I finally transitioned from a banana slowly roasted in oak embers to a bread made from the bananas and a black walnut miso. I topped it with a quenelle of cultured butter from Animal Farm Creamery and aged Schrenckii caviar. We poured a warm toffee made from nocino and candied black walnuts in front of the guests, just melting the butter and barely warming the caviar.

---

burnt banana bread

AP flour	190g
kosher salt	2g
baking soda	4g
butter, softened	115g
granulated sugar	150g
eggs, lightly beaten	2ea
burnt bananas, mashed into a puree	270g
walnut miso	118g
vanilla extract	4g
candied green walnuts, chopped into ¼" pieces	70g

Preheat the oven to 350°F. Sift the AP flour, salt, and baking soda and set aside. Cream the butter and sugar together until smooth, using the paddle attachment of a stand mixer. Next, add the eggs until fully incorporated, followed by the banana puree. Next, add the sifted dry ingredients until fully incorporated, being sure not to overmix. Lastly, mix in the miso, vanilla, and green walnuts until mixed in well. Spray a 9" × 5" bread pan with nonstick spray. Bake for 45 minutes or until a cake tester comes out clean when placed in the center. Allow to fully cool in the pan before removing.

black walnut toffee

sugar	450g
butter	400g
salt	5g
toasted black walnut, roughly chopped	300g
walnut miso	45g
nocino	75g

Bring the sugar, butter, and salt to 300°F while whisking constantly. Remove from the heat and add the toasted black walnuts, walnut miso, and nocino. Cool on a Silpat-lined tray and transfer to an airtight container.

truffle dashi

dashi	660mL
mirin	250mL
white shoyu	250mL
kuzu starch	15g
cold water	28g
black truffle paste	45g

Bring the dashi, mirin, and shoyu to a simmer. Mix the kuzu starch and cold water and slowly whisk into the dashi base. Bring back to a simmer, allow to simmer for 2 minutes. Pass through a fine-mesh strainer. Stir in the truffle paste and cool.

finished walnut toffee sauce

truffle dashi	240g
black walnut toffee	85g
candied green walnuts, chopped fine	35g

Bring to a simmer over medium heat, stirring constantly with a whisk until well combined. Reserve in a warm place until needed.

additional ingredients & to finish

Schrenckii caviar
Maldon salt
good cultured butter at room temperature

Slice the bread into 2" × 1" × ¼" slices, removing the crust. Gently warm in a low oven but do not let the bread dry out. Place the bread in the bottom of a bowl. Place a teaspoon-size quenelle of cultured butter on the bread and make a small indentation with the back of the spoon. Place desired amount of caviar in the butter, add a pinch of salt, and pour the warmed finished walnut toffee sauce over the caviar.

YEAST DONUT, FOIE GRAS, CANDY CAP MUSHROOMS

This version of the donut is probably my favorite and was also a favorite of many of our regulars. For New Year's Eve, we did a bold menu inspired by breakfast for dinner. My sous chef Ian had done a dessert that was a frozen waffle dressed in a syrup made from candy cap mushrooms, which were then smoked and fried, tasting of bacon. Candy cap mushrooms naturally have an intense smell of maple syrup. I told Ian this had to be the next donut! Inspired by maple-and-bacon donuts, we would turn the candy cap mushroom syrup into a glaze and finish the donut by topping with the chopped pieces of the candied mushroom "bacon."

---

candy cap mushrooms

dried candy cap mushrooms	50g	Combine mushrooms, water, and sugar, and pressure-cook on high pressure for 45 minutes. Strain through a fine-mesh strainer and reserve the liquid and mushrooms separately. Reduce the liquid to 500g and cool.
filtered water	1L	
granulated sugar	200g	

candy cap mushroom glaze

reduced cooking liquid (from above)	500g	Combine ingredients. Blend with an immersion blender until smooth. Cool and reserve until needed.
10x sugar	260g	
Ultra-Tex 3	7g	

candy cap bacon

reserved mushrooms from above	Cold-smoke for 30 minutes. Fry at 325°F until no moisture remains. Be sure not to burn. Transfer to a dehydrator set at 110°F for 12 hours. Allow to cool, chop into ¼" pieces, and reserve in an airtight container.

additional ingredients

donut dough (see page 66)	Make a small hole in the side of the donut and fill with the pastry cream. Glaze the top of the donut and season with the sea salt. Finish with desired amount of chopped Candy Cap Bacon Bits.
foie pastry cream (see page 66)	
Maldon sea salt	

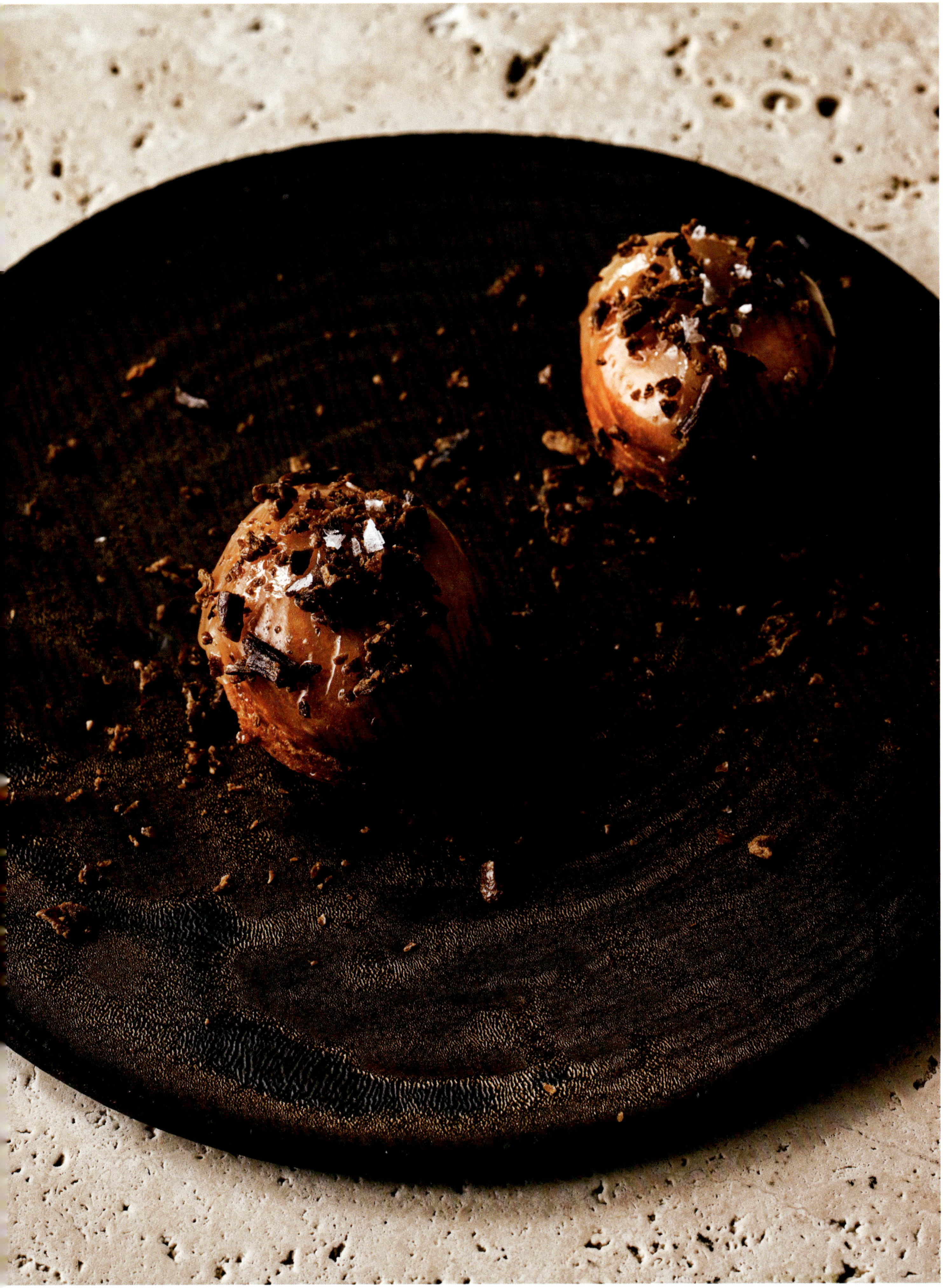

SPRING 2022

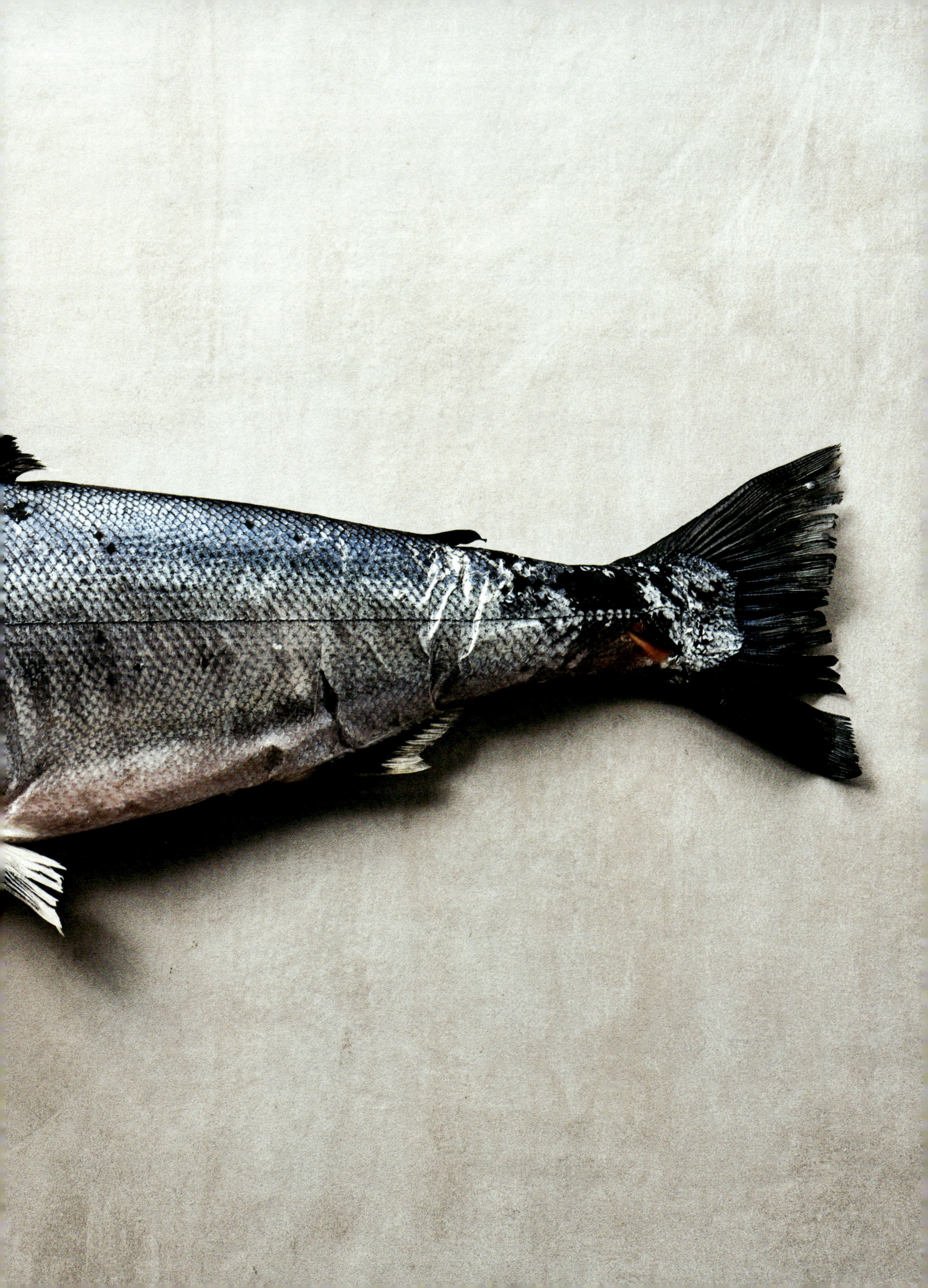

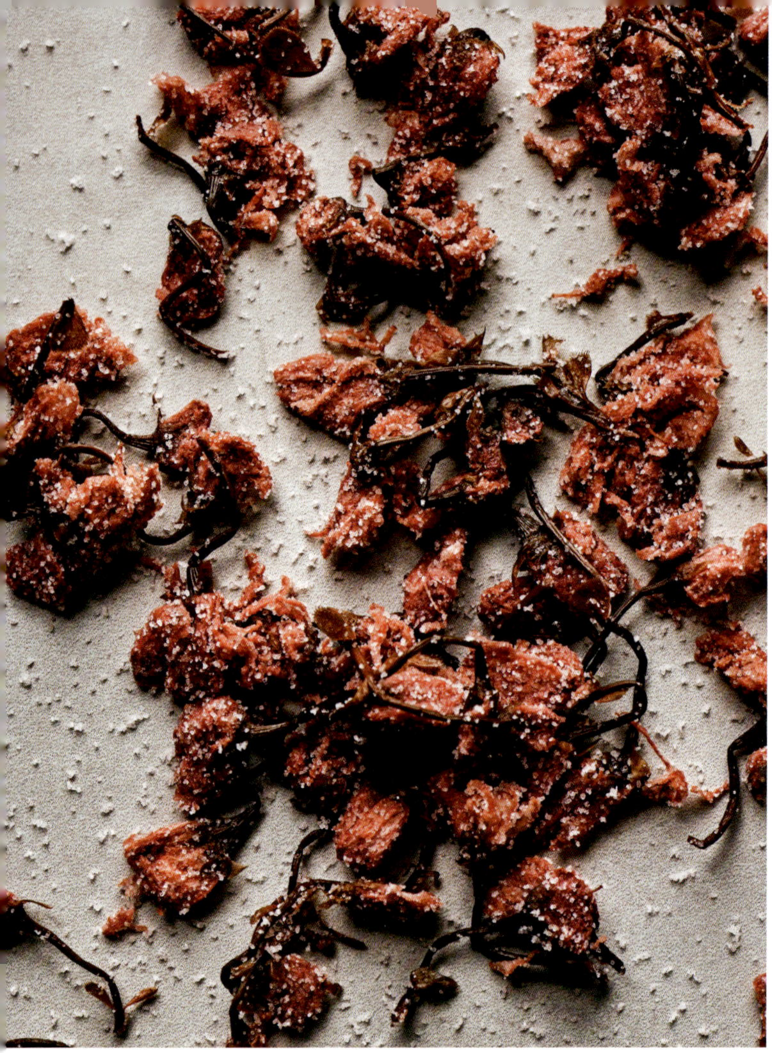
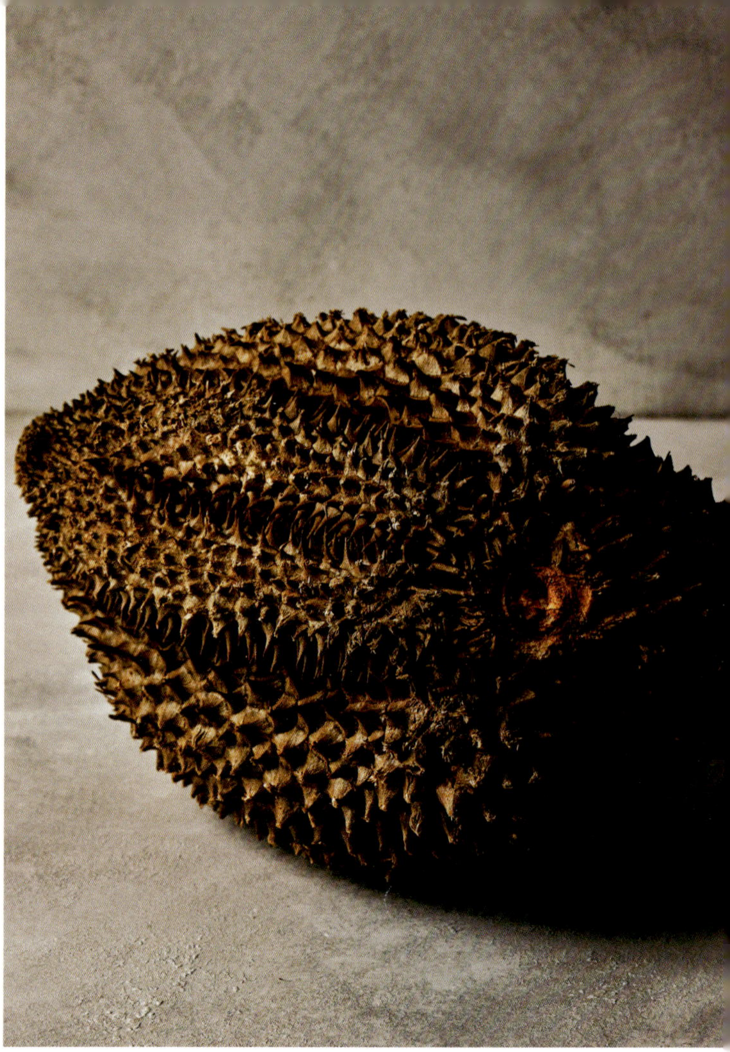
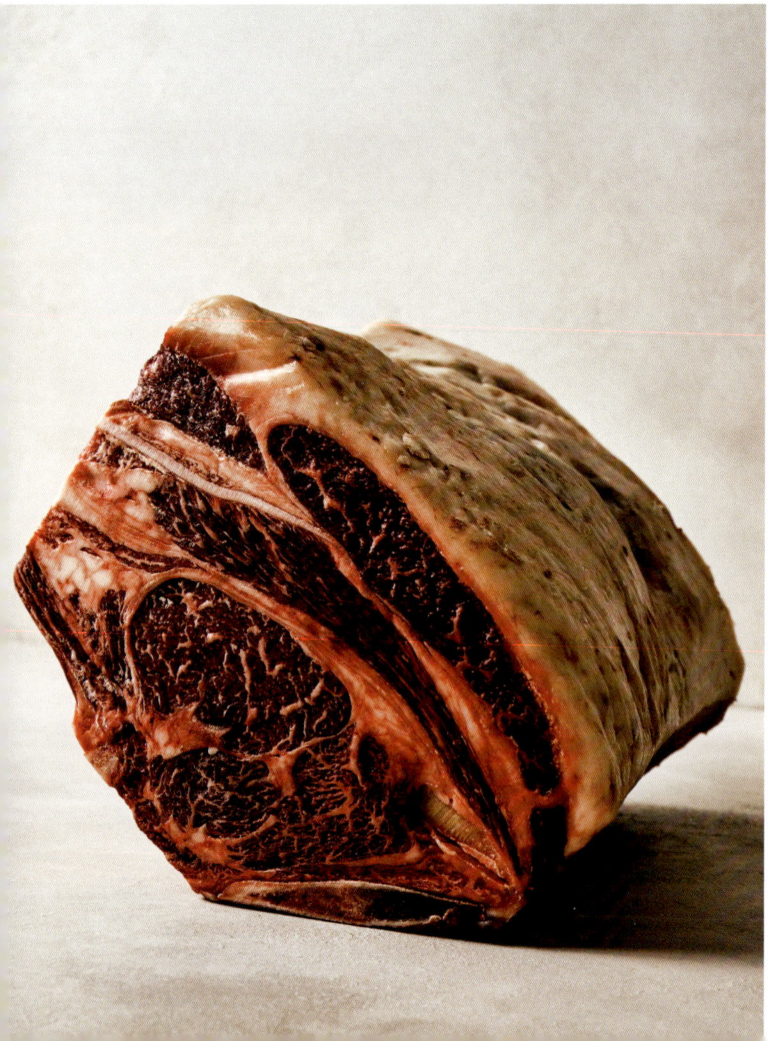
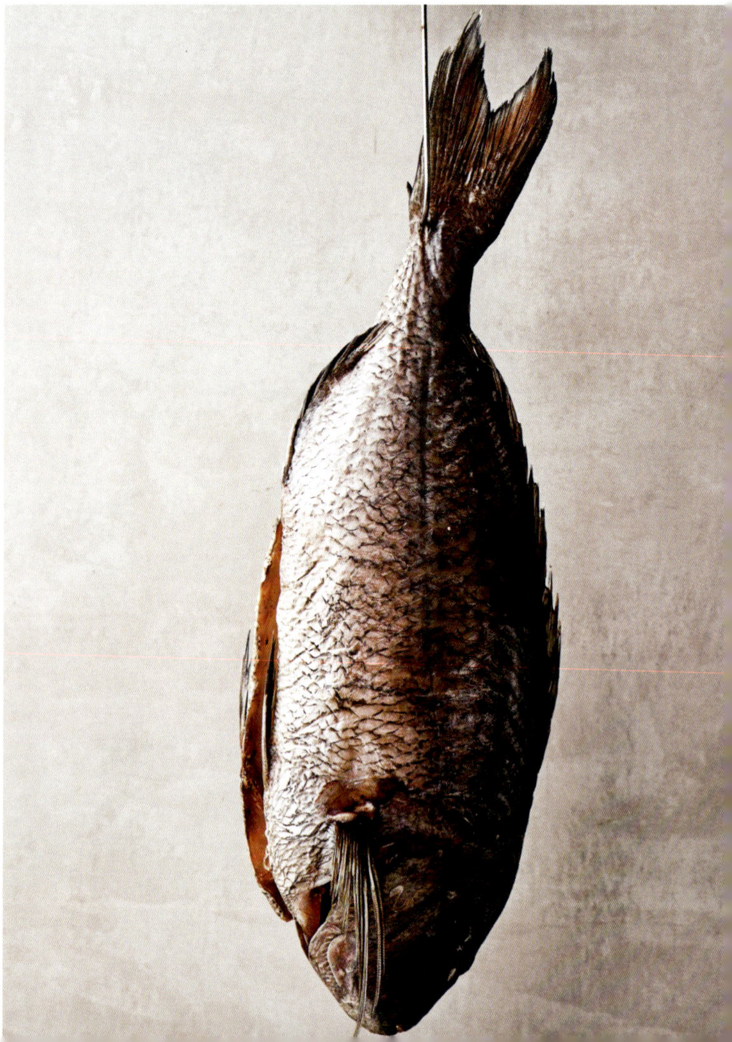

This particular spring season had me going in a few wildly different directions, utilizing Cuban, Japanese, and Vietnamese influences in some of the diverse dishes on this menu. Some trips I took had a profound effect on me, such as the excursion to New York City to eat at Shion 69 Leonard Street, commemorated by the prawn dish with daylilies below (see page 238). Others were more fly-by-the-seat-of-my-pants, like the random side trip we took to a Vietnamese market in Oklahoma City while there for a pop-up with Nonesuch Restaurant. I had never tried durian fruit before, and seeing it at the market in various forms inspired me to try a few new dishes with it once I got back to Nashville (see page 253). A similar thing happened when I visited an Asian market near Buford Highway in Atlanta, discovering nancé fruit, a yellow, cherrylike fruit that tasted somewhat sour. Unripened nancé has oxalic acid, the same compound in rhubarb, which gives it that bright, sour characteristic. As I mentioned in "Cooking with Confidence" (see page 138), being open to new flavors and ideas and trusting your gut and internal flavor library can lead to some fun new directions in your cooking. During this season, that openness led me to try new ingredients that I wouldn't have been as receptive to experimenting with in the past.

Since spring seems to inspire bold floral dishes—after the rustic flavors of fall and winter—I continued to use wild and foraged ingredients, including Sakura cherry blossoms preserved at their peak, which add incredible complexity to dishes. I also used wild daylilies—a flower aptly suited to spring dishes, as they have a flavor reminiscent of asparagus and fresh English peas. Another wild edible to seek out if you live in the middle of the country is pineapple weed, common from Minnesota on down to Alabama, an herb and flower that tastes like chamomile on a tropical vacation.

As in other seasons, a few of my favorite food memories growing up in Florida made their way onto the menu in completely reimagined forms. The crab salad (see page 245), so common at markets in Florida, was enlivened by ramp capers preserved from the previous spring. The Cuban sandwiches I grew up eating near Tampa were enshrined by a dry-aged pork coulotte and plantain dish (see page 254) that was a favorite for many of our guests. We were especially proud of the fermented plantain bread. And speaking of bread, I even took a stab at a playful yet meaty take on avocado toast using Denver steak, one of the most flavorful cuts of meat we incorporated into this very fun spring season.

Credit: Todd Saal

SPRING 2022 MENU

carabinero prawn shiokara, daylilies & koshihikari rice **238**

aged buri belly, chutoro, smoked oyster & seaweeds **241**

dry-aged otoro, tosazu, preserved coriander berries **242**

florida blue crab, sunchoke dauphine, ramp capers **245**

sakura masu, sakura blossom, salted white peach **246**

shaved bear creek farm denver steak, fava bean & stilton cheese **249**

fire-exploded kidney flowers, bamboo shoot & baby leeks **250**

dry-aged pork shoulder, fermented durian & black sesame **253**

dry-aged pork coulotte & plantain **254**

plantain gnocchi, preserved tomato & castelvetrano olives **256**

fermented plantain bread, bob woods ham, plantain syrup **257**

―――――――――

plantain cafécito **259**

nancé, triple cream cheese, pineapple weed & schrenckii caviar **260**

cauliflower ice cream, milk chocolate & black ants **263**

CARABINERO PRAWN SHIOKARA, DAYLILIES & KOSHIHIKARI RICE

This dish was inspired by a trip that my sous chef Connor and I took to New York. We ate at Shion 69 Leonard Street, an amazing seafood-focused experience in Tribeca. My friend Pedro Iglesias (see the Foreword on page viii) had called ahead and ordered the chinmi for us. Chinmi, or "rare taste" in Japanese, usually refers to seafood dishes that are salt-preserved, fermented, or pickled. Each region has its own version of chinmi, and they are meant to be eaten with sake. One of the most flavorful and intense things I have ever eaten was the prawn shiokara I tried that day. The flavor was as if I had just pulled a prawn straight out of the water, ripped off the head, seasoned it with a good helping of salt, and sucked out all the juice. We had been getting Carabinero, or red prawns, from Spain, which have a sweet, intense shrimp flavor. I wanted our guests to be able to experience this same mind-blowing flavor that we did, though I figured we'd have to make it a little more composed for some of our clientele. We ended up serving it on warm koshihikari rice and dressing it in a dashi made from dried daylily blossoms.

---

daylily dashi

kuzu	20g
filtered water	30g
dashi	850g
mirin	150g
sake	150g
white soy	150g
dried daylily flowers, stems removed	25g

Mix the kuzu and water into a slurry. Bring all the ingredients to a boil besides the kuzu and water. Whisk in the slurry and boil for one minute. Let cool to room temperature, chill, and reserve until needed.

prawn shiokara

Carabinero prawns, peeled and deveined	500g
kosher salt	15g
mirin	30g
sake	30g
kombu, rinsed	10g
rice koji	18g

Toss all ingredients together well and seal in an appropriately sized Cryovac bag. Ferment under refrigeration for 2 weeks. Slice into ½" pieces before serving.

koshihikari rice

koshihikari rice, washed well until the water runs clear, then soaked for 30 minutes	180g
filtered water	200mL
sushi vinegar (see below)	t.t.

Combine rice, water, and vinegar in a medium pot. Cover with a tight-fitting lid and bring to a boil over medium heat. Reduce the heat to low and cook for 12 minutes. Remove from the heat and let rest for 10 minutes. Remove the lid and fluff the rice with a rubber spatula or rice paddle. Season to taste with additional sushi vinegar and reserve covered in a warm place until needed.

sushi vinegar

rice vinegar	70g
sugar	50g
sea salt	10g

Combine and warm gently in a sauce pot until everything is dissolved. Set aside to cool.

to finish

Place a spoonful of the seasoned rice in the center of a bowl. Top with a few pieces of the diced shrimp and dress with a couple of ounces of the rewarmed daylily dashi.

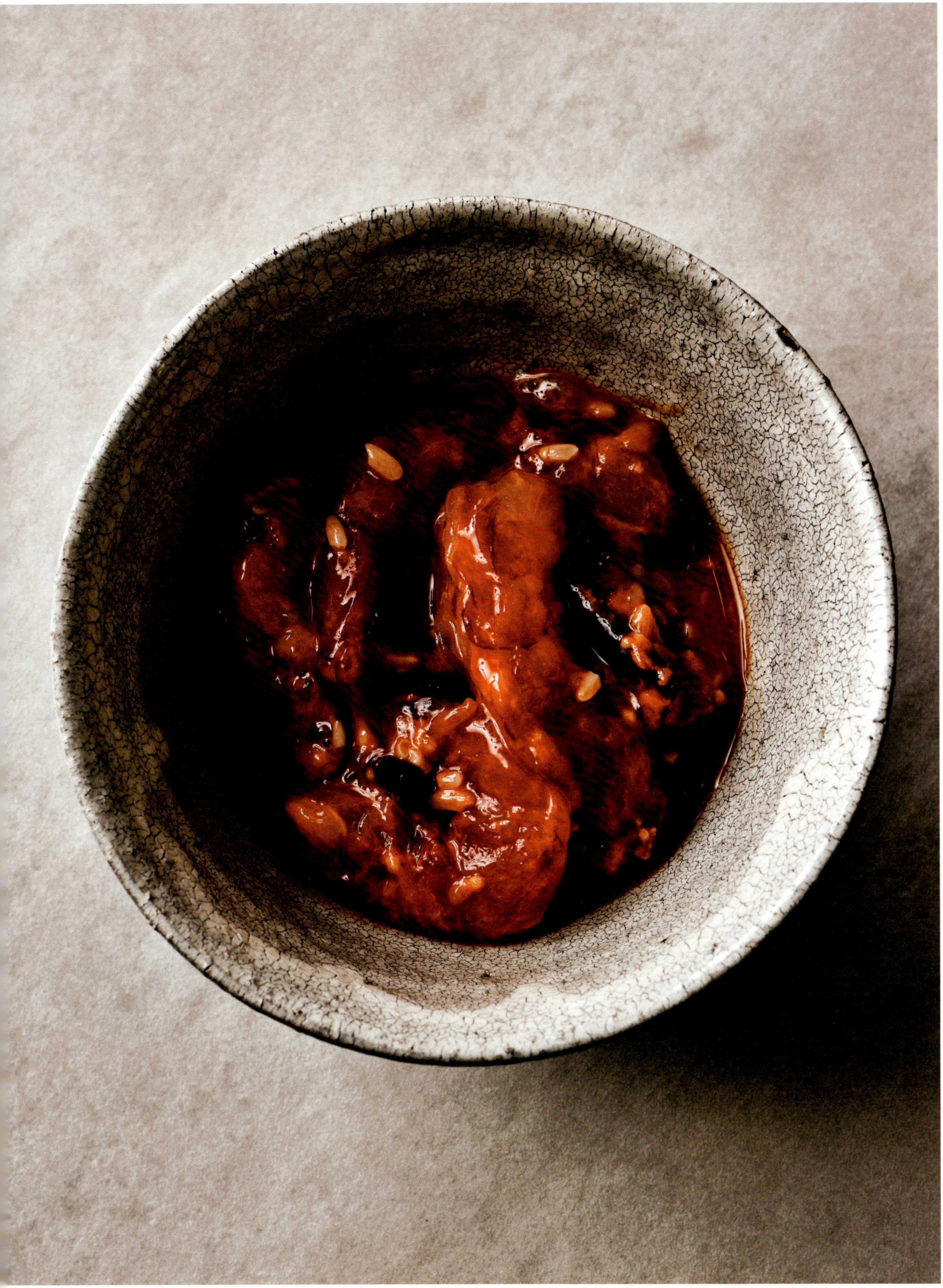

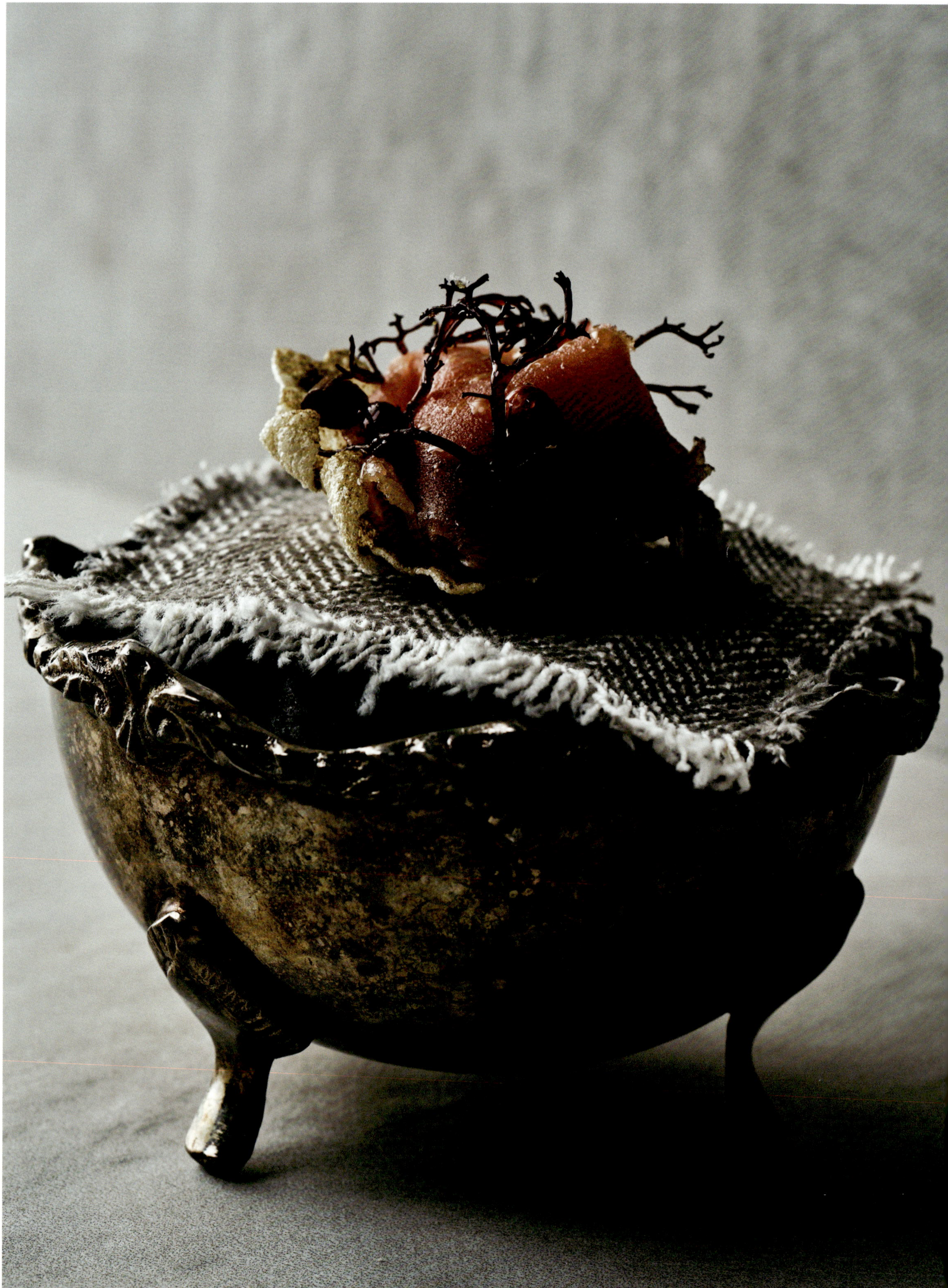

AGED BURI BELLY, CHUTORO, SMOKED OYSTER & SEAWEEDS

The next two dishes here are a progression of toro, or tuna belly. The first is chutoro, less fatty than the otoro, which is the fattiest part of the tuna belly. We sliced it thin and served it over a tartare of the akami, or lean meat of the fish. We mixed the diced tuna with onions that had been marinated in a smoked shoyu and smoked oyster emulsion, and served with a mix of fresh and pickled seaweeds on top of a dashi cracker seasoned heavily with bonito.

---

smoked oyster mayo

cured and smoked oysters, not dried	100g
egg yolk	1ea
yuzu juice	25mL
smoked bone oil (see page 272)	200mL
hot water	10mL

Puree oysters with egg yolk, water, and yuzu juice until completely smooth. Slowly emulsify in the oil.

dashi cracker

glutenous rice flour	300g
dashi	300g
smoked oyster shiro dashi	30g

Combine ingredients until completely mixed and a sticky dough forms. Roll out golf-ball-size portions between two layers of plastic wrap (spray with pan spray) or in a 9 × 12 Cryovac bag. Steam at 100°C for 5 minutes. Dehydrate at 57°C for 5 hours and place at room temperature to dry for an additional 10 hours. Fry at 325°F until puffed.

pickled seaweed

Omed sherry vinegar	240mL
tsuyu soup base	120mL
filtered water	60mL
sugar	125g
seaweed, such as velvet horn, dulse, or sea grapes	100g

Bring all the ingredients except the seaweeds to a boil. Pour the liquid over the seaweeds and allow to cool to room temperature. Transfer to a refrigerator and store for at least 48 hours before using.

additional ingredients & to finish

diced buri belly
chutoro
fresh ogo seaweed
Pacific sea salt

Dress the diced buri belly in some of the smoked oyster mayo. Fold in some of the chopped, pickled seaweed. Break the crackers into bite-size pieces, top with a spoonful of the buri belly mixture, and cover with a slice of the chutoro. Season with Pacific sea salt and fresh ogo seaweed.

DRY-AGED OTORO, TOSAZU, PRESERVED CORIANDER BERRIES

For the next bite, we served the sliced otoro, the fattiest part of the tuna, in a chilled tosazu, an oil made from cured and smoked fish bones, with coriander berries from our garden that we'd preserved like capers the previous summer. We instructed our guests to first eat the tuna and then drink the chilled tosazu to cleanse the palate.

---

tosazu

kombu	25g	Steep kombu in filtered water overnight. Strain and add all remaining ingredients except katsuobushi. Bring to a boil, pour over katsuobushi, and allow to steep overnight in the refrigerator. Strain, chill, and reserve.
filtered water	300mL	
rice vinegar	150mL	
mirin	75mL	
white shoyu	125mL	
katsuobushi	20g	

additional ingredients & to finish

smoked bone oil (see page 272)
otoro, aged 16 days
coriander capers (see page 270)

Place a slice of the otoro in a chilled bowl. Dress with a tablespoon of the chilled tosazu, a few drops of bone oil, and a few coriander berries.

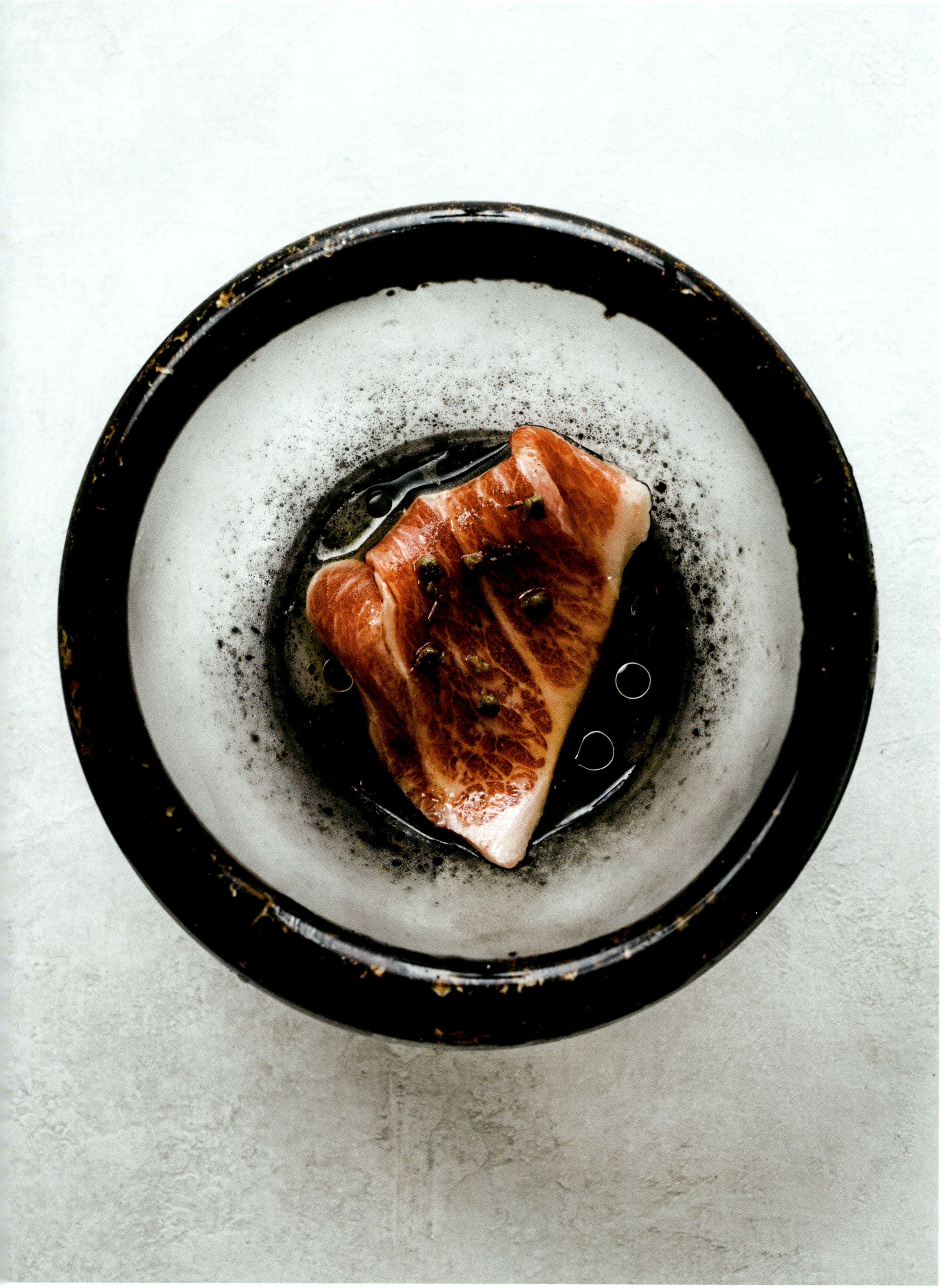

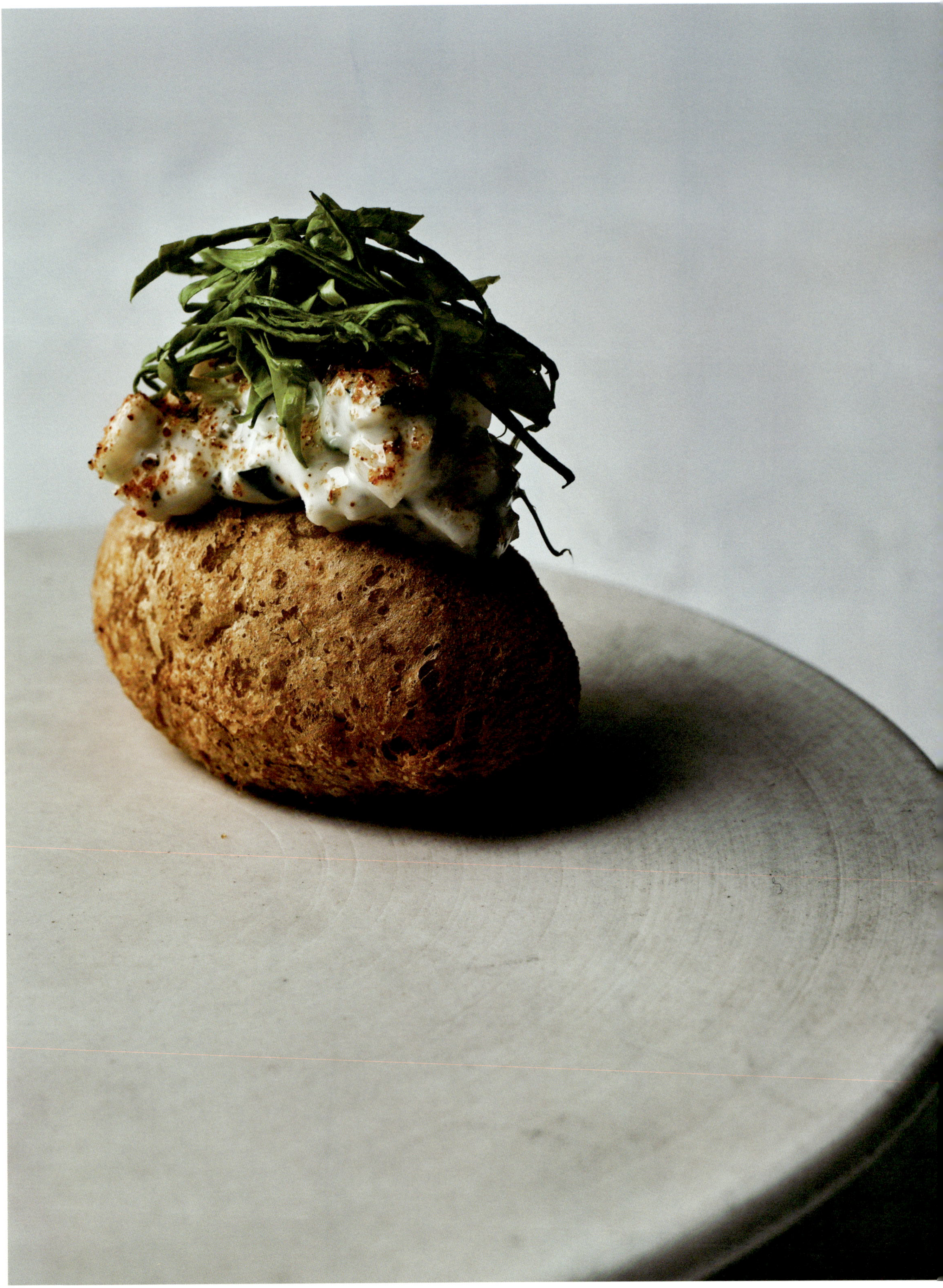

FLORIDA BLUE CRAB, SUNCHOKE DAUPHINE, RAMP CAPERS

Crab salad is not rare to see on a menu in St. Petersburg, Florida, not far from where I grew up—especially at one of the many fish joints down on Gulf Boulevard. This is our take on a crab salad served on top of a crispy sunchoke dauphine. Dauphine is traditionally made with potato (pommes dauphine) and served as a puree mixed with a choux dough. The creaminess of this version replaces the creaminess of avocado, often served with crab salad. The dressing here is a sauce gribiche made with capered ramp buds from the previous year's spring harvest.

---

sunchoke dauphine

filtered water	250mL
butter, cubed	80g
salt	1g
AP flour	125g
eggs	4ea
sunchoke puree	275g

Bring the water, butter, and salt to a boil in a sauce pot over medium-high heat. Quickly whisk in the flour and stir rapidly with a rubber spatula or wooden spoon until a tight dough forms and it pulls away from the sides of the pot. Whip in the eggs, one at a time, making sure each is fully incorporated before the next addition. Mix in the sunchoke puree until well combined and reserve in a covered container until needed.

sauce gribiche

capered ramp buds, chopped (see page 270)	60g
pickled ramps, minced	10g
pickled ramp juice	20g
Duke's mayonnaise	385g
tarragon, minced	15g
parsley, minced	10g
chives, minced	20g
lemon zest	10g
yellow mustard powder	10g
green yuzu kosho	20g
eggs, boiled and passed through a large-holed conical metal strainer	8ea

Mix all the ingredients together until well combined.

additional ingredients & to finish

yuzu juice
blue crab, picked of shells
celery leaves
Pacific sea salt

Set a fryer at 325°F. Dip two spoons of identical size into the fryer to coat with oil. Quenelle the dauphine batter and fry until golden brown and hot all the way through. The mixture should still be creamy on the inside. Dress the crab with desired amount of sauce gribiche, season to taste with Pacific sea salt and yuzu juice, and finish with a chiffonade of the celery leaves.

SAKURA MASU, SAKURA BLOSSOM, SALTED WHITE PEACH

Sakura masu, also known as cherry salmon, is at its peak in the spring during Sakura season. Sakura refers to Japanese cherry blossoms. The blossoms are picked when in full bloom. For this dish, they are salted for a few days, pickled in umezu (green plum or "Ume" vinegar), slowly dried, and steeped in boiling water to make a tea. I wanted to highlight the salmon and cherry blossoms together. We aged the salmon for a few days, quickly grilled it to lightly char the skin, and dressed it in a cream sauce made from a reduction of sparkling rosé, Sakura blossoms, and umezu. I wanted to find a way to highlight the bitter almond flavor of the Sakura blossom, so we added a puree made from lacto-fermented white peach from the previous summer and an oil made from pach pits.

---

sakura cream

shallot	40g
salted Sakura blossoms	30g
sparkling rosé	220mL
sake	75mL
white shoyu	70mL
heavy cream	250mL
cherry vinegar	30mL
umezu, ume plum vinegar	8mL

Bring the shallot, Sakura blossoms, rosé, and sake to a simmer over medium heat. Cook until all the alcohol has burned off. Add the shoyu and cream. Bring back to a simmer and reduce by ⅓. Add the vinegars and bring back to a simmer for one minute. Transfer to a Vitamix and puree on high speed until completely smooth. Pass through a fine-mesh strainer and reserve.

salted peach puree

lacto-fermented white peaches	250g
lacto-fermented white peach juice	75g
xanthan gum	.15g
peach pit oil	75mL

Puree the lacto-fermented peaches and juice in a Vitamix on high speed until completely smooth. Add the xanthan gum and emulsify in the peach pit oil. Pass through a fine-mesh strainer and reserve.

additional ingredients & to finish

peach pit oil
sakura masu, aged 8 days and cut into 8-ounce filets

Grill the salmon skin-side down until lightly charred. Cook the bottom side if needed, aiming for a medium-rare temperature. Slice into 2-ounce portions. Place on the plate with a spoonful of the lacto-fermented peach puree. Rewarm the Sakura cream and fold in a spoonful of peach pit oil. Finish the plate with the sauce.

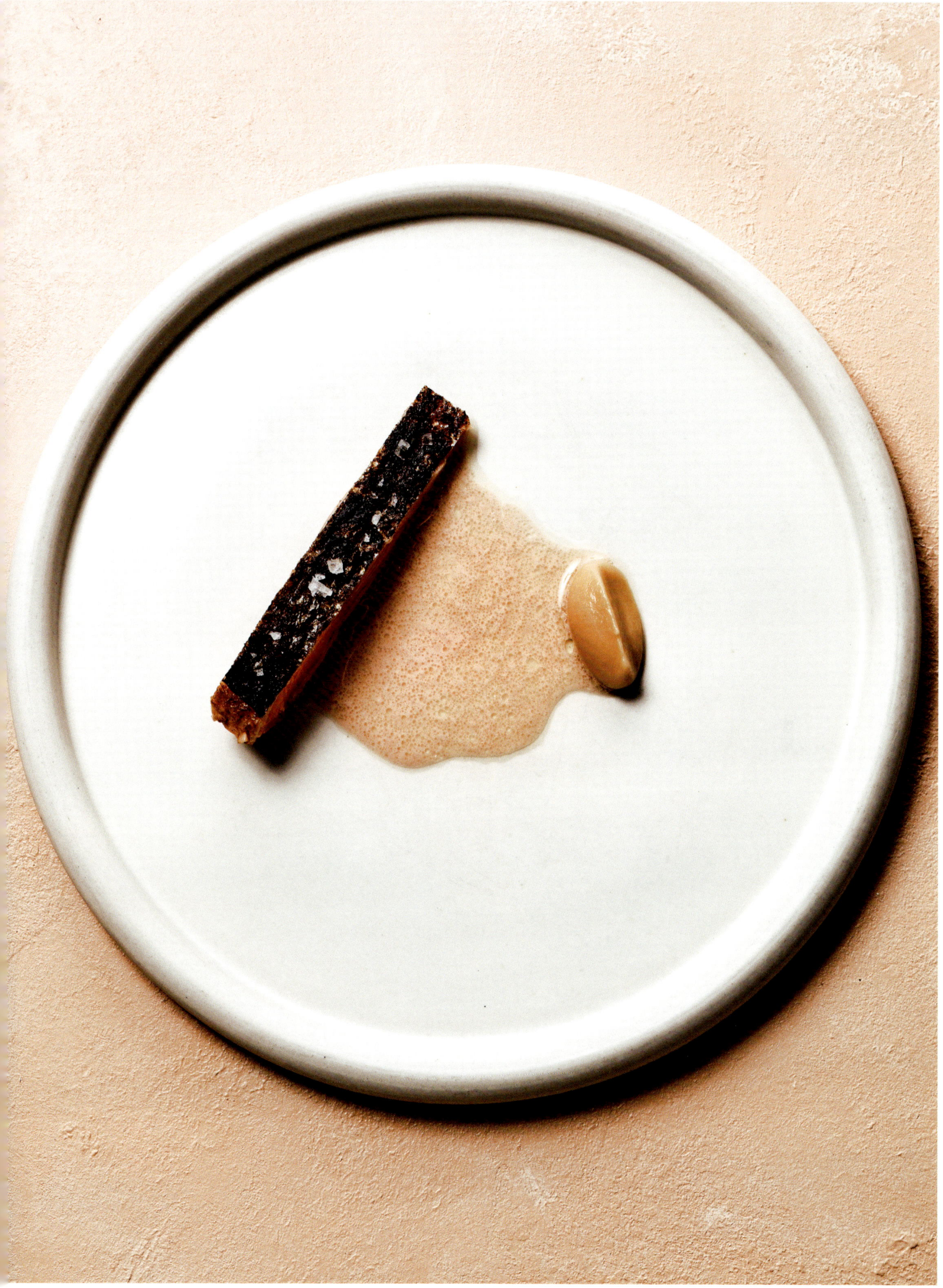

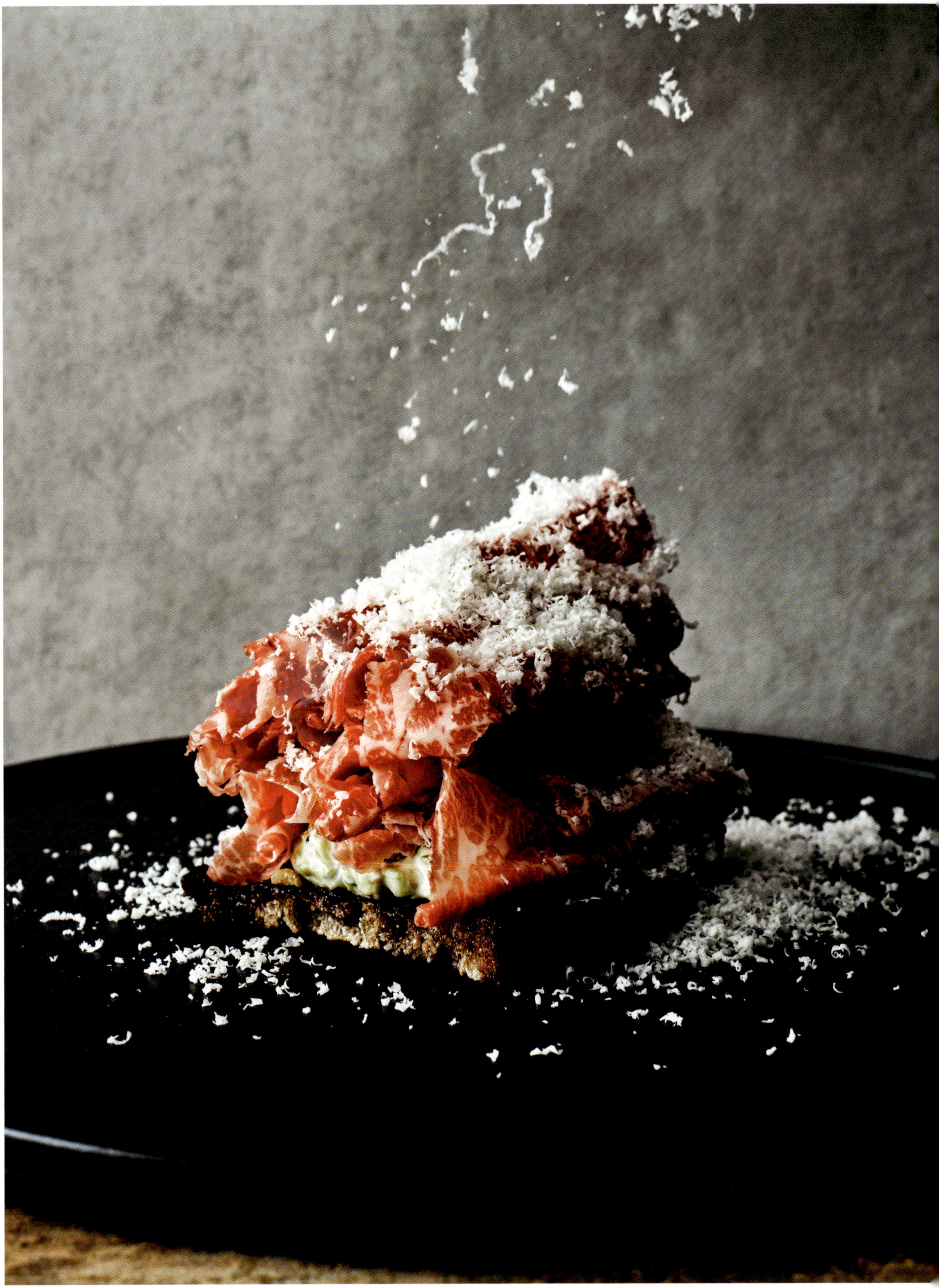

SHAVED BEAR CREEK FARM DENVER STEAK, FAVA BEAN & STILTON CHEESE

This dish was loosely inspired by avocado toast. I wanted something that was a little bit lighter for spring but that still highlighted beef from Bear Creek Farm. We soaked sourdough bread in a rich bordelaise sauce and grilled it, then topped it with layers of a fava bean relish and shaved Denver steak. The center of the chuck, Denver steak has a high fat content and is easily one of the most flavorful cuts of beef. We finished the dish by shaving a considerable amount of frozen Stilton blue cheese on top.

---

sauce perigueux

beef tallow	100g
shallot, sliced thin	300g
mushroom stems, sliced	120g
dried mushroom such as maitake or morel	60g
Madeira	750mL
truffle juice	500mL
demi-glace (see page 274)	3,500g

Melt the beef tallow. Once hot, add shallot and mushrooms and cook until a deep golden brown is achieved. Add the Madeira and truffle juice and cook on medium heat until reduced by ¾ of its original volume. Add the demi-glace and reduce to 1L. Strain through a fine-mesh strainer and reserve.

fava relish

fava beans, shelled and white embryo removed	230g
garlic, minced fine	2g
pecorino	50g
Mint, minced fine	5g
lemon zest	1g
lemon oil	50g
kosher salt	t.t.

Blanch the fava beans for 10 seconds and shock immediately. Pulse the fava beans, garlic, and pecorino in a robot coupe until a paste begins to form. Add the mint and lemon zest. Slowly emulsify in the oil. Season to taste with salt and reserve.

additional ingredients & to finish

Denver steak, cut into 3" × 4" steaks and frozen
Stilton cheese, frozen
Maldon salt
black peppercorn
sourdough, sliced 3" × 4" × ¼" thickness

Shave the Denver steak as thin as possible on a meat slicer. Reserve in the freezer until needed. Soak the bread in the perigueux sauce. Grill over hardwood embers on one side to lightly char. Cover with a spoonful of the fava relish. Top with an ounce of the shaved steak, shave desired amount of cheese over the steak, then season with the Maldon salt and freshly cracked black peppercorns.

FIRE-EXPLODED KIDNEY FLOWERS, BAMBOO SHOOT & BABY LEEKS

This dish was also inspired by a recent trip to New York and a lunch that I had at Hot Kitchen Szechuan Style in Flushing, Queens. Sauteed pig's kidney is marinated in Shaoxing wine and quickly stir-fried with fermented bamboo shoots, baby leeks, celery, and pickled green Szechuan chilies, or Pao Jiao. The pickled green chilies pack so much flavor that I always enjoy snacking on them, even though they do have quite a kick. We quickly learned it was best to sell this dish as Sichuan-inspired stir-fried pork, as the word "kidney" seemed to turn people off. Then the bowls were always licked clean.

for the kidney

Brine the whole kidney in ice water with 10% salt for 30 minutes. Drain and dry well. Cut the fresh kidney in half lengthwise. Lay the outside of the kidney flat on a cutting board. With your knife parallel to the board, gently remove all the membrane from the inside of the kidney so you are left with a smooth pink interior. Flip the kidney over so its inside is flat against the cutting board. Make thin slits at a slight angle in ⅛" intervals the entire length of the kidney. Be sure not to cut all the way through the kidney. Rotate the kidney 90° and repeat, going crosswise. Cut into ¾" strips and reserve.

kidney marinade

cut kidneys	450g
potato flour	20g
Shaoxing wine	80mL

Marinate the kidney in the flour and wine for 30 minutes.

fermented bamboo shoots

bamboo shoots, cleaned and cut into ¼" half-moons	500g
kosher salt	10g
white peppercorns, ground fine	2g

Toss the bamboo, salt, and white peppercorn together. Seal in a Cryovac bag at full pressure and store in a warm place for 14 days. Burp the bag as needed as it fills with gas, and reseal in a clean vacuum bag.

sauce base

rice wine	240mL
pickled Szechuan chile brine	100mL
white shoyu	50mL

Combine in a small sauce pot, bring to a boil, and cool.

additional ingredients & to finish

pickled Szechuan chilies, cut into ⅛" half-moons
baby leeks, halved, washed well, and cut into ½" dice
celery, washed and peeled, cut into ¼" half-moons
scallion greens, cut into ¼" slices on a bias
garlic, minced
ginger, minced
neutral oil, for stir-frying
sesame oil

Place a wok over high heat. Once the pan is hot, add 2 tablespoons of neutral oil to the pan. Once the oil reaches 350°F, add the marinated kidney, season with a pinch of salt, and sauté, stirring quickly with a metal spoon. Once the kidneys begin to flower open, add the garlic and ginger. Continue to sauté until aromatic, about one minute. Add the bamboo shoots, leeks, celery, and chilies, and sauté until they just begin to soften for another minute or so. Add enough sauce just to coat, and toss quickly. Finish with a teaspoon of the sesame oil and scallions. Serve immediately.

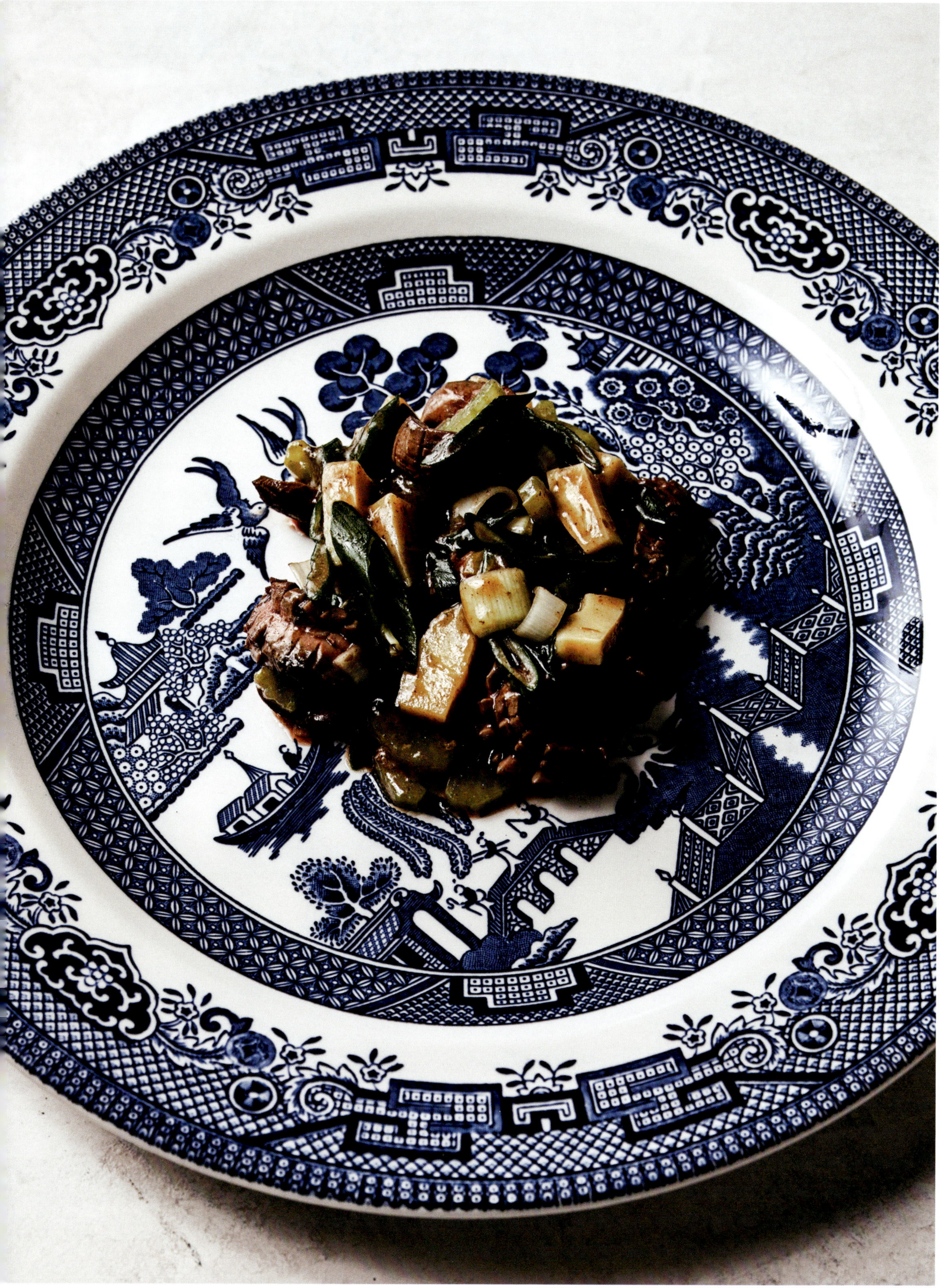

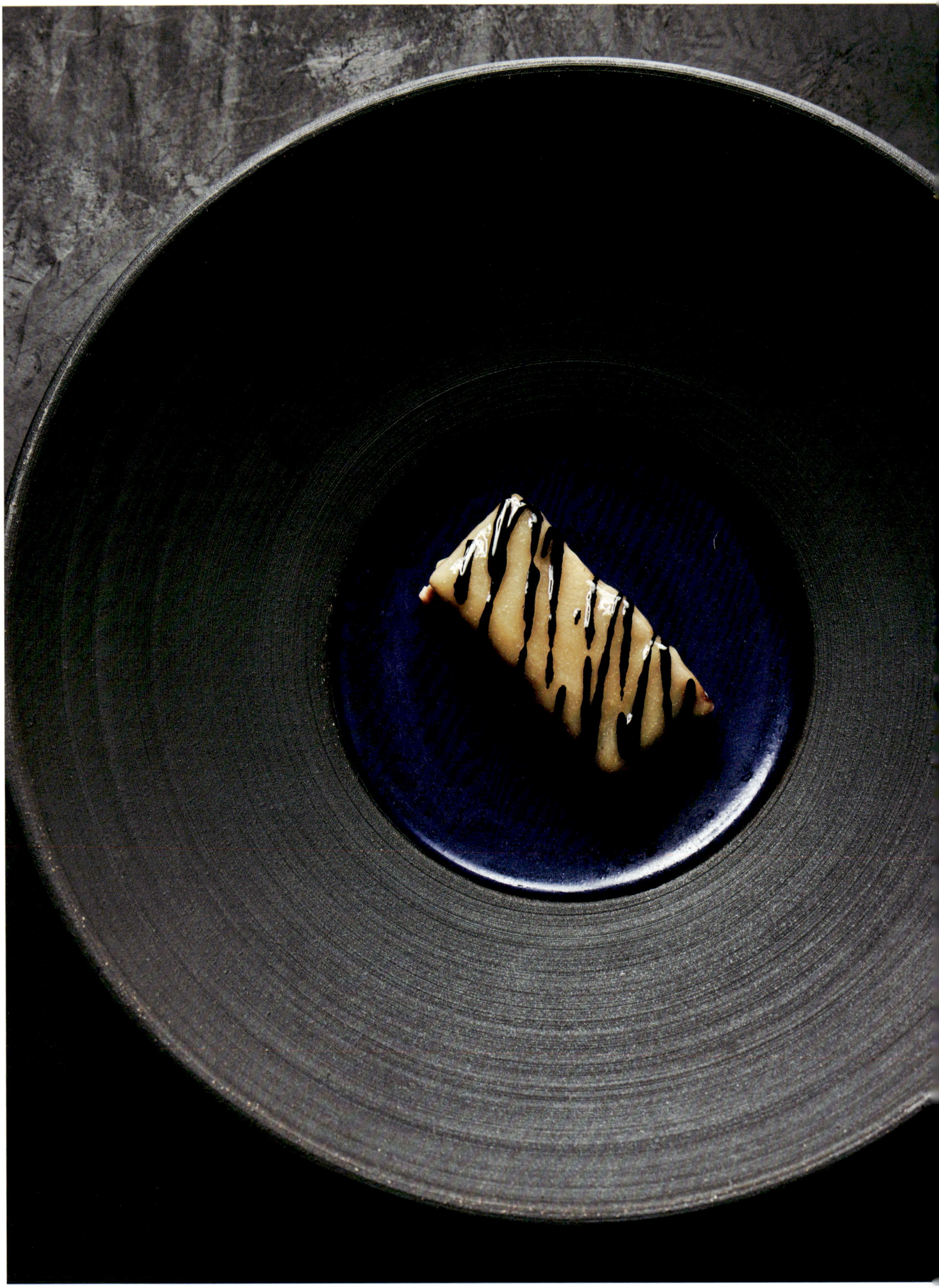

DRY-AGED PORK SHOULDER, FERMENTED DURIAN & BLACK SESAME

We had the opportunity to cook with our friends at Nonesuch Restaurant in Oklahoma City, an amazing restaurant and kindred spirits for us in Nashville. A couple of our buddies came out to hang with us for the weekend and attend the dinner. The first day, Connor, my buddy Chad Koeplinger, and I took a self-guided tour of the city. Once we learned there was a large Vietnamese population in OKC, we quickly found ourselves at the market Super Cao Nguyen. We had already written the menu, but I was thinking about tweaking a banana dish we were doing, substituting durian. I had never had durian, and thankfully they had it in about every form you could imagine: fresh, fully ripened and frozen chunks, candies, and even durian extract. I bought them all. The clerk asked me if I had ever had it, and I told him no, but I really wanted to try it. He told us to eat it as close to frozen as possible, because the texture may be more appealing. So, we proceeded to unwrap the fully ripened frozen chunks and eat them in the parking lot. What a wild ride. It started as an interesting sweet, almost allium flavor; and as it slowly thawed, it displayed an intense flavor of toasted sesame. I instantly fell in love with it. Right then and there I knew this would be good with pork and sesame. I let the fresh one ripen in my hotel room for the rest of the weekend. Once we got back to Nashville, I began to play around with different variations. First it was a dessert of fresh durian curd with black sesame and crispy pork skin (chicharron). What we finally landed on was fatty pork shoulder that had been brined, cooked sous vide, and then seared hard until crispy. We glazed it in a sauce made from a reduced pork stock and fermented durian. To balance the acidity, we added the fresh durian custard and, finally, black sesame paste. Everyone was pleasantly surprised by this one—except the few guests who already had their minds made up about their durian preference from having had it in its native countries.

durian custard

granulated sugar	130g	Combine and process in a Thermomix until the mixture reaches 90°C. Allow to set overnight. The next day, puree in a Thermomix until the mixture is completely smooth. Pass through a fine-mesh strainer into a piping bag and reserve.
maple sugar	130g	
salt	1g	
butter, cubed	170g	
whole eggs	2ea	
egg whites	2ea	
iota carrageenan	5.8g	
kappa carrageenan	5.8g	
ripe durian, pits removed	225g	

durian jus

light brown sugar	60g	Bring the brown sugar and fish sauce to a boil and reduce by half. Whisk in the pork jus and reduce by ⅓. Whisk in the fermented durian and bring back to a simmer. Transfer to a Vitamix and puree on high speed until completely smooth. Pass through a fine-mesh strainer and reserve until needed.
fish sauce	60g	
pork jus	800g	
fermented durian	200g	

pork brine

water	.5L	Mix together until completely dissolved.
salt	50g	
maple sugar	50g	
white pepper	5g	
makrut lime leaf		

pork shoulder

pork shoulder	2lbs	Cryovac the shoulder and the brine on full pressure. Cook at 71°C for 12 hours. Shock immediately in an ice bath to cool. Drain the brine from the bag, pat the pork dry, and cut into 1½"-thick steaks. Reserve until needed.
pork brine	.5L	

additional ingredients & to finish

black sesame paste		Brush the pork shoulder with a small amount of oil. Bring a cast iron to just before smoke point on medium-high heat and sear the shoulder until caramelized well on both sides and warm all the way through. Slice the pork shoulder into 1"-wide slices, glaze the shoulder in the durian sauce, drizzle a small amount of black sesame paste over the sauce, and serve immediately.

DRY-AGED PORK COULOTTE & PLANTAIN

There is a huge Cuban population in Tampa, Florida, the birthplace of the Cuban sandwich. I wanted to create a dish that was inspired by my love for Cuban sandwiches; however, it slowly evolved into a course highlighting pork and plantains. The main course here was a dry-aged coulotte marinated in our version of mojo and slowly roasted. We served it with rice and black beans, or Moros y Cristianos, and a sauce made from the roasted pork juices and mojo.

---

for the pork
sour orange marinade

garlic head, halved	1ea
onion, sliced thin	100g
sour orange juice, such as Seville orange	240g
kosher salt	12g
black peppercorns, ground	12g
Mexican oregano	8g
olive oil	80mL

Combine all ingredients and mix until the salt is completely dissolved. Allow to sit under refrigeration for 24 hours. Strain and reserve.

pork rub

dry oregano	15g
dry thyme	15g
dry basil	10g
dry marjoram	6g
dry parsley	18g
granulated garlic	35g
chipotle powder	10g
smoked paprika	35g
kosher salt	100g

Mix until well combined, and reserve in an airtight container.

moros y cristianos

bacon, cut into 2" pieces	210g
onion, minced	115g
bell pepper, deseeded and minced	100g
garlic, minced	25g
cumin, ground	2g
Mexican oregano, ground	1g
bay leaves	2ea
long grain rice	550g
cooked black beans, liquid reserved	1,115g
thyme sprigs	2ea
salt	t.t.
chicken bouillon granules	t.t.
lime juice	t.t.

In a large sauté pan, sweat the bacon over medium heat until the fat begins to render. Add the onions, bell pepper, and garlic and continue to sweat until translucent. Add the spices, and toast for one minute. Next add the rice and toast until aromatic, 2 to 3 minutes. Lastly, add the black beans and mix well. Add enough of their liquid to cover the rice by ¼". Add water if needed. Bring to a simmer, then cover with a tight-fitting lid. Reduce the heat to low and cook for 18 minutes. Do not remove the lid. After 18 minutes, remove from the heat and rest for 5 minutes longer. Remove the lid, stir gently with a rubber spatula, and season to taste with salt, lime juice, and chicken granules.

additional ingredients
& to finish

pork
Maldon sea salt
lime juice

For the pork coulotte Cryovac the pork with 8 oz of the marinade and let sit under refrigeration for 6 hours. Remove from the bag and discard the marinade. Rub the pork in the pork rub and slowly roast over hardwood coals until the outside begins to caramelize. Wrap in aluminum foil and transfer to a half-sheet pan lined with a roasting rack. Cook in a 325°F oven until an internal temperature of 118°F is achieved. Let rest for 30 minutes.
For the sauce To make the sauce, carefully unwrap the foil and transfer all the juices to a pot. Add equal parts by volume of sour orange marinade, and bring to a boil. Finish the Moros y Cristianos with fresh lime juice to taste. Place a spoonful in the center of a serving plate. Slice the pork and place over the rice and beans. Dress with an ounce or so of the pork sauce and season with Maldon sea salt.

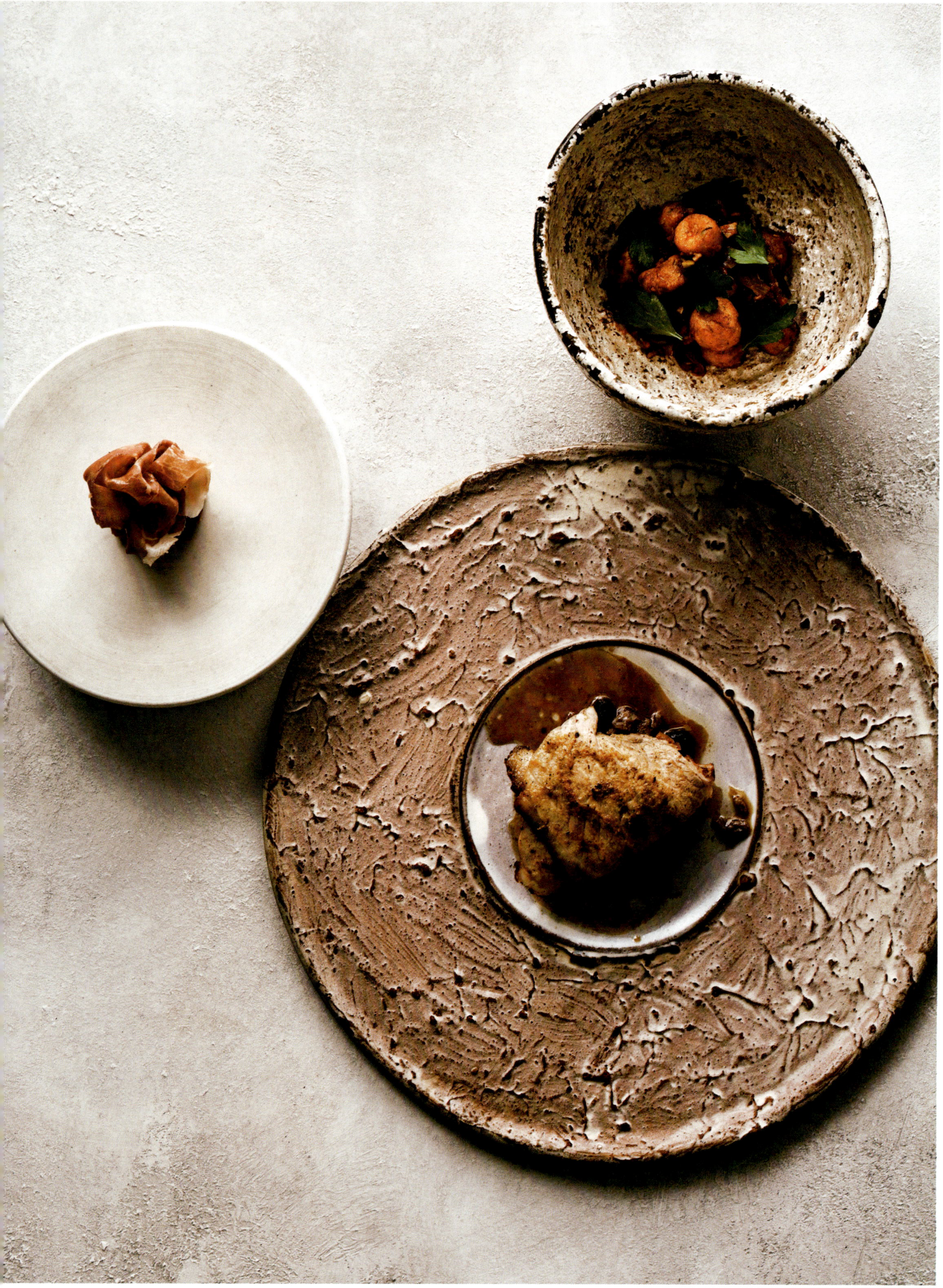

PLANTAIN GNOCCHI, PRESERVED TOMATO & CASTELVETRANO OLIVES

This component was less about being a traditional Cuban dish and more about replacing fried plantains with something more in the style of my upbringing as chef. I made a Parisian gnocchi from plantain flour, then fried it in brown butter and topped with a sofrito of preserved tomato and Castelvetrano olives. We finished the dish with a good bit of lemon and parsley leaves.

---

plantain gnocchi

filtered water	675g
butter, cubed	336g
dried Mexican oregano	3g
salt	t.t.
plantain flour	325g
AP flour	250g
eggs	10ea
pecorino	150g
parsley leaves, minced fine	50g
olive oil as needed	

Bring the water, butter, dried oregano, and salt to a boil in a sauce pot over medium-high heat. Quickly whisk in the flours and stir rapidly with a rubber spatula or wooden spoon until a tight dough forms and it pulls away from the sides of the pot. Whip in the eggs, one at a time, making sure each is fully incorporated before the next addition, followed by the cheese and the parsley. Reserve in piping bags.

Bring a large pot of salted water to a heavy simmer. Cut a ½" opening into the tip of the piping bag. Slowly squeeze the bag over the pot of water. Using a paring knife, cut the dough into 1"-length strips and simmer until they begin to float and are cooked through, 3 to 4 minutes. Remove from the water and toss in a small amount of olive oil just to glaze. Cool on a sheet pan lined with parchment paper and store under refrigeration until needed.

sofrito

preserved tomatoes, strained with juice reserved	940g
white onion, minced	150g
garlic, minced	20g
serrano chile, deseeded and minced fine	20g
capers, minced fine	80g
olive oil	75g
sweet vermouth	90mL
Castelvetrano olives, pitted and brunoised	100g
guajillo chile powder	.75g
chipotle Morita powder	.25g

Chop the tomatoes into a small dice. Sweat the onion, garlic, olives, serrano, and capers in the oil over medium heat until soft and the onions begin to become translucent. Deglaze with the vermouth. Add the remaining ingredients, including the reserved tomato juice, and cook until most of the moisture has evaporated. Season to taste with salt. Cool and reserve.

additional ingredients & to finish

parsley leaves, picked and washed
lemon juice
lemon zest

Melt some butter over medium-high heat. Once it begins to bubble, add a handful of gnocchi, and slowly roast in the butter, keeping the pan moving constantly. Once golden brown and warm all the way through, remove from the pan and drain on a paper towel. In a separate sauce pot, warm a couple of tablespoons of sofrito, add the gnocchi, and coat completely. Season to taste with lemon juice, lemon zest, and salt. Transfer to a serving bowl and garnish with fresh parsley leaves.

FERMENTED PLANTAIN BREAD, BOB WOODS HAM, PLANTAIN SYRUP

The next bite was a piece of grilled fermented plantain bread inspired by the restaurant Amass's fermented potato bread, which is probably the best bread I've ever tasted. One of our cooks at the time, Evan, took this idea and ran with it. On top, we layered cream cheese, Bob Woods ham, and a glaze made from a reduction of fermented guava.

---

fermented plantain

unripe plantains, peeled and cut into 1½" rounds	10lbs
allspice	30ea
cloves	10ea
star anise	5ea
cinnamon sticks	5g
coriander, whole	3g
cumin seed, whole	3g

Place all the ingredients in a pressure cooker, cover with twice the amount of water, and pressure-cook 30 minutes on high pressure. Strain, reserving the liquid, and completely cool. Cryovac with 2% salt by weight of the plantains. Ferment for 7 to 10 days.

plantain syrup

reserved plantain cooking water	500mL
sugar	500g

Slowly reduce over medium-low heat until a maple syrup consistency is achieved. Keep in mind that once cooled the syrup will be more viscous. Cool and reserve until needed.

fermented plantain bread

fermented plantain, passed through a food mill or potato ricer	1,200g
yogurt	900g
AP flour	1kg
salt	36g

Combine ingredients and mix well in a stand mixer fitted with a dough hook until a smooth dough is formed. Transfer to a mixing bowl and wrap well with plastic. Let rest in the fridge for 3 days before using. Ball the dough out into 30g portions. Roll ¼"-thick circles, brush with olive oil, and grill over hardwood embers until caramelized on both sides and cooked through.

lacto-fermented guava reduction

lacto-fermented guava juice	1L
sugar	70g

Combine guava juice and sugar. Reduce slowly over medium-low heat until a thick glaze is achieved.

additional ingredients & to finish

cream cheese
country ham, sliced thin

Place a spoonful of cream cheese on the bread, top with a slice of ham, and drizzle with the guava reduction.

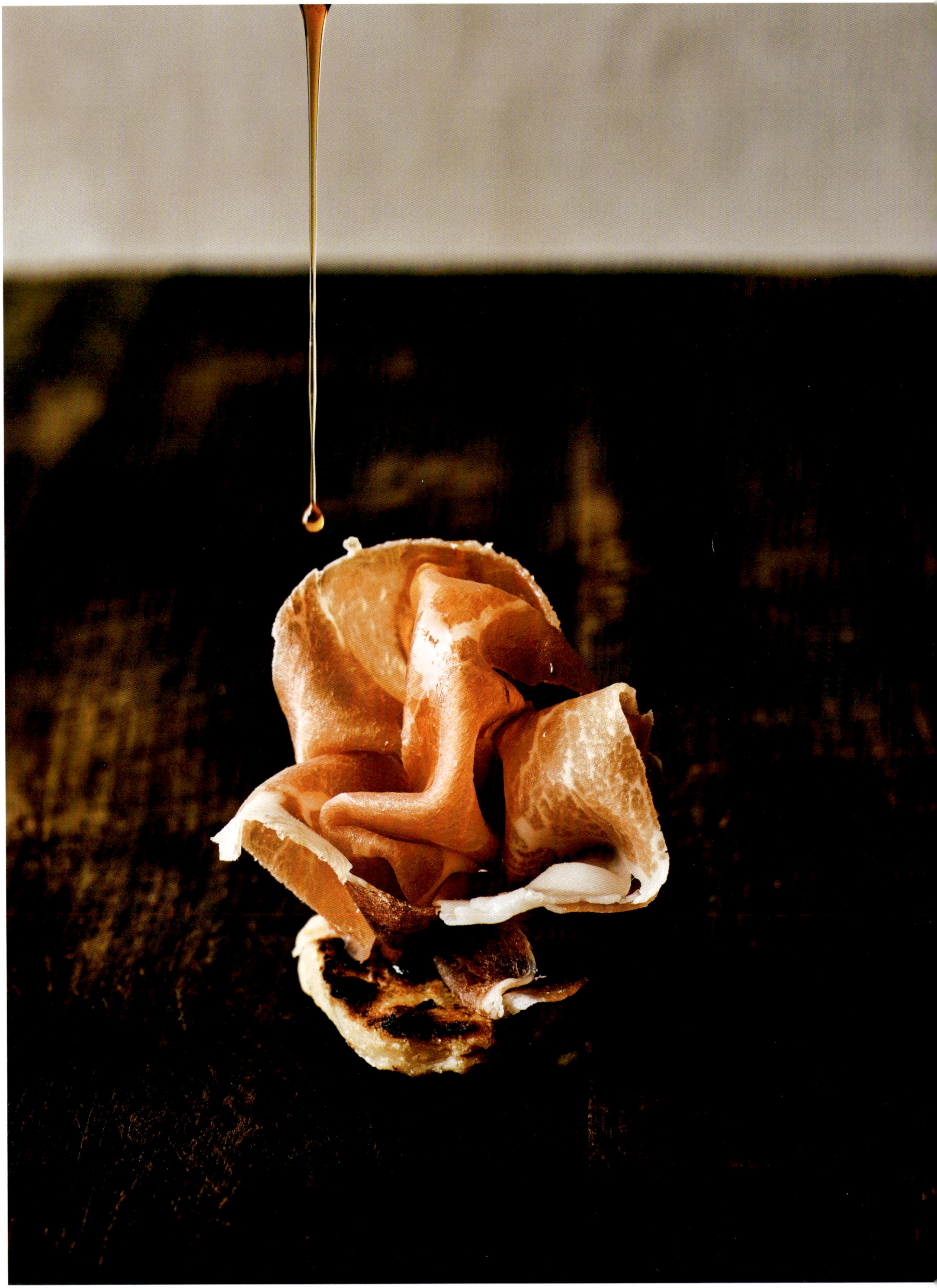

PLANTAIN CAFÉCITO

We finished with a Cafécito, or Cuban coffee, made from a mixture of roasted ripe and unripe plantains, Willett barrel-aged coffee beans, and fresh sugarcane juice.

---

unripe plantains, sliced ¼" thick	20g
ripe plantains, sliced ¼" thick	25g
bourbon barrel-aged coffee	12g
fresh sugarcane juice	
filtered water	300mL

Roast the plantains at 300°F until deep golden brown and completely dried through. Grind the coffee and plantains in a spice grinder to a coarse texture. Place in a French press and bring the water to 200°F. Pour over the ground plantain/coffee mixture and steep for 4 minutes. Press and transfer to a separate pot and weigh the liquid. Whisk in equal parts by weight fresh sugarcane juice. Whisking vigorously, bring to a boil. Immediately spoon into espresso cups and serve.

NANCÉ, TRIPLE CREAM CHEESE, PINEAPPLE WEED & SCHRENCKII CAVIAR

When in Atlanta, I always like to stop at the Buford Highway Farmers Market. On my most recent visit, I saw stacks and stacks of this weird yellow fruit named nancé that I had never seen or heard of. I quickly looked it up and was intrigued to read about its cheeselike aroma and banana/litchi flavor. I decided to impulse-buy 2 gallons. I had no idea what I was going to do with it, but I slowly snacked on them all the way back to Nashville. By the time I got back, I knew I wanted to cook it into a jam and pair it with an Époisses-style cheese and some pineapple weed, a wild edible which smells and tastes like tropical chamomile. After punching all the pits out, I realized there was a decent amount of the fruit stuck to it, so I decided to make a "cheese" that I could shave over the top right in front of the guests. To round out the dish, I needed some salt, so I decided to add a salty, flavorful Chinese caviar from Astrea.

---

nancé jam

nancé, pitted and halved (100 percent)	1,162g	Combine and cook the mixture over medium heat, stirring constantly until it reaches 220°F. Allow to cool to room temperature, then process in a robot coupe until finely chopped.
sugar (50 percent)	581g	
Omed cider vinegar (25 percent)	290g	

nancé pit "cheese"

nancé pits and scraps	500g	Cryovac all ingredients on full pressure and place in a pot of boiling water for 4 hours. Pass through a fine-mesh strainer and portion into silicone molds the shape of small wheels of cheese. Freeze and store in an airtight container in the freezer until needed.
coconut fat	400g	
cocoa butter	100g	
pineapple weed, stems and broken blossoms	50g	

additional ingredients & to finish

triple cream cheese, Époisses-style cheese, fully ripened at room temperature
granulated sugar
pineapple weed
Schrenckii caviar

Gently remove the tops and sides of the cheese. Spread into a ½" layer, sprinkle with the granulated sugar, and brulee as if finishing a crème brulee. Once the sugar has set, carefully move an ounce of the cheese to a plate and top with equal parts nancé jam and caviar. Add 3 pineapple weed buds. Right before serving, shave a good amount of the frozen nancé cheese over the caviar: serve immediately.

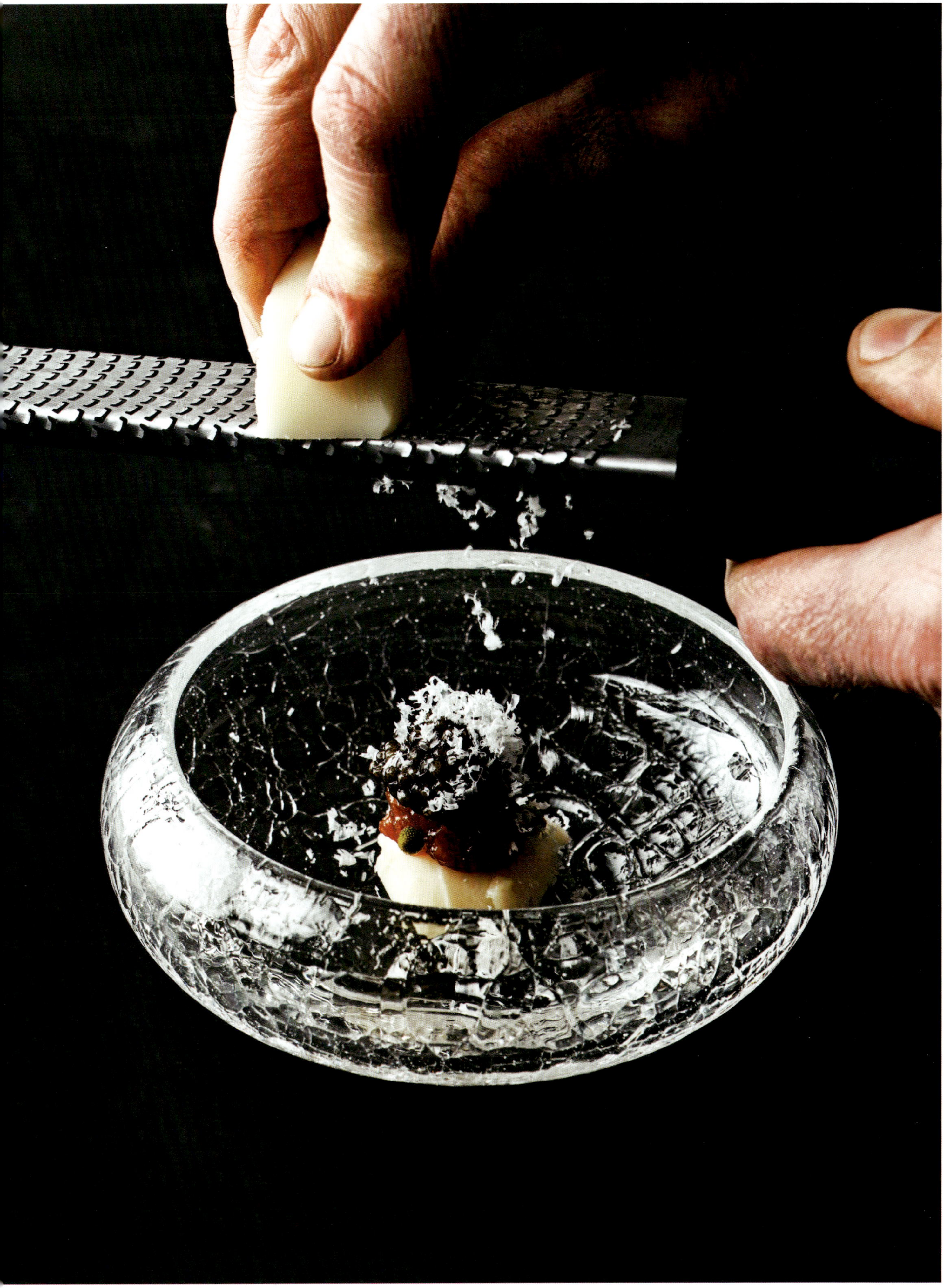

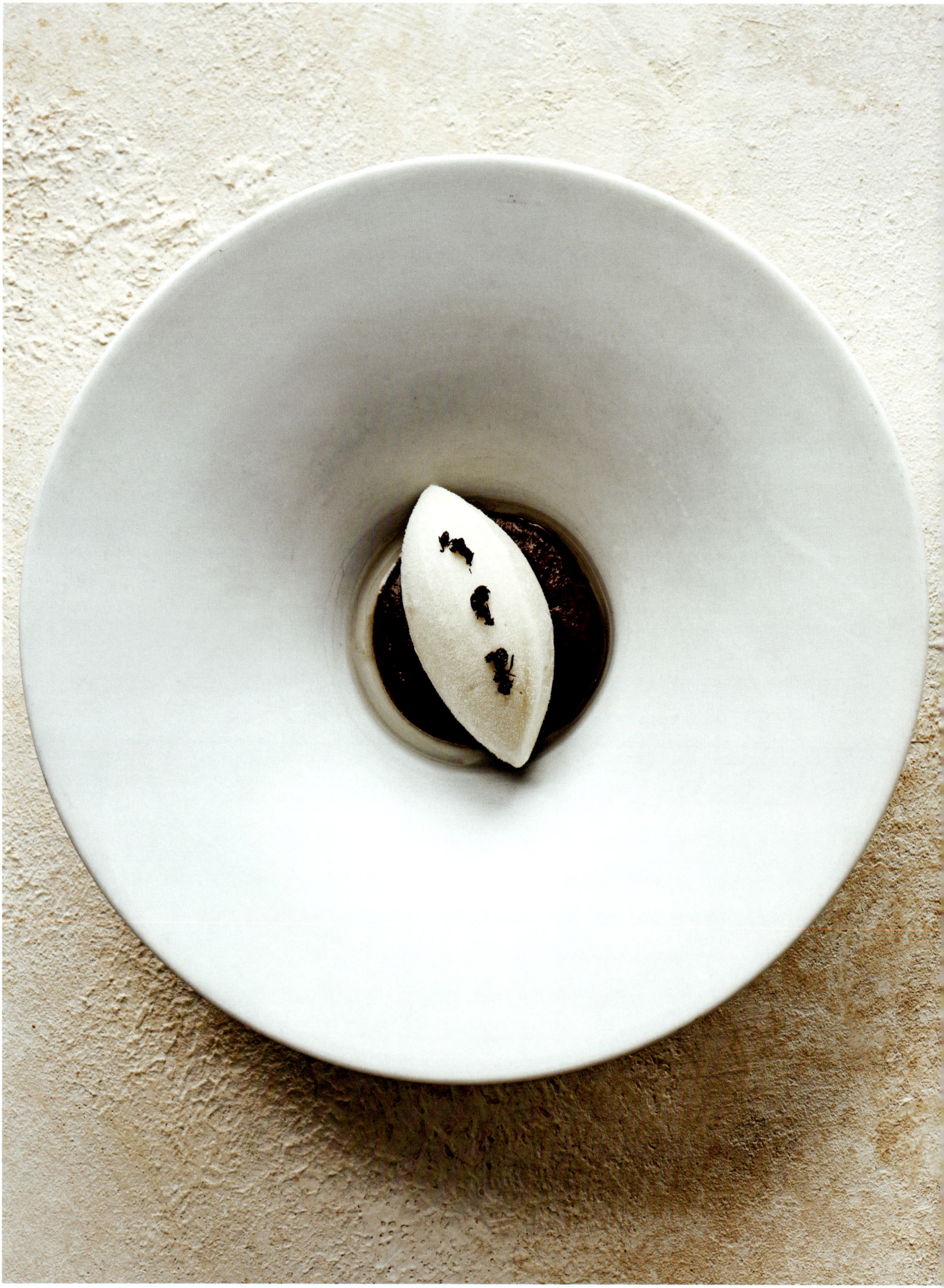

CAULIFLOWER ICE CREAM, MILK CHOCOLATE & BLACK ANTS

When I was a chef de partie at McCrady's, we used to have project nights. It was the opportunity for us as young cooks to create dishes and get mostly constructive feedback. One dish I always wanted to revisit from a project there was a dessert of cauliflower and milk chocolate. This version is a sweet ice cream with a rich milk-chocolate-heavy mole and black ants. Black ants have formic acid, which gives them a citric acid flavor, helping to cut through the richness of the cauliflower and mole. It's also a good way to sneak in your vegetables!

cauliflower gelato

cauliflower puree	1265g	Warm the cauliflower puree over medium heat, transfer to a blender, and puree with remaining ingredients. Season to taste with salt. Pass through a fine-mesh strainer into a Paco canister and freeze. Spin 30 minutes before using.
cream cheese	225g	
50:50 simple syrup	450g	
honey	175g	
kosher salt	t.t.	

mole

butter	100g	Toast all the nuts and spices until toasted and aromatic. Cool completely. Grind the chilies, nuts, and spices as finely as possible and reserve. Fry the black fruits and dried sunchoke in butter for 5 minutes. Add root beer leaf, and sauté another 5 minutes. Add the ground nuts and spices and smoked cocoa nib. Cook until a deep aroma is achieved, 10 to 15 minutes more, stirring constantly. Add the sorghum and oat milk. Bring to a simmer. Reserve and keep warm.
Pasilla pepper, toasted and seeded	20g	
cascabeche, toasted and seeded	10g	
smoked Aleppo	2g	
clove	8ea	
allspice	.75g	
cinnamon stick	6g	
star anise	1g	
fermented honey nut or other squash seeds	60g	
sesame seeds	30g	
hazelnut flour	60g	
dry ginger	.5g	
black garlic	10g	
black chestnut	30g	
black apples	40g	
dried sunchoke	60g	
butter	120g	
oja santa or root beer leaf, dried	2g	
smoked coco nibs	20g	
sorghum	45g	
oat milk	250g	

oat milk	500g	In a separate pot, bring the oat milk to a boil. In a Vitamix, shear in the lecithin. Emulsify in the chocolates followed by the hazelnut oil. Next, add the mole base and blend on high speed until completely smooth. Pass through a fine-mesh strainer and reserve in a warm place until needed.
soy lecithin	.5%	
milk chocolate	35g	
gianduja	220g	
hazelnut oil	25g	

additional ingredients & to finish

black ants	Warm a couple of ounces of the mole. Place a spoonful in the bottom of a bowl and top with a quenelle of the cauliflower gelato. Season the quenelle with a pinch of Maldon sea salt and a few black ants. Serve immediately.
Maldon sea salt	

reflections

As I reflect on the past three years—yes, as I write this I have just passed my third anniversary as the chef at The Catbird Seat—I can't help but be extremely proud of what we were able to accomplish. When we first opened in June 2020, we were only able to serve 24 to 28 people per service, depending on the different party sizes of the reservation. As the country began to slowly reopen after the lockdown and capacity limitations were lifted, we were still limited to 14 people per turn to maintain safe distances for the customers, due to the size and layout of the restaurant. This wasn't ideal, but it allowed us to slowly ease into the space and get our footing before we eventually opened all 20 seats. Over that first year, we met a lot of new people who continued to come back monthly, quarterly, and yearly for different occasions. In the second year, although familiar with these regulars and their faces, we became a new face to them as mask mandates were lifted. I am very thankful for all the guests who continued to support us those first two years. I am thankful for the guests who allowed us to move their reservations to a future date instead of canceling when they had Covid, and apologize to the guests who we had to cancel or reschedule because of our due diligence when a staff member had come in contact with someone infected by Covid. We made it through when many restaurants didn't, and I will never take for granted the support we received from our community, guests, and owners.

I know I said that I try not to pay attention to the lists; but there is a competitive nature that I have from being an athlete for so long that I have a hard time letting go of. I was happy we moved up in OAD's list of best restaurants, but deep down I was pissed we were eleventh and not in the top ten. The easy thing to do would've been to look at what the best restaurants in the world were doing and try to mimic them; but I've never wanted to copy someone else's creations. However, I do believe that we can use them as inspiration, learn from other people, and see techniques and make those techniques unique to our style of food. For example, Noma has been inspirational to many people all over the world—like El Bulli before them—and the knowledge that they share will only make the industry better.

So we continued to try to keep playing with different flavors that I thought were unique or things that I had never seen or had together. A few examples are Sea Urchin Butterscotch Pudding, Mussels and Foie Gras, or razor clams served raw for dessert with horseradish ice cream. We continued to build our larder, utilizing what would normally be thrown out and turning it into a miso, vinegar, garum, or oil, or smoking and infusing different flavors of Shiro dashi with it. Sustainability is something we always try to be cognizant of. If we weren't so limited with space, we would love to work with giving farmers vegetable scraps for their animals and/or composts, which will definitely be something I'll make sure my next project will focus on. After all the hard work and continued dedication from my staff, I wasn't surprised when in May 2023 we had finally been voted as the tenth-best restaurant in the United States by OAD. I felt a sense of pride seeing my name listed close to many whom I've looked up to, but know that I couldn't have done it without my amazing beverage director Sarah Salim, sous chef Connor Carlson, kitchen staff Brennan, Jalen, Kosta, Shivam, and Tristen, support staff Kaylah and Genevieve, and our backbone on the pots and pans, Rohan. Together we were able to work as a team and achieve something that we were all proud of; but most importantly, we continue to build a growing list of guests who come back time and again. I feel like we have built something special here and will be sad when it's over, but I am ready for what the future has in store for me. I will continue to focus on sustainability and community, and look forward to showcasing many of the amazing local products that Middle Tennessee has to offer.

Credit: Todd Saal

BASE RECIPES

Fermentation, preservation, and allowing deeper flavors to develop on some of our favorite ingredients over time was something I started thinking about before ever stepping into the kitchen at The Catbird Seat. I felt a little pressure right away to begin the process on day one. Now that I'm on the other side of two years and change, it has become natural to think of ingredients in a few different ways. I ask: How can I capture the delicious vibrancy of something when it's fresh and at its peak, and how can I dry, cure, or ferment the ingredient to use to bolster something else down the line? This bifurcated approach has become second nature. As I approached year two at Catbird (and even had some great ferments going by the time the first fall rolled around), I was fortunate to have an entire larder of ingredients to add touches of acid, depth, and umami.

Many of these recipes can be tailored to different ingredients you may have in your neck of the woods. The eggplant and sweet potato recipes could just as easily work with rhubarb and even mango. The idea for swordfish ham (page 273) could also work for other types of seafood and—with a little creativity—could even be modified for a vegetarian. Using your senses to see how these flavors change and develop over days, weeks, and months will allow you more command over these ingredients over time. My appreciation, for both the cucumber blossom sitting attached to the vine of the plant and the freshness of biting into fresh cucumber after it's been picked, is only part of the equation. The tang of cucumbers pickled with a variety of spices and the depth of lacto-fermented cucumber juice is another. I hope these base recipes inspire a whole new appreciation for the ingredients you use and add more depth to your cooking.

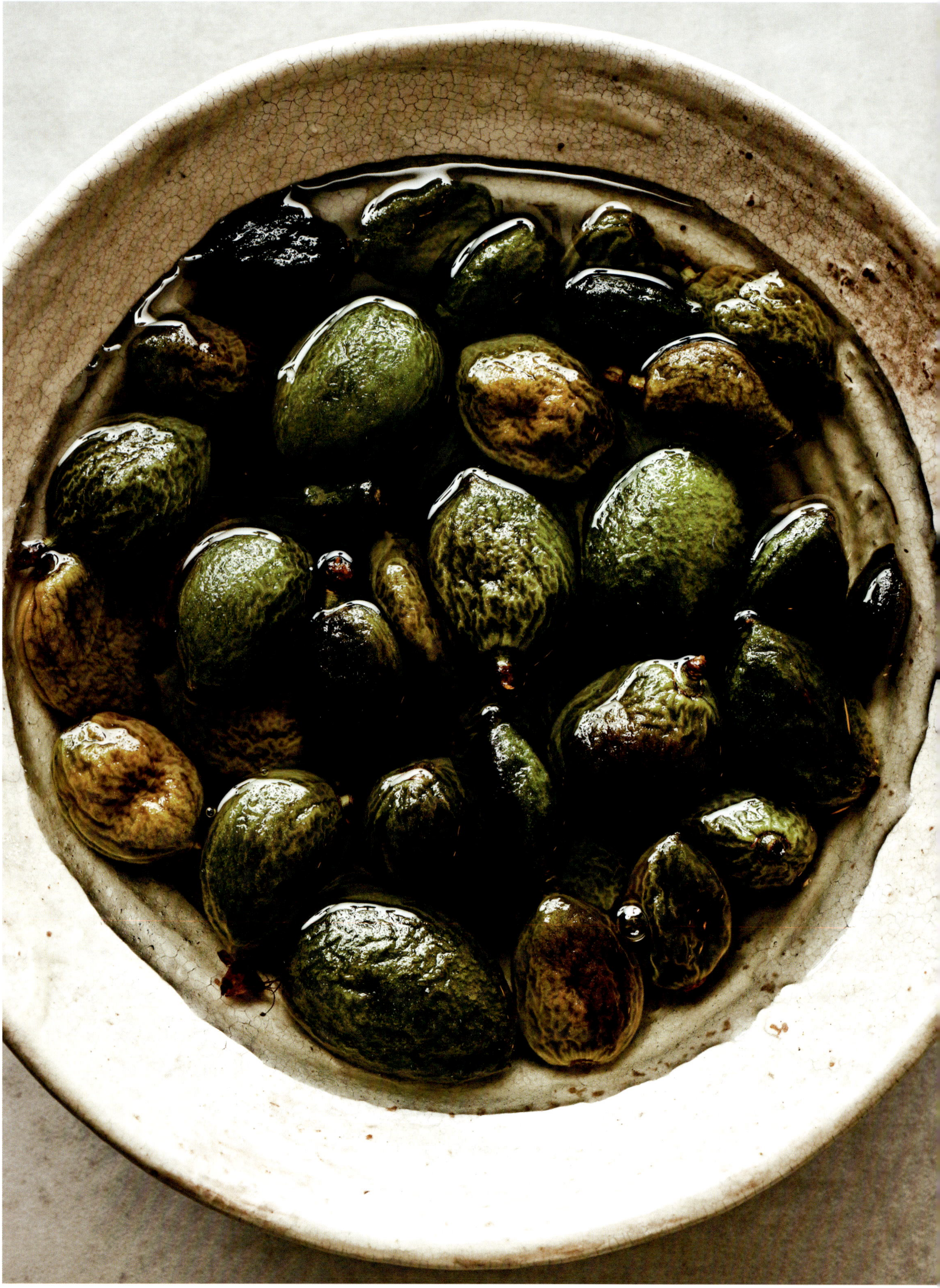

CURED, DRIED & FERMENTED VEGETABLES

cured & dried eggplant

eggplant, washed and peeled	1kg
kosher salt	60g
granulated sugar	30g

Toss all the ingredients together to coat well. Cryovac for 5 days. Remove from the bag, rinse, and dry well. Cold-smoke for 8 hours. Dehydrate at 120°F until completely dry all the way through. Store in an airtight container in a cool dark space.

cured & dried sweet potatoes

sweet potatoes, washed and peeled	1kg
kosher salt	60g
granulated sugar	30g

Poke the sweet potatoes multiple times with a fork or cake tester. Process like the cured and dried eggplant (above).

fermented white asparagus

white asparagus, washed and peeled, peels reserved for other use	1kg
kosher salt	20g

Snap the woody parts of the white asparagus off the bottoms and set aside with the peels. Toss the asparagus with salt, and Cryovac it. Reserve in a warm place for a minimum of 10 days or until desired sourness is achieved.

fermented sea buckthorn juice

sea buckthorn berries, pulsed in a robot coupe to break up	1kg
kosher salt	20g

Puree on low in a Vitamix until well combined. Cryovac and ferment in a warm place for a minimum of 14 days. If needed, burp the bag as it fills with gas, transfer to a clean bag, and reseal. Continue to ferment until desired sourness is achieved.

fermented white asparagus juice

white asparagus peels and stems	1kg
kosher salt	20g

Toss the asparagus with salt and pulse in a robot coupe until a fine paste is formed. Cryovac and keep in a warm place for a minimum of 10 days or until desired sourness is achieved.

fermented gooseberry juice

green gooseberries	1kg
kosher salt	20g

Puree in a Vitamix until smooth. Cryovac and ferment in a warm place for a minimum of 14 days. If needed, burp the bag as it fills with gas, transfer to a clean bag, and reseal.

lacto-fermented pear juice

Shinko pears	1kg
kosher salt	25g

Juice the pears and pass through a fine-mesh strainer. Process like the fermented gooseberry juice above.

fermented turnip juice

hakurei turnip juice	1kg
kosher salt	20g

Process like the fermented gooseberry juice above.

fermented kohlrabi juice

kohlrabi juice	1kg
kosher salt	20g

Process like the fermented gooseberry juice above.

fermented tomato juice

fresh tomato juice	1kg
kosher salt	20g

Juice the tomatoes, reserving the pulp for another use like tomato nduja (or ferment with 2% salt for fermented tomato pulp). Mix the juice with salt. Cryovac and keep in a warm place for a minimum of 10 days or until desired sourness is achieved.

fermented tomato reduction

fermented tomato juice	1kg
granulated sugar	70g

Slowly reduce in a heavy-gauge sauce pot until a syrupy consistency is achieved. Be sure not to let simmer too fast, or the sugars will begin to caramelize and become bitter. Pass through a fine-mesh strainer and chill until needed. (For smoked-tomato reduction, smoke the tomato juice for 30 minutes before mixing with the salt and fermenting.)

tomato bouillon

tomato juice	200g
shallot, small dice	200g
fermented tomato pulp	200g
tomato paste	200g
carrot, small dice	200g
grapeseed oil	200g
garlic cloves, peeled	60g
fresh brick yeast	50g
kombu	10g
tomato vinegar	50g

Process the shallot, carrot, tomato paste, and fermented tomato pulp until a rough paste is achieved. Transfer to a stainless steel bowl. Add the peeled garlic, vinegar, oil, tomato juice, yeast, and kombu to the paste. Wrap it tight and ferment overnight at room temperature. Next day, cook it at a low temperature for 2 to 4 hours, until the paste has cooked to a point where the garlic cloves can be smashed with a fork and most of the moisture has evaporated. Blend until smooth. Spread it all into a Silpat-lined dehydrator tray and place in a dehydrator set at 75°C for 12 hours. The next day, blend until smooth and season with the tomato vinegar. Cool and store in an airtight container until needed.

fermented pineapple juice

pineapple juice	1L
kosher salt	20g

Mix the juice with salt. Cryovac and store in a warm place for a minimum of 21 days or until desired sourness is achieved.

fermented pineapple reduction

fermented pineapple juice	1kg
sugar	70g

Reduce the pineapple juice over low heat until a syrupy consistency is achieved.

fermented apple cider

fresh apple juice	1L
kosher salt	30g

Mix the juice with salt. Cryovac and store in a warm place for a minimum of 21 days or until desired sourness is achieved.

fermented raspberry juice

raspberry juice	1L
kosher salt	20g

Mix the juice with salt. Cryovac and keep in a warm place for a minimum of 14 days or until desired sourness is achieved.

charred brassica stems

brassica stems, leaves, woody parts	1kg
kosher salt	20g

Grill the brassicas and then cold-smoke for 30 minutes. Cool completely, then Cryovac and ferment in a warm place for a minimum of 14 days.

coriander capers

coriander berries	125g
filtered water	125g
white vinegar	125g
kosher salt	10g

Bring the water, vinegar, and salt to a simmer to dissolve the salt. Cool completely. Cryovac with the coriander berries and store at room temperature for 5 days. Transfer to a refrigerator for at least a month before using.

ramp capers

unopened ramp buds	125g
filtered water	125g
Lindera Farms ramp vinegar	125g
kosher salt	10g

Bring the water, vinegar, and salt to a simmer to dissolve the salt. Cool completely. Cryovac with the ramp buds and store at room temperature for 5 days. Transfer to a refrigerator for at least a month before using.

pickled ramps

ramps, washed well, greens and stems removed	1kg
filtered water	850mL
white vinegar	840mL
granulated sugar	600g
lemongrass stalks, bruised and cut into 3" pieces	1ea
ginger, 3" piece, peeled and sliced thin	1ea
mace	1g
allspice berries	3ea
bay leaves	4ea
cloves	3ea
cinnamon stick, 3" pieces	1ea
Thai long peppercorns	5ea

Mix ingredients together. Bring to a boil and pour over the cleaned ramps. Allow to cool at room temperature and store in the refrigerator for at least 1 week before using.

preserved meyer lemons

Meyer lemons, washed well	1kg
kosher salt	500g
coriander berries, toasted and cooled	25g
bay leaves	5ea

Score the lemons from the tip of the fruit crossways, cutting only ¾ of the way into the fruit. Toss all the ingredients together and Cryovac. Store in a warm place, preferably directly in the sun, for a minimum of three months. At this point, they can be transferred to a refrigerator or freezer.

fermented chile powder

cayenne peppers, deseeded and chopped	1kg
garlic, minced fine	20g
kosher salt	25g

Robot-coupe all the ingredients until a paste is formed. Cryovac and ferment in a warm place for a minimum of one month. Save as a paste to use as sambal or dehydrate at 110°F until completely dry. Grind to a fine powder and reserve.

preserved dill stems

dill stems	120g
filtered water	120g
white vinegar	120g
kosher salt	17g

Bring the water, vinegar, and salt to a simmer to dissolve the salt. Cool completely. Cryovac with the dill stems and store at room temperature for 5 days. Transfer to a refrigerator for at least a month before using.

porcini garum

porcini mushroom	800g
egg whites	200g
rice koji	225g
kosher salt	240g
filtered water	800mL

Puree the porcini mushrooms, koji, and egg whites and salt in a robot coupe until a coarse paste is formed. Transfer to a sanitized container and mix with the filtered water. Cryovac on full pressure and transfer to a dehydrator set at 140°F for a minimum of 6 months. When ready to use, allow to strain through a coffee-filter-lined fine-mesh strainer. Reserve the leftover paste for another use.

smoked onion shiro dashi

sweet onions, such as Vidalia, sliced thin	1kg
shiro dashi	1L

Lay the onions in a thin layer and smoke for 6 hours. Place in the dehydrator at 120°F until completely dry. Place the onions and the shiro dashi in a Cryovac bag and seal on full pressure. Transfer to a dehydrator set at 140°F for a minimum of 14 days but up to a month. When ready to use, allow to strain through a coffee-filter-lined fine-mesh strainer.

rose kosho

rose petals	100g
fresh cayenne pepper	75g
kosher salt	35g

Puree in a mortar and pestle until a relatively uniform paste is achieved. Store in an airtight container or Cryovac bag and allow to ferment in a warm place for 1 week. After 1 week, you can use the kosho or transfer to a refrigerator and store for up to 3 months.

shio koji

filtered water	540mL
rice koji	410g
kosher salt	96g

Blend all ingredients together and seal in a Cryovac bag on full pressure. Allow to ferment in a warm spot for 7 days.

burnt hay oil

neutral oil	300g
hay	75g

Place the hay and oil in a large pot with a tight fitting lid. Remove the lid and light the hay on fire with a torch. Cover with the lid and allow to slowly burn out. After it has finished smoking, stir with a metal spoon and repeat the process 2 more times. Pass through a coffee filter–lined fine mesh strainer. Cool and reserve until needed.

CURED, DRIED & PRESERVED SEAFOOD & MEAT

scallop garum

scallop abductor muscles, or leftover scallops sliced 1/8" thick	1kg
rice koji	225g
kosher salt	240g
filtered water	800mL

Puree the scallops, koji, and salt in a robot coupe until a coarse paste is formed. Transfer to a sanitized container and mix with the filtered water. Cryovac on full pressure and transfer to a dehydrator set at 140°F for a minimum of 6 months. When ready to use, allow to strain through a coffee-filter-lined fine-mesh strainer. Reserve the leftover paste for another use.

mussel garum

blue mussels	1kg
rice koji	225g
filtered water	800g
kosher salt	240g

Follow the same process as the scallop garum.

uni garum

sea urchin	900g
egg whites	100g
rice koji	225g
kosher salt	240g
filtered water	800mL

Process the same as the scallop garum.

smoked oyster shiro dashi

smoked and dried oysters	200g
shiro dashi	1L

Process like the smoked onion shiro dashi (see page 271).

fish butter

butter	4lb
fish bones, scrap and trim	1kg
garlic head, halved	1ea
thyme sprigs	7–8ea
bay leaves	4ea
black peppercorns	15g

Melt the butter, add all the remaining ingredients, and bring to a simmer. Cook over medium heat until all the moisture has cooked out of the fish, 1 hour or so.

smoked and dried oysters

oysters, shucked	1kg
country ham cure	60g

Toss the ingredients together well and Cryovac. Store under refrigeration for 8 hours. Discard any brine that has formed, rinse, and allow to dry overnight to form a pellicle. Cold-smoke for 4 hours and transfer to a 120°F dehydrator until completely dried all the way through. Store in an airtight container in a cool dark space.

smoked and dried clams

clams, shucked	1kg
country ham cure	60g

Toss the ingredients together well and Cryovac. Store under refrigeration for 8 hours. Discard any brine that has formed, rinse, and allow to dry overnight to form a pellicle. Cold-smoke for 4 hours and transfer to a 120°F dehydrator until completely dried all the way through. Store in an airtight container in a cool dark space.

smoked fish bones

fish bones, reserved from filleting	500g
kosher salt	200g
granulated sugar	50g

Mix the salt and sugar together. Split in half. Rub the fish bones with half of the cure and store in a non-reactive container for 4 days. Drain and apply the remaining cure for another 4 days. Rinse and allow to dry under refrigeration overnight. Smoke for 8 hours and hang to slowly dry over a fire or in a dehydrator set at 140°F. Once dried, store in a cool dry place.

smoked bone oil

smoked fish bones	500g
neutral oil	250g

Cryovac and place in a pot of boiling water for 4 to 6 hours, adding water as needed. Allow to cool in the oil overnight and pass through a coffee-filter-lined fine-mesh strainer. Cool and reserve until needed.

swordfish ham

swordfish loin	1kg
country ham cure (see below)	985g

Rub the swordfish loin in half of the cure and cover for 5 days. After 5 days, rub with the remaining cure and cover again for another 5 days. After day 10, rinse the swordfish loin and place on a rack in the reach-in to form a pellicle overnight. Cold-smoke for 8 hours and place in a curing chamber. Continue to dry until 30% weight loss has been achieved. Trim away any of the fish that is too dry, portion into manageable blocks, freeze, and slice on a meat slicer to desired consistency.

anchovy powder

anchovy, drained and rinsed	205g
garlic, minced fine	112g
capers, drained	290g

Puree in a robot coupe until smooth. Bake at 250°F until completely dried. Do not let it get too dark, or it will become bitter. Grind in a spice grinder or dry Vitamix and pass through tamis. Store in an airtight container.

wagyu ham

wagyu strip loin	2kg
country ham cure (see below)	20g

Rub the wagyu in half of the cure and Cryovac for 8 days, flipping every day. Remove from the bag and repeat with the remaining cure for an additional 8 days. After day 16, remove from the cure, wipe any excess salt away, and allow to dry overnight to form a pellicle. Cold-smoke for 8 hours and return to the refrigerator. The next day, cold-smoke for another 8 hours. Wrap in cheesecloth soaked in whiskey, with the excess liquid wrung out. Age for a minimum of 6 months.

country ham cure

kosher salt	1,800g
brown sugar	454g
chile flake	30g
black peppercorns, coarsely ground	30g
smoked paprika	10g
Cure #2	6g

Mix and store in an airtight container.

BASE RECIPES

STOCKS

beef stock and demi-glace

beef bones	25lbs

Place bones on rack-lined sheet trays and steam at 212°F in a combi oven for 20 minutes. Remove from the oven and wash under cold water until all impurities have been removed from the surface. Place into a 100-quart stock pot. Cover with cold water and bring to a boil. Turn off the heat and add 22 quarts of ice. Remove any fat or impurities that solidify on the surface. Return the pot to a simmer over medium heat and skim again. Reduce the heat to a low enough temperature to drop to a lazy simmer, allowing just a few bubbles to emerge. Cook for 8 hours, skimming constantly. Remove the bones from the liquid, strain through a fine-mesh strainer into a smaller pot, return to the heat, and bring to a low simmer. As the stock reduces, constantly strain through a fine-mesh strainer into a smaller pot. Reduce until 4 liters remain, pass through a fine-mesh strainer, and chill until needed. We use this reduction once it reaches 4 liters as our demi-glace. If you feel that you want a roasted flavor in your beef stock, this is the point that I recommend adding any roasted bones or caramelized meat scraps. The reason for this is to limit the amount of bitterness in the final sauce after reduction.

chicken stock

chicken cages, washed well until no blood remains and skin removed	20lbs
chicken feet	1000g

Place washed cages and chicken feet in a 100-quart stock pot. Cover in water. Bring up to a simmer over medium-high heat. Add 22 quarts of ice. Remove any fat or impurities that solidify on the surface. Return the pot to a simmer over medium heat and skim again. Reduce the heat to a low enough temperature to drop to a lazy simmer, allowing just a few bubbles to emerge. Cook for 6 hours, skimming constantly. Remove the bones from the liquid, strain through a fine-mesh strainer into a smaller pot, return to the heat, and bring to a low simmer. As the stock reduces, constantly strain through a fine-mesh strainer into a smaller pot. Reduce until 4 liters remain, pass through a fine-mesh strainer, and chill until needed.

duck stock

duck carcasses, reserved from carving	8ea
reduced chicken stock	4L

Lightly char the duck carcasses over embers. Place into a stock pot, cover with the chicken stock, and add the garlic and guajillo. Cook on low heat, covered, for 6 hours. Strain through a fine-mesh strainer and reduce slowly to 1,785mL, skimming constantly. Pass through a fine-mesh strainer and chill.

squab stock

smoked squab carcasses, reserved from carving	15ea
reduced chicken stock	2L
garlic head, halved	1ea
dried guajillo chile	1ea

Lightly char the squab carcasses over embers. Place into a stock pot and cover with the chicken stock. Cook on low heat, covered, for 6 hours. Strain through a fine-mesh strainer and reduce slowly to 650mL, skimming constantly. Pass through a fine-mesh strainer and chill.

clam stock

littleneck clams or razor clam shells/trimmings	10lbs
sweet vermouth	750mL

If using the littlenecks, add the clams and the vermouth to a rondeau and bring to a rapid simmer, covered. Once the clams have opened, remove the meat from the shells. Place back in the rondeau and cover with enough filtered water to just cover. Slowly simmer until the liquid has reduced by half. Pass through a fine-mesh strainer. Weigh the mixture and add 1% of its weight in bloomed gelatin and return to the heat until it is melted. Freeze. Place in a cheesecloth-lined perforated pan over a deeper pan. Allow to defrost under refrigeration overnight. Reduce the clarified liquid until a concentrated stock is achieved.

If using razor clams, cover with the vermouth, and cook until all of the alcohol has evaporated. Cover with water and proceed with the same method.

spiny lobster stock

spiny lobster heads, split	12ea
spiny lobster tail shells	12ea
white miso	200g
cream sherry	750mL
bay leaves	6ea
filtered water	4L

Rub the inside of the split lobster heads with the miso and roast on a rack-lined sheet tray at 425°F for 15 minutes or until caramelized. Place heads and remaining shells in a rondeau, cover with sherry and bay leaves. Cook on medium-high heat until the sherry has reduced by ¾. Cover with the filtered water and continue to reduce, skimming any impurities that rise to the top, until the liquid volume has reduced to 1,320 ml. Strain and reserve.

mussel stock

mussels, washed	2lb
sweet vermouth	500mL
shallots, sliced thin	200g
garlic, sliced thin	20g
saffron threads	1g
gelatin, bloomed	3g

Place all ingredients except gelatin in a pot and cover well. Bring to a simmer of medium-high heat and cook until all the mussels have opened. Cover with hay, light the hay on fire, and cover with a tight-fitting lid until completely burned out. Keep covered for 20 minutes. Remove the mussels, cool them, remove from the shells, and debeard them. Reduce the liquid over medium heat to 300mL. Add the gelatin and stir until melted and well combined. Strain through a fine-mesh strainer. Freeze in a shallow tray. Once frozen, place over a mesh strainer lined with cheesecloth and allow to defrost completely. Reserve the clarified liquid until needed.

dashi

filtered water	1.1L
kombu, rinsed	25g
dry shiitake	50g

Place all ingredients in a Cryovac bag sealed on full pressure. Cook at 60°C for 45 minutes. Remove from the water bath and allow to steep an additional hour. Strain through a fine-mesh strainer and reserve.

kombu stock

kombu, rinsed	500g
filtered water	5L

Bring to 60°C over medium heat. Transfer to a Cambro and cool. Allow to steep overnight or for 12 hours. The next day, pass through a fine-mesh strainer and reduce by half of its original volume.

onion jus

sweet onions, peeled and sliced	25lbs
kombu, rinsed	250g

Place the sliced onions and kombu in a 100-quart stock pot and cover with filtered water. Bring to a simmer, reduce the heat to low so no bubbles are visible, cover, and cook for 12 hours. Strain through a fine-mesh strainer and reduce until the stock is a napé consistency. As the stock reduces, constantly strain through a fine-mesh strainer into a smaller pot. Pass through fine-mesh strainer and chill until needed.

EPILOGUE

NEW ADVENTURES

Mike Wolf

As I sit and write this on a hotel rooftop in Nashville, looking out at the changing Nashville skyline, a tourist in my own town, I can see the exact location of what will be the gleaming new home of The Catbird Seat, wrapped around the 8th floor of the Bill Voorhees building a few blocks south of the heart of downtown Nashville. In fact, they're still building it out and I can see a few workers drilling into steel beams with fiery orange sparks flying across their shielded faces. Sister restaurant/cocktail bar the Patterson House will also be moving and will continue to be connected at the hip to Catbird. Looking to the rolling hills in the countryside just southwest of Nashville, plans are taking shape for Chef Baxter's possible new culinary adventure in a historic home built in the 1890s, a concept he's been honing with the same ownership group of the Catbird Seat, Strategic Hospitality. He's also working up plans for a restaurant in Nashville. Across from the Bill Voorhees building on 8th Avenue sits the former home of Arnold's Country Kitchen, shuttered by the owners after almost forty years in business, a culinary mecca for this city and the throngs who would eat there every week. Looking West to Charlotte Avenue, I can see where the potential new home of Arnold's may end up, if the rumors are true. By the smokestacks to the northwest, I can see the renovation of Nelson's Green Brier Distillery, a fourth-generation operation where I'll be starting a new job very soon. Winds of change are blowing around the wind tunnels created by the shiny new skyscrapers all around, reflecting a changed culinary landscape in a town mostly known for hot, spicy fried chicken. There's still plenty of that to go around too.

I called Chef Josh Habiger (see his introduction on page x), the first co-chef of The Catbird Seat and one of the minds behind that first kernel of an idea that became the counter-style tasting-menu format, to see which direction the new Catbird Seat might be taking. He's still with the company as chef and part owner of lauded local restaurant Bastion, and he's consulting on the new direction and the hiring of the new chef who will soon replace Chef Baxter. What he said told me a lot about the limitations of the previous space, and the value of having a chef involved in making big decisions about balancing the prioritization of budgeting between the back of house and the front of house:

Josh *"One of the ideas that's been really important is to still have the Patterson House and Catbird Seat somewhat connected, hopefully even more connected. They'll be sharing one floor and one footprint, so hopefully they'll be able to work together even more. They're like siblings, so it's great to see them grow together and push forward, but still do all the things they're both known for. Space is probably the most important thing in terms of being able to execute what we want for this new chapter. Equipment is good to have, but honestly no one has ever gone to a restaurant and said 'the food was so good, you must have an excellent oven,' or anything like that, so equipment can only get you so far. But the design of the space will make things much easier for the people working there. The prior Catbird Seat had a walk-in* *downstairs and a really tiny dish area and things like that, so hopefully this new version can be an even better place to work.*

"It was amazing to see what Chef Baxter and his team could do at the old space with all the limitations placed on them. The new space will have a wine room, and the floor plan will be more open and beautiful, so it's really exciting. But selfishly I'm looking at the stuff behind the curtain and in the back of the house, where the money isn't exactly made. Typically, restaurant consultants are like 'Hey, fuck everything behind the curtain, we have to spend money on the things that the guests can see, like the lighting and the artwork and stuff like that.' But having worked there early on and seen how those limitations can be tough for a chef and the team, I'm looking forward to making it an easier, more efficient place to cook food and keep pushing forward creatively."

As for Chef Baxter, he's looking ahead to the future and furthering his love of all things from the ocean, passed down from his relatives on the Florida coast, inspired to bring better seafood to this landlocked land in the rolling Middle Tennessee hills. As for the name, exact location, and style of food, we'll know that by the time this book is hitting shelves. All we know is that it will be delicious, wholly original, and that people will come in from all over to taste it. He'll open a new restaurant with all the hard-won wisdom, experience, and accolades from his time spent cooking and serving guests at the diner-style counter in The Catbird Seat.

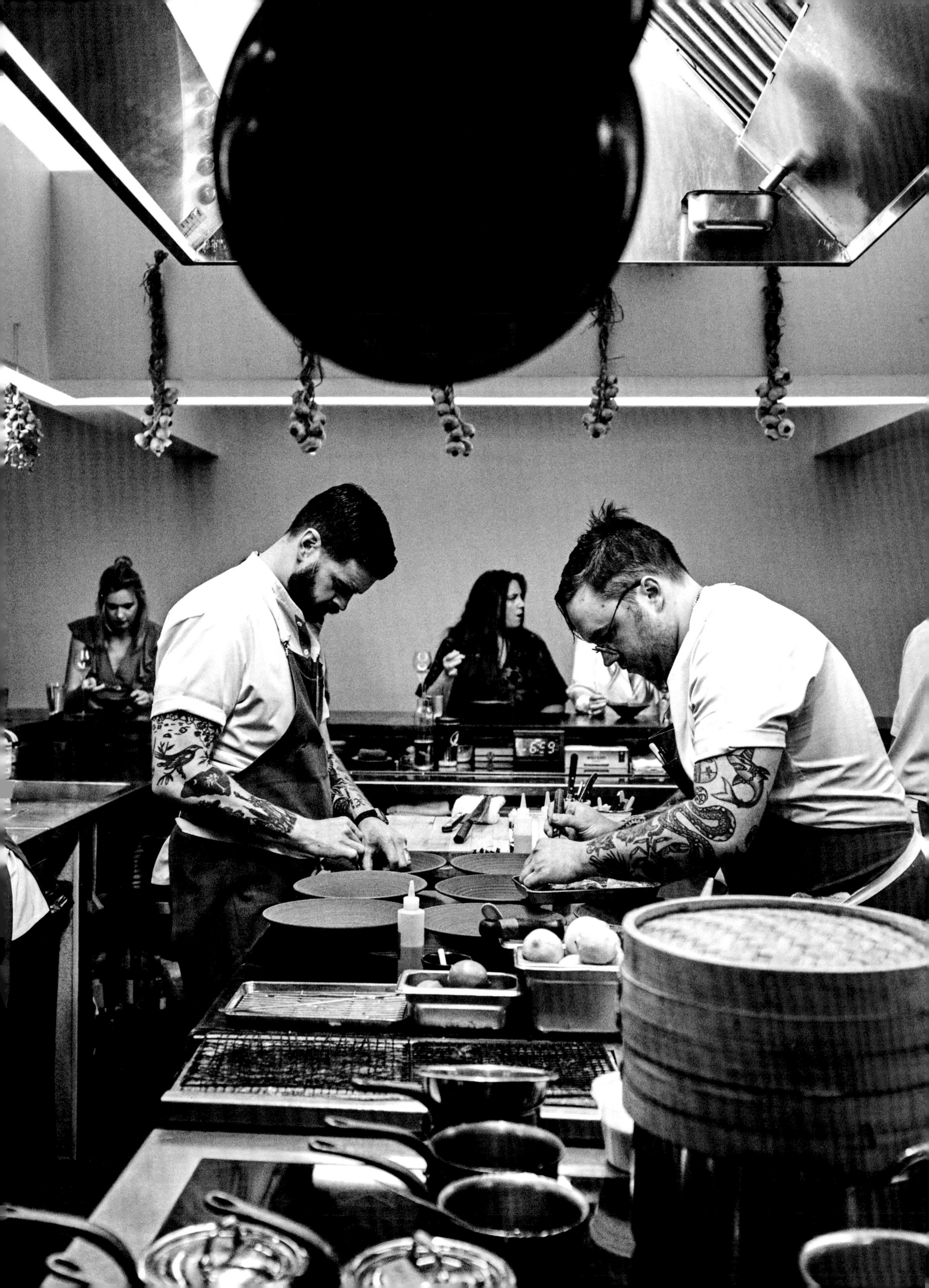

ACKNOWLEDGMENTS

BRIAN BAXTER Thank you to my loving wife, Michaela, for believing in me and allowing me to follow my dream and take the time away from my beautiful kids, Noah and Ella. Thank you to my parents, my sisters Bekah and Rachel, my grandmothers, and my family for believing in me and supporting me over the years. Thank you to the following people for believing in me enough to invest either their time, money, or for their friendship over the years: Roommate (Ben Cashatt), Aaron Izaguirre, Andrew Klamar, Andrew Thomas Lee, Ben Goldberg, Brennan Flemming, Buddy Sleasman, Chad Koeplinger, Chris Windus, Cole Just, Connor Carlson, Cooper Sudbrink, Daniel Alba "JR," Dano & Bethany Heinze, Erik Anderson, Evan LoJacono, Genevieve Bamber, Ian W-H, James Clark, Jayce Knight, Johnny Spero, Jonny Corcoran, Jon Whitebird Newman, Jordan Farrell, Josh Habiger, JP Hanover, Kevin Botout, Kevin Gillespie, Kosta "the Greek," Kyle Lamb, LeeAnn and Bill Cherry and family, Logan Gray, Matt Halleyburton, Matty Matheson, Max Goldberg, Mike Wolf, Nate Leonard, Pat Martin, Patrick McMahon, Rob Ciborowski, Ron Egan, Ryan Bloodworth, Ryan Poli, Ryan Ratino, Sam Jett, Sarah Salim, Sean Brock, Shivam Khullar, Son Pham, Todd Saal, Trevor Moran, Tristen Naquin, Walker Bauer, and all of our regulars who supported us over the past two years. Lastly, thank you to my heavenly father for giving me the ability to be creative and for sending his son to die for us.

MIKE WOLF Thanks to my amazing wife Kate, my beautiful daughter Leila Mae, my incredible son Henry James, the animal crew: Boone, June, George, Jett, my Mom and Dad for always encouraging my writing, my brother Matthew Schmielha, we couldn't do it without the love and guidance of Cathy and Don Barnett, Bob and Ashley Souder, our hero Sherri, the Singing Grandma, Roger, Lisa, my badass niece Anabelle, Stephanie Bowman for your wit and wisdom, Ryan, Amanda, Todd and everyone at Turner, booze news anchor Kenneth Dedmon, Chris, Michael Eades, Matt Campbell, Brian Baxter and the entire team at Catbird Seat, Jordan and the team at Strategic Hospitality, Josh Habiger, Erik Anderson, Charlie Nelson, Jessica Backhus, Kevin King, Vilda Gonzalez, Kenny Lyons, Sean Brock, Sam Jett, Erica Dahlgren, Ed Kolb and the entire team at Nelson's Green Brier, Colby Rasavong, and my neighbor forever in my heart, David Berman.

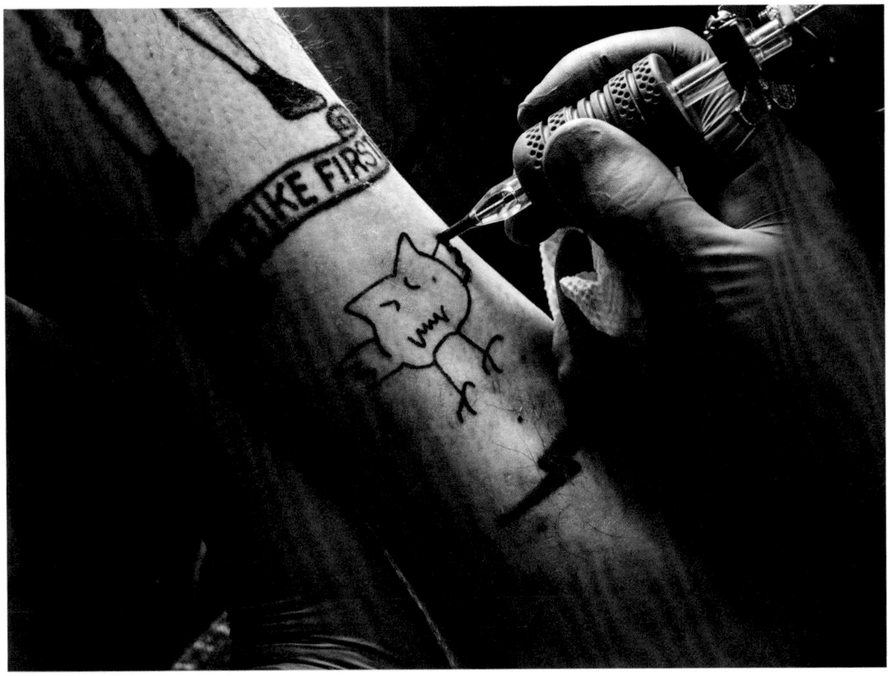

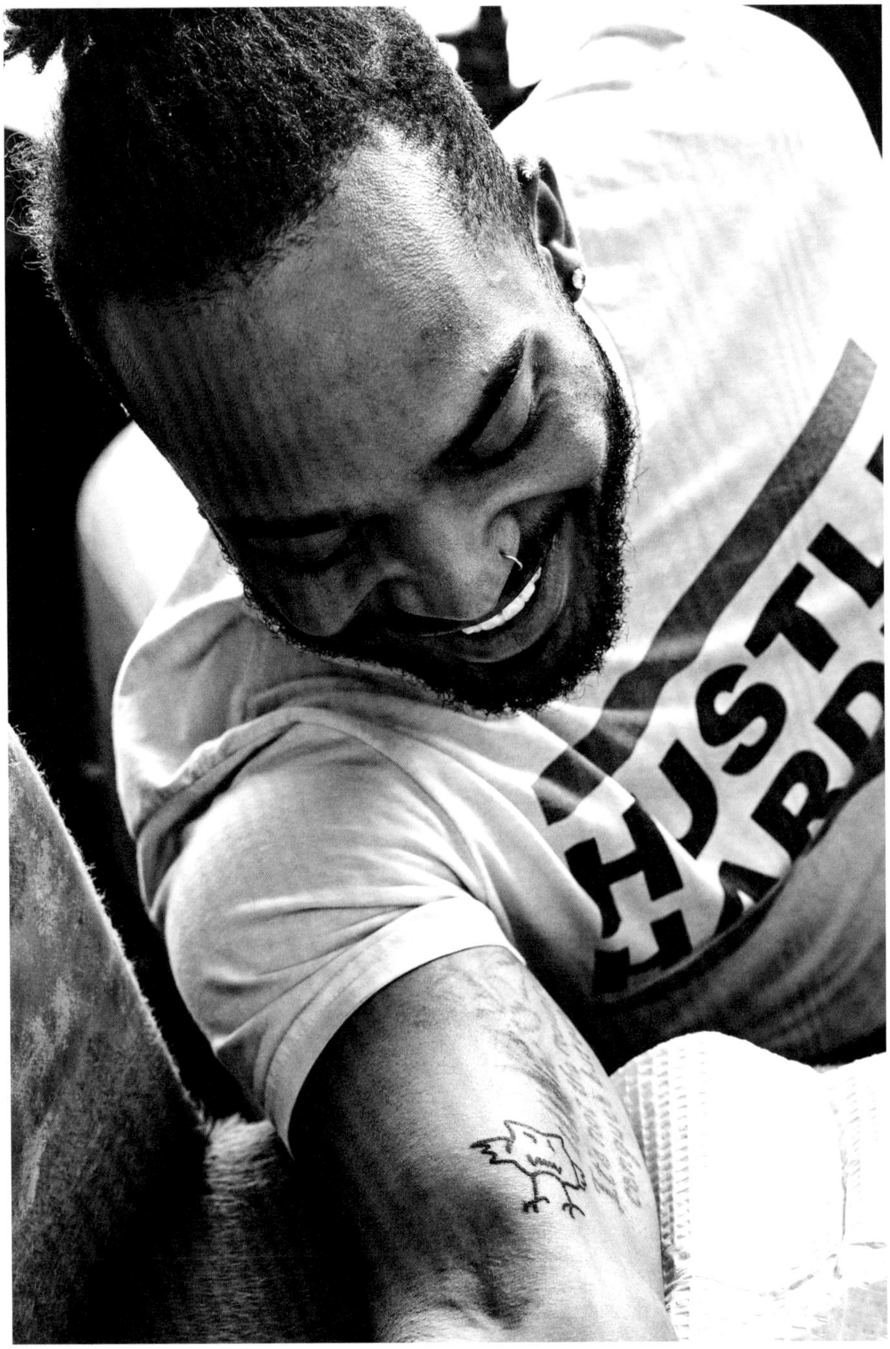

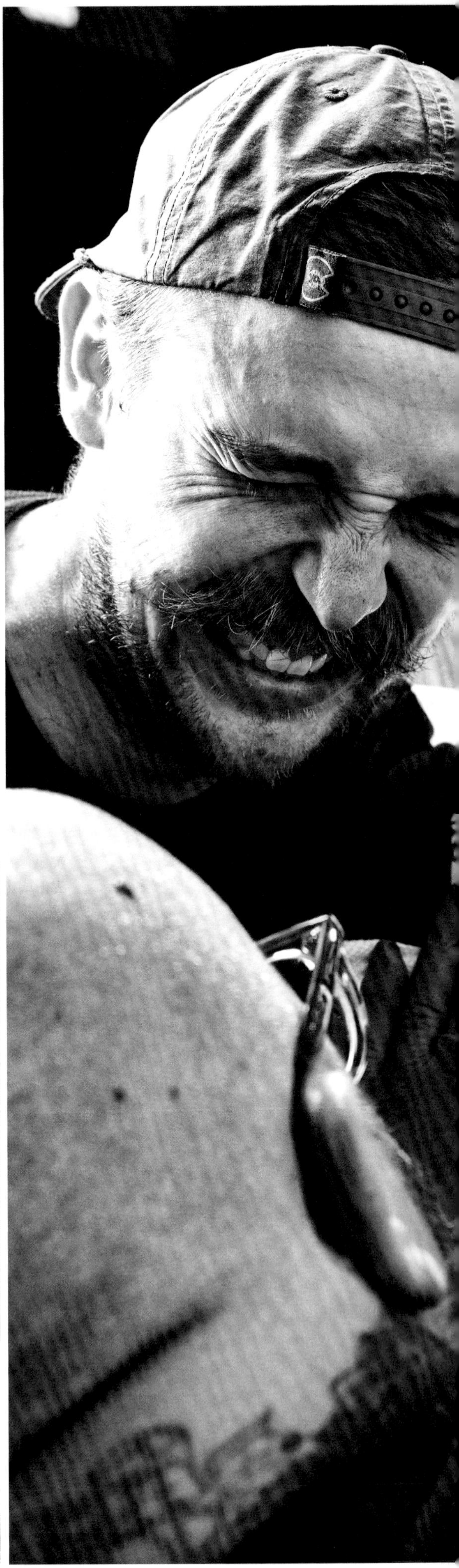

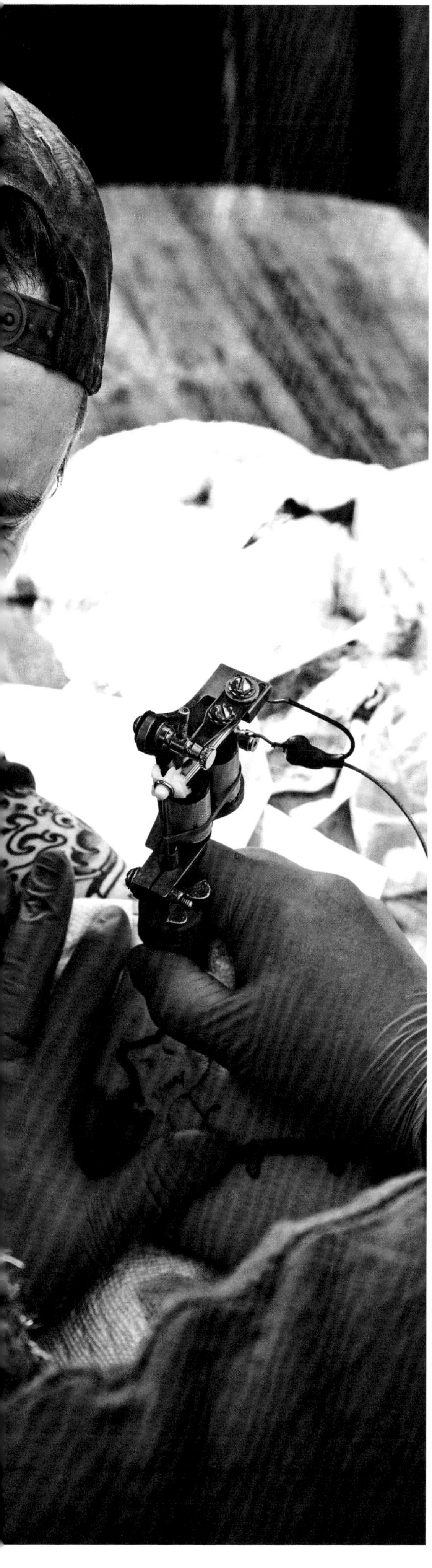

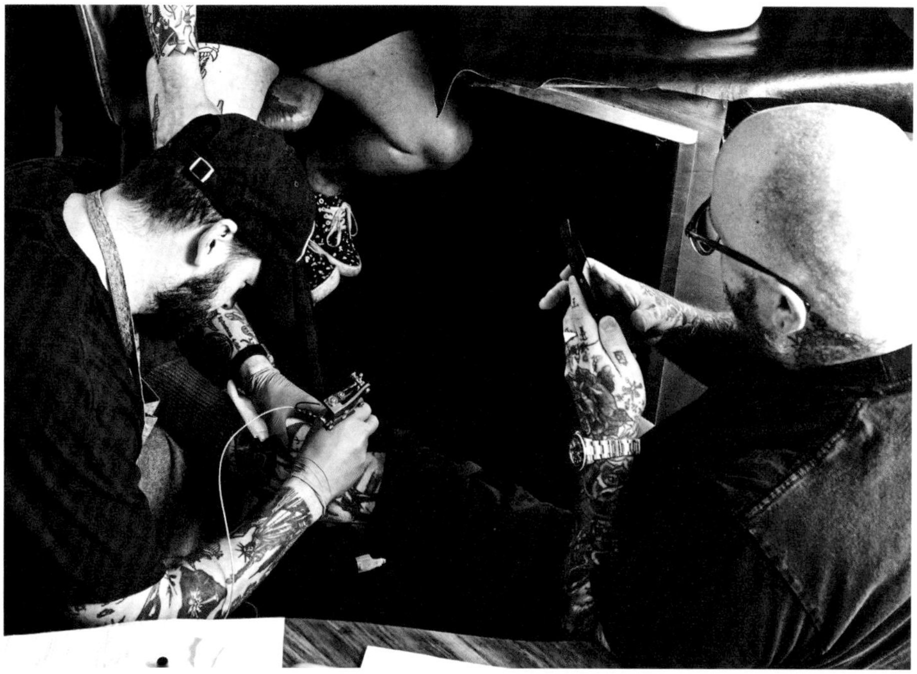

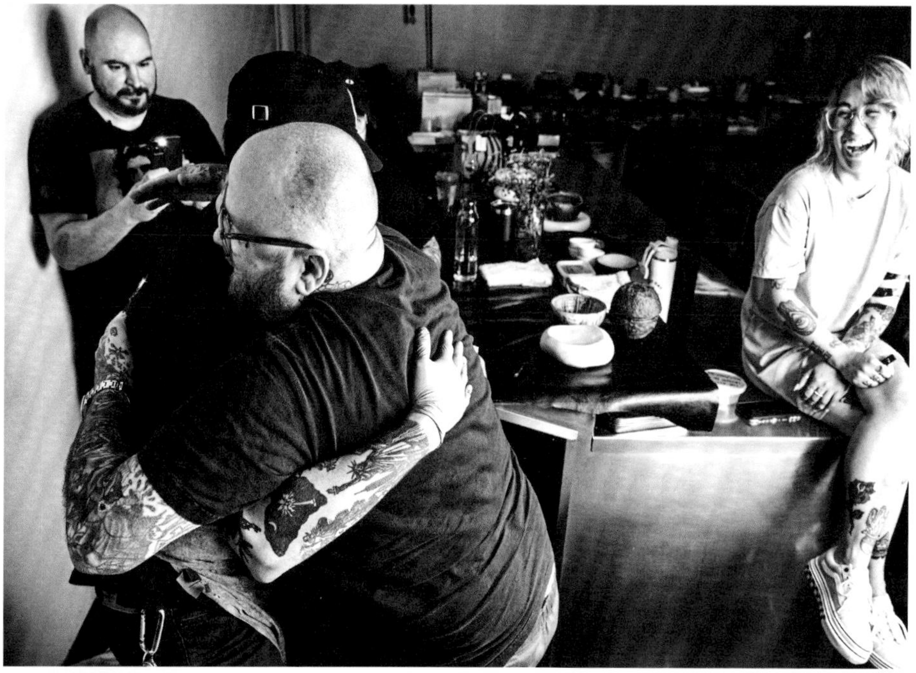

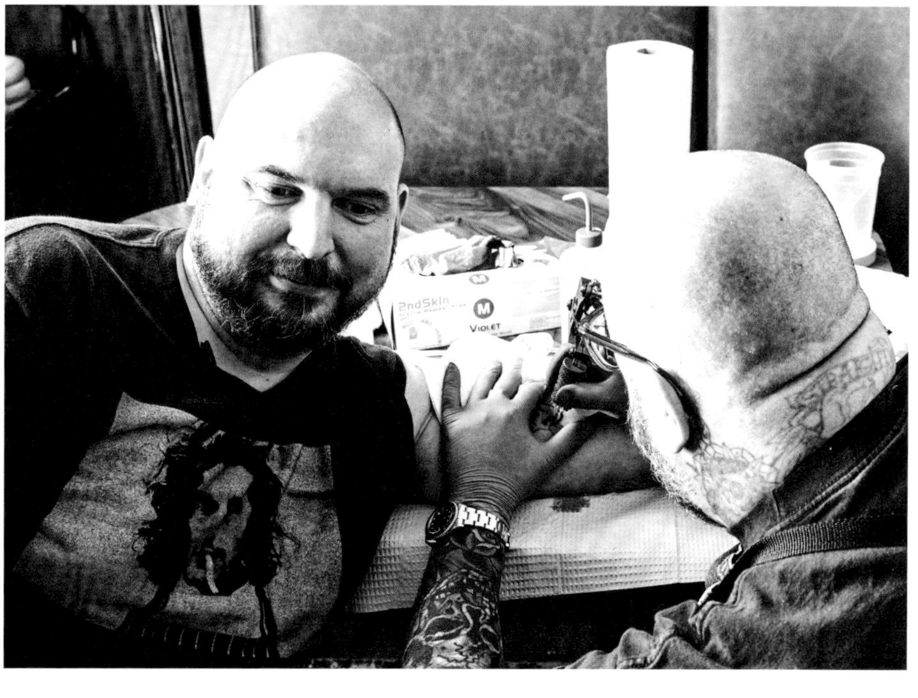
2ndSkin
M
VIOLET

INDEX

Page references in *italics* indicate photographs.

A

Aged Buri Belly, Chutoro, Smoked Oyster & Seaweeds, *240*, 241
Alabama Blue Crab & Courgette, *18*, 19
Almond Angelica Puree, 156
Amadai with a Curry of Fermented Golden Beet, 160, *161*
Ambrosia Salad, *166*, 167
anchovies
    Hollandaise, 190
    Powder, 273
Angelica Root Meringue, 167
apples
    Black Apple Butter, 66
    Fermented Apple Cider, 270
    Fried Apples, 66
    Granny Smith Gelee, 80
    Pink Moon Oysters with an Ice of Mountain Rose Apple & Fresh Wasabi, *78*, 79
    Yeast Donut, Foie Gras, Black Apple, 66, *67*
Asian Pear & Kimchi, *224*, 225
asparagus
    Fermented White Asparagus, 269
    Fermented White Asparagus Bearnaise, 27
    glazed in a Sauce of Smoked Trout Bones with Everything Bagel Spice, *112*, 113
    in Sakura Blossom Butter, 117
Avocado, Grilled, Mayo with, 163

B

bacon
    in Braised Collard Greens, 96
    Candy Cap Bacon, 230
    in Moros y Cristianos, 254
    in Preserved Tomato Broth, 212
    in Scallop XO, 118
    in Scallops Wrapped in 45-Day Aged Pork Belly, Fermented Pumpkin & Smooth Black Truffle, 216, *217*
    in Sorghum Vinaigrette, 99
bamboo, Fermented Bamboo Shoots, 250
bananas, Burnt with Black Walnut, Cultured Butter & Caviar, *228*, 229
Barbecued Carrot, Blue Mussels & Fermented Sea Buckthorn, *184*, 185
Barbecued Spiny Lobster, Fermented Pineapple, Burnt Fresno Chilies, 50, 51, *52*, 53
Barely Cooked Scallops with Brown Butter Roasted Hazelnut, *188*, 189

Baxter, Brian, viii–ix, 37, 138–39, 265, 277
beans
    in Moros y Cristianos, 254
    See also leather britches
Bear Creek Farm Lamb with Swiss Chard & Cashew Milk, 130–31, *132–33*
Bear Creek Farm Pork Coulotte, Clams & Brassicas, 91
beef
    Belly Ham with Kimchi & Asian Pear, 76, *77*
    in Fava Bean & Stilton Cheese, *248*, 249
    Ribloin with Savoy Cabbage, Black Walnut & Périgord Truffle, 222–23, *223*
    Stock and Demi-Glace, 274
    Wagyu Ham, 273
beef fat
    & Laphroaig Sponge Candies, *102*, 103
    Beefsteak Tomato Roasted in Dry-Aged Beef Fat, Porcini, Sauce Marchand De Vin, *22*, 24, *25*
    in Sauce Perigueux, 222, 249
Beefsteak Tomato Roasted in Dry-Aged Beef Fat, Porcini, Sauce Marchand De Vin, *22*, 24, *25*
beets
    Beet Syrup, 68
    Golden Beet Vadouvan, 160
    Lacto-Fermented Golden Beet Juice, 160
Benton, Alan, 205
berries
    Crispy Pig Tail with General Tso's Sauce Made from Strawberry & Fermented Jimmy Nardello Pepper, 114, *115*
    Dry-Aged Ora King Salmon, Raspberry & Angelica, 156, *157*
    Dry-Aged Tennessee Duck with Wild Mushrooms & Preserved Summer Berries, *60*, 61–62, *63*
    Fermented Cranberries, 65
    Fermented Raspberry, Rose & Horseradish Ice Cream, *226*, 227
    Fermented Raspberry Juice, 270
    Fermented Raspberry Vinaigrette, 226
    Pickled Huckleberries, 61
    Preserved Strawberries, 69, 136
Black Apple Butter, 66
Black Apple Glaze, 66
Black Currants, 219
Black Garlic Hoisin, 194
Black Trumpet Shortbread, 68, 100
Black Walnut Toffee, 229
Blue Crystal Prawn Tartare, Fermented Kiwi, Belgian Osetra Caviar, *210*, 211

Bone Oil, 181
Boniato, Smoked Tofu & a Vin Blanc of Last Year's Cured & Dried Sweet Potatoes, *120*, 121
Bonito Butter, 121
Bradford, Nat, 205
Braised Collard Greens, 96
Brassica Butter, 223
Brassica Stems, Charred, 270
broccoli
    with Anchovy & Cured Tuna Heart, 190, *191*
    Broccoli Marinade, 190
Brown Butter Roasted Hazelnuts, 189
buri belly, with Chutoro, Smoked Oyster & Seaweeds, *240*, 241
Burnt Banana, Black Walnut, Cultured Butter & Caviar, *228*, 229
Burnt Chile Mayo, 51
Burnt Hay Oil, 271
Burnt Pine Oil, 193
Burnt Vanilla Ice Cream, 68
buttermilk
    Salted Buttermilk, 15, 151, 226
    Wasabi Buttermilk, 79
butters
    Black Apple Butter, 66
    Bonito Butter, 121
    Brassica Butter, 223
    Crab Butter, 84
    Fermented Butternut Squash Butter, 54
    Fermented Celery Butter, 87
    Fish Butter, 272
    Green Garlic Butter, 28
    Green Tomato Beurre Blanc, 125
    Half-Sour Ramp Butter, 159
    Langoustine Butter, 159
    Lobster Sherry Butter, 215
    Mussel Butter, 47
    Pumpkin Butter, 58
    Sakura Blossom Butter, 117

C

cabbage
    Cabbage Puree, 222
    Fried Cabbage, 223
Candy Cap Mushrooms, Yeast Donut with Foie Gras, 230
cantaloupe
    Candied Cantaloupe, 35
    Cantaloupe Kimchi, 152
    Cantaloupe Syrup, 35
    Sherbet with Sake & Elderflower, *34*, 35
capers
    Coriander Capers, 270
    in Florida Blue Crab, Sunchoke Dauphine, Ramp Capers, *244*, 245
    Ramp Capers, 270
Carabinero Prawn Shiokara, Daylilies & Koshihikari Rice, 238, *239*

Caramelized Onion Hoisin, 220
Caramelized Walnuts, 65
carrots
    in Crab Butter Base, 19
    in Crab-Butter Base, 84
    Mussel & Carrot BBQ, 185
    Roasted Carrots, 185
cashews
    Cashew Curry, 130
    Cashew Milk, 130
    Cashew Yogurt, 131
Catbird
    in June 2020, 2–5
    in Summer 2020, 9
    in Fall 2020, 41
    in Spring 2021, 107
    in Winter 2020–2021, 73
    in Summer 2021, 145
    in Fall 2021, 175
    in Spring 2022, 235
    new directions, 276–77
cauliflower
    Cauliflower Gelato, 263
    Cauliflower Ice Cream, Milk Chocolate & Black Ants, *262*, 263
caviar
    with Burnt Banana, Black Walnut, Cultured Butter, *228*, 229
    with Nancé, Triple Cream Cheese, Pineapple Weed, 260, *261*
Cayenne Pepper Vinegar, 96
cedar
    Cedar & Coconut Curry, 110
    Cedar Green Curry Paste, 110
Celeriac, Puree, 211
celery
    Celery Leaf Powder, 167
    Celery-Leaf Oil, 87
    Fermented Celery Butter, 87
    in Fire-Exploded Kidney Flowers, Bamboo Shoot & Baby Leeks, 250, *251*
    in Oyster Root Stew, 32
Charred Brassica Stems, 270
Charred Broccoli, Anchovy & Cured Tuna Heart, 190, *191*
Charred Cucumber Gelee, 15
Charred Cucumber Salsa Verde, 148
Charred Zucchini, Salted Buttermilk & Marjoram, *150*, 151
cheese
    Fava Bean & Stilton Cheese, *248*, 249
    Nancé, Triple Cream Cheese, Pineapple Weed & Schrenckii Caviar, 260, *261*
Cherry Wood Oil, 117
chicken
    Schmaltz, 48
    Stock, 274
Chile Lime Salt, 51
Chimichurri, 96, 151
Chocolate, Tempered, 103

chutoro, with Aged Buri Belly, Smoked Oyster & Seaweeds, *240*, 241
clams
    & Leather Britches Tea, 16
    Clam Furikake, 16
    Clam Mayo, 95
    Clam Stock, 274
    with Cured Pork Fat & Coriander Capers, 92
    with Fermented Raspberry, Rose & Horseradish Ice Cream, 226, *227*
    with Leather Britches & Chicken Fat, 48
    Smoked and Dried, 272
    Smoked Clam Oil, 95, 110
    Smoked Clam Vinaigrette, 16
coconut
    Coconut Crème Fraiche, 167
    Coconut Meringue, 199
    Golden Beet Vadouvan, 160
    in Nancé Pit "Cheese," 260
coffee, in Plantain Cafécito, 259
Collard Greens, Braised, 96
Confit Sweet Potatoes, 121
Confited Scallops, 189, 216
Confited Sunchoke, 194
coriander berries, Preserved, with Dry-Aged Otoro, Tosazu, 242, *243*
Coriander Capers, 270
corn
    Corn Chawanmushi, 24-Month Aged Ham, Winter Truffle Dashi, 20, *21*
    Corn Ice Cream, 168
    in Crawfish Boil, 122
    Huitlacoche Butterscotch, 168
    Tamales, 162
country ham
    about, 205
    Country Ham Dashi, 20
    Country Ham Vinaigrette, 92
    Cure, 273
    Fermented Plantain Bread, Bob Woods Ham, Plantain Syrup, *255*, *257*, *258*
    Swordfish Ham, 273
    Wagyu Ham, 273
crab
    Crab Butter, 19, 84
    Crab Butter Base, 19, 84
    with Sunchoke Dauphine, Ramp Capers, *244*, 245
Cranberries, Fermented, 65
crawfish
    Crawfish Boil, 122
    Crawfish Nage, 122
Crispy Pig Tail with General Tso's Sauce Made from Strawberry & Fermented Jimmy Nardello Pepper, 114, *115*
cucumber(s)
    & Melon Salad, Salted Buttermilk, Country Ham Gelee, *14*, 15
    Charred Cucumber Salsa Verde, 148
    Fermented Cucumber Curd, 171

INDEX   283

Cured Egg Yolk, 47
Cured Foie Gras, 61, 155
Cured Pork Fat (Lardo), 92
Cured Swiss Chard Leaves, 130
Cured Tomatoes, 31
currants
    Black Currants, 219
    Currant-Black Pepper Jam, 62
    Reginette Pasta with Grilled Mussels Dressed in Foie Gras & Preserved Black Currants, *218*, 219
Curry Butter, 19

D

daikon
    in Asian Pear & Kimchi, *224*, 225
    See also radishes
Dashi, 275
Daylily Dashi, 238
Devil's Gulch Ranch Squab, Romanesco & Pechuga, 162–63, *164–65*
Dill Stems, Preserved, 271
Dolma Spice, 131
Donut Dough, 66
donuts
    with Foie Gras, Black Apple, 66, *67*, 136
    with Foie Gras, Candy Cap Mushrooms, 230, *231*
    with Foie Gras, Strawberry & Elderflower, 136, *137*
Dried Chile Powder, 32
Dry-Aged Bear Creek Farm Ribloin, Savoy Cabbage, Black Walnut & Périgord Truffle, 222–23, *223*
Dry-Aged Buri with Granny Smith Apple, Fermented Green Gooseberry & Sea Lettuce, 80, *81*
Dry-Aged Devil's Gulch Ranch Squab with Sunchokes, Black Garlic & Malted Milk, 194–95, *196*
Dry-Aged Ora King Salmon, Raspberry & Angelica, 156, *157*
Dry-Aged Otoro, Tosazu, Preserved Coriander Berries, 242, *243*
Dry-Aged Pork Coulotte, Razor-Clam Chimichurri & Braised Collards, 96, *97*
Dry-Aged Pork Coulotte & Plantain, 254, *255*
Dry-Aged Pork Shoulder, Fermented Durian & Black Sesame, *252*, 253
Dry-Aged Tennessee Duck with Wild Mushrooms & Preserved Summer Berries, *60*, 61–62, *63*
duck
    Chevreuil, 62
    Confit, 61
    Presse Jus, 61
    Stock, 274
Dukkah, 160
durian
    Durian Custard, 253
    Durian Jus, 253

E

Eggplant, Cured & Dried, 269
elderflowers
    Pickled Elderflower, 35
    in Preserved Strawberries, 69, 136
English Peas, Louisiana Crawfish, Fermented Green Gooseberry Juice, 122, *123*
Eucalyptus Anglaise, 199
Everything Spice, 113

F

fat back, Cured Pork Fat (Lardo), 92
Fava Bean & Stilton Cheese, *248*, 249
fennel
    in Crab Butter Base, 19
    in Crab-Butter Base, 84
    Pickled Wild Fennel, 212
    in Preserved Tomato Broth, 212
Fermented Chile Powder, 271
ferments
    Apple Cider, 270
    Asian Pear & Kimchi, *224*, 225
    Bamboo Shoots, 250
    Barbecued Carrot, Blue Mussels & Fermented Sea Buckthorn, *184*, 185
    Butternut Squash Butter, 54
    Celery Butter, 87
    Chile Powder, 271
    Cranberries, 65
    Cucumber Curd, 171
    Dry-Aged Pork Shoulder, Fermented Durian & Black Sesame, *252*, 253
    Golden Beet Juice, 160
    Gooseberry Juice, 269
    Guava Reduction, 257
    Kiwi, 211
    Kohlrabi Juice, 269
    Lacto-Fermented Pear Juice, 269
    Pineapple Juice, 270
    Pineapple Reduction, 270
    Plantain Bread, Bob Woods Ham, Plantain Syrup, 257, *258*
    Ramp Powder, 95
    Raspberry Juice, 270
    Raspberry Vinaigrette, 226
    Salted Peach Puree, 246
    Sea Buckthorn Juice, 269
    Tomato Jam, 28
    Tomato Juice, 269
    Tomato Reduction, 28, 269
    Turnip Juice, 269
    White Asparagus, 269
    White Asparagus Bearnaise, 27
    White Asparagus Juice, 269
    See also pickles
Fig & Coconut, *197*, 199
Filet Beans with Smoked Clams & Leather Britches Tea, 16, *17*
Finished Walnut Toffee Sauce, 229
Fire-Exploded Kidney Flowers, Bamboo Shoot & Baby Leeks, 250, *251*
fish. *See under* names of individual species
Fish Butter, 272
Fish Sauce Vinaigrette, 220
Flatbread, 95
Florida Blue Crab, Sunchoke Dauphine, Ramp Capers, *244*, 245
flowers
    Daylily Dashi, 238
    Sakura Blossom Butter, 117
    Sakura Masu, Sakura Blossom, Salted White Peach, *246*, 247
foie gras
    Cured Foie Gras, 61, 155
    Foie Parfait, 61, 219
    Foie Pastry Cream, 66
    Halibut Confited in Foie Gras Fat with a Sea-Truffle Dashi, 88
    in Porcini Puree, 62
    Reginette Pasta with Grilled Mussels Dressed in Foie Gras & Preserved Black Currants, *218*, 219
    in Squab Liver Mousse, 182
    in Tart Dough, 182
    Yeast Donut, Foie Gras, Candy Cap Mushrooms, 230, *231*
    Yeast Donut, Foie Gras, Strawberry & Elderflower, 136, *137*
Fried Apples, 66
Fried Bread, 57
Fried Cabbage, 223

G

Garam Masala, 131
garlic
    Black Garlic Hoisin, 194
    Garlic Fry Bread, 28
    Green Garlic Butter, 28
Goat-Milk Kefir Ice Cream, 65
Golden Beet Vadouvan, 160
gooseberries
    in Clam & Leather Britches Tea, 16
    English Peas, Louisiana Crawfish, Fermented Green Gooseberry Juice, 122, *123*
    Fermented Gooseberry Juice, 269
    Green Gooseberry Vin, 80
Granny Smith Gelee, 80
grapes
    in Ambrosia Salad, *166*, 167
    Salad of Green Pepper, Scuppernong & Pistachio, 155
green beans
    with Smoked Clams & Leather Britches Tea, 16
Green Chartreuse Vin, 135
green garlic
    Green Garlic Fry Bread with Fermented Tomato & Aged Sheep's Milk Cheese, *22*, 28, *29*

Green Garlic Soubise, 125
Kue Grouper Buried in Embers, Green Garlic, Fermented Winter Truffle, 126, *127–29*
Green Gooseberry Vin, 80
green onions, in Green Garlic Soubise, 125
green tomatoes
    Green Tomato Beurre Blanc, 125
    Green Tomato Mostarda, 125
greens
    Braised Collard Greens, 96
    Cured Swiss Chard Leaves, 130
    Sourdough Flatbread, Smoked Clams & Mustard Greens, 95
    Swiss Chard Chutney, 131
Grilled Avocado Mayo, 163
Grilled Bucksnort Trout, Fermented Green Tomato Butter & Herbs from Our Garden, *124*, 125
Grilled Maitake Mushroom, Uni Butterscotch, Furikake, 186, *187*
Grilled Mussels & Cantaloupe Kimchi "Jjigae," 152, *153*
Grilled Vanilla Oil, 193
grits
    with Norwegian Langoustine, Fermented Ramps, *158*, 159
    "Redneck Sushi" with Swordfish Ham, Fermented Tomato, 12, *13*
    with Spiny Lobster, Preserved Périgord Truffle, *214*, 215
    Sushi Grits, 12, 208
Ground Cherries, Preserved, 58
grouper
    Kue Grouper Buried in Embers, Green Garlic, Fermented Winter Truffle, 126, *127–29*
    Steamed Kue Grouper, Preserved Tomato & Wild Fennel, 212, *213*
Guava, Lacto-Fermented (Reduction), 257

H

Habiger, Josh, x–xii, 276–77
Half-Sour Ramps, 159
Halibut Confited in Foie Gras Fat with a Sea Truffle Dashi, 88, *89*
ham. *See* country ham
Hay Oil, Burnt, 271
Hay Smoked Mussels with Sauce Poulette, *46*, 47
hazelnuts
    Brown Butter Roasted Hazelnuts, 189
    Hazelnut Puree, 189
Hickory Ice Cream, 100
Hollandaise, Anchovy, 190
horseradish
    Razor Clam, Fermented Raspberry, Rose & Horseradish Ice Cream, 226, *227*
    in Russian Dressing, 83
    in Salted Buttermilk, 151, 226
Huckleberries, Pickled, 61
Huitlacoche Butterscotch, 168

I

ice cream
    Burnt Vanilla Ice Cream, 68
    Cauliflower Gelato, 263
    Corn Ice Cream, 168
    Goat-Milk Kefir Ice Cream, 65
    Hickory Ice Cream, 100
    Horseradish Ice Cream, 226
    An Ice Cream Sundae of Beets Preserved like Luxardo Cherries with Shio Koji Caramel, 68, *69*
    Lovage Ice Cream, 99
    Matsutake Mushroom Ice Cream, 200
    Seaweed Ice Cream, 171

J

jams
    Currant-Black Pepper Jam, 62
    Fermented Tomato Jam, 28
    Nancé Jam, 260
    Onion Jam, 182
    Tomato Jam, 99

K

Kani Miso Chawanmushi, Burnt Vanilla, Matsutake & Virginia Pine, *192*, 193
kefir, Goat-Milk Kefir Ice Cream, 65
Kidney Marinade, 250
Killed Lettuces, *98*, 99
kimchi
    Asian Pear & Kimchi, *224*, 225
    Shinko Pear Kimchi, 76
King Crab, 83
kiwi, Fermented, 211
Kohlrabi, Fermented Juice, 269
kohlrabi, in Crab Butter, 84
Koji Bucatini, Fermented Kohlrabi & King Crab Butter, 84, *85*
Kombu Stock, 275
Korean BBQ Glaze, 76
Koshihikari Rice, 238
Kue Grouper Buried in Embers, Green Garlic, Fermented Winter Truffle, 126, *127–29*

L

lacto-ferments
    Golden Beet Juice, 160
    Lacto-Fermented Guava Reduction, 257
    Lacto-Fermented Pear Juice, 269
    See also ferments
lamb
    Lamb Dolma, 130
    Lamb Mop, 131
    Lamb Ribs, 131
langoustines, with Fermented Ramps, Hickory King Corn Grits, *158*, 159
leather britches
    in Clam & Leather Britches Tea, 16
    Leather Britches, 48
    Leather Britches Oil, 48
Lemon Verbena Oil, 15
lemongrass, in Cedar Green Curry Paste, 110
lettuce
    dressed with Fermented Cranberries, Walnuts & Goat-Milk Kefir, *64*, 65
    Killed Lettuces, 99
Lime Leaf Oil, 54
Littleneck Clams, Cured Pork Fat & Coriander Capers, 92, *93*
Littleneck Clams, Leather Britches & Chicken Fat, 48, *49*
lobster
    Lobster Glace, 215
    Lobster Sherry Butter, 215
    with Preserved Périgord Truffle, Hickory King Corn Grits, *214*, 215
    Red Curry, 54
    Spiny Lobster Stock, 54
    Stock, 54, 75
Long Island Cheese Pumpkin, Makrut Lime, Red Curry, 54, *55*
Loquat Oil, 156
lovage
    Ice Cream, 99
    Oil, 181

M

Maitake Marinade, 186
Malt Cream, 194
masu, Sakura, with Sakura Blossom, Salted White Peach, 246, *247*
Matsutake Mushroom Ice Cream, Preserved Virginia Pine Cones, Pine Nut Milk, *198*, 200
Matsutake & Pine Dashi, 193
mayonnaise
    Burnt Chile Mayo, 51
    Clam Mayo, 95
    Grilled Avocado Mayo, 163
    in Russian Dressing, 83
    in Sauce Gribiche, 245
    Smoked Oyster Mayo, 241
    in Turnip Top Dressing, 57
Mole, 263
Moros y Cristianos, 254
Mountain Rose Apple Ice, 79
muscadines. *See* scuppernong
mushrooms
    Black Trumpet Shortbread, 68, 100
    Candy Cap Bacon, 230
    Candy Cap Mushroom Glaze, 230
    Candy Cap Mushrooms, 230
    Confited Porcini, 24

mushrooms (continued)
    Maitake Marinade, 186
    Matsutake Dashi, 32
    Matsutake Mushroom Ice Cream, 200
    Matsutake & Pine Dashi, 193
    Poached Matsutakes, 32
    Porcini Garum, 271
    Porcini Puree, 62
    in Preserved Winter Truffle Puree, 222
    in Sauce Marchand de Vin, 24
    in Sauce Perigueux, 222, 249
    in Truffle Puree, 126
    Yeast Donut, Foie Gras, Candy Cap Mushrooms, 230, 231
mussels
    & Carrot BBQ, 185
    Butter, 47, 185
    Fudge, 47, 185
    Hay-Smoked Mussels, 47
    Mussel Garum, 272
    Paste, 152
    Poulette Sauce, 47
    Poulette Spice, 47
    Reginette Pasta with Grilled Mussels Dressed in Foie Gras & Preserved Black Currants, 218, 219
    Soup Base, 152
    Steamed, 152, 219
    Stock, 275

N

Nancé, Triple Cream Cheese, Pineapple Weed & Schrenckii Caviar, 260, 261
Norwegian King Crab, Rose & Horseradish, 82, 83
Norwegian Langoustine, Fermented Ramps, Hickory King Corn Grits, 158, 159
nuts
    Barely Cooked Scallops with Brown Butter Roasted Hazelnut, 188, 189
    Burnt Banana, Black Walnut, Cultured Butter & Caviar, 228, 229
    Caramelized Walnuts, 65
    Dry-Aged Bear Creek Farm Ribloin, Savoy Cabbage, Black Walnut & Périgord Truffle, 222–23, 223
    Pork Ribs, Winter Squash & Peanut, 220, 221
    Roasted Pecan Dressing, 167

O

oil(s)
    Bone, 181, 272
    Burnt Hay Oil, 271
    Burnt Pine, 193
    Celery-Leaf, 87
    Fig Leaf, 199
    Grilled Vanilla, 193
    Herb, 84, 125
    Kombu, 178
    Lime Leaf, 54
    Loquat, 156
    Lovage, 181
    Prawn Shell, 211
    Ramp Root, 118
    Sea Lettuce, 80
    Sea-Truffle, 88
    Smoked Bone Oil, 272
    Smoked Clam, 110
    Smoked Pea Shell, 122
    Tarragon, 135
olives, in Sofrito, 256
onion, spring, in Green Garlic Soubise, 125
Onion Jus, 275
onions
    Caramelized Onion Hoisin, 220
    Gravy, 126
    Jam, 182
    Jus, 275
    Marinade, 131
    Smoked Onion Nikiri, 208
    Smoked Onion Shiro Dashi, 271
oranges, Sour Orange Marinade, 254
otoro
    with Redneck Sushi & Wagyu "Ham," 208, 209
    with Tosazu, Preserved Coriander Berries, 242, 243
oysters
    with Aged Buri Belly, Chutoro & Seaweeds, 240, 241
    with Charred Cucumber, Succulents, 148, 149
    Gelee, 15
    Glaze, 178
    Pie with Porter Beer Cream, 178, 179
    Root Stew, Matsutake Mushroom, Dried Chilies, 44, 45
    Shiokara, 178
    Smoked and Dried, 272
    Smoked Oyster Mayo, 241

P

parsnips
    with Black Trumpet Shortbread, Hickory, 100, 101
    Parsnip Cake, 100
pasta
    Koji Bucatini, Fermented Kohlrabi & King Crab Butter, 84
    Plantain Gnocchi, 255, 256
    Reginette Pasta with Grilled Mussels Dressed in Foie Gras & Preserved Black Currants, 218, 219
peaches, Salted Peach Puree, 246
Peanut Crumble, 220
pears
    Asian Pear & Kimchi, 224, 225
    Asian Pear Snow, 225
    in Korean BBQ Glaze, 76
    Lacto-Fermented Pear Juice, 269
    in Radish Dressing, 225
    Shinko Pear Kimchi, 76
peas
    in Crawfish Nage, 122
    in Green Chartreuse Vin, 135
    with Green Strawberries & Green Chartreuse, 134, 135
    with Louisiana Crawfish, Fermented Green Gooseberry Juice, 122, 123
    Smoked Pea Shell Oil, 122
pecans, Roasted Pecan Dressing, 167
Peppercorn Spice, 15
peppers, hot
    Cayenne Pepper Vinegar, 96
    Fermented Chile Powder, 271
    Mussels Soup Base, 152
peppers, sweet
    in Moros y Cristianos, 254
    in Salad with Scuppernong & Pistachio, 155
    in Strawberry General Tso's, 114
Perigueux, Seasoned, 222
Pickled Ramps, 270
pickles
    about, 107
    Elderflower, 35
    Green Strawberries, 135
    Half-Sour Ramps, 159
    Huckleberries, 61
    Ramps, 270
    Sea Lettuce, 80
    Seaweed, 241
    Watermelon Rind, 110
    Wild Fennel, 212
    See also ferments
Pig Tails, 114
pine
    Burnt Pine Oil, 193
    Pine Nut Meringue, 200
    Preserved Virginia Pine Cones, 200
pineapple
    BBQ, 51
    Catsup, 51
    Fermented Pineapple Juice, 270
    Fermented Pineapple Reduction, 270
    Granita, 32
    Reduction, 51
Pink Moon Oysters with an Ice of Mountain Rose Apple & Fresh Wasabi, 78, 79
pistachios
    Dukkah, 160
    Pistachio Dressing, 155
    Toasted Pistachio, 171
plantain
    & Dry-Aged Pork Coulotte, 254, 255
    Fermented Plantain, 257
    Gnocchi, Preserved Tomato & Castelvetrano Olives, 256
    Plantain Cafécito, 259
    Plantain Syrup, 257

Popcorn Shio, 159
porcini mushrooms. *See* mushrooms
pork
    in Braised Collard Greens, 96
    Cured Pork Fat (Lardo), 92
    Dry-Aged Pork Coulotte & Plantain, 254, *255*
    in Durian Jus, 253
    Kidney Marinade, 250
    in Moros y Cristianos, 254
    Pork Brine, 253
    Pork Ribs, Winter Squash & Peanut, 220, *221*
    Pork Rub, 254
    Pork Shoulder, 253
    Scallops Wrapped in 45-Day Aged Pork Belly, Fermented Pumpkin & Smooth Black Truffle, 216, *217*
potatoes
    in Crawfish Boil, 122
    in Green Garlic Soubise, 125
Poulette Sauce, 47
Poulette Spice, 47
poultry
    chicken schmaltz, 48
    Chicken Stock, 274
    Squab Chorizo, 160
    Squab Jus, 163
    Squab Liver Mousse, Onion Jam, Crispy PX Sherry, 182, *183*
    Squab Spice, 163
    Squab Stock, 274
    Squab with Sunchokes, Black Garlic & Malted Milk, 194–95, *196*
prawns
    Prawn Shell Oil, 211
    Prawn Shiokara, 238
    Tartare, Fermented Kiwi, Belgian Osetra Caviar, *210*, 211
Preserved Dill Stems, 271
Preserved Ground Cherries, 58
Preserved Meyer Lemons, 271
Preserved Strawberries, 69, 136
Preserved Sudachi, 181
Preserved Tomato Broth, 212
Preserved Virginia Pine Cones, 200
Preserved Winter Truffle Puree, 222
pumpkin
    Butter, 58
    -Vin Jaune Sauce, 216
    See also squash, winter

Q
quail, in Squab Liver Mousse, 182

R
radishes
    in Asian Pear & Kimchi, *224*, 225
    Radish Dressing, 225
    See also daikon

Ramp Capers, 270
ramps
    about, 107
    Fermented Ramp Powder, 95
    in Green Garlic Butter, 28
    Half-Sour Ramp Butter, 159
    Pickled Ramps, 270
    Ramp Capers, 270
    Ramp Root Oil, 118
    Sauce Gribiche, 245
raspberries
    with Dry-Aged Ora King Salmon & Angelica, 156, *157*
    Fermented Raspberry Juice, 270
    Razor Clam, Fermented Raspberry, Rose & Horseradish Ice Cream, 226, *227*
    Razor Clam, Fermented Raspberry, Rose & Horseradish Ice Cream, 226, *227*
    "Redneck Sushi" Crispy Grits, Swordfish Ham, Fermented Tomato, 12, *13*
Redneck Sushi with Aged Otoro & Wagyu "Ham," 208, *209*
Reginette Pasta with Grilled Mussels Dressed in Foie Gras & Preserved Black Currants, 218, *219*
Rhubarb Granita, 167
ribloin, with Savoy Cabbage, Black Walnut & Périgord Truffle, 222–23, *223*
rice, in Popcorn Shio, 159
Roasted Carrots, 185
Roasted Pecan Dressing, 167
romanesco, with Devil's Gulch Ranch Squab & Pechuga, 162–63, *164–65*
Rose Kosho, 271
Rose Salt, 83
Russian Dressing, 83

S
Sakura Blossom Butter, 117
Sakura Cream, 246
Sakura Masu, Sakura Blossom, Salted White Peach, 246, *247*
Salad of English Peas, Green Strawberries & Green Chartreuse, *134*, 135
Salad of Green Pepper, Scuppernong & Pistachio, *154*, 155
salmon
    with Raspberry & Angelica, 156, *157*
    Sakura Masu, Sakura Blossom, Salted White Peach, 246, *247*
salsa
    Charred Cucumber Salsa Verde, 148
    Salsa Macha, 162
salsify, in Oyster Root Stew, 32
Salted Buttermilk, 15, 151, 226
Salted Peach Puree, 246
salts
    Chile Lime Salt, 51
    Rose Salt, 83

sauces
    Anchovy Hollandaise, 190
    Black Garlic Hoisin, 194
    Caramelized Onion Hoisin, 220
    Fermented White Asparagus Bearnaise, 27
    Finished Walnut Toffee Sauce, 229
    Marchand de Vin, 24
    Pineapple BBQ, 51
    Pumpkin-Vin Jaune Sauce, 216
    Sauce Base, 250
    Sauce Chorón, 31
    Sauce Gribiche, 245
    Sauce Perigueux, 222, 249
scallops
    Confited Scallops, 189, 216
    with Fairytale Pumpkin & Preserved Ground Cherries, 58, *59*
    with Fermented Celery Butter & Alba Truffle, *86*, 87
    Mi-Cuit, Fermented White Asparagus, Sakura Blossom, *116*, 117
    Scallop Cracker, 118
    Scallop Garum, 272
    Scallop XO Cracker, 118, *119*
    wrapped in 45-Day Aged Pork Belly, Fermented Pumpkin & Smooth Black Truffle, 216, *217*
Schmaltz, 48
scuppernong, in Salad of Green Pepper, Scuppernong & Pistachio, 155
sea buckthorn
    with Barbecued Carrot, Blue Mussels, *184*, 185
    Fermented Sea Buckthorn Juice, 269
sea lettuce
    Pickled Sea Lettuce, 80
    Sea Lettuce Oil, 80
Sea Urchin Butterscotch Pudding, 171
seafood. *See under* names of individual species
Seasoned Dashi, 88
Seasoned Matsutake Dashi, 193
Seasoned Perigueux, 222
sea-truffle
    Sea-Truffle Dashi, 88
    Sea-Truffle Oil, 88
seaweed
    Ice Cream, Fermented Cucumber & Sea Urchin Butterscotch Pudding, *170*, 171
    Pickled Seaweed, 241
    Shaved Bear Creek Farm Denver Steak, Fava Bean & Stilton Cheese, *248*, 249
Shigoku Oyster, Charred Cucumber, Succulents, 148, *149*
Shinko Pear Kimchi, 76
Shio Koji, 271
Shio Koji Caramel, 68
Shiro Dashi Custard, 181
Smoked and Dried Clams, 272
Smoked and Dried Oysters, 272
Smoked Bone Oil, 272
Smoked Clam Oil, 95, 110
Smoked Clam Vinaigrette, 16

Smoked Fish Bones, 272
Smoked Onion Nikiri, 208
Smoked Onion Shiro Dashi, 271
Smoked Oyster Mayo, 241
Smoked Oyster Shiro Dashi, 272
Smoked Pea Shell Oil, 122
Smoked Tofu, 121
Smoked Tomato Nikiri, 12
Smoked Trout Cracker, 113
Smoked Trout Dip, 57
Sofrito, 256
sorghum
    in Shio Koji Caramel, 68
    Sorghum Vinaigrette, 99
Sour Orange Marinade, 254
Sourdough Flatbread, Smoked Clams & Mustard Greens, 94, 95
spice blends
    Dolma Spice, 131
    Dukkah, 160
    Everything Spice, 113
    Garam Masala, 131
    Peppercorn Spice, 15
    Squab Spice, 163
    Sweet Potato Furikake, 121
spiny lobster. *See* lobster
Sponge Candy, 103
squab
    Chorizo, 160
    Jus, 163
    Liver Mousse, Onion Jam, Crispy PX Sherry, 182, *183*
    Spice, 163
    Stock, 274
    with Sunchokes, Black Garlic & Malted Milk, 194–95, *196*
squash, winter
    with Makrut Lime, Red Curry, 54, *55*
    with Pork Ribs & Peanut, 220, *221*
    Pumpkin Butter, 58
    Pumpkin-Vin Jaune Sauce, 216
steak, with Fava Bean & Stilton Cheese, 248, *249*
Steamed Kue Grouper, Preserved Tomato & Wild Fennel, 212, *213*
Steamed Mussels, 152, 219
stocks, 274–75
strawberries
    Pickled Green Strawberries, 135
    Preserved Strawberries, 69, 136
    in Rhubarb Granita, 167
    Strawberry General Tso's, 114
    Strawberry Glaze, 136
succulents, with Shigoku Oyster, Charred Cucumber, 148, *149*
Sudcahi, Preserved, 181
sunchokes
    Confited Suncoke, 194
    Sunchoke Dauphine, 245
sunflowers
    Sunflower Seed Puree, 194
    Sunflower-Miso Puree, 19

Sungold Tomatoes Oscar, 22, 26, 27
Surf Clam, Cedar Tips Green Curry & Pickled Watermelon Rind, 110, *111*
Sushi Grits, 12, 208
Sushi Vinegar, 238
Sweet Corn Ice Cream, Huitlacoche & Australian Winter Truffle, 168, *169*
sweet potatoes
    Boniato, Smoked Tofu & a Vin Blanc of Last Year's Cured & Dried Sweet Potatoes, *120*, 121
    Confit Sweet Potatoes, 121
    Cured & Dried, 269
    Sweet Potato "Bushi" Cream, 121
    Sweet Potato Furikake, 121
swiss chard
    Cured Swiss Chard Leaves, 130
    Swiss Chard Chutney, 131
Swordfish Ham, 12, 273
Syrup, Beet, 68

T

tallow. *See* beef fat
Tamales, 162
tarragon
    Oil, 135
    Vinegar, 27
Tart Dough, 31, 178, 182
Tartare of Toro Sawara & Otoro with Japanese Citrus & Shiro Dashi Custard, *180*, 181
Tempered Chocolate, 103
Tiny Tomato Pie, 22, *30*, 31
Toasted Pistachio, 171
Tofu, Smoked, 121
tomatoes
    Beefsteak Tomatoes, 24
    in Charred Zucchini, Salted Buttermilk & Marjoram, *150*, 151
    Cured Tomatoes, 31
    Fermented Tomato Jam, 28
    Fermented Tomato Juice, 269
    Fermented Tomato Reduction, 28, 269
    Green Tomato Beurre Blanc, 125
    Green Tomato Mostarda, 125
    Preserved Tomato Broth, 212
    in Russian Dressing, 83
    in Sauce Chorón, 31
    Smoked Tomato Nikiri, 12
    in Sofrito, 256
    Sungold Tomatoes, 27
    Tiny Tomato Pie, 22, *30*, 31
    Tomato Bouillon, 270
    Tomato Jam, 99
    Tomato Nduja, 31
    Tomato Salad with Pineapple & Litchi Blossom, 32, *33*
    Tomato Tea, 32
    Tomato Vinaigrette, 31
Tosazu, 242

trout
    with Fermented Green Tomato Butter & Herbs from Our Garden, *124*, 125
    Smoked Trout Cracker, 113
    Smoked Trout Dip, 57
    Trout Bone Glaze, 113
truffles
    in Cabbage Puree, 222
    in Duck Presse Jus, 61
    with Maine Scallop & Fermented Celery Butter, 87
    Preserved Winter Truffle Puree, 222
    with Ribloin, Savoy Cabbage & Black Walnut, 222–23, *223*
    in Sauce Perigueux, 222, 249
    with Scallops Wrapped in 45-Day Aged Pork Belly, Fermented Pumpkin, 216, *217*
    in Seasoned Dashi Base, 20
    in Seasoned Perigueux, 222
    Sea-Truffle Dashi, 88
    Sea-Truffle Oil, 88
    with Sweet Corn Ice Cream, Huitlacoche, 168, *169*
    Truffle BBQ, 216
    Truffle Dashi, 229
    Truffle Puree, 126
tuna, with Charred Broccoli, Anchovy, 190, *191*
turnips
    Fermented Turnip Juice, 269
    Turnip Top Dressing, 57

U

Uni Butterscotch, 186
Uni Garum, 272

V

vanilla
    Burnt Vanilla Ice Cream, 68
    Grilled Vanilla Oil, 193
vinaigrettes
    Fermented Raspberry Vinaigrette, 226
    Fish Sauce Vinaigrette, 220
    Smoked Clam Vinaigrette, 16
    Sorghum Vinaigrette, 99
    Tomato Vinaigrette, 31

W

Wagyu Ham, 273
walnuts
    with Burnt Banana, Cultured Butter & Caviar, *228*, 229
    Caramelized Walnuts, 65
    with Dry-Aged Bear Creek Farm Ribloin, Savoy Cabbage & Périgord Truffle, 222–23, *223*

Warm Salad of Hakurei Turnips, Lovage & Smoked Bucksnort Trout, *56*, 57
Wasabi Buttermilk, 79
watermelons, Pickled Watermelon Rind, 110
Wolf, Mike, xiii–xvii, 276–77

Y

Yeast Donut, Foie Gras, Strawberry & Elderflower, 136, *137*
yeast donuts
    with Foie Gras, Black Apple, 66, *67*
    with Foie Gras, Candy Cap Mushrooms, 230, *231*
    with Foie Gras, Strawberry & Elderflower, 136, *137*
yogurt
    Cashew Yogurt, 131
    in Fermented Plantain Bread, 257

Z

zucchini, with Salted Buttermilk & Marjoram, *150*, 151